THE END OF THE WEST?

The End of the West?

Crisis and Change in the Atlantic Order

EDITED BY

Jeffrey Anderson

G. John Ikenberry

Thomas Risse

Cornell University Press

Ithaca and London

First published 2008 by Cornell University Press
First printing, Cornell Paperbacks, 2008

Printed in the United States of America

Library of Congress Cataloging-in-Publication Data

The End of the West? : crisis and change in the Atlantic order / edited by Jeffrey Anderson, G. John Ikenberry, Thomas Risse.
    p. cm.
    Includes bibliographical references and index.
    ISBN 978-0-8014-4639-9 (cloth : alk. paper) — ISBN 978-0-8014-7400-2 (pbk. : alk. paper)
    1. Europe—Foreign relations—United States. 2. United States—Foreign relations—Europe. I. Anderson, Jeffrey J. II. Ikenberry, G. John. III. Risse, Thomas. IV. Title.
    D2025.5.U64E53 2008
    327.4073—dc22   2007039504

Cornell University Press strives to use environmentally responsible suppliers and materials to the fullest extent possible in the publishing of its books. Such materials include vegetable-based, low-VOC inks and acid-free papers that are recycled, totally chlorine-free, or partly composed of nonwood fibers. For further information, visit our website at www.cornellpress.cornell.edu.

Cloth printing   10 9 8 7 6 5 4 3 2 1

Paperback printing   10 9 8 7 6 5 4 3 2 1

CONTENTS

CONTRIBUTORS

JEFFREY ANDERSON is the Graf Goltz Professor and Director of the BMW Center for German and European Studies of the Edmund A. Walsh School of Foreign Service, and Professor of Government at Georgetown University.

MICHAEL BYERS holds the Canada Research Chair in Global Politics and International Law at the University of British Columbia.

DIETER FUCHS is Professor of Political Theory and Comparative Analysis of Democracies at the Institute for Social Sciences, University of Stuttgart.

JOHN A. HALL is Professor of Sociology at Dartmouth College.

GUNTHER HELLMANN is Professor of Political Science at Johann Wolfgang Goethe–Universität Frankfurt am Main.

WILLIAM I. HITCHCOCK is Professor of History at Temple University.

G. JOHN IKENBERRY is the Albert G. Milbank Professor of Politics and International Affairs in the Department of Politics and the Woodrow Wilson School of Public and International Affairs at Princeton University.

HANS-DIETER KLINGEMANN is Professor emeritus of Political Science, Freie Universität Berlin and Wissenschaftszentrum Berlin für Sozialforschung.

CHARLES A. KUPCHAN is Professor of International Affairs at Georgetown University and a fellow at the Council on Foreign Relations.

KATHLEEN R. MCNAMARA is Associate Professor of Government and International Affairs in the Department of Government and the Edmund A. Walsh School of Foreign Service at Georgetown University.

HENRY R. NAU is Professor of Political Science and International Affairs at the Elliott School of International Affairs, George Washington University.

THOMAS RISSE is Professor of International Politics, Freie Universität Berlin, and Coordinator of the Collaborative Research Center 700 "Governance in Areas of Limited Statehood."

JENS VAN SCHERPENBERG is a nonresident senior fellow at the Stiftung Wissenschaft und Politik, Berlin.

ACKNOWLEDGMENTS

"Patience is the companion of wisdom." We found frequent consolation in Saint Augustine's words during the nearly five years it took to bring this project from nascent idea to bound volume. We were not simply making a virtue out of necessity. In fact, it would have been intellectually reckless to rush into print an academic perspective on the state of the transatlantic relationship while the reverberations of September 11, 2001—to say nothing of the invasion of Iraq in March 2003—were in full swing.

During that time, we incurred many debts. We begin by thanking colleagues who provided keen advice and commentary to us as editors and to individual authors: Helga Haftendorn, Ingo Peters, Georg Nolte, Jürgen Gerhards, and Manfred Görtemaker. We also acknowledge the commentary and research support given by graduate students connected to the project at various stages: Josh Busby, Tobias Heider, Caroline Fehl, and Thomas Wright. Philip Schunke, Heide Strecker, Allison Hillegeist, and Calluna Euving made invaluable contributions to workshop and conference planning. Finally, we express our gratitude for the financial and logistical support provided by the following organizations: the Max-Planck-Gesellschaft; the Alexander von Humboldt Foundation; Stiftung Deutsch-Amerikanische Wissenschaftsbeziehungen of the Stifterverband der Deutschen Wissenschaft; the BMW Center for German and European Studies of the Edmund A. Walsh School of Foreign Service, Georgetown University; the Mortara Center for International Studies, also of the Walsh School; and the American Consortium on European Union Studies, Washington, D.C.

JEFFREY ANDERSON
G. JOHN IKENBERRY
THOMAS RISSE

Washington, D.C.
Princeton
Berlin

THE END OF THE WEST?

1 EXPLAINING CRISIS AND CHANGE IN ATLANTIC RELATIONS

An Introduction

G. JOHN IKENBERRY

The first years of the twenty-first century will long be remembered as a time of political upheaval in Atlantic relations. The United States embarked on a controversial war in Iraq opposed by most Europeans and many of their governments. For the first time in the postwar era, a German chancellor opposed Washington in full public view on a fundamental issue of security and even made opposition to Bush policy a part of his reelection campaign. At the United Nations, France publicly lobbied Security Council members to oppose a resolution that would authorize the United States' use of force in Iraq. European hostility to the United States—its polity, power, and policy—reached historic levels. Long-standing social and cultural differences between America and Europe in areas such as energy consumption, global warming, the death penalty, transnational justice, and religion were inflamed. In the eyes of many Americans, Europe and the Western alliance were no longer central to the pursuit of U.S. global security. In the eyes of many Europeans, the United States had become a superpower that now must be resisted and contained. Some observers even speculated about the "end of the West."[1]

The political storms that swirled so violently across the Atlantic over the Iraq War have since calmed, and new leaders have taken office in Western countries seeking to move beyond the conflicts of the recent past. Yet as the conflicts between the United States and Europe over the Iraq War and Bush-era foreign policy recede into the past, questions remain about the longer-term significance and impact of this upheaval on Atlantic relations. The policy agenda of the Western alliance has moved beyond Iraq, but it is less clear that the crisis of the

---

1. See, for example, Charles A. Kupchan, "The End of the West," *Atlantic Monthly*, November 2002, 42–44; David Marquand, "Goodbye, the West," *Prospect* (August 2004); and David Frum, "The End of the Transatlantic Affair," *Financial Times*, 31 January 2005.

old Atlantic partnership is really over. The conflicts have receded but the questions have not, at least not the scholarly questions about the logic and character of the Atlantic political order and its future. With the greater distance and perspective that time provides, it is now possible to look more deeply into the structures and foundations of the Western order and into the ways in which the recent conflict exposes the operating logic and trajectory of that order.

The two most important questions in the contemporary debate about conflict and crisis across the Atlantic are how serious is the U.S.-European discord as it was recently experienced and what are its sources? The cover of the February 15–21, 2003, issue of the *Economist* posed the first question—"How deep is the gulf?" In part this question is about how to describe the nature of the recent Atlantic political conflict. Journalists and public intellectuals have evoked a wide variety of terms to capture what is happening—divorce, estrangement, rift, dividing fates. These terms tend to beg a deeper question about the character of the crisis. Is it a political conflict that has been particularly intense but will come and go—as it has in the past—or are we witnessing a more fundamental break and transformation of U.S.-European relations? That is, is the Atlantic world—or more concretely the Western alliance—breaking apart in some meaningful sense or simply evolving, adjusting, and accommodating itself to new realities?

The second question focuses on the sources of the crisis. Is this recent crisis really about the Bush administration and the war in Iraq or is it driven by deeper fissures that will continue to open up and erode Atlantic relations after the Bush administration and the Iraq War no longer occupy center stage? That is, how "structural" should our analysis be of the troubles that have recently beset U.S.-European relations? To be sure, there are many historic shifts in the international political system that bear on Atlantic relations: the end of the cold war, the rise of U.S. unipolarity, the fits and starts of European unification, the emergence of new security threats, the growing geopolitical importance of Asia, and the globalizing impact of modernity. Does one or several of these transformations auger ill for Atlantic cooperation and community? Would a crisis in U.S.-European relations have erupted if George W. Bush had not been elected or if he had not launched the Iraq War? If there are deep and growing sources of conflict in Atlantic relations, how are they manifested? Some world historical developments may serve to pull America and Europe apart. This is the famous claim of Robert Kagan, who argues that growing power disparities between the United States and Europe breed divergent strategic cultures and interests, which in turn lead to conflicts over rules and institutions, the use of force, and the basic organizing principles of international order.[2] But other world historical developments may be pushing

---

2. Robert Kagan, *Of Paradise and Power: America and Europe in the New World Order* (New York: Knopf, 2003).

America and Europe back together. The relentless forces of trade and investment and the proliferation of Western transnational civil society are also strengthening the interests and social ties across the Atlantic. Structural shifts can cut both ways.

This volume has three purposes. First, the volume is aimed at improving our theoretical understanding of the logic of conflict and crisis within Western and international order. What do we actually mean by conflict, crisis, breakdown, and transformation in the Atlantic order? What precisely are the theoretical claims that are in play in our judgments about continuity and change in U.S.-European relations? What is new in this current moment of Atlantic crisis and what is not? Political conflict—by itself—does not say much about the functioning of a political order. Political conflict can trigger the rupture, breakdown, and transformation of a political system. It can, however, also be a normal part of the operation of a stable and mature political system. After all, political conflict is ubiquitous within Western democratic societies—and indeed it is essential to the operation of such democracies. So the question is: how do we make sense of political conflict across the Atlantic? Are the recent tensions and disputes between the United States and Europe a reflection of deep problems, contradictions, and dysfunctions of the Atlantic political system or part of the healthy functioning of a stable political order?

When political conflict turns into a genuine crisis within the political order, additional questions arise. What is a crisis and what are the various logics of change that follow from crisis? In this volume, *crisis is defined as an extraordinary moment when the existence and viability of the political order are called into question*. That is, it is a historical juncture at which conflict within the political order has risen to the point that the interests, institutions, and shared identities that define and undergird the political system are put in jeopardy. The settled rules, expectations, and institutions that constitute the political order are rendered unsettled. Conflict has pushed the very existence of the political order to the brink.

Defined in this way, crisis can lead in several different directions. Crisis can lead to resolutions that reestablish the old rules and institutions of a political system, it can lead to a transformation of that political system, or it can lead to a fundamental breakdown and disappearance of the old political system. Developing a theoretical sense of how conflict and crisis operate within the Atlantic political order and what the current conflict and crisis mean for the future of the Atlantic system is a central inquiry of this volume.

A second purpose is that we seek to identify the new interdisciplinary research agenda on Atlantic relations. The public debate is lively and full of insights. But what do scholars have to offer? The answer is historical perspective, theoretical clarity, and empirical rigor. This response does not mean that scholars agree on the character and sources of Atlantic conflict, but they can help illuminate the categories and forces that are at work in generating conflict and cooperation. The authors of these chapters draw on established research traditions and knowledge in political science, history, economics, sociology, and law that sharpen and deepen the debate about the character and sources of Atlantic discord. In doing so, they tend to take the long view of U.S.-European relations, putting the recent troubles in postwar historical context.

Finally, the authors in this volume use the Atlantic crisis as a contemporary laboratory to examine the relevance of various theories of politics and international relations. Crises expose fault lines, deep structures, and historical trajectories, so we want to use the current situation to reassess old theories and scholarly debates. Power, interests, culture, historical legacies, and personalities are all at play in the current disputes between the United States and Europe. How can we use this current moment to draw more general conclusions about the usefulness of time-honored realist, liberal, and social constructivist theories about core features of the advanced industrial world?

In recent decades, the transatlantic order has not been a place where basic debates about international relations theory have been conducted. Those have occurred elsewhere. Debates about U.S.-European relations have tended to be less theoretical and focused on empirical issues of policy and diplomacy. This lack of theoretical vibrancy in the study of Atlantic relations is not entirely surprising, inasmuch as the Atlantic relationship has been so steady and predictable for many decades. The upheavals in world politics have occurred outside the West. Great social theories and debates tend to emerge in response to historic disruptions and grand upheavals—social revolutions, wars, civil violence—rather than in response to the calm and dull equanimity of a stable political order. The recent disruption in the relatively placid Atlantic landscape offers an opportunity to probe theories of power politics, alliance relations, democratic community, capitalist society, and Western order.

Indeed, in response to the new Western discord, a growing body of scholarship has started to appear. Some writers have drawn detailed empirical portraits of the policy disputes that have risen between the United States and Europe in recent years—quarrels over trade, the International Criminal Court, the Kyoto Protocol, and the Israeli-Palestinian stalemate as well over the Iraq War.[3] Others offer scholarly studies of the political, economic, cultural, and ideological dimensions of the crisis in Atlantic relations as it appeared in 2003 with the Iraq War. David M. Andrews and his colleagues, for example, have recently explored the various ways in which changes in the

---

3. Elizabeth Pond, *Friendly Fire: The Near Death of the Transatlantic Alliance* (Washington, DC: Brookings Institution Press, 2003); Philip Gordon and Jeremy Shapiro, *Allies at War: America, Europe, and the Crisis over Iraq* (Washington, DC: Brookings Institution Press, 2004); and David M. Malone, *The International Struggle over Iraq: Politics in the UN Security Council, 1980–2005* (New York: Oxford University Press, 2006).

post–cold war international environment have tended to undercut support for Atlanticism in both the United States and Europe.[4] Still others have explored the deeper question of the fate of the Atlantic political order. While some scholars argue that the special characteristics of the transatlantic order—built on a foundation of shared democracy and security cooperation—prevent conflict from spiraling out of control, others have questioned the permanence of this security community. Michael Cox writes that "[a] few years ago, it was normal to refer to something called the West; liberal theorists could also talk (and did) about a 'security community.' Today, it is doubtful whether we can talk of either with the same degree of confidence."[5]

It is here that this book enters the debate. The title of the book—*End of the West?*—is meant to be a provocation. By "the West," we mean the transatlantic order or security community, embodied as it is in the Atlantic alliance. The book's title signals our collective purpose: to probe the shifting foundational structures of the Atlantic political order. In fact, none of the authors in this volume argues that the West—defined in our terms—is going to disappear. Charles Kupchan makes the most thoroughgoing argument that the old postwar Atlantic world is passing away. But no one argues that war or even old-style balance-of-power politics or security competition is on the horizon. Yet the authors take seriously the notion of a crisis that calls into question the old assumptions and bargains of Atlantic political order. In this sense, the "end of the West" really means an end of the old grand strategic partnership between the United States and Europe. The result will not be a complete breakdown in Atlantic political community but rather its transformation into a new type of Western political order.

4. David M. Andrews, ed., *The Atlantic Alliance under Stress: U.S.–European Relations after Iraq* (New York: Cambridge University Press, 2005). See also Thomas S. Mowle, *Allies at Odds: The United States and the European Union* (New York: Palgrave, 2004); Laurent Cohen-Tanugi, *An Alliance at Risk: The United States and Europe since September 11* (Baltimore: Johns Hopkins University Press, 2003); Gustav Lindstrom, *Shift or Rift? Assessing U.S.-EU Relations after Iraq* (Paris: Institute for Security Studies, 2003); and William Anthony Hay and Harvey Sicherman, eds., *Is There Still a West? The Future of the Atlantic Alliance* (Columbia: University of Missouri Press, 2007).

5. Michael Cox, "Beyond the West? Terrors in Transatlantia," *European Journal of International Relations* 11, no. 2 (2005): 203–33, quotation at 209. Other authors in this debate include the following: Thomas Risse, "Beyond Iraq: The Crisis of the Transatlantic Security Community," in *American Power in the 21st Century*, ed. David Held and Mathias Kosnig-Archibugi (Cambridge, MA: Polity Press, 2004); Erik Jones, "Introduction," in "The Transatlantic Relationship," special issue, *International Affairs* 80, no. 4 (2004): 595–612; Alice Ackermann, "Why Europe and America Don't See Eye to Eye," *International Politics* 40, no. 1 (2003): 121–36; Tod Lindberg, ed., *Beyond Paradise and Power: Europe, America, and the Future of a Troubled Partnership* (New York: Routledge, 2004); Charles A. Kupchan, *The End of the American Era: U.S. Foreign Policy and the Geopolitics of the Twenty-First Century* (New York: Knopf, 2002); and Timothy Garten Ash, *Free World: Why a Crisis of the West Reveals the Opportunity of Our Time* (London: Penguin, 2004).

In the concluding chapter, Thomas Risse draws out these collective arguments. Most of the authors do in fact see a crisis in the Atlantic order, defined as
a moment when the existence and viability of that order are called into question.
Yet they also tend to see not an "end of alliance" but an evolution away from or
transformation in the rules, institutions, and bargains of the old postwar partnership. As Risse observes, the disagreements in this volume are mostly over the
sources and causes of the crisis. In one sense, these disagreements are not surprising inasmuch as the authors come to the problem from widely divergent theoretical and disciplinary backgrounds. But the authors also offer unexpected and
counterintuitive findings about the impact of economic interdependence, conceptions of sovereignty, and sociopolitical values on Atlantic conflict and crisis.

The old transatlantic order has exhibited a remarkable robustness over the
postwar decades. The crisis of today reflects changes in the interests, institutions, and identities of the United States and Europe as they operate within the
Atlantic political space. The old order, as Thomas Risse argues in the conclusion, has outlived itself and needs to be adjusted to the challenges of the twenty-
first century. This statement is not surprising. The global system has itself been
transformed in the six decades since the end of World War II. The West has
been plunged into crisis before—indeed, it has consumed itself in war and
depression—but regained its footing and developed new forms of political and
economic community. If history and theory are a guide, it will do so again.

Points of Departure

We begin by making clear our common points of departure, which are fourfold. First, the authors in this volume agree that the United States and Europe
have created and operate within a relatively distinct and coherent postwar regional political order that goes by various labels, such as the North Atlantic
community, the Atlantic political order, or the Western system. This Atlantic
order obviously predates the end of World War II, but it was really only after
1945 that it took on its current shape. It has security, economic, political, and
ideational dimensions. It has institutions and norms that reflect a functioning—
if loosely organized—political order.

Second, we argue that this community is also a distinctive political order—
although we may not fully agree on the specific features that make it distinctive. Karl Deutsch's famous depiction of the North Atlantic region as a
"pluralistic security community" is probably the most frequently evoked way
to identify what is distinctive about this order.[6] It is a regional interstate

---

6. Karl W. Deutsch, Sidney B. Burrell, and Robert A. Kann, *Political Community and the
North Atlantic Organization in the Light of Historical Experience* (Princeton: Princeton University
Press, 1957). For a reexamination of the conception of security community, see Emanuel Adler
and Michael Barnett, eds., *Security Communities* (New York: Cambridge University Press, 1998).

system in which war or the threat of force to settle disputes within the region is unthinkable. It is a stable "zone of peace." Moreover, this security community character of the Atlantic order is reinforced by shared values, economic and societal integration, and political institutions that regulate and diffuse political conflict. In this and other ways, the postwar Atlantic political order operates in a manner that set it apart from other regions of the world and political orders of past eras.

Third, over the last several years—and most dramatically in the run-up to the Iraq War in 2003—this political order has encountered extraordinary turbulence and disruption. This conflict may or may not be unprecedented. Indeed, in their chapters William Hitchcock and Henry Nau argue that today's conflict is not altogether different from previous disputes that roiled Atlantic relations. And the current crisis may or may not alter the preexisting order. We agree, however, that the recent conflict between the United States and Europe is serious and forces us to ask basic questions about the character and future of the Atlantic relationship.

Fourth, there is also consensus among the authors that our scholarly theories need to grapple more effectively with the problem of continuity and change in the international political order. As Gunther Hellmann argues, international relations scholarship has not been well equipped to conceptualize change in the Atlantic political order. In applying a typological framework developed by Paul Pierson to study large-scale processes of change, Hellmann discusses what types of causal accounts have been dominant in the international relations literature in explaining change with regard to NATO, in particular—and what this may tell us about particular strengths, biases, and potential blind spots in coming to grips with current events. In essence he argues that the structures of the most prominent explanations of change have often been similar—regardless of paradigmatic origins. In spite of major differences in expected paths of NATO's future development, the main theories—realist, liberal, and constructivist—have almost always relied in equal fashion on causal arguments that emphasize large-scale causal processes. These arguments were almost always framed in statist structural terms, even though they essentially entailed slow-moving causal processes. This temporal dimension of the causal processes was rarely spelled out, however. Hellmann argues that, as a result of this theoretical stance, scholarly arguments about NATO have tended to oscillate between two extremes: the position that NATO was (and is) certain to survive and the position that NATO was (and is) certain to collapse. Hellmann sees a possible solution to this structural bias in theory in moving from the fairly abstract level of structural analysis to theoretically structured stories.

Against this backdrop, the authors in this volume set out to take a fresh look at the Atlantic relationship. Collectively the authors seek answers to a series of questions. First, what precisely is the character of the Atlantic order? Lots of concepts are advanced by scholars to depict the elements of this order, including pluralistic security community, cooperative security alliance, political community, economic region, Western civilization, and constitutional order. Each of these notions carries with it a notion of the underlying sources of cohesion and logic of politics within it. The first task of the book is to explore these alternative notions of political order and their relevance in capturing today's Atlantic political order.

Second, what is the character of the current change? If the Atlantic order is undergoing some sort of change—evolving, eroding, breaking down, or altering—what is it? There are lots of different ways to talk about change. Is change manifest as disruption, crisis, transformation, or politics as usual? Change can lead to maturation and deepening of the order, but it can also lead to erosion and breakdown of the order. In making these queries we are searching for an answer to the basic question of whether, in the current cycle of conflict and crisis, the Atlantic political order is functioning or malfunctioning?

Third, what are the sources of continuity and change? If U.S.-European relations are becoming more divided, separate, and conflict-ridden, are these changes the result of ephemeral factors such as leadership styles and personalities or of the unique conjuncture of events? Or are they the result of shifts in power, values, society, economy, or global developments? Several alternative master sources of change focus on underlying shifts in power, interests, and values. In asking about the sources of change in Atlantic relations, however, we must also ask questions about what forces are at work in maintaining stability and cohesion.

Atlantic Political Order

To begin, it is useful to see U.S.-European relations as a distinct political order. The postwar origins of this Atlantic political order are well known.[7] Emerging out of the turmoil of the world wars and depression of the first half of the twentieth century, it took coherent shape during the cold war. It is held together by military alliance, economic integration, shared values, and networks of political and diplomatic governance. Democracy, capitalism, and a common civilizational heritage also give it shape. This sense of an Atlantic political community was evoked in Walter Lippmann's observation in 1943 that the ocean that separated the United States and Europe is actually an "inland sea" around which a common people live.[8]

7. See G. John Ikenberry, *After Victory: Institutions, Strategic Restraint, and the Rebuilding of Order after Major War* (Princeton: Princeton University Press, 2001).

8. Walter Lippmann, *American Foreign Policy: Shield of the Republic* (Boston: Little, Brown, 1943).

The Atlantic political order, however, is not just a common political space that sprang naturally to life. It is a constructed political order, built around U.S. hegemony, mutual interests, political bargains, and agreed-upon rules and norms. The blueprints of this political order were not as formal or specific as, say, the founding documents and visions of the European political community. But the ideas of an Atlantic political community do exist in a sequence of diplomatic acts: the Atlantic Charter of 1941, the Bretton Woods agreements of 1944, the United Nations Charter of 1945, the Marshall Plan of 1947, and the Atlantic Pact of 1949. In different ways, these acts laid down principles, institutions, and commitments that formed the foundations of Atlantic order.[9]

The core of the Atlantic political order is the NATO security pact. It provided the most formal and durable link between the United States and Europe. But the alliance and the larger array of formal and informal economic and political institutions are not simply products of the cold war. The political construction of the Atlantic political order after 1945 was facilitated by the visions and principles of Western order that predated and emerged semi-independently of the cold war. Even the birth of the Atlantic Pact in April 1949 had a positive vision behind it as reflected in British foreign minister Ernst Bevin's call in December 1948 for a "spiritual union" of the Western democracies. That is, NATO was part of a Western community and not just a military alliance. John Foster Dulles made the same point in 1954 when he argued that the major emphasis of the Atlantic alliance was "on cooperation for something rather than merely against something."[10] It is this democratic community impulse that must be recalled when searching for the underlying bases of Atlantic political order.

This Atlantic order is built on two historic bargains that the United States has made with Europe. One is a realist bargain and grows out of the United States' grand strategy of the cold war. The United States provides its European

9. A wide-ranging literature exists that explores the political, economic, and intellectual foundations of the postwar Atlantic order. See, for example, Robert Strausz-Hupé, James E. Dougherty, and William R. Kintner, *Building the Atlantic World* (New York: Harper and Row, 1963); James Robert Huntley, *Uniting the Democracies: Institutions of the Emerging Atlantic-Pacific System* (New York: New York University Press, 1980); Harold van B. Cleveland, *The Atlantic Idea and Its European Rivals* (New York: McGraw-Hill, 1966); Tony Smith, *America's Mission: The United States and the Worldwide Struggle for Democracy in the Twentieth Century* (Princeton: Princeton University Press, 1994); Richard Gardner, *Sterling-Dollar Diplomacy: Anglo-American Collaboration in the Reconstruction of Multilateral Trade* (Oxford: Clarendon Press, 1956); Robert A. Pollard, *Economic Security and the Origins of the Cold War, 1945–1950* (New York: Columbia University Press, 1985); Melvyn P. Leffler, *A Preponderance of Power: National Security, the Truman Administration, and the Cold War* (Stanford: Stanford University Press, 1992); and Marc Trachtenberg, *A Constructed Peace: The Making of the European Settlement, 1945–1963* (Princeton: Princeton University Press, 1999).

10. As quoted in Mary N. Hampton, "NATO at the Creation: U.S. Foreign Policy, West Germany, and the Wilsonian Impulse," *Security Studies* 4, no. 3 (Spring 1995): 625.

partners with security protection and access to U.S. markets, technology, and supplies within an open world economy. In return, these countries agree to be reliable partners that provide diplomatic, economic, and logistical support for the United States as its leads the wider Western postwar order. The result has been to tie the United States and Europe together—to make peace "indivisible" across the Atlantic. The binding of security ties also provides channels for consultation and joint decision making. Common security threats gave shape to unprecedented security cooperation embodied in the NATO alliance.[11]

The other is a liberal bargain that addresses the uncertainties of U.S. asymmetrical power. East Asian and European states agree to accept U.S. leadership and operate within an agreed-upon political-economic system. In return, the United States opens itself up and binds itself to its partners. In effect, the United States builds an institutionalized coalition of partners and reinforces the stability of these long-term mutually beneficial relations by making itself more user friendly—that is, by playing by the rules and creating ongoing political processes with these other states that facilitate consultation and joint decision making. The United States makes its power safe for the world, and in return Europe—and the wider world—agrees to live within this U.S.-led system. These bargains date from the 1940s. The status of these bargains today is open to question, but the legacy of these bargains helps the political context of norms, understandings, and expectations that feed into today's Atlantic disputes. The identification of these historic bargains also helps us measure how far away from the older Atlantic order the United States and Europe have moved.[12]

The Atlantic political order also allowed for the United States and Europe to pursue their own, semi-independent political projects. The U.S. project was the building and management of a wider hegemonic system—alliances, open markets, special relationships, multilateral regimes, regional protectorates, and so forth. U.S. power, geography, ideals, and history animated this global ambition. So too did the geopolitical realities of the bipolar cold war struggle. Europe was an essential partner in many of these endeavors, but the United States essentially pursued a separate, non-Atlantist foreign policy agenda in its dealings with Asia, Latin America, and the Middle East.

The European project was the unification and integration of Europe. The United States initially played a direct supporting role in helping to launch the European integration project. The United States insisted that a European security grouping (the Brussels Pact) be established before it would enter into a

---

11. See Thomas Risse-Kappen, *Cooperation among Democracies: The European Influence on U.S. Foreign Policy* (Princeton: Princeton University Press, 1995).

12. G. John Ikenberry, "The Political Foundations of Atlantic Order," in *The New Transatlantic Agenda: Facing the Challenges of Global Governance*, ed. Hall Gardner and R. Stefanova (Aldershot, U.K.: Ashgate, 2001), 17–29.

North Atlantic security commitment. The United States also channeled Marshall Plan funds to Europe in a way that was contingent on increased European economic cooperation. But as the agenda of European integration took off, the United States largely stepped aside and allowed Europe to chart its own course.

The conflict between the United States and Europe can be seen, at least in part, as a breakdown of these great historical bargains coupled with a growing clash between the U.S. and European projects. The security bargain has eroded in the aftermath of the cold war, even as the NATO alliance has expanded into eastern Europe. U.S. commitment to norms of consultation and multilateral cooperation has also been thrown into question. In the meantime, the U.S. project and the European project seem to coexist less comfortably than in the past. The rise of unipolarity and the transformation in international threats make it easier—and perhaps necessary—for the United States to act alone and in ways that conflict with Europe's security orientation. At the same time, as the European project travels a pathway that is increasingly separate and distinct from that of the United States or the old Atlantic partnership, and as Europe's size and geopolitical influence grow and become less connected to the United States, Europe's conflicts with the United States' global leadership aspirations are increasing.

Conflict, Crisis, and Transformation

One of the central aims of this volume is to assess the nature and consequences of the recent conflict in U.S.-European relations. We want to develop a more precise understanding of what drives current conflict in the Atlantic political order and whether that conflict is leading to crisis and change. It is useful, therefore, to specify what the various conflict pathways are. These are sketched in figure 1.1.

We start with political conflict. In the current period of Atlantic relations, political conflict has been triggered by the war in Iraq and the deeper disagreements between the United States and Europe over the post-9/11 international order. Conflict can lead to two sorts of outcomes. One is resolution of the conflict within the existing rules and institutions of the Atlantic political order. In effect, a disagreement emerges between the two parties, and it is settled within the political framework that has long operated to deal with such problems. This settlement can take one of two forms. One is simply a resolution that leaves the existing rules and institutions as they were before. The other actually alters incrementally the rules and institutions of the political order.

For example, the United States and Europe can disagree over the roles and purposes of NATO, such as its "out-of-area" missions. This conflict can play itself out in established channels of consultation and policy development. The resolution of the conflict may entail some modification of NATO's mission or

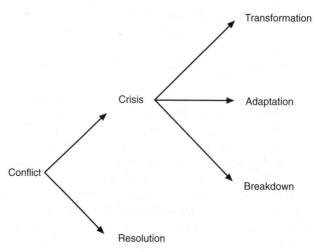

Figure 1.1. Pathways of political conflict

not. But the conflict and its settlement take place within the existing institutional framework of the Atlantic security partnership—and there is no extraordinary questioning of the underlying premises of that partnership. The underlying commitment to the Atlantic order is not questioned by any of the parties, and that order is not imperiled. Under these circumstances, transatlantic conflict is not unlike political conflict within domestic Western political systems. It is natural, inevitable, and contained.

Conflict can also escalate into an outright political crisis. As noted earlier, a political crisis is defined as an extraordinary moment when the existence and viability of the political order are called into question. That is, a crisis exists when conflict threatens the integrity of the order. More specifically, for purposes of this volume we define a crisis as a situation in which one or more of four circumstances obtain: (1) a fundamental disagreement breaks out over what at least one side believes is a core interest; (2) a sharp break occurs in market and social interdependence; (3) an institutional breakdown occurs regarding the rules and norms of process; (4) and/or a breakdown occurs in a sense of community.

When the Atlantic order enters into a crisis, there are three possible outcomes. One is breakdown. The old order gives way to disorder. The rules and norms of the order are thrown into question and found wanting. In this situation the order does not reconstitute itself. No new rules and institutions replace the old rules and institutions. It may be that in place of the postwar Atlantic system, a crisis and breakdown occur and result in estrangement and ongoing fundamental disagreement about the Atlantic and international political space that the United States and Europe mutually inhabit. This "disorder" may actually result in a phase of strategic rivalry and great power counterbalancing. Such a breakdown of order may—in the eyes of some observers—be a sort of order. At the extreme it may look like a return to a sort of nineteenth-century balance-of-power system—which is a sort of ordered disorder. Charles Kupchan explores the logic of breakdown of the Atlantic system's might by looking at previous cooperative political orders that fell apart.

A second outcome of crisis is for the Atlantic system to be transformed. In this outcome, the two sides fundamentally restructure their relationship, but they ultimately do so by renegotiating its basic rules and norms. Here the basic rules and norms of the partnership are thrown into question, but they are reinvented. At the end of the cycle of conflict and crisis, the two sides find a new set of arrangements that are mutually satisfactory. A new settled agreement of how the order should operate takes hold. In the case of the Atlantic order, this might take the form of a new set of governance mechanisms for handling security and economic issues. The old postwar bargains are replaced with a new set of bargains that leaves the United States and Europe together within a common political order.

A third outcome is something in between. This one might be called the adaptation of the Atlantic order. In this case, the old order is not completely wiped away, but new rules and arrangements are added to it to cope with the new disagreements. It may be difficult to fully distinguish this outcome from the evolutionary outcome that emerges when the political order settles a conflict short of a deep political crisis. In the case of the Atlantic order, this outcome might entail a reworking of the NATO bargain that keeps the joint security arrangements in place but alters the formal mechanisms for consultation and decision making. Thus, in the case of NATO there are clear alternative pathways of transformation, adaptation, and breakdown. Transformation would entail an eventual restructuring of NATO to deal with out-of-area conflicts as transformation. Adaptation would be seen in a continuation of coalitions of the willing (as manifest in some NATO members' current roles in Afghanistan and Iraq). And breakdown would involve a significant downgrading of NATO, repeated U.S. unilateralism, or a separate EU defense force (as envisaged by French president Jacques Chirac) unattached and uncoordinated with NATO.[13]

These various conflict and crisis pathways help clarify the level of discord that may beset the Atlantic system and also spell out the various ways that conflict and crisis can alter the political order and cause it to evolve. The analogy to domestic constitutional systems is instructive. Where disagreements within the polity are handled by the existing domestic legal system, this solution is the method of conflict resolution that is short of crisis. Where a new sort of conflict

---

13. Henry Nau discusses these alternative pathways in his chapter.

emerges that threatens the basic framework and legitimacy of the domestic political order, a crisis exists. Crisis that leads to breakdown is something akin to a civil war that results in division and separation. A crisis that leads to transformation is akin to constitutional crises that lead to what Bruce Ackerman calls "higher rule making."[14] In the American experience, this sort of process is analogous to the renegotiation of the constitutional framework that occurred during and after the Civil War and the Great Depression.

Explaining Conflict and Crisis

Each author in this volume makes a distinct argument about the sources and character of conflict and crisis. In explaining this conflict and pathway of continuity and change, each tends to focus on one of four clusters of variables: power, markets, institutions, and identity. These variables are invoked in various ways as both indicators of crisis and sources of crisis. In sketching these clusters of explanatory variables, I am not seeking to construct a deductively derived causal framework for analysis but rather am engaging in the inductive identification of general categories of causal factors that can be found in the individual chapters.

Power and Security

One set of explanations for U.S.-European discord focuses on shifts in the disparities of power and security threats. The most basic variable is the changing distribution of power. The journalist Robert Kagan points to these power shifts as key to the Atlantic conflict. The United States has become a unipolar military power with global security imperatives, while Europe has lost its capacity and willingness to project power abroad. The United States operates as the preeminent global power in a Hobbesian world of threats and insecurities, while Europe has grown satisfied and secure within its Kantian zone of peace. These objective differences in power capabilities—which are in part reflections of choices and historical legacies—in turn help shape divergent American and European strategic cultures. These divergent security cultures shape the way Washington and European elites think about and act in the wider global arena in regard to issues that include arms control, peace in the Middle East, the use of force, and the war on terrorism. So constituted, the United States and Europe find themselves in different geopolitical worlds—and conflict is inevitable.[15]

Charles Kupchan also sees power disparities between the United States and Europe as the critical dynamic shaping Atlantic relations—but he draws

14. Bruce Ackerman, *We the People*, vol. 1, *Foundations* (Cambridge: Harvard University Press, 1993).

15. Kagan, *Paradise and Power*.

different conclusions. It is not Europe's weakness but its rising power and expanding global ambitions that generate conflict. Conflict today is a sign of incipient geopolitical rivalry between the United States and Europe and the breakdown of the postwar Atlantic order.[16] In this volume, Kupchan argues that the Atlantic relationship is in the midst of a fundamental transition. America and Europe no longer have the same strategic interests that they did during the cold war, and their identities have become more oppositional as opposed to shared. The events of the past four years constitute a critical breakpoint, comprising key features of the order that existed from World War II through to the end of the twentieth century. Kupchan argues that scholars and policymakers need to embrace a new conceptual framework and associated vocabulary in dealing with the Atlantic community.

In capturing today's Atlantic breakpoint, Kupchan identifies four key periods of Atlantic relations: the Revolutionary War to the early 1900s; the early 1900s through the events of Pearl Harbor and the United States' entry into World War II in 1941; World War II through the events of September 11; and post–September 11. It is the undermining of the postwar security order that, Kupchan argues, is critical for bringing the United States and Europe to this breakpoint. It is too early to tell where the new stable resting point is for Atlantic relations, but Kupchan looks at various possibilities—and he looks at how events could conspire to make arms conflict between the two parts of the West "thinkable" again and what steps could be taken to avert the worst consequences of this historic shift in the Atlantic community.

In contrast to Kupchan, who sees the current crisis as part of a long-term erosion and breakdown of the Western alliance, William Hitchcock argues that the Atlantic alliance possesses remarkable flexibility and adaptability, and has shown itself over the past sixty years able to contain serious divergences among its members over core interests and values. The ties that bind the alliance—common security interests, democratic governance, and economic interdependence—have proven themselves to be powerful adhesives that counteract the fissiparous dynamics of period crises. Equally important, many crises within the alliance over the past half century have been resolved by the creation of new rules and institutions that have allowed member states to remain within the community. Thus the Western alliance endures largely through a process of adaptation and flexibility. Hitchcock notes, however, that the basic strategic argument at the heart of the Iraq debate has yet to be resolved. The alliance is in a holding pattern, as members cooperate effectively in some areas (Afghanistan and the Balkans, for example) while agreeing to disagree over Iraq. The long, slow burn of the Iraq crisis has yet to lead to adaptation or creative solutions to bring the alliance back into unanimity. Only a resolution of the war itself, argues Hitchcock, can accomplish that.

16. Kupchan, *End of the American Era.*

In addition to shifting disparities of power, the changing character of U.S. and European perceptions of external threats can also be invoked to explain recent Atlantic conflict. The end of the cold war entailed the loss of a common threat that served as a transcendent source of cohesion and cooperation. With the disappearance of this threat, the cost of disagreement has been reduced. But the cold war also gave the United States and Europe a common identity: they together constituted the vanguard of the Free World. They were thrown together in struggle, and this common effort helped give shape to a common Western identity. The rise of new threats from the Middle East and the diffuse worry about transnational terrorism do not enhance solidarity in the same way that the cold war threats did; indeed they provide new sources for strategic disagreement.

In his chapter, Henry Nau argues that threat plays an important role in shaping transatlantic community responses. At the outset, the Soviet threat was a major, perhaps the major, factor creating NATO. Shared values in the Western world were weak—the United States let Great Britain stand or fall on its own in 1940—and it was some years after World War II before common democratic values permeated the alliance. Although common values defined Soviet communism as an unacceptable political system, NATO was inconceivable without perceived Soviet threats in Berlin and Korea. Today, according to Nau, the absence of a common threat on the scale of the Soviet Union and the existence of differing perceptions of the terrorist threat weaken the transatlantic community. But now shared values and habits of institutional cooperation are much stronger, and Nau is optimistic that the community may narrow future perceptions of the terrorist threat or hang together, as it seems to be doing in Afghanistan and Iraq, even if different threat perceptions persist. Nau's approach, consistent with his other work, combines equal focus on the role of power and identity, while underplaying the influence of institutional factors.[17]

Although not directly discussed by the authors of these chapters, another power-based explanation for Atlantic discord focuses on the rise of unipolarity. The end of the cold war did not result in a return to a multipolar distribution of power but rather reinforced U.S. dominance. The United States started the 1990s as the world's only superpower, and it grew faster than the other major states during the decade.[18] This power preeminence has implications for Atlantic relations. First, the United States finds it easier to act outside of multilateral rules and alliances. Washington does not need to accommodate

17. Henry Nau, *At Home Abroad: Identity and Power in American Foreign Policy* (Ithaca: Cornell University Press, 2002).

18. On the general impact of American unipolarity on international relations, see G. John Ikenberry, ed., *America Unrivaled: The Future of the Balance of Power* (Ithaca: Cornell University Press, 2002); and Ethan Kapstein and Michael Mastanduno, eds., *Unipolar Politics: Realism and State Strategies after the Cold War* (New York: Columbia University Press, 1999).

itself to or compromise with other states as it did during the cold war. This stance inevitably leads to disputes with Europe, particularly because the European embrace of multilateralism and rules-based order has only increased. Second, unipolarity provides new reasons for Europe both to free ride on U.S. leadership and to resist U.S. power. Both reactions—free riding and resistance—erode Atlantic cooperation. Third, unipolarity creates legitimacy problems for the United States. During the cold war, Europe and other countries were readily able to see U.S. power and leadership as good for the wider system. A one-superpower world eliminates this source of normative cover for U.S. power. To be sure, the U.S. unipolar provision of global public goods—security protection, underwriting of economic openness, and so forth—might still be appreciated around the world and generate normative acceptance of unipolarity. But unipolarity also appears to diminish the American willingness to provide those public goods. Finally, the rise of unipolarity appears to generate incentives for the United States to renegotiate its institutional bargains with other countries, including Europe. Unipolarity may not lead to outright U.S. rejection of multilateralism and rules-based order, but it seems to prompt a rethinking of the cold war–era rules and bargains that underlie the Atlantic political order.

These various power-based explanations of Atlantic discord provide important insights into the deep logic of the system. In assessing the role of these factors, several considerations are relevant. First, if the power disparities and lost common threats do not break up the Atlantic order, this lack of change says something about the necessity of a common threat to hold the Atlantic order together. As Henry Nau argues, common threat may be less necessary today than it was in 1949 to hold the community together. Changing distributions of power and threat perceptions may have far-reaching implications for Atlantic conflict and cooperation, but these variables might be best seen in combination with other factors that reinforce or mute their impact.[19] Second, if the type of conflict in U.S. relations with Europe is also evident in U.S. relations with other countries outside the Atlantic world, this comparison provides some evidence that the causes of conflict are not unique to the Atlantic region. It might, for example, strengthen the argument that the new dynamics of unipolarity are important in causing conflict. Alternatively, the conflicts generated by unipolarity might be manifest differently in different regions of the world. Henry Kissinger, for example, noted in 2004 that Europeans are more distressed by the unilateral assertion of U.S. power than are East

---

19. The fact that the end of the cold war did not lead to the immediate unraveling of the U.S.-European security partnership has been used to identify the importance of other factors in binding the Atlantic countries together. See, for example, G. John Ikenberry, "Institutions, Strategic Restraint, and the Durability of Western Order," *International Security* 23, no. 3 (Winter 1998–99): 43–78.

Asians.[20] These regional comparisons can also help isolate variables that amplify and mute structural power dynamics.

Economic Interests and Market Relations

There are many ways in which Atlantic economic relations help explain Atlantic cooperation and discord. One type of variable is the degree of economic integration between America and Europe, which can be measured through trade and market dependence, the shifting concentration of imports and exports, and levels of foreign direct investment. Growth of Atlantic economic integration can have various impacts on the political relations between the United States and Europe, influencing the opportunity costs of conflict. Kathleen McNamara surveys the various mechanisms that link Atlantic economic relations to the wider political order. Generally speaking, the growth of Atlantic economic interdependence has reinforced political cooperation, but market exchange only has a pacifying effect if it coexists with a host of other factors.

In McNamara's view, there are three ways that growing economic interdependence can strengthen political relations between the United States and Europe. One way that growing economic integration reinforces cooperation is by generating an array of vested interests—such as commerce, banking, and investment groups—that favor stable and continuous relations. International business groups have tangible interests in a steady and predictable political environment, but these interests are much more likely to matter today than in the past. Also, the growth in Atlantic economic interdependence has created incentives for U.S. and European leaders to develop governance mechanisms to facilitate orderly economic relations. The G-7/8 summit process was created in the 1970s to help the advanced economies govern an increasingly interdependent world economy. This intergovernmental process in turn provided mechanisms for governments to discuss and resolve Atlantic policy disputes. A third impact of growing economic interdependence is the reconfiguration of national economic interests. As national economies become more fused, the costs of major political disruptions grow. But beyond this, as trade and investment tie countries together it becomes harder for national leaders to act nationally. In particular, growing foreign investment has this impact. It is harder to know which companies within the United States or Europe are domestic and which are foreign—a problem further compounded when domestic workers are employed by foreign companies. Economic boundaries are blurred, interests and identities redefined, and this ambiguity undercuts the ability to pursue radically nationalist policies.

Of course, growing economic interdependence also can generate new forms of conflict. As noted earlier, one response to these problems of interdependence

---

20. Henry Kissinger, "A Global Order in Flux," *Washington Post*, 9 July 2004.

is to build more extensive Atlantic and global governance mechanisms. But conflict can nonetheless grow as well. New regulatory issues and controversies emerge. National differences in social welfare, labor standards, corporate taxation, environmental standards, and so forth are brought more directly into Atlantic political relations. Moreover, there is no necessary and inevitable link between economic interdependence and Atlantic strategic cooperation. The United States and Europe can still disagree on how to deal with the Middle East or over the rules for the use of force.

Another aspect of the Atlantic economic relationship is the seigniorage role of the U.S. dollar. From the early postwar years until today, the U.S. dollar has acted as global reserve currency—and this role provides the United States with special advantages.[21] Countries around the world use the dollar in international transactions and hold the dollar as a reserve asset, which allows the United States to run current account deficits without putting the dollar under pressure. The size of the U.S. economy, the centrality of its currency, and the relative safety of U.S. assets give the United States political advantages and are an often-hidden aspect of U.S. hegemony. In the context of U.S.-European relations, the dollar system can be seen as part of the power structure within which Washington and the other Atlantic governments operate. In the 1960s, it was grist for strident French and European attacks on U.S. foreign policy because the dollar's position allowed the Johnson administration to wage the Vietnam War and launch the Great Society. Today it is Japan and China that are buying U.S. Treasury bonds and thereby helping to finance the U.S. current account deficit. But the important point is that the dollar-based monetary system is integral to the wider U.S.-centered political order and not just a narrow aspect of exchange rates.

Jens van Scherpenberg offers a note of caution concerning the argument that transatlantic economic interdependence is a stabilizing factor for political relations between Europe and the United States. Contrary to the liberal perspective, he argues that the low level of conflict in regular trade relations should not be taken as an indication of a low level of conflict intensity in transatlantic economic relations in general. In pointing out a number of actual and potential transatlantic "strategic" economic conflicts, van Scherpenberg draws on the classic realist argument—the linkage and spillover between economic and security relationships. A look at particular contentious issues such as direct investment in strategic industries, trade in strategic goods—for example, passenger aircraft (the Airbus-Boeing subsidies dispute) and satellite navigation (GPS versus Galileo)—and economic relations with China underpins his argument that underneath the surface of the highly integrated transatlantic economy lies latent distrust and rivalry.

21. For a discussion of the seigniorage role of the dollar, see Robert Gilpin, *The Challenge of Global Capitalism: The World Economy in the 21st Century* (Princeton: Princeton University Press, 2000).

Van Scherpenberg thus identifies critical political-economic variables that bear on the future of the Atlantic order. The coming strategic economic conflicts and instabilities that the author sees will be most consequential if they are magnified by security conflict—of the sort seen during the controversies that attended the Iraq War. Although such an outcome would imply a breakdown of any factual burden sharing between the United States and Europe in global security and stabilization policies, it is not inevitable. Well-negotiated burden-sharing arrangements, based on a cooperative, nonrival approach to transatlantic relations in strategic economic areas, are still a realistic possibility—the more so if Europe stands on its own.

In stepping back from the specific economic variables that bear on U.S.-European relations, we see several questions to raise. First is the question of how economic incentives for Atlantic cooperation will perform in the face of serious deterioration of security or value-based splits. That is, how much weight of discord can the economic dimension of the Atlantic order bear? French and U.S. businessmen, for example, made public calls for moderation and dialogue at the height of the U.S.-French dispute over the Iraq War. How much these countervailing business interests in cooperation can succeed in muting or reversing serious strategic disagreement remains to be seen. Historically, as McNamara points out, such economic interdependence had little effect on political conflict in World War I and the Suez crisis. Second, if the NATO alliance in fact erodes into insignificance, the big question is what the impact of this change will be on Atlantic economic relations. Certainly, the postwar U.S.-led security umbrella facilitated the building of open market relations between Europe and America—as it did between East Asia and America. The indivisibility of peace went hand in hand with the construction of an open world economy. But what would a growing division of security realms—or, even more, the rise of rival security spheres—mean for the functioning of an open world and Atlantic economy?

Institutions, Law, and Sovereignty

Another set of variables that explains the unfolding of Atlantic conflict is composed of the underlying institutions and conceptions of law and sovereignty. The dense array of institutions that span the Atlantic world is itself a manifestation of decades of growing interdependence as well as shared values and interests that have brought America and Europe together. These institutions exist in various guises: in the myriad intergovernmental and multilateral institutions and regimes that were established for specific functional purposes over the decades; in the wider legal and normative rules and institutions that reflect long-established agreements on how states should act and relate to each other; and in the deeper—and often buried—conceptions of state sovereignty that spell out the location and character of political authority within and between states.

These multilayered institutions enter into the current Atlantic crisis in two ways. First, the institutions—security, economic, political—that make up the political order provide the mechanisms and channels through which the United States and the European countries do business with each other—advancing their interests and settling their disputes. A rich international relations literature traces the ways that institutions, and international regimes, can affect the likelihood of cooperation by facilitating flows of information and establishing credible commitments.[22] There is also a literature that shows how the density of institutional connections between states is related to the propensity for the peaceful settlement of disputes.[23] In various ways, this array of institutions operates primarily as a moderating role in the face of periodic political conflict.

Institutions, however, can enter Atlantic disputes in another way: in the guise of international law and ideas about sovereignty that establish normative standards for the proper conduct of government policy. These norms can be procedural or substantive, but either way they provide standards and benchmarks that states use to evaluate the rectitude of their own or other governments' action. These legal-based normative standards can impact disputes between the United States and Europe in several ways. They can act as constraints on conflict by providing procedural or substantive guides that help states find their way back to common ground. In effect, the legal norms provide a language for negotiation and mutual adjustment. But legal norms—and the wider set of rules and norms about the proper conduct of foreign policy—can also play the opposite role. They can provide the normative grist for disagreement. The Atlantic relationship—perhaps more than any other major region of the world apart from the European Union itself—is infused with legal-based norms about how relations should operate. To the extent that the United States or Europe seeks to pull back from these established norms—for example, the norms relating to multilateralism or to the use of force—these perceived violations or transgressions can trigger disputes from the other side.

In his chapter Michael Byers offers insights of this sort. In his rendering, international law as it relates to the use of force and the resolution of disputes over legal interpretations creates a process that brings the parties together over the terms of the debate. In this sense it "domesticates" disputes. Even at the worst moments of the controversy at the UN Security Council over the military intervention in Iraq, the conflict played itself out within the framework

---

22. See Stephen Krasner, ed., *International Regimes* (Ithaca: Cornell University Press, 1982); Robert Keohane, *After Hegemony: Cooperation and Discord in the World Economy* (Princeton: Princeton University Press, 1984); and Andreas Hasenclever, Peter Mayer, and Volker Rittberger, *Theories of International Regimes* (Cambridge: Cambridge University Press, 1997).

23. See Bruce Russett and John O'Neal, *Triangulating Peace: Democracy, Interdependence, and International Organization* (New York: Norton, 2001).

and terms of international law. As Byers sees it, international law provides a "field of contest." The United States did not break out of the international legal system, and indeed both sides want to see the legal foundations remain.

In particular, Byers examines the role of international law in the current U.S.-European conflict. He asks the question: is there common ground on the application of international law? His argument is that the Atlantic order—at least as it is defined in terms of international law—is not at stake. Indeed, the international legal system's central position in the political conflict that consumed the Atlantic community in the year leading up to the 2003 Iraqi War makes it an ideal focus for considering whether relations between the United States and Europe have changed fundamentally, as least with respect to the rules and norms of process that regulate the relationship. Byers focuses on two firmly established rules of international law, namely, the right of self-defense and the general rule of interpretation, and follows their course through the geopolitical transformations of the last two decades. He finds that the approaches taken by the United States and European countries to these foundational rules have remained remarkably consistent. This consistency may reflect the fact that similarities in identities and interests within the Atlantic community still outweigh the differences. Indeed, the contemporary international legal system is predominantly a joint creation of Western Europe and the United States; these countries therefore have a strong interest in maintaining, strengthening, and only occasionally—and cautiously—altering the rules. For Byers there is no transatlantic crisis, at least not with respect to foundational rules.

Jeffrey Anderson, in his chapter, looks not at international legal frameworks and norms but at each side's conceptions of the supremacy of the national state's legal and political authority. Anderson addresses the question of whether the crisis in transatlantic relations stems in part from differing conceptions of sovereignty operating in foreign policy-making circles within the United States and Europe. Employing Stephen Krasner's fourfold classification scheme, he shows that there are in fact marked differences between the United States and Europe in one aspect of their approach to sovereignty—specifically, their willingness to accept limitations on domestic authority structures, or what Krasner terms Westphalian sovereignty. Along other dimensions, however, the United States and Europe are similar, both in terms of rhetoric and behavior. Thus, whatever tangible differences exist between U.S. and European conceptions of sovereignty, they have not played a significant role in the unfolding of the transatlantic crisis since 9/11. To the extent that differing approaches to sovereignty have mattered at all, the effects have been felt on the margins, and only then as loose cognitive frames that appear to rule in certain strategies while ruling out others. In the main, however, the recent and at times sharp political conflicts over threat definition, the doctrine of preemption, the use of military force versus diplomacy, and other bones of contention in the transatlantic relationship have not flowed from differing conceptions of the proper scope and validity of national sovereignty.

Values and Political Identity

Ideational and normative variables can also be used to explain Atlantic conflict and its resolution. Indeed, at the most general level, it is useful to see the Atlantic community as a reflection or manifestation of shared Euro-American political identity, a constructed or imagined community that has evolved over the decades. David Easton talked about political community in terms of a "we feeling"—that is, a sense that American and European peoples are part of a single political grouping that stands apart from the world outside the Atlantic community.[24] If a shared sense of community exists across the Atlantic, the questions are how is it manifest, in what ways does it matter, and how is it changing?

John Hall provides, in his chapter, an analytic narrative of the character and significance of Atlantic community. Hall makes an initial distinction along a spectrum of possible transatlantic identities and identifies sentiments typically attached to human relationships. At one extreme is love, followed by bargaining, resentment, separation, and, at the other extreme, divorce. Hall's argument is that the European relationship with the United States exists somewhere between bargaining and resentment. Bargaining implies a negotiated and—in the end—mutually satisfactory relationship. It is manifest as a political community in which political relations are based on compromise, diffuse reciprocity, equality of form, and voluntary participation and compliance within the political order. Resentment implies a more coerced relationship. It is manifest as hierarchy, political inequality, necessity, and imposition of rule. Hall suggests that the Atlantic relationship has gone back and forth between these two relational types. Today, the United States still provides leadership in the form of security protection and support for an open world economy— hegemonic services that Europe enjoys. But the end of the cold war has made Europe and the United States need each other less. Europe does not have the will or capacity to generate an alternative order that reduces its reliance on the United States, but resentment of the United States has grown nonetheless.

John Hall argues that there are historically and socially derived American and European images of belonging that have risen and fallen and transformed over the last century. In the late-nineteenth century, Anglo-American identity had genuinely transnational aspects. The flow of immigrants in the late nineteenth century also gave the Atlantic world a sense of shared community. After the world wars, and particularly after 1945, a new generation of U.S. and European elites saw themselves as part of a common political community. Hall argues that these transnational Atlantic loyalties and attachments have

24. David Easton, *A Systems Analysis of Political Life* (New York: John Wiley, 1965).

waned in recent decades, although the erosion of a sense of shared belonging has not translated directly into a breakdown of Atlantic political order.

Another way that political identity can be manifest is in shared and divergent U.S. and European conceptions of democracy, liberal society, and sovereignty. In the most diffuse sense, the United States and Europe share the common heritage of Western civilization, a heritage that embraces constitutional democracy, market society, civil rights, and the rule of law. These shared commitments make it easier for the United States and Europe to affiliate with each other, to cooperate, and to imagine themselves operating within a shared community of values and interests. Practical problems of cooperation are less onerous between liberal democracies.[25] Differences between liberal and social democracy are still differences within the democratic family.[26] But within this common civilizational setting, differences also exist— and in some ways are indeed growing. Continental Europe's tradition of social democracy is different from the United States' liberal democratic tradition. Political values about the proper scope of the state within the economy and society are different, and this diversity can fuel political conflict.

More specific social and political values can also become the grist of Atlantic conflict. Gun control, capital punishment, religion, environmentalism— all these contentious issues are rooted in social and political values that are differently distributed and manifest in Europe and the United States. Political cycles—in which either right- or left-of-center political parties rule in Europe and the United States—can minimize or exacerbate these differences.[27]

In this regard, Dieter Fuchs and Hans-Dieter Klingemann, in their chapter, look closely at public opinion survey data to identify underlying differences in values. They find variations in political orientations among the United States and European countries in areas such as religion, political participation, and civic engagement. These gaps in value orientation are particularly striking between the United States and core European countries such as France and Germany. The differences are not ones that go to the heart of values associated with Western civilization. Europe and the United States both embrace basic liberal democratic values such as support for human rights, political equality, and tolerance of others. But differences exist in the way the two parts of the West think democracy should be institutionalized. Americans are more likely to evince libertarian attitudes—supporting ideas such as a minimal state, self-responsibility, and competition in the market place. Europeans

25. For a recent statement of this argument, see Charles Lipson, *Reliable Partners: How Democracies Have Made a Separate Peace* (Princeton: Princeton University Press, 2003).

26. The threshold is when, in the view of the United States, social becomes authoritarian or, in the view of Europe, liberal becomes lawless. See Nau's chapter for a discussion of thresholds between political values and implications for political conflict.

27. This point is stressed in Nau's chapter. See also Timothy Garten Ash, *Free World: America, Europe and the Surprising Future of the West* (New York: Random House, 2004).

evince more traditional social democratic attitudes—supporting ideas such as state intervention to advance social welfare and equality. Fuchs and Klingemann argue that these differences are likely to increase as central and eastern European countries are integrated into the EU. Yet they also show that value gaps exist within Europe and the United States. These variations in the attitudes of Americans and Europeans make the lines of value cleavage more complex and shifting, which in turn reduce the sharpness of the disputes that play out across the Atlantic.

Stepping back, we find that shared values and political identity can impact Atlantic relations in several different ways. One mechanism is the transnational and trans-societal connections between the United States and Europe in which politics takes place. Where U.S. and European citizens sense that they are all members of a common Atlantic political community or Western society, this sentiment can provide support for government cooperation. Shared values reduce the depth of the disagreements that come and go within the Atlantic political community. Disagreements are not over the fundamental character or direction of the advanced world. Shared liberal democratic norms and institutions also facilitate processes of dispute resolution.[28] When these shared values and beliefs about a common political identity erode, the political order will be more prone to more fundamental and destabilizing forms of conflict.

Values can also shape political issues within the United States and European countries, which in turn impacts transatlantic relations. A lot of these national policies—such as ones concerned with the environment, the death penalty, or genetically modified food—are essentially domestic issues but indirectly spill over into international relations. It remains an interesting question whether these sorts of value-derived policy issues are more or less important in Atlantic relations in twenty-first century than they were in earlier decades or within the domestic societies. It also is an open question whether the values divide between Europe and the United States is growing or declining. The political salience of these value-derived policy differences—that is, the extent to which differences get "kicked up" into transatlantic politics—also varies.

In evaluating the role of values and political identity in Atlantic conflict, we find that several considerations seem particularly important. First, these variables are by their nature slow to change, so they need to be linked to other variables or circumstances to explain abrupt outbreaks of conflict. For example, the long-term erosion of a common political identity—or image of belonging—may only be manifest in the Atlantic political arena when it is combined with more proximate shifts in government leadership and policies.

It is also important that we focus on process norms and mutual understandings. Part of what gives the Atlantic political order its distinctiveness is that it

28. See Risse-Kappen, *Cooperation among Democracies*.

is infused with shared understandings and expectations about how political business will be conducted between the United States and Europe. Norms of consultation and reciprocity, for example, are key features of the postwar Atlantic security and economic partnership. These process norms and expectations can exist at least partially independently of substantive norms and values. It is important that when we assess whether a fundamental breakdown is emerging in Atlantic relations, we not just track the rise of new policy disputes but also look closely at the norms and rules that exist to handle or resolve these disputes. What makes Western constitutional democracies so stable is not that they are immune to political conflict—because they certainly are not—but that they are infused with norms, rules, institutions, and expectations about how the political system will deal with conflict.

Conclusion

The Atlantic political order has just passed through a dramatic moment of crisis. Serious observers argue that the essential character of that order—forged after World War II—is at risk. Some see the conflict between the United States and Europe over Iraq and over the rules and institutions of international order as part of a longer-term breakdown and dissolution of the Atlantic order. Europe and the United States will not disappear, but the interests, identities, and institutions that give the alliance its essential character as a functioning political order are disappearing. The authors of the chapters in this book provide analytic and empirical arguments that allow us to grasp and evaluate this debate about the future of Atlantic order.

At one level, these authors illuminate both the sources of conflict in contemporary U.S.-European relations and the logics that explain their significance and pathways of resolution. Hitchcock, Nau, and Kupchan shed light on the recent Atlantic crisis by placing it in postwar historical perspective. At another level, the authors also illuminate the different logics that exist when conflict emerges in a political order. Some show why the Atlantic order is losing its old character and why latent underlying shifts may unleash more breakdown and change in the future. Kupchan shows that the "security community" character of the West, manifest in the NATO alliance, has unraveled. Van Scherpenberg identifies submerged economic imbalances and dysfunctions that could yet emerge to divide the Atlantic countries. Yet many of the other authors identify factors that reinforce continuity in Atlantic relations. Byers shows—perhaps paradoxically—that although the most intense conflict between Europe and the United States dealt with disputes over international law, it was the deeper infrastructure of laws and norms that guided, muted, and resolved the dispute.

In these various ways, the authors in this book collectively offer a sophisticated portrait of Atlantic relations. Conflict is inherent in political orders, whether those orders are domestic or international. How conflict is managed, channeled, and resolved tells us a great deal about the character of the political order itself. Most of the authors in this volume see the recent crisis in U.S.-European relations as very real and consequential. But the long-term impact of this crisis is likely to push the Atlantic political order in new directions—to alter and loosen its older postwar rules, institutions, and bargains. Thomas Risse sketches possible trajectories of change in the conclusion. The Western order may simply adapt to a new array of interests and power realities that were brought into play by the recent crisis. Or it may be transformed into something strikingly different.

2 INEVITABLE DECLINE VERSUS PREDESTINED STABILITY

Disciplinary Explanations of the Evolving Transatlantic Order

GUNTHER HELLMANN

I don't think of transformation as something that starts un-transformed and goes to something that is transformed. I think of it as a process where we are forced by the nature of our world in this 21st century to continue, and it's more a matter of culture and attitude than it is technologies or platforms. It's more a question of recognizing that in the world today we are faced with things that come at you very fast.

> *Secretary of Defense Donald H. Rumsfeld, remarks at the forty-first Munich Conference on European Security Policy, Munich, Germany, February 12, 2005*

The evolution of NATO (and the Atlantic order more broadly) has been a hotly debated topic at the center of international relations discourse since the end of the cold war.[1] To some extent this interest was an expression of two motives that indeed should drive academic research: (1) genuine curiosity about the major factors influencing the alliance's development and (2) a widespread consensus that whatever happened to the alliance would have major effects well beyond the immediate confines of the transatlantic area. There was, however, a third motive behind the burgeoning interest in NATO (in

---

1. Donald Rumsfeld's remarks, as quoted in the epigraph, can be found at http://www.usembassy.it/file2005_02/alia/a5021102.htm (accessed 4 February 2007). In this chapter I use the term "Atlantic order" (as John Ikenberry does in the introduction) to refer to the overarching cooperative framework linking European and North American states and societies. When I speak of NATO, I am referring more narrowly to the military alliance between European states and the United States.

particular) in the 1990s: given the significance as well as the nature of the issue for disciplinary debates, the past, present, and future of NATO and the Atlantic order almost inevitably became an obvious research target for practically any established "paradigm." Not surprisingly, the issue also moved to the center of some of the usual paradigmatic battles.[2]

The evolution of the Atlantic order has not only been an important topic for the discipline but also a difficult one. In part this is because the concept of change underlying evolution or transformation is as dazzling as it is necessary. As Donald Rumsfeld, one of the key actors in transatlantic relations over the last few years, put it, transformation should not be looked at as something that "starts un-transformed and goes to something that is transformed." Rather, it ought be conceived of as "a process where we are forced by the nature of our world . . . to continue" from where we find ourselves. Although Rumsfeld had something different in mind when he referred to process and transformation in the context of institutional change at NATO (basically applying a technical term from NATO's vocabulary on weapons modernization), the underlying notion of change is much the same one with which international relations scholarship has had to come to grips since the end of the cold war. The discipline has examined the question of how NATO will be affected by the demise of its former adversary, the Soviet Union. In a simplified version, most of the answers to this question fell into one of two rubrics: scholars close to the realist tradition basically argued that NATO was bound to dissolve eventually, as any historical military alliance has done when confronted with the loss of its former enemy. In contrast, scholars closer to the liberal tradition (broadly conceived) argued that the Atlantic order was more likely to adapt successfully to the new environment because it was more than a military alliance. In many respects, these two strands also survived the aftermaths of 9/11 and even the clash between the Bush administration and some western European NATO members over Iraq in 2002–3.

One of the starting points of this book project has been that this theoretical indeterminacy is not a satisfactory state of affairs. Contributors mostly agreed that the Atlantic order is currently experiencing some major changes. Yet although there is broad consensus that the depth as well as the pace of these changes are more far-reaching than in past decades, it is unclear exactly how deep and how far these changes reach.[3] To come to grips with these changes,

2. Cf. Gunther Hellmann, "A Brief Look at the Recent History of NATO's Future," in *Transatlantic Tug-of-War: U.S.-EU Relations in the 21st Century. In Honor of Helga Haftendorn*, ed. Ingo Peters, Christopher Daase, and Susanne Feske, 181–215 (Münster: Lit Verlag, 2006).

3. For other recent works examining the crisis in transatlantic relations, see Ivo Daalder, Nicole Gnesotto, and Philip Gordon, *Crescent of Crisis: U.S.-European Strategy for the Greater Middle East* (Washington, DC: Brookings Institution Press, 2006); Thomas L. Ilgen, *Hard Power, Soft Power and the Future of Transatlantic Relations* (Aldershot, U.K.: Ashgate, 2006); Peters, Daase, and Feske, *Transatlantic Tug-of-War*; Roland Dannreuther and John Peterson, eds., *Security Strategy and Transatlantic Relations* (London: Routledge 2006); David

most of the authors in this book explore the character as well as the sources of these changes. In this chapter I approach the topic from a metaperspective by examining how the discipline has dealt with the question of change in the Atlantic order in the past. I argue that the discipline has not been well equipped conceptually to deal with the kind of transformational processes under examination here, that is, large-scale processes of change. In applying a typological framework developed by Paul Pierson, I discuss what types of causal accounts have dominated within the international relations literature—and what this domination may tell us about particular strengths, biases, and potential blind spots in coming to grips with the evolution of the Atlantic order in the past and possibly in the future. In essence I argue that the *structure* of the most prominent explanations is often similar, irrespective of paradigmatic ancestry. In spite of major differences—in spite, even, of mutually exclusive predictions—as to the expected path of change, realist, liberal, and constructivist accounts heavily rely in equal fashion on causal arguments that emphasize large-scale causal processes that are almost always framed in fairly statist *structural* terms, even though they essentially entail slow-moving causal processes.[4] This temporal dimension of the causal processes presumably shaping the course of developments is seldom spelled out in detail, however. For instance, threats play a crucial role both in realist accounts of bringing NATO into existence

---

M. Andrews, ed., *The Atlantic Alliance under Stress: U.S.-European Relations after Iraq* (Cambridge: Cambridge University Press, 2005); Matthew Evangelista and Vittorio E. Parsi, eds., *Partners or Rivals? European–American Relations after Iraq* (Milan: V&P, 2005); Hall Gardner, ed., *NATO and the European Union: New World, New Europe, New Threats* (Aldershot, U.K.: Ashgate, 2004); Philip Gordon and Jeremy Shapiro, *Allies at War: America, Europe and the Crisis over Iraq* (New York: McGraw-Hill, 2004); Elizabeth Pond, *Friendly Fire: The Near-Death of the Transatlantic Alliance* (Pittsburgh: European Union Studies Association; Washington, DC: Brookings Institution Press, 2004).

4. I focus here on contributions that either are self-consciously located in a specific paradigmatic tradition by their authors or easily fit into such a category. This is not to say that NATO or the Atlantic order more broadly has only been a topic of research for scholars associated with one of the three schools currently figuring prominently in international relations. As a matter of fact, some of the most original research on these topics stems from authors whose work either shuns such paradigmatic labels or is obviously hard to categorize under any of them, given the particular theoretical or methodological approach they chose. For a sample of important contributions that are difficult to locate in a paradigmatic context, see Peter J. Katzenstein, *A World of Regions: Asia and Europe in the American Imperium* (Ithaca: Cornell University Press, 2005); Ole Waever and Barry Buzan, "An Interregional Analysis: NATO's New Strategic Concept and the Theory of Security Complexes," in *Bound to Cooperate: Europe and the Middle East*, ed. Sven Behrendt and Christian-Peter Hanelt, 55–106 (Gütersloh: Bertelsmann Foundation Publishers, 2000); Barry Buzan and Ole Waever, *Regions and Powers: The Structure of International Security* (Cambridge: Cambridge University Press, 2003); and Michael C. Williams and Iver B. Neumann, "From Alliance to Security Community: NATO, Russia, and the Power of Identity," *Millennium* 29, no. 2 (June 2000): 357–87. The significant contributions of these authors notwithstanding, the future of transatlantic relations has gained most prominence in international relations in the context of paradigmatic exchanges.

and in causing its collapse. Yet neither the pace nor the duration of the temporal categories "appearance of threat" and "disappearance of threat," which figure as the key independent variables in realist accounts of NATO's origins as well as of its demise, is usually specified. This notion applies in similar fashion to comparable liberal or constructivist accounts. Thus, if one examines the debate as a whole, one sees a picture of international relations scholarship that essentially oscillates between two extremes: the position that NATO/the Atlantic order was (and is) certain to survive and the position that NATO/the Atlantic order was (and is) certain to collapse. What is more, these extremes on a spectrum of possible positions between breakdown on the one hand and successful adaptation on the other are not hypothetical but actually propagated by some of the most reputable scholars in the discipline. In other words, rather than gravitate toward the center (that is, a position that, for instance, envisages a looser but still cordial relationship) after the usual give-and-take of exchanging scholarly arguments, the debate has for a long time accentuated paradigmatic differences, sometimes to the extreme. In this chapter I illustrate this point in some detail and discuss potential remedies.

Explaining the Evolving Atlantic Order

Regardless of whether we conceive of the future of the Atlantic order in terms of institutional breakdown, transformation, or adaptation, we are always observing a process, that is, a moving outcome.[5] The vocabulary that usually figures prominently in our conceptual or theoretical schemes in analyzing processes of change (or continuity) also implies that we are dealing with phenomena in which time plays a significant role. However, this temporal dimension is seldom specified. Kenneth Waltz's prominent statement from the fall of 1990 is a good example: "NATO is a disappearing thing. It is a question of how long it is going to remain as a significant institution even though its name may linger on."[6] As of early 2007, NATO's process of "disappearing" was slowly moving toward completion of the second decade after the end of the cold war. In the meantime, even Waltz himself seems to have grown uncertain about whether it had already fully disappeared. In an article in *International Security* in 2000, Waltz at first seemed to grant that NATO's "outliving [of] its purpose" looks like a "strange case." Yet this initial judgment was quickly reversed. As Waltz put it, "I expected NATO to dwindle at the Cold War's end and ultimately to disappear. In a basic sense, the expectation has been borne out. NATO is no longer even a treaty of guarantee because one cannot answer

---

5. See John Ikenberry's introduction to this volume.
6. Kenneth N. Waltz, "Relations in a Multipolar World," Hearings before the Senate Committee on Foreign Relations, U.S. Congress, 102nd Cong., 1st sess., 26, 28, and 30 November 1990 (Washington, DC: U.S. Government Printing Office, 1991), 210.

the question, guarantee against whom?" What remains of it serves in the way that alliances have always been useful: as a tool at the disposal of their most important member(s)—which of course is, in NATO's case, the United States. To the extent that one may still say that NATO exists, Waltz wrote in 2000, it is "a means of maintaining and lengthening America's grip on the foreign and military policies of European states" and thus "the ability of the United States to extend the life of a moribund institution nicely illustrates how international institutions are created and maintained by stronger states to serve their perceived or misperceived interests."[7]

By quoting Waltz at length I do not mean to score easy points against realism. The same can be done for other (realist and nonrealist) scholars as well. In the mid-1990s, for instance, Robert Keohane and Celeste Wallander predicted that NATO would easily adjust to the new international environment and not disappear at all. To the contrary, NATO was expected to have a good chance to continue as an effective security management institution "to a ripe old age."[8] The main point in quoting these prominent examples is that the phenomenon to be tackled is as important as it is complex. More importantly, as the following analysis shows, the disciplinary study of

---

7. Kenneth N. Waltz, "Structural Realism after the Cold War," *International Security* 25, no. 1 (Summer 2000): 5–41, quotation at 18–20.

8. Celeste A. Wallander and Robert O. Keohane, "Why Does NATO Persist? An Institutional Approach," manuscript, Center for International Affairs, Harvard University, 1996, 37. More recently Keohane was asked in an interview whether he was "surprised by the way the Bush administration has tipped the balance against international organizations and toward a unilateral response" when it invaded Iraq. Keohane stated he was "not surprised, because they came into office talking against international organizations, although in a different form." However, he granted that it was "very disappointing from a professional point of view, because when those of us who emphasize and value the role of institutions in world politics think we won the debate (which I think we did, intellectually, in the academy), it's disappointing to see these throwbacks—people (some of them old, like Rumsfeld; some of them not so old, like Rice) who still just don't get it. An academic teaching people over a period of twenty years hopes, at least, they will learn some of these newer truths. So that's disappointing." These throwbacks notwithstanding, Keohane still believed that "the overall story, although it has more bumps in the road than I expected, is a story which shows the importance of international institutions, because the test of that doesn't come when a regime of people who are in favor of international institutions is in power. The test comes when people are in power who are opposed to them, instinctively. When they have to go back to them, then that tells you something." Since the United States did "go back" to the UN in the latter half of 2003, Keohane thought that "the overall lesson of Iraq . . . sustains the view that international institutions are terribly important, even in this high politics security area." See Robert O. Keohane and Harry Kreisler, "Theory and International Institutions," Conversations with History, Institute of International Studies, University of California at Berkeley, 9 March 2004, http:—globetrotter.berkeley.edu–people4–Keohane–keohane -con0.html (accessed 4 February 2007). For an early effort at predicting NATO's future in which I participated, see Gunther Hellmann and Reinhard Wolf, "Neorealism, Neoliberal Institutionalism and the Future of NATO," *Security Studies* 3, no. 1 (Autumn 1993): 3–43, esp. 21–26 (as to the specificity of competing realist and institutionalist predictions).

the evolution of the Atlantic order has been characterized by an overdose of highly aggregated variables at the macrolevel, which often left underspecified how the postulated (or implied) causal processes of change actually worked. In other words, in most accounts—whether they were of realist, liberal, or constructivist descent—structure almost always trumped action or process.

In a major conceptual article, Pierson examined how we can come to grips with a particular type of causal process—macrosocial processes, that is, processes that are "big, slow-moving, and . . . invisible," as he put it in his title. In an analogy with the natural sciences, he distinguished four basic types of causal accounts, as reproduced in table 2.1: (1) a tornado-like occurrence that involves quickly unfolding causal processes, that is, a rapidly developing storm, leading to equally rapid outcomes; (2) an earthquake (long-term causal process/quick outcome); (3) a meteorite hitting the earth (quick/slow); or (4) global warming (slow/slow).[9]

If we take this typology as a foil, the scholarship on the evolution of the Atlantic order reveals some interesting patterns relating to both the conceptualization of the outcome (or the dependent variable, that is, the evolution of the Atlantic order) and the preferred causal accounts.

The Evolving Atlantic Order as a Slow-Moving Outcome Akin to Global Warming

As far as the outcome is concerned, the landscape of international relations research is diverse. In comparison to other problems on the agenda of international relations research, the community as a whole appears to face not only the standard challenge of identifying the proper causes of established facts but, in addition, a higher than usual uncertainty about what is to

Table 2.1. Time horizons of different causal accounts

		Time horizon of outcome	
		Short	Long
Time horizon of cause	Short	I Tornado	II Meteorite hit
	Long	III Earthquake	IV Global warming

Source: Pierson, "Big, Slow-Moving," 179.

9. Paul Pierson, "Big, Slow-Moving, and . . . Invisible: Macrosocial Processes in the Study of Comparative Politics," in *Comparative Historical Analysis in the Social Sciences*, ed. James Mahoney and Dietrich Rueschemeyer, 177–207 (Cambridge: Cambridge University Press, 2003), here at 178–79.

be explained in the first place. When we examine the evolution of NATO, are we focusing essentially on a military alliance?[10] Are we dealing with a "security management institution" that is much more than a narrowly defined "treaty of guarantee" in the realist sense?[11] Is NATO even a security community that is based on neither threat nor rational interest calculation but primarily on a common set of shared values?[12] Or is NATO best conceived of inclusively, as a broad political order encompassing political dimensions (democracy), economic dimensions (capitalism), and a common civilizational heritage?[13]

It is obvious for anyone familiar with the established language games of the discipline that these concepts are highly connotative as far as particular theoretical assumptions are concerned. Thus, one of the first (and least surprising) observations about international relations research on the evolution of the Atlantic order (as a shorthand for all of these conceptualizations of the dependent variable) is that nearly two decades after the end of the cold war in 1989–90 and after a surge in theoretical work, the real nature of the beast is as contested as ever.

A second, less obvious observation relates to the predominant nature of causal accounts. Irrespective of diverging conceptual preferences and theoretical assumptions, most scholars implicitly agree that it is necessary to approach the analysis with a longer time horizon both as far as the outcome and the causal side are concerned. In other words, there is a convergence even among the most conflicting approaches around quadrant IV (global warming). A few illustrations across the paradigmatic dividing lines illustrate the point.

Realists, for instance, have long argued that the end of the cold war would bring an end to NATO eventually, even if the precise time frame could not be specified given the nature of the (structural) causes and how

10. See, e.g., Stephen M. Walt, "Why Alliances Endure or Collapse," *Survival* 39, no. 1 (Spring 1997): 156–79; Stephen M. Walt, "The Ties That Fray: Why Europe and America Are Drifting Apart," *National Interest*, no. 54 (Winter 1998–99): 3–11; Stephen M. Walt, "The Imbalance of Power: On the Prospects for Effective American-European Relations," *Harvard Magazine* 106, no. 4 (March–April 2004): 32–35; Waltz, "Relations in a Multipolar World"; Waltz, "Structural Realism after the Cold War."

11. Helga Haftendorn, Robert O. Keohane, and Celeste A. Wallander, eds., *Imperfect Unions: Security Institutions over Time and Space* (Oxford: Oxford University Press, 1999).

12. Thomas Risse-Kappen, *Cooperation among Democracies: The European Influence on U.S. Foreign Policy* (Princeton: Princeton University Press, 1995); Thomas Risse-Kappen, "Collective Identity in a Democratic Community: The Case of NATO," in *The Culture of National Security: Norms and Identity in World Politics*, ed. Peter J. Katzenstein, 357–400 (New York: Columbia University Press, 1996); Thomas Risse, "The Crisis of the Transatlantic Security Community," in Peters, Daase, and Feske, *Transatlantic Tug-of-War*, 111–41; Frank Schimmelfennig, "NATO-Enlargement: A Constructivist Explanation," *Security Studies* 8, nos. 2–3 (Winter 1998–99, Spring 1999): 198–234.

13. G. John Ikenberry, "The End of the Neo-Conservative Moment," *Survival* 46, no. 1 (March 2004): 7–22.

they would translate at the cognitive level. Even before the upheaval of 1989, Stephen Walt argued that alliance cohesion was bound to decline given the vanishing perception of threat.[14] Moreover, "without a clear and present threat," Walt added in June 1990, "neither European politicians nor U.S. taxpayers are likely to support a large U.S. military presence in Europe. Although NATO's elaborate institutional structure will slow the pace of devolution, only a resurgence of the Soviet threat is likely to preserve NATO in anything like its present form."[15] In subsequent articles Walt granted that NATO "has proven to be more resilient than many pessimists predicted."[16] He then argued that alliances may persist even if the conditions under which they were originally formed had changed substantially. Referring mainly to NATO, he listed four factors in particular—a large asymmetry of power within the alliance, shared values, a highly institutionalized relationship, and a strong sense of common identity—factors that usually do not figure prominently in realist analyses and that are difficult to pin down precisely in terms of a causal time horizon.[17] Still, on balance, Walt continued to question whether this reasoning would provide strong enough evidence to believe that NATO would persist. Given the absence of a major threat, strains among its members were bound to increase, eventually leading to its demise.[18]

Other realists with a stronger bias toward the "defensive" version of realism, such as Barry Posen, have stretched this time horizon ("eventually") further as more time has passed. In their view, new factors have to be added that tend to further lengthen the time horizon. For example, because the United States is not perceived as a direct security threat to its European allies, an argument that even realists widely share, bandwagoning rather than balancing is seen to be a viable as well as a cost-effective option after all. In this perspective, European security and defense policy (ESDP) "is not quite a balancing project, but certainly an effort by Europeans, including many who bandwagon in their NATO guise, to develop an alternative security supplier" just in case the United States does not turn out to be as reliable and trustworthy a partner as the staunch Atlanticists within NATO believe.[19] Yet the fact that U.S. hegemony in Europe might be challenged if ESDP proved to be successful may be a reason for the United States "to be more interested in Europe's special

14. Stephen M. Walt, "Alliances in Theory and Practice: What Lies Ahead?" *Journal of International Affairs* 43, no. 1 (Summer–Fall 1989): 1–18, here at 8–9.

15. Stephen M. Walt, *The Origins of Alliances* (Ithaca: Cornell University Press, 1990), vii.

16. Walt, "Why Alliances Endure or Collapse," 171; see also Walt, "Imbalance of Power."

17. Walt, "Why Alliances Endure or Collapse," 164–70.

18. Ibid., 173; see also Walt, "Ties That Fray"; for a more guarded perspective, see more recently Walt, "Imbalance of Power."

19. Barry Posen, "ESDP and the Structure of World Power," *International Spectator* 39, no. 1 (2004): 5–17, here at 12.

security concerns than would otherwise be the case."[20] In other words, U.S. hegemony (and therefore NATO cohesion) can be preserved as long as this hegemony appears to be fairly benign. Yet to the extent that U.S. hegemony is benign might increasingly imply a tolerance of more European security independence, which in itself would imply a more far-reaching change in the nature of the alliance, with Europe less willing to play the role of a "docile ally of the U.S. in a decade or two."[21] Again, as in Walt's case, the causal processes that presumably drive NATO's transformation are stretching far back (and forth) in terms of the time horizon.

From an "offensive realist" point of view, this time horizon may not be as long, yet even here the causal processes will take some time to lead to NATO's demise. John Mearsheimer, for instance, sees NATO's future largely in terms of its utility to the United States' role as an effective offshore balancer. Given that NATO has lost this function, he foresees an increase in the distancing of the United States' European allies as well as a dwindling of interest on the American side for maintaining a significant U.S. troop presence. Without a major reversal of the distribution of power on the Continent (as it prevailed around the millennium), Mearsheimer thinks that the United States "is likely to pull its forces out of Europe . . . in the immediate years ahead."[22] Against this background, "the most likely scenario" would be an increase in German defense spending (possibly including an attempt to acquire nuclear weapons) in order to compensate for the removal of the nuclear umbrella by the United States but also in order "to dominate central Europe." Because other big powers (such as Russia and France) would not sit by idly, "serious security competition" would result. Obviously, or so goes the implicit argument, it would be hard to imagine NATO persisting under these circumstances.

In contrast to Walt's and Posen's arguments, Mearsheimer's causal story is less complex, focusing mainly on U.S. policy as the driving force. Moreover, the speed of the causal process also seems to be faster because it is driven by one actor above all. Still, the common denominator of all realist accounts is the fact that the major security equation has changed since the end of the cold war. In this sense they belong in either quadrant III or IV of Pierson's matrix. On the outcome side, the time horizon may be somewhat shorter (Mearsheimer) or somewhat longer (Walt, Posen), yet there can be little doubt that the time horizon at the causal level is always long rather than occurring

---

20. Ibid., 16. See also Christopher Layne, "The Unipolar Illusion Revisited: The Coming End of the United States' Unipolar Moment," *International Security* 31, no. 2 (Fall 2006): 7–41, here at 34–36.

21. Posen, "ESDP and the Structure of World Power," 17.

22. John J. Mearsheimer, *The Tragedy of Great Power Politics* (New York: Norton, 2001), 394, 395.

suddenly. Power shifts don't happen overnight, and threats do not vanish (nor do new ones arise) in a matter of weeks or even months. Yet the political effects of both will show over time. In this reading, the crisis over Iraq served as a trigger to unleash the forces that have been accumulating (in Pierson's sense of an earthquake) for some time. But it was not the first one to shake the alliance, and even some realists (such as Walt) at least implicitly still grant that it has not (yet) been the ultimate one, finally putting an end to an extended process of "disappearing."[23] Rather, in this interpretation of NATO's transformation, pressure has been building ever since the end of the cold war, releasing energy repeatedly as in the Balkans in the early 1990s, in Kosovo toward the end of the 1990s, in Afghanistan after 9/11, and then in Iraq. There is also broad agreement in this camp that the likelihood is high that the underlying seismic shifts are almost inevitably driving Europe and the United States apart. However long the long term may be, the collapse of NATO is seen to be as certain as is the heating up of the atmosphere in Pierson's quadrant IV scenario of global warming.

The same kind of story can also be told with regard to the work of liberals of both rationalist and constructivist descent. They too best fit in quadrant IV, although for different reasons. As is to be expected from an institutionalist, for instance, Robert Keohane has long been emphasizing an extended time horizon in accounting for the persistence and/or adaptation of international institutions in general.[24] There were some early hints in his writings that short-term calculations of interests might drive NATO's transformation, including, explicitly, a breakdown scenario.[25] Subsequent, more-detailed analyses almost always emphasized slow-moving causal factors, such as institutional inertia and more dynamic and adaptive institutional processes of more flexible and hybrid security management institutions.[26] The factors

23. Walt, "Imbalance of Power."

24. Cf. Robert O. Keohane, *After Hegemony: Cooperation and Discord in the World Political Economy* (Princeton: Princeton University Press, 1984); Robert O. Keohane, *International Institutions and State Power: Essays in International Relations Theory* (Boulder, CO: Westview, 1989); Robert O. Keohane and Joseph S. Nye, "The End of the Cold War in Europe," in *After the Cold War: International Institutions and State Strategies in Europe, 1989–1991*, ed. Stanley Hoffmann, Robert O. Keohane, and Joseph S. Nye, 1–19 (Cambridge: Harvard University Press, 1993).

25. In the early 1990s Keohane explicitly stated that he was unwilling to predict that NATO would still be around in the year 2000 "because it is not clear that both the US and Europe will regard NATO as continuing to be in their interest." Robert O. Keohane, "Institutionalist Theory and the Realist Challenge after the Cold War," manuscript, Center for International Affairs, Harvard University, 31n16.

26. Keohane and Nye, "End of the Cold War in Europe," 19; Keohane, "Institutionalist Theory and the Realist Challenge," 25; see also Wallander and Keohane, "Why Does NATO Persist?"; Celeste A. Wallander and Robert O. Keohane, "Risk, Threat, and Security Institutions," in Haftendorn, Keohane, and Wallander, *Imperfect Unions*, 21–47; Celeste A. Wallander, "Institutional Assets and Adaptability: NATO after the Cold War," *International Organization* 54,

driving institutional processes all seemed to assure that NATO would persist to a ripe old age.[27]

A similar argument was put forth by constructivists building on Karl Deutsch's work on NATO as a pluralistic security community, which has been around longer than any of the (rational) institutionalist challengers of realism. As in the case of Deutsch, scholars working in this line of tradition emphasized slow-moving identity-building processes that tended to foster a sense of community. As Thomas Risse or Frank Schimmelfennig has argued, the Atlantic order was best conceived of as "an institutionalized pluralistic security community of liberal democracies," an alliance representing the military branch of a broader "Euro-Atlantic or 'Western' community."[28] From this perspective, the end of the cold war did not only "not terminate the Western community of values" but even "extend[ed] that community into Eastern Europe and, potentially, into even the successor states of the Soviet Union, creating a 'pacific federation' of liberal democracies from Vladivostok to Berlin, San Francisco, and Tokyo." The important point here was, however, that the institutional form of NATO was considered less critical than the underlying community of values: "liberal theory does not necessarily expect NATO to last into the next century. It only assumes that the security partnership among liberal democracies will persist in one institutional form or another."[29] In other words the key processes driving the Atlantic security community were moving even slower than expected among institutionalists. In this reading the Soviet threat may have helped foster a sense of common purpose within the Atlantic order, but "it did not create the community in the first place." Rather, "the collective identity led to the threat perception, not the other way around."[30] Thus, democracies were seen to form alliances

---

no. 4 (Autumn 2000): 705–36. For a discussion of the relationship between organizational theory (emphasizing bureaucratic inertia) and institutional theory more broadly, see Robert B. McCalla, "NATO's Persistence after the Cold War," *International Organization* 50, no. 3 (Summer 1996): 445–75, here at 456–69; and Helga Haftendorn, "Sicherheitsinstitutionen in den internationalen Beziehungen: Eine Einführung," in *Kooperation jenseits von Hegemonie und Bedrohung: Sicherheitsinstitutionen in den internationalen Beziehungen*, ed. Helga Haftendorn and Otto Keck, 11–34 (Baden-Baden: Nomos, 1997), here at 27–28; for a more skeptical analysis of NATO's adaptability, especially with regard to NATO's capacity for peace operations drawing on collective action theory, see Joseph Lepgold, "NATO's Post-Cold War Collective Action Problem," *International Security* 23, no. 1 (Summer 1998): 78–106; see also Fred Chernoff, *After Bipolarity: The Vanishing Threat, Theories of Cooperation, and the Future of the Atlantic Alliance* (Ann Arbor: University of Michigan Press, 1995), which draws on institutionalist as well as cybernetic theory, arguing that NATO's outlook is not as pessimistic as realists suppose but more pessimistic than institutionalists allow.

27. Wallander and Keohane, "Why Does NATO Persist?" 37.

28. Risse-Kappen, "Collective Identity in a Democratic Community," 397; Schimmelfennig, "NATO-Enlargement," 213–14.

29. Risse-Kappen, "Collective Identity in a Democratic Community," 396.

30. Risse-Kappen, *Cooperation among Democracies*, 32.

with each other not because of a unifying external threat but because they perceive each other as peaceful.[31] As a result, the key causal processes driving the Atlantic order's evolutionary development were slow moving indeed. Moreover, they were clearly pointing in one direction: communitarian stability. More recent events, however, have challenged constructivists to specify what had always been granted in general terms without really spelling out the details—that is, those mechanisms that might lead to the *disintegration* of a security community.[32] Thomas Risse has emphasized that "norms of democratic decision-making among equals emphasizing persuasion, compromise, and the non-use of force or coercive power" are crucial in accounting for the persistence of a security community.[33] As long as these norms are not violated, there is little reason to question the community's solidity. In this regard, recent events in the context of the Iraq War have certainly raised some new questions since "unilateral and even imperial tendencies" in the United States' approach have "violate(d) constitutive norms on which the transatlantic community has been built over the years, namely multilateralism and close consultation with allies."[34] If these tendencies were to persist or even worsen, the foundation of the alliance could indeed be endangered. However, these developments should not be overdramatized, since other trends

31. Risse-Kappen, "Collective Identity in a Democratic Community," 371; on the underlying theoretical rationale, see also Emanuel Adler and Michael Barnett, "Security Communities in Theoretical Perspective," in *Security Communities*, ed. Emanuel Adler and Michael Barnett, 3–28 (Cambridge: Cambridge University Press, 1998); Emanuel Adler and Michael Barnett, "A Framework for the Study of Security Communities," in Adler and Barnett, *Security Communities*, 29–65.

32. Constructivists have spent most of their time outlining how and why security communities come about and how and why they persist. In the abstract there was always room for the collapse (or disintegration) of a security community. Yet in contrast to the vast theoretical literature on the origins and persistence of security communities, there has been little (and underspecified) theoretical work on the disintegration of security communities. In comparison to the almost twenty pages that Adler and Barnett invest in outlining a theoretical framework to examine how security communities may come into existence, they discuss disintegration in only half a page, basically arguing that "the same forces that 'build up' security communities can 'tear them down.' Therefore, *many* of the same social processes that encourage and serve to reproduce the security community are also associated with its decline." Adler and Barnett, "Framework for the Study of Security Communities," 58. Reflecting on the disintegrating tendencies in transatlantic relations, more recent research is starting to look into these factors more thoroughly; see Harald Müller, "A Theory of Decay of Security Communities with an Application to the Present State of the Atlantic Alliance," paper presented at the conference Mars vs. Venus: America, Europe and the Future of the West, 6–7 April 2006, University of California at Berkeley.

33. Risse-Kappen, "Collective Identity in a Democratic Community," 369; see also Risse-Kappen, *Cooperation among Democracies*, 33.

34. Thomas Risse, "Beyond Iraq: Challenges to the Transatlantic Security Community," AICGS/German-American Dialogue, Working Paper Series (Baltimore: American Institute for Contemporary German Studies, Johns Hopkins University, 2003), 3, http://www.atasp.de/downloads/aicgs.pdf; Risse, "Crisis of the Transatlantic Security Community," 113.

continue to nourish the vitality of the alliance. Other authors who also emphasize ideational factors over material power have more recently come to more pessimistic conclusions. Ted Hopf, for instance, shares a Deutschian appreciation of the ideational foundation of transatlantic relations with Risse and Schimmelfennig. In conceptual terms he only replaces the concept of a security community with what he calls an authoritative alliance. Yet in contrast to Risse's and Schimmelfennig's guarded optimism about the solidity of the Atlantic order, he sees 9/11 as "a catalyst for processes in both Europe and the United States that promise not a closer alliance . . . but rather an acceleration of a seismic reordering of global affairs" based on identity differences.[35] The crucial point here is that it is not material power but conflicts over values and incompatible visions of world order that drive Europe and the United States apart and that may eventually even bring the Europeans to soft balance against the United States.[36]

In short, the overall story from a constructivist point of view easily fits in Pierson's quadrant IV as well: a complex set of slow-moving causes is at work. Yet constructivists differ among themselves in regard to what effects such causes are likely to produce. Initially, constructivists mostly saw a solidifying effect for the transatlantic security community. More recently, ideational factors—identity drift, as Hopf puts it[37]—have come to be seen as causes that may actually drive Europe and the United States apart. In this sense the time horizon has been shorted recently in the context of the Iraq War. In Pierson's conceptual vocabulary, the crisis over Iraq can be compared with a tornado: it arose quickly, and it has certainly caused some damage. Yet constructivists disagree about its medium-term and long-term consequences. For some, a set of (closely connected) events that caused the fallout over Iraq is unlikely to turn out eventually as a meteorite, that is, a highly destructive hit out of the blue with effects reaching far into the future. Others tend to accord more weight to these kinds of events, while emphasizing macrophenomena (identity drift) as key variables nevertheless.

From a still broader liberal perspective based on material as well as ideational factors, John Ikenberry has argued that the links across the Atlantic were more than a classical alliance. In his reading, the postwar order was made up of two kinds of settlements: the containment order, based on countering the Soviet threat via NATO, and a more diffuse although equally profound liberal democratic order, made up of "a wide range of new institutions

---

35. Ted Hopf, "Dissipating Hegemony: U.S. Unilateralism and European Counter-Hegemony," in Evangelista and Parsi, *Partners or Rivals?* 39–59, here at 42.

36. See Olav Knutsen, "NATO in Crisis—or Why the Transatlantic 'Security Community' May Have Come to an End," paper presented at the National Conference of the Norwegian Political Science Association, Trondheim, 3–5 January 2007, available at http://www.google.de (accessed 4 February 2007).

37. Hopf, "Dissipating Hegemony," 52.

and relations among the Western industrial democracies, built around economic openness, political reciprocity, and multilateral management of an America-led liberal political system."[38] What is more, this order did not come about as the unintended result of a random mix of policies and events but was deliberately brought about by a "distinctively American liberal grand strategy."[39] In this view, the end of the cold war did not mark a significant break but an accentuation of a major trend: at the least it amounted to a "mild hegemonial authority" in the form of a loose informal concert of the strongest powers, with the United States standing at the top.[40] In a more far-reaching interpretation, the end of the cold war ushered in a benign imperial system, a "world democratic-capitalist empire" that could actually be called the American system because of the preponderance of the United States.[41] This system was thought to be "expansive and highly durable" because of a bundle of powerful causes: U.S. military as well as economic power; the benefits of geography, rendering the United States an "offshore" power; the "liberal character of American hegemony" with its inbuilt "mechanisms to make itself less threatening to the rest of the world"; and the United States' "deep alignment with global developmental processes— . . . the 'project of modernity'."[42]

In comparison with liberal constructivists, this argument emphasized two additional factors driving transformation processes: (1) slow-moving material causes at the level of the international system and (2) material as well as ideational causes at the level of the most important state of this system, the United States. In this sense it mirrored Mearsheimer's argument on the liberal side. Whereas Walt and Waltz on the one hand and Risse and Schimmelfennig on the other focus mostly on the state-transcending international level—the latter primarily on the ideational side, the former mostly on the material side—Mearsheimer and Ikenberry added "causal speed" by granting a major role in driving the transformation process to one key player in the system, the United States. In Mearsheimer's argument the United States was

38. G. John Ikenberry, "The Myth of Post-Cold War Chaos," *Foreign Affairs* 75, no. 3 (May–June 1996): 79–91, here at 81.

39. G. John Ikenberry, "America's Liberal Grand Strategy: Democracy and National Security in the Post-War Era," in *American Democracy Promotion: Impulses, Strategies, and Impact*, ed. Michael Cox, G. John Ikenberry, and Takashi Inoguchi, 103–26 (Oxford: Oxford University Press, 2000), here at 104.

40. This argument is advanced by Adam Watson, *The Limits of Independence: Relations between States in the Modern World* (London: Routledge, 1997), 132, 126. Although Watson places developments in a still larger historical context than Ikenberry does, there are similarities in the arguments they advance although the conceptual language differs. In Watson's description, the hegemonial authority pursued three aims in particular: the promotion of peace, economic prosperity, and Western standards of civilization (ibid. 127).

41. G. John Ikenberry, "American Power and the Empire of Capitalist Democracy," special issue, *Review of International Studies* 27 (2001): 191–212, here at 192.

42. Ibid., 193–94.

driving NATO apart as a consequence of new policies resulting from global power shifts and accompanying changes in the incentive structure of the potential hegemon. In Ikenberry's account the United States was both well positioned strategically and predisposed by its own historical experience and identity to guarantee the stability of the liberal order. As a result the U.S. empire appeared to be robust and durable.[43] In both cases, assumptions about the forces driving U.S. foreign policy turned out to be a crucial factor in the transformation of the Atlantic order.

To sum up, from a bird's-eye view the scholarly debate about the evolution of the Atlantic order reveals some interesting parallels and fault lines. Two preliminary conclusions stand out. First, overwhelming evidence indicates that the most prominent accounts place a heavy emphasis on a long time horizon at the causal level, that is, structural variables carry the main explanatory burden. Most of these accounts easily fit into Pierson's quadrant IV (global warming), with a few potential outliers in quadrant III (earthquake/realists) and II (meteorite/constructivists; see the summary in table 2.2). Moreover, with a few exceptions on both sides (Mearsheimer among the realists, and Ikenberry among the liberals), agency does not figure prominently in accounting for change—and even if it does, it refers mainly to the biggest player, the United States. So the key consensual point up to here is that the analysis of the evolution of the Atlantic order must come to grips with complex causal processes mostly covering long time horizons. Judgments diverge, however, as to which slow-moving causal processes are most important and, even more so, what effects they will yield. This interim result may look familiar in terms of the usual kind of scientific progress achieved in scholarly debate. However, it is certainly not satisfactory in terms of a desirable synthesis of knowledge.

The Evolving Atlantic Order as Driven Mainly by Cumulative Causes

This unsatisfactory state of affairs does not improve significantly when we examine the study of the evolution of the Atlantic order from yet another angle. A third observation thus relates to the form of causal accounts usually offered. Pierson distinguishes three types of slow-moving causes: cumulative causes, threshold effects, and extended causal chains. Cumulative causes point to changes in an independent variable that are continuous but extremely gradual. The potential effects of demographic changes for a country's social welfare system are a case in point. Globalization and the spread of democracy as potential causes of changing state policies are other examples. As Pierson points out, cumulative causes of this kind are often treated as fixed in analyses that focus on outcomes with a short time horizon.[44] If the crisis over Iraq, for

43. Ibid., 193.
44. Pierson, "Big, Slow-Moving," 181–82.

Table 2.2. Dominant time horizons of typical IR accounts of the transatlantic relationship

		Time horizon of outcome	
		Short (e.g., intra-alliance conflict over Iraq, 2002–3)	*Long* (e.g., "stable peace"/ "inevitable decline")
Time horizon of cause	Short (e.g., neoconservative administration/bad diplomacy)	I (tornado)	II (meteorite) constructivists
	Long (e.g., threats/values)	III (earthquake) realists	IV (global warming) realists and constructivists

Note: It is worth highlighting a few subtleties about this table. First, it is not at all clear that IR theorists pay much attention at all to phenomena located in quadrant I (tornados). Second, the placement of constructivists in quadrant II and realists in quadrant III carries less certainty in my mind than does the placement of both in quadrant IV.

instance, figures prominently in an attempt to examine the evolution of the Atlantic order, the potential effects of globalization or global changes in the spread of democracy will most likely be downgraded or even ignored, thus essentially treating them as fixed. However, it would be more difficult to do so if we were to conceive of this process of change as one that covers a longer time frame, from the late 1980s until the present.

Threshold effects focus on a particular stage in a longer causal process. Cumulative causes or causal chains may play a role here as well, but they don't lead to visible effects unless they reach some critical level, triggering major changes. Pierson uses the example of an earthquake or avalanche to illustrate how a slow buildup of pressure unleashes rapidly once a critical level has been reached (see fig. 2.1). Iraq and Kosovo may once again help to illustrate the point. In the literature it is well established by now that the war in Kosovo served as a catalyst in the push for ESDP. Plans had been made for some time, but for the European allies (the British, in particular) it took the experience of being sidelined by the United States in the conduct of the Kosovo War to trigger a major new advance with more independent European military capabilities. For some observers, Iraq has had the same effect with regard to NATO: basically the war marks a threshold that, when crossed, underlines that NATO is dead.[45]

45. Cf. Steven E. Meyer, "Carcass of Dead Policies: The Irrelevance of NATO," *Parameters: U.S. Army War College Quarterly* 33, no. 4 (Winter 2003–4): 83–97; Thomas Donnelly, "Learning to Live without Europe," American Enterprise Institute (National Security Outlook), May 2004, http://www.aei.org/docLib/20040513_NSOmay2004graphics.pdf (accessed 4 February

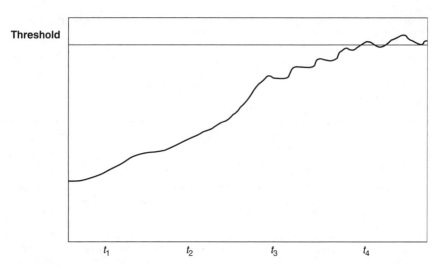

Figure 2.1. A basic threshold model

The third type of slow-moving causes, causal chains, focuses on a long-term causal process in which a sequence of distinct and crucial developments is linked into a tightly coupled chain. Establishing the tightness of the links is the difficult thing here, so it is not surprising that in causal chain arguments, agency-related causes usually play a bigger role than structural causes because they appear to be more easily identifiable. A (fictitious) causal chains account of NATO's decline from a realist perspective, for instance, would have to connect vanishing perceptions of a Soviet/Russian threat with increasing internal divisiveness and declining cohesion (e.g., from the Balkans in the early 1990s, to Kosovo in 1999, Afghanistan in 2001, up to Iraq in 2002–3). To my knowledge there is little work along such lines (from either realist or nonrealist scholarship) that also reflects on the intuitions of the scientific community more broadly; the analysis of the evolution of the Atlantic order is a complex matter indeed.

Once again, we see interesting parallels. Irrespective of paradigmatic preference in most causal accounts, complexity trumps parsimony. Causal chain arguments are rare. John Mearsheimer's scenario of U.S. troop withdrawal from Europe as propelling German rearmament, which in turn leads to intense security competition, perhaps comes closest to such a situation. In most other accounts, however, cumulative causes and particularly threshold effects dominate. I have already referred to Stephen Walt's and Kenneth Waltz's

2007); John C. Hulsman, "European Arrogance and Weakness Dictate Coalitions of the Willing," Heritage Lectures, no. 777, delivered 19 December 2002, http://www.heritage.org/Research/Europe/hl777.cfm (accessed 4 February 2007).

arguments about NATO's decline. Here the end of the cold war and the waning of a common threat figure as the key development that pushes the transformation process below the threshold of the causal dynamic that originally necessitated an alliance. Yet there are differences. For Walt things still seem to hang in the balance, although the pressure is clearly downward. For Waltz the threshold has already been crossed, with NATO no longer being an alliance.

Rationalist institutionalist and constructivist accounts have become more guarded recently in comparison with earlier accounts. Yet they too focus (implicitly or explicitly) on some kind of threshold. As Keohane already stated in his work on international institutions in the 1980s, changes in the distribution of power "create *pressures* on . . . regimes and *weaken* their rules."[46] It remains unclear, however, at what point it can be said that an institution has ceased to exist.[47] At a very general level NATO's collapse was certainly possible, but the theoretical arguments developed basically explained why it was unlikely that some abstract threshold might be crossed.[48] Only recently did Keohane hint at a complex set of "divergences of interests, values and social structures" between Europe and the United States that amounted to a "widening Euro-American breach" and that is now said to be so significant that Europe and the United States might in the medium term even "favour a parting of ways."[49] Yet it remains unclear once again when this implicit threshold would actually have been crossed. The same applies to arguments put forth by Risse and Ikenberry. The continuous violation of constitutive norms such as multilateralism and consultation would represent such a threshold from a constructivist security community perspective.[50] In Ikenberry's interpretation, the United States' unexpected move toward an aggressive strategy in pursuit of a unipolar world could have had similar effects if it had turned out to be a lasting change.[51]

Regardless of the fact that not all of these statements imply a specific future path (i.e., that a broad range of outcomes is possible for perspectives such as Risse's or Ikenberry's), these examples illustrate the key challenge in explanations focusing on threshold effects: the difficulty of identifying observables that enable us to argue that something qualitatively different separates

---

46. Keohane, *International Institutions and State Power*, 168.

47. To be sure, pinpoint predictions are not an appropriate standard against which to measure the explanatory power of theories. Yet if the overall picture of an academic discipline's cumulative findings on the same phenomenon is as contradictory as has long been the case for a lot of macroperspective theorizing on transatlantic relations, this picture does not reflect positively on the discipline.

48. See Wallander and Keohane, "Why Does NATO Persist?"

49. Robert O. Keohane, "Ironies of Sovereignty: The European Union and the United States," *Journal of Common Market Studies* 40, no. 4 (2002): 743–65, here at 760, 761.

50. Risse, "Beyond Iraq"; Risse, "Crisis of the Transatlantic Security Community."

51. G. John Ikenberry, "America's Imperial Ambition," *Foreign Affairs* 81, no. 5 (September–October 2002): 44–60, here at 49–55.

two distinct phases—a phase in which NATO can still be said to be working as an alliance from a phase in which it has ceased to do so; or a phase in which a security community is said to be stable compared to a phase in which it has disintegrated. This problem of identifying thresholds is the same one that Karl Deutsch faced when he invented the security communities concept. In discussing the issue of how he and his collaborators distinguished between integration and nonintegration, Deutsch wrote that the achievement of a security community would have to involve "something like the crossing of a threshold." The problem was that "somewhat contrary to our expectation . . . some of our cases taught us that integration may involve a fairly broad zone of transition rather than a narrow threshold; that states may cross and recross this threshold or zone of transition several times in their relations with each other; and that they might spend decades or generations wavering uncertainly within it."[52]

If we focus our attention on a process outcome—such as the evolution of the Atlantic order, Deutsch's formation of a security community, Waltz's disappearance of an alliance, or Keohane's parting of the ways of actors thus far heavily linked in a tight institutional network—we are necessarily hard-pressed to identify thresholds, even if we may not be able to put these in precise terms similar to point predictions. Yet identifying thresholds is precisely not what international relations research on NATO/the Atlantic order has been good at in the past. The preferred self-location of realists, institutionalists, and constructivists in Pierson's quadrant IV implies that they had a theoretical predisposition in favor of cumulative or incremental causes in which change in a causal variable is continuous but extremely gradual (see tables 2.2 and 2.3).

This is another way of saying that scholars from all paradigmatic traditions are focusing mostly on a process outcome that unfolds somewhere at

Table 2.3. Time horizons of different causal accounts

		Time horizon of outcome	
		Short	Long
Time horizon of cause	Short	I	II Cumulative effects
	Long	III Thresholds; causal chains	IV Cumulative causes

Source: Pierson, "Big, Slow-Moving," 192.

52. Karl W. Deutsch, *Political Community and the North Atlantic Area* (New York: Greenwood Press, 1957), 32–33.

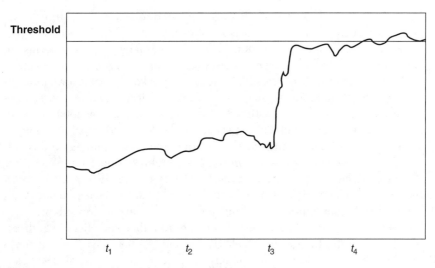

Figure 2.2. A threshold model with a structural cause

time t_4 in figure 2.1. The problem is that our theoretical predispositions direct us at causes that are mostly located at times t_1–t_4 or at times t_1–t_3 in figure 2.2.[53]

No matter what type of cause we prefer, it is difficult to arrive at a consensual conclusion because likely the most fitting description of the evolution of the Atlantic order is one resembling Karl Deutsch's point about a "fairly broad zone of transition" in which "states may cross and recross this threshold or zone of transition several times in their relations with each other; and that they might spend decades or generations wavering uncertainly within it." Unless the threshold is crossed decisively in either direction, this indeterminacy enables both realists and liberals/constructivists to stick with their basic narrative.

Conclusions: Linking Micro and Macro in the Study of the Evolving Atlantic Order

Two concepts figure prominently in the conceptual framework of this volume: (political) conflict and crisis. The project as a whole tries to come to grips with the question of whether the Atlantic order finds itself on a trajectory that is more aptly described in terms of conflict or crisis.[54] The conflict trajectory would yield one of two outcomes: resolution within the existing rules and

53. The former tends to be a model that could be shared by both realists and liberals; the latter is a model that depicts a realist story emphasizing the structural cause "disappearance of Soviet threat" at time t_3.

54. See Ikenberry's introductory chapter to this volume.

institutions or escalation to a crisis stage defined by one or more of three characteristics: (1) fundamental disagreement over what at least one side believes to be a core interest; (2) institutional breakdown as far as rules and norms are concerned; or (3) a breakdown in a sense of community. A crisis is conceptualized as leading to three possible outcomes: breakdown, transformation (in the sense of an intentional renegotiation of the institutional framework, leading to a new set of mutually satisfactory arrangements), and adaptation (as an intended or unintended outcome between breakdown and transformation).

In this chapter, in contrast to most of the other contributions to this volume, I have not addressed in a *substantive* fashion the question of whether transatlantic relations are on a conflict trajectory or a crisis trajectory (and if the latter, which outcome is more likely). Instead, I have reflected on the ways in which prominent international relations theories have addressed this question in the past—and what we may conclude from those practices in addressing the current situation in which the Atlantic order finds itself. From a bird's-eye perspective, the disciplinary discourse since the early 1990s appears disillusioning. A simplified summary would go something like the following. As a discipline we have known since the mid-1990s (at the latest) that the Atlantic order was both doomed to collapse and destined to persist. Some of the most highly respected scholars from the discipline have come out with strong statements as to what we know. Yet the way in which our theoretical heritage has been put to fruition seemed to leave only two mutually exclusive and equally teleological futures for the Atlantic order. At the same time, the divisiveness was hardly justified given the inconclusiveness that resulted when theoretical arguments were related to empirical observations (and vice versa). Irrespective of paradigmatic preference (and arguments to the contrary notwithstanding), the structure of the causal accounts generally advanced by all sides in these paradigmatic exchanges was always complex with regard to both a slow-moving outcome (such as a disappearing alliance, a persisting security management institution, or a stable security community) and slow-moving (mostly cumulative) causes (such as a declining threat, common values, etc.). In other words, the determination attached to some of the bold predictions about inevitable decline or everlasting stability was seldom accompanied by a sufficiently differentiating delineation of thresholds, causal mechanisms, or potentially falsifying indicators. Only recently have there been signs of a slow convergence, with some realists implicitly granting that NATO may not be dead after all,[55] and constructivists acknowledging that the fallout over Iraq was indeed a sharp break with established norms of cooperation within the Atlantic alliance.

One possible explanation for this harsh confrontation at the level of paradigmatic exchange has to do with the disciplinary preference for structural

55. See Walt, "Imbalance of Power."

explanations presumably more suited to theory building and an accompanying neglect of the implications of incorporating time and agency in accounting for the evolution of transatlantic relations. As Ronald Aminzade put it with regard to macrosociological studies more broadly, the focus on

> large-scale structures and long-term processes has often discouraged close attention to temporally connected events. . . . The concern is often with identifying key structural variables to incorporate into causal models of outcomes, not with the temporal characteristics of events or the way in which actors in a particular event or process understand and experience the temporal flow of events. By aggregating the attributes of individuals or organizations at given points in time into seemingly enduring variables that are correlated with outcomes, sociologists divorce actors from actions and fail to acknowledge the causal power of connections among events.[56]

Timeless (structural) concepts such as threat, value, identity, or institution dominate at the causal level, often reducing processes to mere conditions. And even if a dynamic component is introduced (e.g., with qualifications such as diminishing threats), we are often left guessing about the duration and pace associated with these qualifications.[57]

One obvious solution to this structural bias in international relations theorizing is to systematically add a historical perspective to the analysis of transformation processes in the way that it has long been advocated by historical sociologists. In many ways this is an obvious via media because it allows us to integrate structural and agentic factors as well as the macro- and the microlevel.[58] The transatlantic confrontation over Iraq in particular has demonstrated that rationalist as well as constructivist approaches have difficulties in systematically accounting for agency, that is, the decisions by individual leaders (Gerhard Schröder and George Bush in particular) or governing elites in key member countries. Many historians consider this dimension to rank among the central factors in causing "a fundamental break with the practice [of NATO] of the preceding fifty years."[59] This fundamental break manifested itself in concrete decisions. For instance, that the German ambassador to the United Nations helped establish and coordinate the opposition to the Anglo-American Iraq strategy by Russia, China, France, and Germany would have

---

56. Ronald Aminzade, "Historical Sociology and Time," *Sociological Methods and Research* 20, no. 4 (1992): 456–80, here at 457.

57. For a more detailed discussion of the concepts "duration" and "pace," see ibid., 459–62.

58. On the difference between the structure-agency link on the one hand and the macro-micro link on the other, see Nicos Mouzelis, *Sociological Theory: What Went Wrong? Diagnosis and Remedies* (London: Routledge, 1995), 155.

59. Geir Lundestad, "Toward Transatlantic Drift?" in Andrews, *Atlantic Alliance under Stress*, 9–29, here at 9. See also Pond, *Friendly Fire*.

been inconceivable even a few months before the crisis escalated.[60] Historians mainly focus on these kinds of events in constructing their causal stories, implicitly arguing that these decisions form patterns that change the underlying dynamic of the overall relationship. Systemic theorists, in contrast, have no consistent place for these historical contingencies, even though bits and pieces of such event-oriented causal stories almost always pop up in their explanations as well, which in and of itself is a significant indication of the importance of these developments since events are recognizable as such only within the frames provided by a cultural structure. The mere fact that analysts who are generally inclined toward structural explanations refer to specific events as significant for constructing a causal story tells a lot about the events' overall importance within this cultural structure.[61]

In this opposition between ideographic and nomothetic approaches, the analyst of the transformation of transatlantic relations seems to be confronted with a choice between treating this transformation in theoretical (and therefore ahistorical) terms or treating it as a sui generis process. Although many political as well as academic arguments can be put forward in defense of treating this transformation process as unique, this aspect need not imply that we cannot gain some theoretical mileage along the way. Two venues come to mind in this context.

First, analysts could move from the abstract level of structural analysis to theoretically structured stories explicating trajectories such as the two broadly sketched at the outset of this project. In trying to account for evolutionary processes along the trajectory of either conflict or crisis, one has to specify how seemingly timeless deep-structure variables such as threats, common values, or institutional inertia relate to sequences of actions and events that produce the stipulated outcomes (i.e., breakdown, transformation, or adaptation in a crisis situation). For instance, a realistic account of a crisis trajectory potentially leading to breakdown would have to specify how shifts in power and perceptions of threat leave traces in the beliefs and actions of relevant actors. It would, in other words, have to link slow-moving causal process variables at the structural level to concrete actions and events in the flow of time in terms of a theoretically informed narrative. The difficulty, of course, is that in these types of accounts, time and historical processes would have to be taken seriously in a theoretical sense. Analysts would have to construct causal arguments that identify beginnings (or key choices in path dependency

60. See Stephen F. Szabo, *Parting Ways: The Crisis in German-American Relations* (Washington, DC: Brookings Institution Press, 2004), 35–44; and Gunter Pleuger, *Die Europäische Union als Macht und Makler in den Vereinten Nationen*, presentation at the German Association for the United Nations, Berlin, 28 September 2006, esp. 3, http://www.dgvn.de/pdf/Publikationen/Pleuger%20EU-UN_Redig.pdf (accessed 4 February 2007).

61. See William H. Sewell Jr., *Logics of History: Social Theory and Social Transformation* (Chicago: Chicago University Press, 2005), 197–224.

arguments) if a certain path is presumably being followed; they would have to specify duration and pace of a certain sequence of actions and/or events; they would also have to incorporate contingency in a systematic manner, including the possibility for reversible trajectories.[62]

Second, analysts with a preference to start at the microlevel might be encouraged to systematically connect their causal accounts with longer-term institutional processes. This idea is based on the dual assumption that (1) the Atlantic order manifests itself in institutions (such as NATO or the World Trade Organization [WTO]) as settings of political interaction and that (2) bad diplomacy by individual leaders (such as Gerhard Schröder or George Bush) has to reverberate in such institutional contexts in order to become structurally significant.[63] In other words, transatlantic institutions here become the focal point for studying a broader process of macrotransformation of the Atlantic order, one that encompasses both the individual decisions of "great men" as well as the causal power of bureaucracies in institutional reproduction.[64] One of the underlying assumptions of this perspective is that institutions would not be regarded as "the 'frozen' residue of critical junctures or as the static, sticky legacies of previous political battles."[65] Rather they would be considered to be the prime locus of innovation, embedded in dynamic historical processes.[66]

Taking this systematic link between the microlevel and the macrolevel of theoretically informed accounts of the Atlantic order's transformation more seriously would have several benefits. First, it would put academic debate about a key process in international politics on a more empirically informed basis, thereby removing some of the heat of a paradigmatically charged debate. Second, to the extent that empirical data were incorporated systematically into our accounts, they would increase the falsifiability of theoretical arguments, which in turn would most likely increase the pressure to gravitate toward the

---

62. See Aminzade, "Historical Sociology and Time," 462–67.

63. Even if the analysis were to remain at the microhistorical level of single decisions or events, this occurrence need not be considered atheoretical. For a discussion of the notion of "exceptional typical" in microhistorical research, see Matti Peltonen, "Clues, Margins and Monads: The Micro-Macro Link in Historical Analysis," *History and Theory* 40, no. 3 (October 2001): 347–59.

64. Daniel L. Byman and Kenneth M. Pollack, "Let Us Now Praise Great Men: Bringing the Statesman Back In," *International Security* 25, no. 4 (Spring 2001): 107–46; Michael Barnett and Martha Finnemore, *Rules for the World: International Organizations in Global Politics* (Ithaca: Cornell University Press, 2004).

65. Kathleen Thelen, "How Institutions Evolve: Insights from Comparative Historical Analysis," in Mahoney and Rueschemeyer, *Comparative Historical Analysis in the Social Sciences*, 208–40, here at 211.

66. For an excellent overview of recent work by historical sociology in international relations in general and historical institutionalism in particular, see George Lawson, "The Promise of Historical Sociology," *Internatioal Studies Review* 8, no. 3 (September 2006): 397–423, here at 410–14.

center along the spectrum of potential explanations ranging from inevitable decline to predestined stability. Third, this gravitational pull would sharpen our acceptance of the historically contingent nature of our concepts and increase the likelihood of conceptual innovation. For instance, in contrast to the rough balancing-versus-bandwagoning dichotomy that dominated the (intra)realist debate in the 1980s, new concepts such as soft balancing or balking were suggested during the early 2000s, in order to account for (potentially) new dynamics driving the evolution of the Atlantic order—concepts that may be compatible with theorizing in a liberal/constructivist line of thought as well.[67] Conceptual innovation such as these examples would thus help us to better understand what kind of evolutionary (or revolutionary) change the Atlantic order may be going through beyond a dichotomous "inevitable decline"-versus-"predestined stability" projection. It may thus also help us to fill the conceptual vacuum of an adaptation scenario between the extremes of breakdown and transformation (here defined in terms of cooperative institutional change). Finally, the systematic theoretical linkage between the microlevel and the macrolevel would also be useful from a policy point of view. In specifying competing causal arguments about potential paths to breakdown or (successful) transformation, scholars would offer a point of entrance for informed political deliberation, including the identification of potential intervention points.

67. On soft balancing, see Robert A. Pape, "Welcome to the Era of 'Soft Balancing,' " *Boston Globe*, 24 March 2003; and Frank Schimmelfennig, "Jenseits von Gleichgewichtspolitik und Anpassung: Chancen und Grenzen transatlantischen sozialen Einflusses," *WeltTrends* 11, no. 40 (Autumn 2003): 76–81; on balking, see Seyom Brown, "Balking: The International Community Responds to American Empire," presentation at the American Imperium Conference, Swarthmore College, Swarthmore, PA, 19 April 2004, http://www.realisticforeignpolicy.org/content/view/34/ (accessed 14 July 2004); see also Seyom Brown, *The Illusion of Control: Force and Foreign Policy in the 21st Century* (Washington, DC: Brookings Institution Press, 2003).

3 THE GHOST OF CRISES PAST

*The Troubled Alliance in
Historical Perspective*

WILLIAM I. HITCHCOCK

The Atlantic alliance presents scholars with a glaring paradox. Since its founding in 1949, members of the alliance have engaged in an almost uninterrupted series of conflicts and disputes with each other, on subjects ranging from military interventions, security and defense policy, nuclear strategy, and economic and trade issues. These disputes have often been serious, and some have even threatened the integrity of the alliance. Yet after half a century, the alliance still survives and remains by any measure the strongest and most enduring alliance in modern history. In 2007, as the Western alliance enters its fifth year of sustained crisis over the war in Iraq, scholars differ over how severe the current crisis is and what solutions are available. Chapters in this volume by Henry Nau and Charles Kupchan offer two contrasting opinions. Nau sees the current crisis as only a moderate one, a crisis narrowly focused on a strategic debate about the threat of terrorism, whereas Kupchan suggests that the Iraq debate is symptomatic of the larger collapse of the European-U.S. cold war alliance community. In this chapter I chart a middle path. I argue that the Iraq crisis is a deep, sustained rupture, probably the worst in the history of the Western alliance; yet I also draw some reason for optimism from past crises, which show that the alliance has survived for the simple reason that the ties that bind it together remain stronger than the forces pulling it apart. This vigor remains true in the year 2007: divisions over Iraq persist, yet no American or European leader has expressed a desire to withdraw from the alliance or even to alter its institutions in any fundamental way. This discrepancy suggests that preserving the Atlantic alliance has emerged as perhaps the single dominant shared core interest of the member states. As long as this interest is shared, and as long as the costs of maintaining the alliance are lower than the costs of ending it, it seems unlikely that this strategic community will break up any time soon.

It would be wrong to suggest, however, that just because previous crises in the alliance have been resolved that crises don't matter. Previous crises have revealed the serious differences of core interests and values between the alliance's members. So far, these crises have led to adaptation rather than total breakdown of the alliance because its members, often grudgingly, either created new rules and institutions that allowed for resolution within the framework of the alliance, or because they simply tolerated a degree of unilateral action by a member state and concerted together to modify the impact of such behavior. The reason the crisis over Iraq looms so large in this narrative is because the process of adaptation, new rule making, or compromise has not yet been successfully implemented, even after five years (2003–7) of severe disruption. This lack of adaptation makes the Iraq crisis the most dangerous one the alliance has ever faced.

In this chapter I examine five interalliance crises since 1949: the dispute over German rearmament in 1950–55; the Suez crisis of 1956; the Gaullist challenge of the mid-1960s; the alliance rifts over the war in Bosnia in the early 1990s; and the divisions generated by the Iraq War. (These are not the only crises in the past sixty years, but my selection is designed to enrich and complement those cases examined by Nau in his chapter.) I have chosen these cases because they all reveal the profound differences among leading member states over issues of power, security, and strategy. Also, they are—like the Iraq crisis—not "United States versus Europe" crises but crises in which the United States was able to split the European bloc and pick off allies. And these cases all reveal a degree of adaptation in their resolution, rather than breakdown or transformation of the entire alliance. I argue that taken as a whole, they indicate a fairly typical pattern within the alliance and are consistent with the current period of intra-alliance disputes. I also argue that all of these crises fit in various ways the working definition of a crisis as laid out by John Ikenberry in the introduction to this volume: they all involved disagreements over core interests, a breakdown of institutional norms, and/or the erosion of a sense of shared community. The evidence presented here suggests that Ikenberry's "third outcome" to a crisis—namely, the creation of new rules and arrangements—is typical of alliance disputes. So far, the alliance survives precisely because of its flexibility and its ability to incorporate a pluralistic set of security interests. Such adaptation has not yet occurred in the debate over Iraq.

What does this chapter reveal about the origins of the crises themselves? The sources of interalliance crises invariably relate to national perceptions of power and security. No state within the alliance has surrendered its national prerogative to assert and defend its own security strategy, and in certain historical epochs (during decolonization, for example, or the Balkan wars) alliance members have come to diametrically opposed positions about how best to pursue security. In discussing the Atlantic alliance, it is vital to recall that the alliance is a community of individual sovereign states. The appearance of the European Union sometimes blinds observers to the persistence of the national interest in Europe; this myopic view of Europe should have been shattered by the Iraq crisis, which showed eighteen European states, led by Britain, fighting openly and angrily with France and Germany over how best to defend European security from the threat of global terror. Crises feed on the persistence of the national interest inside what at times appears to be— but is not—some kind of supranational alliance structure.

Compared to previous crises, the most recent dispute over the war in Iraq has led to a more sustained rupture and an unprecedented loss of confidence in the United States' stewardship of the alliance. The Iraq debate has been a qualitatively different level of crisis than anything we have seen before. In this chapter I show that past crises did not develop into a catastrophic collapse of the institutions of the alliance chiefly because leaders worked hard to manage the alliance through its periods of crisis and to find creative solutions to steer the alliance away from the rocks of discord. In the wake of the Iraq War, the health of the alliance depends now—as always—on how well the present membership is able to find common ground in areas other than Iraq, in order to demonstrate continued relevance of the alliance. This debate is not a simple one about tactics; it is a debate about what role the Atlantic alliance will play on the world stage, in response to a host of major and unprecedented challenges from terrorism, Islamic radicalism, nuclear proliferation, the Israel-Palestinian conflict, the rise of China, North Korea, global public health, the environment, and so on. These issues have become interlocked and intertwined in a way that presents the alliance with its greatest challenges ever. Unless there is significant adaptation in the alliance to accommodate Washington's emphasis on the global war on terror and Europe's insistence on nonmilitary responses to terror and its causes, as well as other global security issues, then the Atlantic alliance will cease to be seen as a valuable tool in advancing the interests of its members. Crisis is a way of life within the alliance, yet even so, its longevity at the moment is in question because the usual pathways to adaptation have not yet been followed.

The Crisis over German Rearmament, 1950–1955

One of the worst alliance crises over the past fifty years emerged just at the birth of the alliance, and it centered on the role that West Germany would play in the emerging Atlantic community. This dilemma has gone down in the books as the debate over German rearmament, but in fact it was much more broadly based than that and fits our working definition of crisis well. At the heart of the dispute over German rearmament lay major disagreements about core interests: Who should be a NATO member? What role was West Germany to play in the alliance? What was NATO's purpose—to contain the Russians or hold down the Germans? Could certain structures be arranged to accomplish both tasks? In the end, the crisis led to significant innovations in the institutions of the alliance. Rupture or breakdown was avoided, and in fact the crisis proved to be salutary in that new mechanisms were designed to contain Germany while also benefiting from its presence inside the alliance.

The debate over German rearmament was brought about by the advent of the first great military conflict of the cold war era, the Korean War. The swift U.S. response to the invasion of South Korea by the North pleased European leaders, since it implied that the United States would do at least as much if western Europe were ever menaced by the Soviets. But almost immediately, Washington began to place intense pressure on the European members of the alliance to increase their own defense spending and to pave the way for a German contribution to Western defense. Five years after the end of the Second World War, most Europeans were profoundly uneasy about the prospect of returning to Germany its military sovereignty. Yet the problem was there: how else could Europe defend itself?[1]

Of course it was France that felt most uneasy about rearming Germany. The French leaders had a number of worries, one of which was that they knew the public would be dead set against it. In this context it is important to recall that the French public was deeply divided about the NATO alliance itself, with nearly half the country opposing membership in 1949. To offer a seat at the table, and a rebuilt army, to the Germans was bound to be sharply opposed by French public opinion—and indeed it was. But of even greater concern to the French was the enduring problem of balancing German power in Europe: a rearmed and sovereign Germany, it was thought, would soon eclipse France inside the alliance. Once Germany was rearmed, it would naturally be accorded greater stature and prestige within the alliance and so weaken French influence. This position was intolerable to the French leadership. German rearmament would therefore have to be opposed.[2] To fend off U.S. pressure yet postpone the creation of a German army, the French proposed to create a European army in which German citizens might enlist but that would be entirely governed by and monitored by an international staff and over which German military commanders would have no independent control. The debate over this European Defense Community (EDC) lasted four long, troubled years.

---

1. For an introduction to the strategic situation at the time in Europe, see Melvyn Leffler, *A Preponderance of Power: National Security, the Truman Administration and the Cold War* (Stanford: Stanford University Press, 1992), 361–90; Ernest May, "The American Commitment to Germany, 1949–1955," *Diplomatic History* 13, no. 4 (Fall 1989): 431–60; and Walter LaFeber, "NATO and the Korean War: A Context," *Diplomatic History* 13, no. 4 (Fall 1989): 461–77.

2. See William I. Hitchcock, *France Restored: Cold War Diplomacy and the Quest for Leadership in Europe, 1944–1954* (Chapel Hill: University of North Carolina Press, 1998), 134–47.

What were the issues at stake, and what made this situation such a big deal? For France, as we have seen, the debate was about how to allow for some German role in Western defense while in practice denying any place for Germany inside the Atlantic alliance. France was simply not yet ready to treat Germany as an ally. For the United States, the problem was the reverse: how to reward German chancellor Konrad Adenauer for his pro-Western policies by giving Germany a trusted place alongside the Western powers in a community of nations working to stabilize Europe and contain the Soviets. The United States could stomach the European army only if it was integrated into NATO and if Germany was given NATO membership. This France could not accept. Adenauer himself could not accept a demeaning role inside a French-dominated scheme for a European army. That would open him up to the charge that he had failed to secure Germany the equality among the Western powers that Adenauer had promised his people. It would open up the whole debate about whether Germany should stick with the West or look to make some sort of compromise with the Soviets and the East Germans. The British position, too, was illustrative of the United Kingdom's fundamental opposition to continental union: the British government urged France and Germany to join in the European army but insisted that Britain—because of its empire—could never possibly join such a federalist scheme. The EDC debate revealed that the major states within the alliance had competing national ideas and needs about security strategy.[3]

Disputes within France also slowed the resolution of the crisis. Although the German and U.S. governments were willing to accept the EDC, a powerful coalition of nationalists in the French parliament turned against the scheme. The French governments of the time thus refused to submit the EDC proposal for ratification, knowing it would fail. The Parliament was simply not yet ready to accept the re-creation of a German army—even though the French leaders who had dreamed up the scheme thought it would actually limit German power inside Europe. The debate within France raged: those who favored the plan depicted the choice as one between the Wehrmacht and the EDC; those opposed characterized the plan as a U.S.-sponsored scheme to create a German army with which to wage war on the Russians.

Meanwhile, the Western allies now lost all patience with France and could not understand why a plan proposed by French leaders could now be so violently opposed by the Parliament. The debate eroded confidence in France as an ally. The French were spoken of in contemptuous terms as the sick man of Europe or, in Eisenhower's memorable phrase, as "a helpless hopeless mass of protoplasm." Winston Churchill, once again Britain's prime minister, said in

3. The German position is treated admirably in Thomas Schwartz, *America's Germany: John J. McCloy and the Federal Republic of Germany* (Cambridge: Harvard University Press, 1991), chap. 5.

December 1953 that "three years had been completely wasted in getting what was absolutely necessary, a good strong German army"—not an argument likely to be welcomed in France. Churchill deemed the French so feckless that he actually declared to his French counterparts at a conference in Bermuda that "thank God he still had the Channel" to rely on. For a country in which memories of Dunkirk were still fresh, these were shocking words. It came as little surprise, then, when John Foster Dulles declared in late 1953 that if France continued to block the creation of the EDC, Washington would face "an agonizing reappraisal of basic U.S. policy" toward Europe—meaning the United States would rearm Germany without France and bring Germany into NATO, in direct defiance of France. In June 1954, Eisenhower, Dulles, Churchill, and Anthony Eden agreed at a meeting in Washington that if the EDC could not be passed by the French parliament, the two Anglo-Saxon powers would strike a bargain with the Germans directly and bypass France altogether. The NATO alliance was indeed on the rocks.[4]

In the end the solution to the crisis came in part from Asia. For in the spring of 1954, the French army suffered its humiliating defeat at Dien Bien Phu, and this trouncing so shook the country that the Parliament elected to the premiership a young maverick named Pierre Mendès France. Mendès France was called in to settle the Indochina conflict and get France out, which he did. But he also sought to cut the Gordian knot that had tied up the question of Germany's role in NATO. Mendès France faced a difficult choice: accept Germany in NATO or destroy the young Atlantic alliance. He opted for the former course, but only after some clever and imaginative proposals had been hammered out by the British and French leadership.

The solution to the crisis was adaptation and the making of new rules. The allies agreed to drop the EDC. In any case, it could never achieve ratification in the French parliament. Instead, Germany and Italy would ask to join the Western European Union—a body set up in 1948, before NATO, of which Britain and France both were members. The WEU would be transformed into a kind of "little NATO"—what we now know as the European pillar of Western defense. Best of all, the United Kingdom was already a member, so the French could feel that they had a British link to help balance German power. WEU would open the way to German entry into NATO. Yet WEU would also allow certain discriminatory restrictions on German rearmament to be carried over from the EDC project: German divisions would be limited in number; the German general staff would not be allowed to act independently of NATO; and Germany would never be allowed to produce atomic, biological, or chemical weapons, although France would of course be allowed to

---

4. Hitchcock, *France Restored*, 184–85; and Brian Duchin, "The 'Agonizing Reappraisal': Dulles, Eisenhower, and the European Defense Community," *Diplomatic History* 16, no. 2 (Spring 1992): 201–21.

do so. The WEU would act as a kind of control authority, monitoring German rearmament and overseeing procurement and weapons production inside Germany.

It was not easy for the French to swallow the reestablishment of a German army. But Mendès France persuaded his countrymen that the WEU plan offered the best chance to create a strong Western defense in which France played a major role, while also limiting German power. The alternative was no alliance at all, and a special German-U.S. axis—a nightmare scenario for France. On the last day of December 1954, the French parliament voted to accept German entry into WEU and NATO.

The lessons of the EDC debate are relevant for our own time. Here was a crisis in which a major member state, France, was locked in a struggle to define the terms and goals of the alliance: the French wanted to keep Germany in an inferior position in the alliance. Yet French and German leaders knew they needed NATO and a strong British and American commitment to their defense. The only way to appease American demands for German rearmament was to rewrite the rules of the alliance in a way that allowed for a second-class citizenship for Germany while masking the basic inferiority of the German position by bringing Germany into the alliance as a full member. The alliance held together because the partners wanted it and believed in its strategic value, and because they were able to create new rules and new institutions to balance out the competing needs of the various members.

The Suez Crisis of 1956

No sooner had the alliance emerged from the tempestuous fight over German rearmament than it entered into another crisis, this one related to the decolonization of the European empires that had been under way since the 1940s and was beginning to pick up significant steam in the later 1950s. The interallied dispute that erupted over the British and French response to Egypt's nationalization of the Suez Canal in July 1956 fits our definition of a crisis perfectly: there was a fundamental disagreement over core interests, in this case, Arab nationalism and its challenge to Europe's oil supplies; there was a breakdown in the normal mechanisms of consultation within the alliance, as Britain and France secretly colluded to invade Egypt; and the sense of Atlantic community was seriously eroded. Moreover, even though the "special relationship" between London and Washington was reestablished fairly rapidly in the wake of the Suez fiasco, France remained deeply alienated by the affair and chose a path in its security and alliance policy that would reverberate for the subsequent decade or more.

The Suez Canal was—and still is—one of the world's most important highways of water-borne commerce; in the 1950s, it was still closely identified with British power in the Near East. One-third of the ships that passed through it each year were British, and the British government owned a 44 percent stake in the Suez Canal Company. And the canal was important for all of Europe: some 70 percent of Europe's oil supply passed through the canal. Yet in the context of the postwar world, when Britain had already surrendered its role in India and Palestine, and when France had lost a costly colonial war in Indochina, it was clear that Britain could not maintain formal control over the Suez Canal. Britain would have to resort to other less formal means of exercising influence. In 1954, in fact, Britain had agreed to withdraw its substantial military base near the canal and, along with the United States, offered Egypt substantial economic aid to build a power-producing dam along the Nile River, near Aswan. But Egypt's leader, a dashing young army officer named Gamal Abdel Nasser, proved immune to such blandishments. He championed the cause of Arab nationalism and heaped abuse on the British for their continued pretensions in the region. Nasser even made overtures to the Soviet bloc and accepted a shipment of Czech arms. In response to Nasser's truculence, Britain and the United States withdrew their support for the Aswan Dam project in July 1956. Nasser retaliated by nationalizing the canal, directly challenging Britain's presence in the Near East.

That this dispute over the control of the Suez Canal should erupt into a major international crisis was the result of two factors. First, the British prime minister, Anthony Eden, and his advisers believed that control of the canal was vital to Britain's oil supplies and also to its overall security. Without access to Middle East oil, one top Foreign Office official moaned, Britain would have to spend valuable foreign exchange in acquiring oil elsewhere, leading to depleted gold reserves, the collapse of the sterling bloc, a bankrupt government, and a total implosion of Britain's security posture in Europe and Asia.[5]

The second reason the Suez dispute erupted into a full-blown crisis was the result of France's colonial adventures. Nasser had established the Algerian rebels who were busily fighting for independence from France. He had offered arms and military training to the rebels, and the French were eager to see Nasser punished. It was the French who conceived the infamous plan to urge Israel to invade Egypt. France and Britain would then pose as neutral brokers, insist that the Israelis and Egyptians agree to a cease-fire and, to ensure the peace, would position their own troops in the Suez Canal zone. It was hoped that Nasser would be humiliated by the defeat at the hands of Israel and would be overthrown. In late October, the British and Israelis agreed to this harebrained scheme; on October 29, Israeli forces attacked Egypt and swept through the Sinai Peninsula. The British and French helpfully bombarded Egyptian airfields. Despite a swift denunciation by the UN General

5. Keith Kyle, "Britain and the Suez Crisis, 1955–56," in *Suez 1956: The Crisis and Its Consequences*, ed. W. Roger Louis and Roger Owen, 103–31 (Oxford: Oxford University Press, 1989), 117, 123; Alistair Horne, *Harold Macmillan*, vol. 1, *1894–1956* (New York: Viking, 1988), 396.

Assembly of this operation, British and French paratroopers landed in Port Said on November 5, prepared to seize control of the Suez Canal zone.[6]

The British and French had their reasons, however ill considered, to seek Nasser's ouster and maintain control over the Suez. Yet it was the U.S. reaction to this Anglo-French-Israeli plan that turned this intervention into a serious interallied crisis. Why did President Eisenhower react with such fury to the invasion of Suez, and why was he willing to use U.S. power to restrain, even to humiliate, his two allies? Eisenhower's angry reaction derived from his belief that the Anglo-French use of military action against Nasser would inflame opinion in the Arab world against the West—as indeed it did—and, even if successful, fail to resolve the broader issue of how the West should contain the rising tide of Arab nationalism in the Middle East. As Eisenhower's CIA chief Allen Dulles put it, the British and French wanted "to reverse the trend away from colonialism and turn the clock back 50 years." Further, Eisenhower feared that an invasion would push Egypt and the Arab world into the hands of the Soviet Union. Washington wanted a diplomatic approach to the nationalization and spearheaded a conference of twenty-two nations to design a new framework for international control of the canal. Nasser refused to yield, declaring the canal to be Egyptian. Even so, Washington would not countenance any military action. The French and British leaders nonetheless moved ahead with their plans for a military invasion, meeting with the Israelis and keeping Washington in the dark. Dulles told the National Security Council that relations with France were "strained to a degree not paralleled for a very long time in the past." And tellingly: "We don't know their plans. Never in recent years had we faced a situation where we had no clear idea of the intentions of our British and French allies." The Americans had given clear warnings that they opposed intervention, and when it came anyway, Secretary of State John Foster Dulles solemnly told the French ambassador that it was "the blackest day which had occurred in many years in the relations between England, France, and the United States."[7]

The British and French had believed that an invasion of Egypt would demonstrate the continued resilience of European power in the Middle East. In fact, it had precisely the opposite effect. Washington refused to lend diplomatic or public support to the invasion once it began, and currency traders and banks then rushed to cash in their pounds sterling in exchange for dollars, causing a run on the pound. The Bank of England began hemorrhaging dollars, and Britain faced the depletion of its currency reserves unless the United States would give it a short-term loan. Eisenhower refused and instead let the

---

6. The narrative of the crisis is carefully laid out in Keith Kyle, *Suez* (New York: St. Martin's, 1991).

7. Irwin Wall, *France, The United States, and the Algerian War* (Berkeley: University of California Press, 2001), 39, 47, 57.

British twist in the wind; financial aid would come only after British troops were withdrawn from Egyptian soil. Eden, faced with the imminent collapse of the pound, called his French counterpart Guy Mollet on November 6 to say that Britain was pulling out and abandoning the invasion in midcourse. The French had to follow suit. The humiliation was complete: the invasion was failure, world opinion had turned against the Europeans, and the Atlantic alliance was in tatters.[8]

There is no question that the NATO alliance, and the sense of comradeship between the big three states within it, was seriously harmed by the Suez fiasco. Yet the alliance survived. Why? Chiefly because, in the immediate aftermath of the invasion, Anthony Eden resigned and made way for Harold Macmillan to take the reins of the British government. Macmillan strongly favored a close alliance with Washington and worked hard to recover the confidence of his old World War II friend Dwight Eisenhower. Macmillan knew that by itself, Britain had no hope of running an independent foreign and security policy. The Suez crisis revealed Britain's economic frailty, but Macmillan also knew that his country had a paltry nuclear deterrent that was entirely dependent on the United States for its delivery systems. Far better, Macmillan believed, to make common cause with the Americans than to join forces with the unreliable French. In this sense, the Suez crisis did not permanently damage the special relationship between Washington and London.

Suez did, however, seriously alienate France from the alliance. Eden's last-minute bailout revived France's old prejudices against the "Anglo-Saxons" and reinforced in Paris the idea that Britain could never be trusted as a European partner. Guy Mollet, infuriated by Eden's reversal, moved swiftly on two fronts: he pushed ahead with negotiations on the formation of the European Economic Community, which would come to fruition in 1957, and also accelerated work on France's own nuclear deterrent—a project that would lead to a French nuclear weapon by 1960. While the British sought to return to the fold of the Atlantic partnership after Suez, the French sought greater strategic independence from Washington and nourished a serious grievance against the United States for its lack of support at Suez. The bitterness from Suez would never fully dissipate from Franco-American relations.[9]

The Gaullist Challenge

It is perhaps not surprising, given this history, that for the rest of the century the major controversies within the Atlantic alliance seemed to center around Franco-American disputes. After Suez, the next major challenge to the shape

8. Diane Kunz, *The Economic Diplomacy of the Suez Crisis* (Chapel Hill: University of North Carolina, 1991).

9. Maurice Vaïsse, "Post-Suez France," in Louis and Owen, *Suez 1956*, 335–40.

and integrity of the Western alliance arrived soon after the return to power of French president Charles de Gaulle in 1958. Again, the source of the friction was France, but de Gaulle's challenge to U.S. dominance of the alliance was in fact part of a broad effort to determine what precisely Europe's relationship with the United States would be in the postreconstruction phase of Europe's development. Was Europe to become an independent, powerful community of states, using its economic, military, and cultural assets to influence world affairs? Or would Europe remain a group of cautious, sheltered, inward-looking states, dependent on the United States for its security and its foreign policy choices? Or could it find some happy balance between these two extremes? De Gaulle, of course, desired greater independence from Washington, especially in light of France's nuclear capabilities, its expansive economy, and its leading role among the states of the newly created European Economic Community. De Gaulle's challenge provoked a great deal of hand-wringing and tension. But did the Gaullist challenge to U.S. leadership constitute a crisis? As far as de Gaulle was concerned, he and the United States diverged on core interests in cold war policy, the Vietnam War, and the global position of the dollar. Moreover, de Gaulle was willing to threaten the integrity of NATO to make his point. But this crisis was probably more dependent on de Gaulle himself rather than on any serious, long-term split between France or Europe and the United States. With de Gaulle's departure in 1969, the Atlantic alliance recovered its balance fairly quickly.

The Gaullist challenge to the Atlantic alliance can be reduced to two key components: first, de Gaulle sought to tighten Franco-German relations and so pull Germany away from the Anglo-American center of gravity inside the alliance; second, he sought to free France from what he saw as NATO's control over French military and nuclear policy. In each case, however, the alliance survived intact, perhaps it was even strengthened, and the Gaullist challenge was contained.[10]

The first phase of the Gaullist challenge emerged in 1958 and ran through the signing of the Franco-German Friendship Treaty in January 1963. De Gaulle fired the opening salvo in his memorandum of September 17, 1958, in which he proposed establishing a tripartite directorate within NATO through which the United States, Britain, and France would set policy on strategic and nuclear matters. In part, this proposal grew from his frustration at being left out of U.S. decision making in recent international crises such as those over the offshore Chinese islands Quemoy and Matsu, and U.S.-U.K. intervention in Lebanon and Jordan in 1958, which had seriously increased cold war tensions. De Gaulle, not unreasonably, felt that if a world war was to be triggered, France ought to be involved in the decisions. Also, France was about to become

10. The most complete account of de Gaulle's foreign policy is Maurice Vaïsse, *La grandeur: Politique étrangère du général de Gaulle* (Paris: Fayard, 1998).

a nuclear state—it did so in 1960—and so was now on a different plane from the other nonnuclear states. As such, it should have a seat in the nuclear club.

De Gaulle's memorandum was only the first move in a longer match of wits with the Western states, however. De Gaulle knew his proposals would not be well received. He intended to use their inevitable rejection as a means of triggering a crisis within NATO and opening up a bid for a tighter Franco-German partnership that might weaken Washington's control over Europe. Indeed, de Gaulle presented France's 1959 withdrawal of its fleet from the joint NATO Mediterranean Command as a result of Washington's rejection of his tripartite scheme. But the real crisis in the alliance was moving along another front: as de Gaulle was making trouble in NATO, he was also trying to seduce Adenauer's Germany into joining with France to alter the character of the project for European integration. De Gaulle wished to weaken the federal character of the emerging European community, strengthen its intergovernmental institutions, and bolster continental Europe as a counterbalance to U.S. and British weight in Europe. To that end, he naturally intended to keep Britain out of the EEC. De Gaulle hoped that France and Germany, working together, could strengthen Europe, make European defense less reliant on Washington, and possibly break down the cold war division of the Continent, which worked to keep western Europe under a U.S. security umbrella. De Gaulle seemed to be proposing a Europe-centered conception of the alliance, in contrast to Washington's Atlantic-based conception.

The dual blows of January 1963—when de Gaulle vetoed Britain's application to join the EEC and also signed the French-German Friendship Treaty—appeared to Washington as if Adenauer had been won over to de Gaulle's conceptions, and that France and Germany were going to hijack the EEC and split NATO. President Kennedy called the treaty "an unfriendly act." George Ball, the U.S. deputy secretary of state, came down hard on the Germans and said that Germany "would have to make a difficult choice between its relationship with France and its ties with the rest of Europe and the U.S." Rusk believed that de Gaulle was trying "to force us [the United States] out of Europe," and this had to be resisted with "the greatest effort."[11]

Yet the United States misread the position of the Germans in all this. Adenauer, as early as 1960, had already told his advisers that he did not plan to let de Gaulle wreck NATO or the EEC, and even though he was pleased by de Gaulle's willingness to demand greater equality among the Europeans with Washington, Adenauer had to recognize the desire of most in his political party to ensure the continued close relationship with Washington. Indeed, it was the German Bundestag that insisted on language in the treaty's preamble declaring Germany's support for NATO, for European unity, and for a close

---

11. Geir Lundestad, *The United States and Western Europe since 1945* (London: Oxford University Press, 2003), 124.

alliance with the United States. De Gaulle was in the end unable to bring Germany into a partnership that might replace, or even counterbalance, the Anglo-American dominance of the alliance.

So the result of de Gaulle's first challenge to the alliance was, paradoxically, a strengthening of the ties that bound Germany to the United States. France was forced to confront the fact that for the majority of West Germans, Adenauer's *Westpolitik* had become an article of faith and must be protected from intra-European challenges.

De Gaulle's second challenge, the one to NATO, had a similar outcome. In March 1966, de Gaulle announced that France, while remaining a member of NATO, would withdraw from the integrated military command, and he obliged all NATO organizations and 26,000 U.S. soldiers to leave French soil within the year. Had any other European states followed France's lead, the NATO alliance might surely have come to a crashing end. But none did. De Gaulle's challenge to NATO was based on his own conception of national sovereignty: that states that cannot defend themselves are weak and ineffective; that alliances should be communities of interest without a corresponding loss of sovereignty; and that no one state should be allowed to determine the foreign policies of another. Of course, it is debatable if any of these conditions applied within NATO, but de Gaulle's worldview and his politics required that France distance itself from NATO. Of course he hoped this might signal a gradual loosening of the alliance, not because he opposed the Western states but because he believed the alliance took the initiative in world affairs away from Europe and placed it permanently in the hands of the Americans. Now, de Gaulle believed, France could act as a balancer between the states, not, as he put it, as "a humble auxiliary of one of them." France had taken a bold step, he believed, and "has perhaps given the signal of a general evolution toward international détente."[12]

Taken by itself, this crisis might not have become full blown. To contemporaries, however, de Gaulle looked like a serious threat to the integrity of the alliance. His withdrawal from NATO came at the same time as he was busily denouncing the U.S. war in Vietnam. In 1964 he had given recognition to Communist China. In 1965, de Gaulle sided with the Soviets, the Chinese, and the North Vietnamese in calling for a reopening of the Geneva talks on drawing up a peace settlement in Vietnam. In June 1965, de Gaulle announced—in a remark that has been heard frequently since the start of the Iraq War—that "the United States was the greatest danger in the world today to peace." Polls showed the French public opposed the United States' war in Vietnam by 71 percent to 8 percent. In 1965, 32 percent of French respondents to a poll thought Mao Tse-tung the greatest threat to world peace, and Lyndon Johnson

12. De Gaulle, as quoted in Charles Cogan, *Charles de Gaulle: A Brief Biography with Documents* (Boston: Bedord Books, 1996), 129.

was a close second at 30 percent. When Vice President Hubert Humphrey visited Paris in 1967, his entourage was pelted with eggs, paint, and stones. The French people appeared eager to detach themselves from NATO and Washington's leading strings, exasperating France's longtime U.S. allies. Columnist Russell Baker captured the American perception of de Gaulle when he wrote in one of his pieces that "the General's announcement that France would withdraw from Earth was hardly unexpected."[13]

So, in a broad sense, the Gaullist challenge was a crisis of confidence in U.S. leadership in the alliance, and it particularly revealed that many Europeans, not just French people, were worried that U.S. policy in Vietnam and elsewhere might draw Europe and NATO into a global war. Yet in the end, de Gaulle's challenge failed to shake the alliance in a serious way. Why?

His challenge failed for at least three reasons. First, the rest of the alliance members resisted any temptation to follow de Gaulle's lead. For the Germans, de Gaulle's policies toward NATO were seen as reckless and injurious to west European security: if the German public got the idea that NATO troops should leave German soil as well as French, what would be left of the alliance? Instead, the rest of the alliance was able to reaffirm, in the Harmel report of December 1967 (Pierre Harmel was the Belgian defense minister), a common strategy for NATO: to defend the territorial security of the alliance through a policy of collective defense, while also pursuing a stable relationship with the USSR. In a clear repudiation of de Gaulle's view of world affairs, the report noted that "military security and a policy of détente are not contradictory but complementary. Collective defense is a stabilizing factor in world affairs."[14] Just a year after the crisis of 1966, NATO appeared stable and if anything strengthened by the ordeal.

Second, Lyndon Johnson responded to de Gaulle in a measured fashion calculated to reassure the other allies that NATO's future was secure. As one aide recalled, Johnson declared that when de Gaulle "comes rushing down like a locomotive on the track, why the Germans and ourselves, we just stand aside and let him go on by, then we're back together again." Johnson's "private references to General de Gaulle stretched his considerable talent for colorful language," but in public he maintained his cool.[15] France, President Johnson wrote to de Gaulle, was a valued ally and would remain so, despite its request that U.S. forces leave the country. Johnson later wrote that he thought a full-blown denunciation of the French position "would only further enflame French nationalism" and "created strains among the nations of the EEC."

13. Frank Costigliola, *France and the United States: The Cold Alliance since World War II* (New York: Twayne, 1992), 140–47.

14. Report published in Lawrence S. Kaplan, *NATO and the United States: The Enduring Alliance* (Boston: Twayne, 1988), 223–25.

15. Kaplan, *NATO and the United States*, 117.

Besides, Johnson said, he knew "de Gaulle would not remain in power forever."[16] Johnson had the wisdom to accept French exceptionalism.

The main reason that de Gaulle's challenge did not hurt NATO too seriously, however, was that the alliance proved flexible and adapted to the new realities. With the French out of the way, the other fourteen members of NATO reorganized the Defense Planning Committee and created the Nuclear Planning Group—excluding France but including Germany—to discuss nuclear strategy among its allies. It established new protocols through the Lemnitzer-Ailleret agreements of 1967 on French relations with NATO in case of war. And NATO adopted a policy of forward defense and flexible response that the French had criticized. Far from resulting in the destruction of the alliance, de Gaulle's challenge may have strengthened it. The historian of NATO Lawrence Kaplan has written that the 1966 changes "represented a liberation of the alliance from French negativism."[17]

Bosnia and the Western Alliance: From Crisis to Unity

The 1992–95 war in Bosnia provides yet another, and tragic, example of interallied crisis. In Bosnia, the circumstances were quite different from those of any previous crisis. The cold war was over, and the landscape of the international system appeared unfamiliar. The war in the Balkans was an "out-of-area" problem, and the crisis was not triggered by an internal debate over alliance policy but by a campaign of mass murder and ethnic cleansing inside the former Yugoslavia. The war unfolded in a geographical area about which most Americans and Europeans were ignorant, and most important the war—awful as its consequences were—did not present an immediate security threat to the territorial integrity of the NATO countries (except possibly Greece). As a result, the Western alliance was badly prepared to handle what became the defining international crisis of the 1990s. Does Bosnia fit our definition of a crisis within the alliance? The crisis did not center on a disagreement over core interests—all the alliance members opposed Serb aggression and genocidal tactics in Bosnia and wanted to contain the violence inside Bosnia from spreading to neighboring regions in the Balkans. The disagreements related to process and strategy: How should the Atlantic community respond? What actions—military intervention or peacekeeping—should it take to halt the violence? Whose responsibility were the Balkans, anyway? These were serious issues precisely because of the global context: the cold war had recently ended, the United States had led a coalition in the Gulf War to expel Saddam

16. Alfred Grosser, *The Western Alliance: European-American Relations since 1945* (New York: Vintage, 1982), 215–16.

17. Kaplan, *NATO and the United States*, 116.

Hussein's army from Kuwait, and there had appeared to be a general sense of purpose and confidence within the alliance. The Bosnia case shattered the honeymoon and left the major states embittered and alienated.

This is not the place for a recapitulation of the history of the Bosnian War.[18] The questions we face here are of a different sort. Why did the major states within the Western alliance allow the war in Bosnia to proceed for three and a half years without implementing an effective strategy for putting an end to the worst campaign of genocide in Europe since 1945? What flaws did the Bosnian crisis reveal about the inner workings of the Western alliance? Finally, how did the alliance resolve its internal differences and join forces to end the war?

The answer to the first question—what explains the dilatory response of the alliance to the genocide in the Balkans—has been established by scholars and analysts alike. For the Americans, the war in Bosnia was low on a long list of international commitments. In 1991, the United States had fought and won a war in Kuwait and Iraq, sending half a million troops to the Persian Gulf to protect pro-Western Arab states and secure the West's access to Arab oil. That year, U.S. diplomacy was also focused on the demise of the Soviet Union. By 1992, the U.S. economy was in recession and the president, George H. W. Bush, faced a difficult reelection campaign. The United States simply did not want to get involved.[19]

U.S. inaction left the problem on Europe's doorstep. Europe publicly welcomed the challenge of attempting to bring peace to Yugoslavia. "The hour of Europe has dawned," declared the foreign minister of Luxembourg, Jacques Poos, in June 1991, when his country held the rotating presidency of the EC. After all, if Europe could manage the overthrow of communism and the unification of Germany without resort to violence, surely it could bring its brand of civilized discourse to Bosnia. But there was a problem. The Europeans, like the Americans, refused to see the Bosnian War as one of aggression and genocide by one people against another. Rather, Europeans viewed the conflict as part of a long-term ethnic contest that had been under way for many centuries and whose real origins lay in the murky Balkan past. Because all sides were equally guilty, the argument went, the only solution was to mediate and compromise over territorial issues. Therefore, the Europeans staked their entire effort not on punishing Serb aggression but on securing a cease-fire and administering humanitarian aid to the displaced refugees.

In September 1992, the UN Security Council agreed to deploy troops— mostly French and British—as a UN Protection Force (UNPROFOR) with a mandate to monitor troop movements in Bosnia and protect humanitarian aid convoys. The troops had no authority to use military force. In November,

18. An excellent narrative can be found in Laura Silber and Allan Little, *Yugoslavia: Death of a Nation* (Penguin: New York, 1997).

19. Richard Holbrooke, *To End a War* (New York: Random House, 1998), 23.

6,000 soldiers under UN command arrived in Bosnia. At the same time, peace talks spearheaded by the EC and UN negotiators David Owen and Cyrus Vance proposed the division of Bosnia into ten cantons of ethnic communities. By subscribing to the Vance-Owen plan, the EC accepted in principle that Bosnia would become ethnically divided and its people physically separated. However, the Bosnian Serbs rejected the plan because it required them to give up territory they had already seized and cleansed of Muslims. So the pattern continued: the earnest search for a peace settlement acceptable to all sides, the delivery of humanitarian aid, the declaration by the UN of certain cities as "safe areas"—and the long slow strangulation of the Bosnian Muslims.

The EU countries were clearly misguided in their belief that sanctions, UN resolutions, and threats of diplomatic isolation would intimidate Serbia and their Bosnian Serb proxies. Between 1992 and 1995, under full view of UN troops, the Bosnian Serbs effectively cleansed about two-thirds of Bosnia of its Muslim inhabitants by killing them or pushing them into Bosnian government–held areas. The UN troops on the ground were too weak to oppose Serb troops by force, and in any case their mandate required them to maintain peace between the "warring parties" rather than taking sides. As the British commander of UN troops in Bosnia declared, "You cannot fight a war from white-painted vehicles."[20]

At least the Europeans put troops on the ground. Although the troops were not effective, the action gave the Europeans the moral high ground in their discussions with the United States. Where, by contrast, was the United States' military contribution? Why did the United States fail to engage itself, and indeed the whole NATO apparatus, in the Bosnian conflict early enough to perhaps stave off some of the mass murders of Bosnia's Muslims? Richard Holbrooke, an architect of the Dayton accords that finally ended the war, argued in his memoir that NATO should have been engaged in the war right from the start. "The best chance to prevent the war," he wrote, "would have been to present the Yugoslavs with a clear warning that NATO airpower would be used against any party that tried to deal with the ethnic tensions of Yugoslavia by force. The United States and the Europeans could then have worked with the Yugoslav parties to mediate peaceful . . . divorce agreements between the Republics."[21]

This scenario, however, did not happen. Instead, Washington failed to use the NATO tool to address the problem. In a paradoxical reversal, now the United States feared that the Europeans might drag it into a war if NATO were deployed. Warren Zimmerman, the former U.S. ambassador to Belgrade, recalled his meeting with senior Bush officials in 1992 in which he asked them why the United States could not use NATO and threaten the Serbs with

20. Silber and Little, *Yugoslavia*, 326.
21. Holbrooke, *To End a War*, 28.

air strikes. Lawrence Eagleburger replied that he thought the situation was similar to the quagmire of Vietnam. The United States would gradually get pulled in deeper and deeper until it could not get out. He also said he saw no compelling U.S. national security interest in the conflict. Brent Scowcroft, the national security adviser, told Zimmerman much the same. If air strikes were not effective, he argued, the United States would have to be prepared to put boots on the ground and intervene fully. If the United States was not willing to intervene fully, it should stay out altogether or else risk losing credibility. This reply depressed Zimmerman: "The refusal of the Bush administration to commit American air power early in the Bosnian War . . . was our greatest mistake of the entire Yugoslav crisis."[22] The result of this failure is well known: the United States left the issue in the hands of the Europeans and the UN, and the Bosnian Serbs continued to slaughter Muslims.

What was really going on here, and what weaknesses of the alliance did this sad affair reveal? The ongoing war in Bosnia between 1992 and 1995 poisoned interallied relations. The Americans had abdicated leadership on the Bosnia issue, but then when the UN and European states engineered the Vance-Owen agreement, it was roundly denounced as a sellout to the Bosnian Serbs and seen as rewarding aggression. Instead, some in Washington called for a lifting of the arms embargo on Bosnia, thus allowing the Muslims to arm themselves and level the playing field, and the use of limited bombings of Serb targets. The Europeans roundly denounced this policy, since more arm would likely mean more killing, with the EU peacekeepers caught in the middle. As for limited bombing, the Europeans worried that this tactic would only result in reprisals against their troops—as indeed it did. The stalemate was complete, no coherent joint U.S.-EU policy ever emerged, and the slaughter continued into 1995.

We know, in the end, that this crisis too worked itself out. Thanks to a number of factors—the election of Jacques Chirac to the French presidency; the ever more ruthless and egregious violations of UN safe areas, especially in Srebrenica, by the Bosnian Serbs; and the Croatian assault in August 1995 against the Bosnian Serbs—NATO was finally pressed into service, using U.S. air power for a significant and punishing series of air strikes on Serb targets across the former Yugoslavia. As Holbrooke put it, "in only eighteen weeks in 1995—when the situation seemed most hopeless—the United States put all its prestige on the line with a series of high risk actions: an all-out diplomatic effort in August, heavy NATO bombing in September, a cease-fire in October, Dayton in November and in December the deployment of twenty thousand American troops to Bosnia."[23] The lessons of Dayton were carried on into the late 1990s, and the United States and Europe

22. Warren Zimmerman, *Origins of a Catastrophe* (New York: Random House, 1999), 215–16.
23. Holbrooke, *To End a War*, 358.

were much more effective and swift in dealing with the 1999 crisis over Kosovo, where diplomatic and military action worked to stymie another vast project of ethnic cleansing.

What did this sad episode tell us about the Western alliance in the post–cold war era? The crisis over Bosnia revealed a number of facts about the alliance that bear emphasis. First, the crisis revealed that Europe by itself, without U.S. partnership, was unable to develop and implement a coherent, effective foreign and security policy. It was not for lack of courage or money, but the fact was plain that Europe could not resolve a war in its own backyard without U.S. engagement. This lesson was painful, but it helps explain why European states are as strong in their support of NATO in the post–cold war era as they were during the cold war.

Second, the Bosnian crisis revealed that the United States still has a national interest not only in European security but also in the institutions that underpin that security. Disengagement from Europe, however brief in the early 1990s, was a disaster. It left the EU and UN to their own devices in Bosnia, depriving them of the tools they needed to solve the crisis. Only full U.S. engagement brought about an end to the Bosnian War and later to the Kosovo crisis. The Bosnian crisis forced the United States once again to declare itself a "European" nation, with security interests there that had to be defended.

Third, the Bosnian crisis in the long run opened the way for a strengthening of certain institutions and relationships, in part because all sides recognized the central role of the United States in Europe's security. Dayton, and Washington's recommitment to Europe, produced momentum toward NATO expansion and an improvement in U.S.-Russian relations. And on the ground in Bosnia, U.S. troops worked side by side with Europeans in peacekeeping roles, providing support to the Organization for Security and Cooperation in Europe (OSCE) and EU operations for the reconstruction of Bosnia and Kosovo. Ten years later, they were still there, partners in building stability in the Balkans. Even the worst crises, it seems, have their silver linings.

A New Level of Crisis? The Iraq War and the Atlantic Alliance

This narrative of interallied crises now brings us to the most recent rupture in the alliance: the global debate about Iraq that erupted in the wake of the September 11, 2001, attacks on the United States and continued up to the invasion of Iraq by U.S. and British forces in March 2003. The dispute over intervention in Iraq certainly constitutes a crisis as we have used that term: it grew from divergent perceptions of core interests, in this case over how to ensure security from a perceived threat of terrorism and weapons of mass destruction; it led to a spectacular breakdown of the norms of alliance processes when, at the United Nations, France threatened to veto a proposed resolution that would give UN sanction to the use of force against Iraq; and it also led to a breakdown in the sense of community, with a wave of anti-Americanism crashing across the continent of Europe. Seen from this perspective, the Iraq crisis is certainly the most serious and troubling of the post–World War II era. More worrisome: it has not yet been resolved by significant new rule making or adaptation. The intensity of the crisis has eased somewhat since the electoral defeat in November 2005 of the German Social Democratic leader Gerhard Schröder and his replacement by the more moderate and pro-American Christian Democrat Angela Merkel as German chancellor, but the underlying issues of U.S. unilateralism and European recalcitrance to act on the global stage have yet to be resolved.[24]

Why did the attacks of September 11, 2001, lead to a split inside the Atlantic alliance, at a time when the bold actions of a common enemy—radical Islamic terrorism—should have brought about a new era of alliance solidarity? The origins of the crisis that erupted in 2001 inside the alliance lay in the reactions of the United States and Europe to the threat of terrorism itself. Americans were naturally shocked by the scale of devastation to lower Manhattan, fearful that additional attacks might soon follow, and quickly roused to passionate fury toward the perpetrators. In the wake of the events of that awful day, it was perhaps natural that the United States' entire political discourse would become focused on how to exact revenge and ensure that such things not happen again. The events of 9/11 marked the start of a new period in the United States' military history that the president, George W. Bush, termed "the war on terror."

For Europe, the effect of the attacks was less direct, less personal. Naturally, from across the Continent came expressions of horror, along with a desire to reach out and help an old friend. The editor of the influential French daily *Le Monde* caught the spirit of the moment in an editorial the day after the attack:

> At a moment like this, when words fail so lamentably to express one's feelings of shock, the first thought that comes to mind is that we are all Americans, all New Yorkers, just as inevitably as President John Kennedy pronounced himself to be a Berliner in his famous 1962 speech in what has since become the German capital. As during the darkest hours of French history, there is absolutely no question of not showing solidarity with the United States and its people, who are so close to us, and to whom we owe our freedom.[25]

24. The most thorough account of the interallied controversy on Iraq is Philip H. Gordon and Jeremy Shapiro, *Allies at War: American, Europe, and the Crisis over Iraq* (New York: McGraw-Hill, 2004).

25. Jean-Marie Colombani, "Nous sommes tous américans," *Le Monde*, 13 September 2001.

German chancellor Gerhard Schröder called the attacks a declaration of "war against the civilized world," and church services and candlelight vigils were held across Germany. "I have assured the American president of our unlimited solidarity, and I stress unlimited," Schröder told the Bundestag. British prime minister Tony Blair, whose country lost sixty-seven citizens in the inferno, emphatically declared that his country "stands shoulder to shoulder with our American friends in this hour of tragedy and we, like them, will not rest until this evil is driven from our world."[26] On September 12, NATO, for the first time ever, invoked article 5 of its collective security treaty and declared the terror strikes to be an attack on all nineteen members of the alliance. On September 14, all EU member states held memorial ceremonies. A total of 400 million Europeans joined in shared grief with America.

Despite initial sympathy, however, Europeans were uneasy with the justifiable anger that Americans now directed at their attackers. President Bush delivered a series of terse addresses in the days after the attack that left no doubt that the United States would unleash its formidable power upon any country it deemed a threat to its security. "Whether we bring our enemies to justice," he said, "or bring justice to our enemies, justice will be done." EU foreign ministers, meeting on September 12, sounded a note of caution: the Norwegian Thorbjorn Jagland said, "it's not easy to warn the United States in such a situation, but we must hope that there will not be an irrational revenge." Alain Richard, French defense minister, suggested that if "an act of retaliation leads to a new destabilization, you haven't won anything at all." The German defense minister contradicted President Bush, claiming, "We do not face a war." Instead, he called for stepped up international police measures against terrorism.[27]

Something more than rhetoric was splitting Europeans and Americans apart, however. Even before 9/11, many in Europe had expressed hostility toward President Bush and his policies.[28] In the first year of his administration, Bush took a series of actions that Europeans saw as unilateralist and inconsistent with the emerging post–cold war emphasis on international cooperation. He had withdrawn the United States from the Kyoto Protocol on global warming, turned up his nose at the Rio Pact on biodiversity, declared the antiballistic treaty with Russia to be outdated and defunct, and pursued a U.S. ballistic missile shield, opposed a ban on land mines, and denounced the new International Criminal Court. With such actions in mind, some Europeans

26. Deutsche Presse-Agentur, 11 September 2001; Agence France Presse, 12 September 2001; *Daily Mail*, 14 September 2001.

27. William Drozdiak, "Attack on U.S. Is Attack on All, NATO Agrees," *Washington Post*, 13 September 2001; Deutsche Presse-Agentur, 14 September 2001; George H. W. Bush, address to joint session of Congress, 20 September 2001, http://www.whitehouse.gov.

28. For detailed polling, see Pew Research Center poll of 15 August 2001, "Bush Unpopular in Europe."

suggested that the September attacks, while not justified, were in part a consequence of the United States' ham-handed, self-centered behavior on the world stage.

Therefore, while European states and NATO partners lent support to the invasion of Afghanistan by the U.S. military in early October—an invasion designed to destroy terrorist leader Osama bin Laden and the extremist Afghan regime that had sheltered him—most European citizens refused to sanction a wider military campaign against other states that might harbor hostile intentions toward the United States.[29] Although Bush believed that 9/11 gave him carte blanche to use U.S. power to crush his enemies, Europeans called for precisely the opposite: a calm analysis of the roots of Islamic terror, the development of global solutions to problems such as poverty and ethnic warfare that seemed to fuel anti-Western sentiment, and a renewed effort to resolve the Israeli-Palestinian conflict, which had so radicalized millions in the Islamic world.[30]

Had the affair ended with the invasion of Afghanistan and the overthrow of the Taliban government, the dispute over terrorism might not have led to a crisis in the alliance. However, President Bush sought to carry the war on terror to other states that had the capacity, either through unconventional weapons or religious ideology, or both, to harm the United States. First on his list was Iraq, a country not implicated in the 9/11 attacks but one controlled by an odious tyrant who had used chemical weapons in the past and who had a record of seeking to develop an arsenal of nuclear, chemical, and biological weapons. The growing emphasis in U.S. foreign policy on waging what Bush called a preemptive war on Iraq—get him before he gets us—was made clear in September 2002, when President Bush, visiting New York for the one-year anniversary of the 9/11 attacks, delivered a somber and threatening speech to the UN General Assembly. He alleged that Iraq represented a major threat to the Middle East and the world because of its covert and illegal weapons program, and he called on the UN to marshal its forces against this rogue state. To many Europeans, however, this seemed a brazen bid to win UN approval of a unilateral attack on Iraq. The proposal didn't sell well in Germany, where nationwide parliamentary elections had begun. Facing a tough reelection battle in troubled economic times, Chancellor Schröder played the antiwar card and warned Bush "against

29. In France 64 percent approved of the U.S. invasion of Afghanistan, whereas in Germany 61 percent did so. In Great Britain 73 percent supported the invasion of Afghanistan. "Americans and Europeans Differ Widely on Foreign Policy Issues," Pew Research Center, 17 April 2002. EU foreign policy chief Javier Solana called the U.S.-led military invasion "a legitimate act to find those responsible" for the September 11 attacks. "It has the support of the European Union and it has the understanding of the European people," he said. Agence France Presse, 8 October 2001.

30. A majority of Europeans believed that U.S. foreign policy was in part responsible for the attacks of September 11. See Worldviews 2002, poll of 4 September 2002, http://www.worldview .org.

playing games with war and military intervention." Immediately, Schröder's poll numbers began to improve. In the run-up to the German election, it became acceptable to say almost anything derogatory about Bush. On the eve of the vote, justice minister Herta Daubler-Gmelin, one of Schröder's cabinet colleagues, drew a loose comparison between George Bush's use of his Iraq policy and Adolf Hitler's conjuring of foreign enemies to draw attention away from domestic crises. In response, Bush's national security adviser, Condoleezza Rice, said U.S.-German relations had been "poisoned." She added, "There have clearly been some things said that are way beyond the pale. The reported statements . . . are simply unacceptable." Most awkward of all for Washington was that Schröder won the election.[31]

The gloves now came off. Although Britain's prime minister, Tony Blair, supported George Bush in his bid to lead the international community toward a showdown with Iraq, the European public, especially the French and Germans, were overwhelmingly opposed. They voiced sharp criticism of Bush's saber rattling, and in reply, American pundits launched an unprecedented tirade of bilious anti-European commentary. Editorialists for U.S. newspapers expressed shock at the ingratitude of those Europeans who had forgotten all the sacrifices America had made on their behalf. The U.S. press seemed to enjoy targeting the French in particular, who, it was now declared, were habitual appeasers, cynical back-stabbers, anti-Semitic and pro-Arab, envious of U.S. power, and determined to sabotage the United States' effort to liberate the Middle East from tyranny. Merchants threatened to boycott French wines; the restaurant of the U.S. House of Representatives refused to serve french fries and offered freedom fries instead. Even the moderate and influential columnist for the *New York Times*, Thomas Friedman, called for France's permanent seat on the United Nations Security Council to be revoked.[32]

Bush was if anything emboldened by European criticism. It freed him from the painstaking work of coalition building, which his father, President George H. W. Bush, had skillfully undertaken before the 1991 Gulf War. Instead, Bush simply announced: "you are with us, or you are with the terrorists." By contrast, his secretary of state, Colin Powell—the one administration official

---

31. George H. W. Bush, UN speech, http://www.whitehouse.gov; Associated Press, 5 August, 13 September, and 21 September 2002. The election result was extremely close. Gerhard Schröder remained chancellor only with the help of his Green Party allies.

32. Thomas Friedman, "Vote France off the Island," *New York Times*, 9 February 2003. The most persistently anti-European journalists were Charles Krauthammer, George Will, and William Safire, all syndicated columnists. Robert Kagan, a conservative analyst and writer, coined the phrase that became the standard explanation for the U.S.-European divide: "Americans are from Mars, Europeans are from Venus," which was meant to suggest that Americans understood that military force was a legitimate tool of statecraft, whereas Europeans had come to believe that armed conflict was illegitimate. His book became a best seller: *Of Paradise and Power: America and Europe in the New World Order* (New York: Knopf, 2003).

Europeans hoped would restrain Bush—tried eagerly to win United Nations support for a tough resolution that would place weapons inspectors in Iraq and called for "serious consequences" if Iraq did not fully comply with this disarmament mission. Resolution 1441 of November 8, unanimously approved by the Security Council, declared Iraq in breach of previous UN resolutions and gave it a "final opportunity" to disarm. At the insistence of France and Russia, however, the resolution did not specify what would happen if Iraq did not do so.

Now began a high-stakes debate at the United Nations about what precisely Saddam Hussein would have to do to avoid war. He allowed the inspectors back into Iraq in November, but they did not turn up much. The U.S. position was that Saddam possessed chemical and biological weapons; the fact that the inspectors failed to find them meant that they were incompetent or that Saddam was hiding them, and probably both. Thus, inspections were a farce, and it was time to move to all-out war. For the majority of the fifteen-member Security Council, however, the absence of any major new discoveries in Iraq seemed to argue in favor of prolonging the inspections until weapons could be found and destroyed. Or perhaps Iraq had no banned weapons to begin with. The positions began to harden. The French foreign minister, Dominique de Villepin, became the voice and the face of the growing opposition to the United States within the United Nations. On January 20, he blurted out in a news conference that whatever the wording and intention of Resolution 1441, the French "will not associate ourselves with military intervention that is not supported by the international community. Military intervention would be the worst possible solution." Powell took this statement to be a betrayal of the diplomatic negotiations still under way in New York and never forgave the Frenchman.[33]

Although the Americans believed that Resolution 1441 gave them the legal right to resort to war, America's ally, Britain, wanted a second resolution specifically approving the use of military force to disarm Iraq. Indeed, polls showed that 77 percent of Britons opposed a war without such approval. Colin Powell and Tony Blair, eager to make the strongest case possible, dressed up partial and inconclusive intelligence information to depict Saddam's Iraq as an imminent threat. In a dramatic speech on February 5 at the UN, Powell said U.S. and British intelligence had evidence that Iraq possessed hundreds of tons of chemical weapons, including anthrax and VX nerve gas, had placed such facilities on trucks and rail cars to avoid detection, and most worrisome, had given sanctuary to al-Qaeda terrorist ring operating out of Baghdad. It was a grave bill of particulars, but it was not new information, nor did it necessarily militate for war. France, Russia, China, and Germany (which then occupied a rotating seat on the Security Council) all responded

33. *Financial Times*, 27 May 2003.

that if Powell was right, it was all the more imperative that inspections be continued—indeed, significantly expanded. There was not yet a reason for rushing to war. Powell was stymied.[34]

He was winning some converts in Europe, however. In one of the more fascinating subplots in this tale, a number of European states had moved in the United States' direction in the early weeks of 2003. This shift became strikingly apparent on January 30, when eight governments published a joint declaration in support of a tough, unified position on Iraq. The governments of Britain, Spain, Italy, Portugal, Denmark, Poland, Hungary, and Czech Republic drew attention to the values that America and Europe shared, called on all Europeans to stand by the United States, and urged Saddam Hussein to comply with disarmament resolutions. This position was a political bombshell in Europe, because it shattered the idea that Europe was unified in its opposition to war. (Public opinion in these eight countries, however, was running strongly against U.S. policy.) The U.S. secretary of defense, Donald Rumsfeld, now asserted that Europe had split between a dynamic, forward-looking "new" Europe that wished to cooperate with Washington and a sclerotic, cynical, and envious "old" Europe—France, Germany, Belgium, perhaps Russia—that resented U.S. leadership. That Vaclav Havel—the poster child of nonviolent revolution—was a signatory of the declaration, and had spoken eloquently of the need "to protect human life, human freedom, and human dignity" from tyranny, struck a crashing blow to the antiwar forces.[35]

Back at the UN, however, this show of support did not win the United States any new votes. On March 7, the United States, Britain, and Spain proposed a resolution to the Security Council that Iraq give up its weapons or face war. The fifteen members of the Security Council remained deadlocked, although a majority of them privately stated their opposition to the resolution. Yet a vote was never held. On March 10, the French and Russian foreign ministers made it clear that even if the United States could persuade a majority of the council, they would use their veto privilege to reject a resolution approving war. This prospect allowed the Americans to throw up their hands at the whole diplomatic process—which they were eager to do in any case—and blame France for obstructing the will of the United Nations. The resolution was withdrawn, and on March 17 President Bush gave Saddam Hussein forty-eight

34. "France, Backed by Germany, Calls for Stronger Inspections, but the U.S. Is Unmoved," *New York Times*, 6 February 2003.

35. *Financial Times*, 30 January, 2003; Vaclav Havel, as quoted in the *Washington Post*, 2 December 2002. An additional ten European states—Slovenia, Slovakia, Romania, Bulgaria, Lithuania, Latvia, Estonia, Albania, Croatia, and Macedonia—later issued a second declaration of support for U.S. policy. These ten states were all candidates for membership in NATO and had an incentive to support Washington. Virtually none of them gave any military or economic aid to the war effort. For an excellent review of the diplomatic wrangling on the eve of the Iraq War, see the four-part series in the *Financial Times*, 27–30 May 2003.

hours to leave his country or face war. Absent any reply from the Iraqi dictator, the United States on March 20 launched cruise missiles on Baghdad, while U.S. and British tanks thundered across the Iraqi border.

The war in Iraq that started in 2003 featured a swift defeat of the conventional Iraqi army forces. In a broader sense, however, the war is far from over. Although as of 2007 progress has been made in creating legitimate democratic Iraqi political institutions, over 100,000 U.S. troops remain in Iraq while a bitter, violent insurgency continues to mount attacks across the county. The country is unstable, lawless, and without basic infrastructure or services. The long-term nature of the U.S. military presence in Iraq led President Bush, re-elected in November 2004, to reach out to his European counterparts and to try to breathe new life into the alliance. The visit to France in February 2005 of his newly appointed secretary of state, Condoleezza Rice, led to a brief thaw in public relations. Rice optimistically declared that "history will surely judge us not by our old disagreements but by our new achievements."[36] The problem was that the crisis was not yet "history"—the war in Iraq looked to Europeans like a quagmire, vindicating their own arguments that war and occupation are a poor way of creating democracy and freedom. Worse, the United States' struggles in pacifying Iraq emboldened Iran, which brazenly pursued a nuclear weapons program in defiance of the United Nations. Claims by U.S. officials that Iran was funding and arming Shiite insurgents in Iran seemed to suggest the possibility of a widened war in the region.[37] Meanwhile, polls continued to show that Europeans on a wide scale viewed the United States, its foreign policy, and its leadership as deeply misguided, arrogant, self-centered, and naïve.[38] No European leader has any political incentive to share the Iraqi burden, and indeed, even the token European forces sent to Iraq by Spain, Poland, and Italy were removed or reduced. British prime minister Tony Blair, Bush's most stalwart ally, suffered a significant electoral setback in the parliamentary elections of May 2005; his Labour Party majority was cut by over a hundred seats, as the public punished him for supporting the Iraq War. In June 2006, people in Britain, France, Germany, and Spain were reported to have sharply lower favorability ratings of the United States than they had had in 2000, whereas in those same four countries plus Russia, a third to a half of the public saw the U.S. policy in Iraq as a "great danger" to world peace.[39] In this environment, it can be concluded that until U.S. policy in the Middle East alters course, there will be a deep and growing reservoir of suspicion on the part of Europeans toward U.S. motives.

36. As quoted at http://www.cbsnews.com/stories/2005/02/09/politics/main672569.shtml.

37. Just for one example, see "Military Official: Iranian Millions Funding Insurgency," 28 September 2006, http://www.cnn.com/2006/WORLD/meast/09/28/iraq.iran/index.html.

38. See the report prepared by the Pew Research Center for the People and the Press at http://www.people-press.org.

39. Pew Research Center, "America's Image Slips," 13 June 2006, http://www.pewglobal.org.

Yet we are faced with this glaring paradox: despite the severity of the crisis, the alliance has functioned remarkably well these past few years in Afghanistan, as well as in the Balkans and elsewhere. The International Security Assistance Force has been providing security in Afghanistan since December 2001, and a multinational force of 8,000 troops, including German and French soldiers, works closely and constructively with U.S. counterparts. In Kosovo, KFOR (Kosovo Force) coordinates the work of security forces from thirty-six countries, including NATO and non-NATO states, and has been doing so since 1999. The NATO parliamentary assembly continues to convene parliamentarians from twenty-six NATO members and thirteen associate members for discussions about security cooperation and counterterrorism. And the OSCE, with fifty-five member states, including the United States, runs security missions in southeast Europe, eastern Europe, the Caucasus, and central Asia. Although the public disputes quite rightly attract media attention, the patient work that the alliance does on a daily basis—providing security and pressing ahead on democratization—is rarely discussed. Yet these projects have continued uninterrupted during the Iraq crisis and show how the alliance can function institutionally, even as crises divide the leadership. It is too soon to state, as Charles Kupchan does in this volume, that "the close-knit security partnership of the past five decades is in all likelihood gone for good."

Even so, the process we have observed in previous crises—in which crisis is followed by adaptation—has not yet happened over the Iraq War. The Iraq War remains a U.S. war, in which only Britain plays any supporting role. In early 2007, Britain maintained only 7,000 troops in Iraq, mostly near Basra in the south, and its leaders were under heavy domestic pressure to remove even those soldiers. Yet in January 2007, President Bush announced his intention to send as many as 20,000 more U.S. troops to Iraq to try to quell unrest in the capital, Baghdad. NATO has not been involved in the war and has managed to reduce its involvement to the training of a few units of Iraqi police. Simultaneously, key Europeans sought to discuss areas of common interest with the United States while ignoring Iraq. In January 2007, when German chancellor Angela Merkel visited President Bush in Washington, they conferred over policy regarding the Israeli-Palestinian conflict, Afghanistan, Iran, and Lebanon, overlooking the elephant in the room, Iraq.[40] This stance does not yet represent meaningful adaptation and compromise as much as a wait-and-see approach. The war has not broken the alliance, but the alliance has reverted to a policy of denial and willful blindness: it is a hear-no-evil strategy rather than a conscious effort to grapple with the basic national differences that led the United States to pursue war while France, Germany, and the majority of the European public bitterly protested. Short of this kind of open, public adaptation, we cannot say the Iraq crisis is really over.

40. See http://www.spiegel.de/international/0,1518,458025,00.html.

Conclusions

Crises within the Atlantic alliance have been frequent because its members have often disagreed about national, regional, and global security interests. For France, a weak Germany was a national security interest in the early 1950s, while Washington wanted a strong Germany. In 1956, Britain and France saw Nasser as a threat to regional influence and oil supplies, while Washington saw the persistence of European colonial institutions as the real threat to regional stability. In the 1960s, France wanted less U.S. dominance of the alliance, while Washington believed NATO could not function without U.S. leadership. In Bosnia in the 1990s, Europeans and Americans disagreed on the origins, causes, and preferred solutions to that war. And in 2003, the alliance members diverged on how to respond to the threat of global terror.

In the past, the crises within the alliance have been resolved through a combination of steady leadership, creative adaptation, and new institutions. The basic bargain holding together the Atlantic alliance—that the United States would offer security and integration with Europe in exchange for European respect of the United States' predominant role in the alliance—has produced periodic protest but has never been defied. The alliance has managed to survive almost a half century of conflict within it, and indeed has now expanded to include twenty-six members—ten from the former Soviet bloc. A broad historical narrative such as the one offered here shows that over time, serious disagreements have been frequent but that the U.S.-European alliance system has shown remarkable resilience and flexibility.

The crisis over Iraq, however, remains unresolved. At its heart, the Iraq War, is a global debate about national security. Henry Nau, in his contribution to this edited volume, is right to point out that a major driving factor in the current crisis is the absence of clarity among alliance members over the nature of the common threat. Those states that favored intervention, chiefly the United States and Britain, argued that Iraq was but one front in a global war on terrorism; the regimes that might supply terrorists with sanctuary, weapons, and money must be destroyed. The opponents of the Iraq War argued, by contrast, that an invasion of Iraq would radicalize the Muslim world and destabilize the Middle East while pouring fuel on the fire of anti-Americanism in the Muslim world. It would not fundamentally protect the West from terrorism. Rather, a strategy that emphasized intelligence sharing, savvy police work, and engagement with the Israeli-Palestinian peace process would better serve the long-term interests of the West.

This argument still rages within the alliance, and it has become something bigger—a debate about the common threat of terrorism. At its heart, it reflects a wider cultural shift in the landscape, and here Charles Kupchan and Robert Kagan have got it right: major gaps have opened up between the United States and its allies about what the global order should look like and what role the Western alliance should play in it.[41] The stakes in Iraq are high: both sides in this dispute feel that their strategic arguments will be vindicated. Thus, there is little incentive for either side to concede to the other. The adaptation and creative rule making that have typified previous crises have not yet happened. Leaders on both sides have failed to find a viable middle ground. Of course, the alliance still functions, and quite well, in other global contexts. Yet divisions over Iraq keep the prospect of interallied crisis in constant view. Only a decisive change of the equation—a sudden U.S. victory over the Iraqi insurgents, or a full-scale U.S. pullout, or a change in the U.S. presidency, or the massive engagement of European states in support of the war effort, or a truly catastrophic terrorist attack in Europe by Islamic radicals—could bring about a resolution of the internal feud between major states within the alliance. In this sense, the debate over Iraq has to be seen as far more than a debate about threat perception: it is a debate about the basic responsibilities, obligations, and strategies of the Western states in an unstable world order. The crisis has become much bigger than the war in Iraq, and it is not over.

41. Charles A. Kupchan, *The End of the American Era: U.S. Foreign Policy and the Geopolitics of the Twenty-First Century* (New York: Vintage, 2003); Kagan, *Of Paradise and Power.*

4 IRAQ AND PREVIOUS TRANSATLANTIC CRISES

Divided by Threat, Not Institutions or Values

HENRY R. NAU

How serious is the transatlantic crisis provoked by the Iraq War and how is it likely to be resolved, if at all? I conclude that it is serious but not as serious as several previous transatlantic crises. The current crisis is defined primarily by differences among the allies over the strategic threat posed by terrorism, comparable perhaps to allied differences in the late 1940s over the Soviet threat. It is not characterized by a significant breakdown of transatlantic institutions and economic ties, as were the French withdrawal from NATO in 1966 and the oil crises of the 1970s; nor is it representative of a sharp spike in transatlantic political disenchantment greater than that of the Vietnam era or intermediate-range ballistic missile deployments in the early Reagan years. Political discord, especially over Iraq, may have more to do with political party differences—a conservative Republican Party being in control in the United States, which is more classically liberal and unilateralist than are major parties in Europe—than with a fundamental breach in shared democratic political systems. In fact, transatlantic institutions and values are much stronger today than they were when communism prevailed in half of Europe, and this constitutive bond may help narrow terrorist threat perceptions in the future and transform NATO into a global "out-of-area" alliance, along the lines of NATO's joint combat command in Afghanistan. Failing that, NATO is likely to muddle through or adapt with more flexible institutional fixes such as coalitions of the willing backed by modest NATO training and logistical support, as in Iraq. The least likely outcome is the breakup of NATO. Even if the terrorist threat fades, NATO is likely to continue to act to pacify and expand democracy in a Europe recently made whole and free.

In the first section of this chapter I discuss how the four dimensions of crisis emphasized in this volume—interests, institutions, interdependence, and values—are weighed differently, depending on one's theoretical perspective. Those holding realist perspectives see crises as caused and resolved primarily by shifts in power balances (interests) and threat perceptions; those holding liberal perspectives see them as caused and resolved primarily by disruptions and strengthening of institutions and interdependence; and those holding constructivist perspectives see them as caused and resolved largely by changes in shared or relative identities and values. I emphasize the role that common threat perceptions played in the past to create NATO and the role that shared values and economic ties may play in the future to sustain through the Iraq crisis. In the second section I compare the present crisis with five previous transatlantic crises—Suez, Berlin/Cuba, the French withdrawal from NATO's military command, Vietnam and the oil crises, and NATO missile deployment/Afghanistan. The Iraq crisis is not as severe as earlier ones because it is centered primarily outside Europe rather than, as in the case of the Soviet threat, inside Europe. On the other hand, the terrorist threat is less visible and harder to assess than conventional threats such as Soviet armies and missiles. The Iraq crisis, therefore, is marked by wide disparities among the allies concerning the nature and scope of the terrorist threat. In the third section of this chapter I examine these differing threat perceptions: *imperial* perceptions, held primarily by defense officials in the United States, which define the terrorist threat most expansively and seek to preempt it; *multipolar* perceptions, held primarily by France, which judge the threat of unipolar U.S. power to be more serious than terrorist threats and seek to counterbalance the United States; *multilateral* perceptions, held primarily by European Union officials, which see terrorism largely as a criminal activity to be managed by the rule of law within global (United Nations) rather than alliance (NATO) institutions; *liberal internationalist* perceptions, held mostly by liberal Democrats in the United States and social democrats in Europe, which define the threat primarily in terms of what the consensus will bear within centralized NATO institutions; and *conservative internationalist* perceptions, held chiefly by conservative Republicans in the United States and some Liberals and Christian Democrats in Europe, which see the threat as larger for some countries than others and prefer to deal with it more pragmatically through decentralized initiatives in NATO such as coalitions of the willing.

I conclude that if imperial, multipolar, or multilateral threat perceptions prevail, NATO will eventually break up because each of these threat perceptions moves the center of decision making primarily outside NATO. If liberal internationalist perceptions prevail, NATO will be transformed into a centralized democratic security community to combat terrorism worldwide. And if conservative internationalist perceptions prevail, NATO will muddle through as a more decentralized democratic security community employing periodic ad hoc initiatives to fight terrorism.

Crisis and Community

How do we define crisis and community? If NATO is in crisis, how did it initially become a community? And what can we learn from the process of NATO's formation that may help us assess its potential for breakup, adaptation, or transformation in the current Iraq crisis?

Crisis from Different Theoretical Perspectives

This volume defines a transatlantic crisis in terms of the existence of one or more of four circumstances: (1) disagreement over core security interests; (2) disruption of rules and institutions; (3) sharp breaks in market and social interdependence; and (4) loss of sense of community or shared values.[1] Different theoretical perspectives weigh these circumstances differently. Realists, for example, see crisis largely in terms of diverging core security interests or threat perceptions. Alliances form when perceptions converge around a specific threat and dissolve when those perceptions diverge or the specific threat disappears. Whether member states share common institutions or values is irrelevant.[2] From this realist perspective, a transatlantic crisis already existed after November 11, 1989 (11/9), when the Berlin wall came down and the Soviet threat no longer united the Western allies. Liberal theorists see crisis primarily in terms of the disruption of institutions and interdependence that safeguard common interests and defend against general threats. Collective security institutions and economic interdependence bring member states together, before specific threats emerge, to develop common perceptions of threat and deter them through community action. Thus, for liberal perspectives, the transatlantic crisis dates from September 11, 2001 (9/11), when the United States rejected NATO assistance in Afghanistan and went on to invade Iraq despite the opposition of major allies. Finally, constructivists who focus on shared values or substantive norms date the transatlantic crisis from the time of the Vietnam War and subsequent Reagan era, when the United States appeared to embrace a set of militarist and socially conservative values that alienated much of Europe. They note that many European leaders who opposed U.S. leadership in Iraq (such as Gerhard Schröder and Joschka Fischer in Germany) also protested the U.S. war in Vietnam in the 1960s and 1970s. Other constructivists who focus on procedural norms date the crisis from the

---

1. See John Ikenberry's introduction and Thomas Risse's conclusion to this volume. As Risse emphasizes, these are indicators, not causes, of crisis. Causes involve theoretical perspectives. See Henry R. Nau, *Perspectives on International Relations: Power, Institutions, and Ideas* (Washington, DC: CQ Press, 2006).

2. Threats are a function of both structural realist factors, such as the distribution of power and geopolitical stakes (Kenneth Waltz), and classical realist factors, such as converging or diverging perceptions of threat among alliance members (Steven Walt). I use both measures in this chapter. See table 4.1.

Bush administration's penchant for unilateralism, which on some issues such as the ABM treaty predated 9/11.[3]

The various measures that realists, liberals, and constructivists emphasize to define crises may interact. A crisis over threat, such as 9/11, may precipitate a crisis over institutions, such as U.S. unilateralism. And an institutional crisis in turn may undermine common values, such as respect for the rule of law. The danger in the Iraq crisis is that a crisis over threat perception (if my diagnosis is correct) may undermine common institutions, impede new trade initiatives, and exacerbate value conflicts. On the other hand, as both John Ikenberry and Thomas Risse point out in this volume, common institutions and values may work in the other direction. They may constrain and even narrow threat perceptions, leading to adaptation or transformation of transatlantic relations. Historical path dependence is important in this respect.[4] When transatlantic countries faced their first crisis over threat perception in the late 1940s, they had fewer and weaker institutional, economic, and normative ties to cushion their disagreements. NATO did not exist as a military organization, economic relationships were in their infancy (e.g., the Organization for European Economic Cooperation [OEEC]), and many transatlantic countries were not yet enduring democracies. Today common institutions and democratic values are much stronger and pervade the transatlantic community. These deeper structures, despite continuing value gaps (stressed, for example, by Risse in his chapter), could narrow current threat perceptions and even transform the alliance. Viewed in this light, the crisis over threat in the late 1940s posed a significantly greater challenge to transatlantic relations than the one today.

In all three theoretical perspectives, crisis can lead to breakdown, defined here as the return of the possibility of using violent means to settle disputes within the transatlantic community. When an alliance dissolves, former allies consider once again the need to balance power against one another.[5] When international (or for that matter domestic) institutions and commerce break up, the commitment to resolve disputes peacefully weakens. And when values diverge or clash significantly, trust diminishes and the security dilemma reemerges.[6]

The ultimate crisis in transatlantic relations, therefore, would be one that precipitated a return to balance-of-power politics among Atlantic countries.

---

3. The three major theoretical perspectives—realist, liberal, and constructivist or identity— illuminate many contemporary and historical problems in world affairs and account for policy as well as scholarly disagreements. See Nau, *Perspectives on International Relations*.

4. For an enlightening discussion of different causal paths, see Gunther Hellmann's contribution to this volume.

5. Bruce Bueno de Mesquita, *The War Trap* (New Haven: Yale University Press, 1981).

6. Robert Jervis, "Cooperation under the Security Dilemma," *World Politics* 30 (January 1978): 167–214.

This definition of crisis is an extreme one, however. It may be no more useful than defining crisis in such a way that almost any transatlantic dispute over the past sixty years qualifies. Crises become either so rare or so ubiquitous that they cannot be isolated and studied. We need a way to place crises along a spectrum from more severe to less severe. The comparison of previous crises taken up later in the chapter addresses this issue of relative severity.

Formation of the Transatlantic Security Community

How did the current transatlantic community come into being? What role did threat (interests), institutions, interdependence, and values (ideas/identities) play? What can we learn from the formation of this community about how it might progress or unravel today?

The transatlantic community of democratic states did not exist in 1941. The Atlantic Charter drawn up in August of that year committed the United States and Great Britain to respect the right of all people to self-determination, and the two countries shared common democratic values at home.[7] But they did not share common foreign policy aims or threat perceptions. The United States stood by while Britain almost fell to Nazi conquest in winter 1940–41. And it is at least questionable when, if ever, the United States would have entered the European war had not Japan attacked Pearl Harbor and Hitler, four days later, gratuitously declared war against the United States. In U.S.-British relations at the time, common values alone were not sufficient to create a security community.

Transatlantic security ties did not emerge until the Nazi threat imperiled the entire world. Even then these ties took the form of a traditional alliance that included the Soviet Union, a totalitarian state, and aimed only to defeat the specific threat of Nazi Germany. To be sure, plans to go beyond a wartime alliance and create a postwar collective security arrangement that would defend against unspecified threats were begun already in 1942. The United Nations that resulted from these plans made the wartime allies permanent members of the Security Council to safeguard international peace and security, but veto powers given to permanent members ensured that the UN would not be able to intervene in conflicts among the great powers themselves.

Such a great power conflict sidelined the United Nations after 1945–46, and another traditional alliance, this time at the regional transatlantic level, emerged to contain the Soviet Union. NATO likely would not have come into existence without the emergence of a specific Soviet threat in central Europe.[8] Common values and institutions were too weak at the time, as NATO

7. John Lewis Gaddis, *The United States and the Origins of the Cold War, 1941–1947* (New York: Columbia University Press, 1972), 12.

8. In his chapter in this volume, William I. Hitchcock details NATO's difficulties in formulating common perceptions of threat even in the face of a visible Soviet army in eastern Europe.

initially included several nondemocratic states. Nevertheless, common political values framed some aspects of early threat perceptions. From the outset, core democratic values in Great Britain and the United States defined the Soviet threat as much in ideological as geopolitical terms. Although the Soviet Union held a decisive conventional military advantage in central Europe, U.S. nuclear superiority offset this advantage. The real danger in 1946–47, therefore, was not an imminent attack by Soviet forces in central Europe. It was instead the political threat that communist parties in western Europe, supported by Moscow, might impede the restoration of democracy in allied countries such as France and the creation of new democracies in defeated fascist countries such as Italy and Germany. The Marshall Plan announced in 1947 addressed political concerns of governmental weakness and economic chaos in western Europe, not immediate military needs to defend against a Soviet attack.

The Marshall Plan invited central and eastern European states to participate. Like the UN, it sought to go beyond the wartime alliance against a specific enemy to deal with unspecified (not excluding or targeting specific countries) enemies of economic and political disorder. Why didn't this offer revive the prospects of common institutions and the United Nations? The answer is straightforward. Each side saw a different "unspecified enemy." For the Soviet Union, it was capitalism in eastern Europe. For the United States, it was communism in western Europe. Diverging domestic political identities created a gulf between the superpowers and made it difficult to accommodate common institutions.[9] The Marshall Plan threatened to extend capitalism and democratic governments deep into the heart of Soviet-controlled territory, a political threat to the Soviet Union as real as the threat to the United States and Great Britain of communist governments in western Europe.[10] When the Western powers took the first steps to implement the Marshall Plan by consolidating the three Western zones of occupied Germany and introducing a common currency, the Soviet Union reacted with military force. The Berlin blockade and airlift precipitated the formation of NATO, and the Korean War led to its militarization.

9. Constructivist studies talk about shared and relative identities. On shared identity, see Alexander Wendt, *Social Theory of International Politics* (Cambridge: Cambridge University Press, 1999). On relative identities and the distribution or ideological distance among domestic political identities, see Henry R. Nau, *At Home Abroad: Identity and Power in American Foreign Policy* (Ithaca: Cornell University Press, 2002); and Mark L. Haas, *Ideological Origins of Great Power Politics, 1789–1989* (Ithaca: Cornell University Press, 2005).

10. Thomas Risse-Kappen, "Collective Identity in a Democratic Community: The Case of NATO," in *The Culture of National Security: Norms and Security in World Politics*, ed. Peter Katzenstein, 357–400 (New York: Columbia University Press, 1996). See also Henry R. Nau, "Rethinking Economics, Politics and Security in Europe," in *Reshaping Western Europe*, ed. Richard N. Perle, 11–39 (Washington, DC: AEI, 1991).

In the context of the 1940s, threat and geopolitics did the heavy lifting to shape transatlantic community ties. Relatively speaking, institutions and interdependence in this period were weak or nonexistent, and common values influenced threat perceptions significantly only after geopolitical interests shifted. In winter 1940–41, the United States tolerated the spread of fascism on the Continent. It was uncommitted and prepared to stand by even if Great Britain had succumbed to Nazi conquest. Geopolitical isolation still seemed to provide the United States with a sufficient margin of safety. After Germany declared war on the United States, however, the United States committed its military power to the Continent. By 1945, U.S. geopolitical stakes in Europe had risen substantially, and the United States now identified more readily with the politics and institutions of western Europe.

Duration of the Transatlantic Community

NATO went on to confront and resolve the conflict with the Soviet Union. But unlike traditional alliances, it did not break up once the Soviet Union disappeared. Nor did NATO evolve into a broader, universal collective security community. Although there was some flirtation with the idea of reviving Great Power cooperation under the UN Security Council (e.g., the Clinton administration's policy of assertive multilateralism in 1993), those plans died with U.S. soldiers in the streets of Mogadishu, Somalia. NATO, not the UN, went on to lead joint military actions in Bosnia and Kosovo. Conceived in 1949 only because of the Soviet military threat, NATO lived on after 1991 without a Soviet threat or any other significant military challenge. NATO had become a security community. Common values drove institutional development more than threat perceptions. NATO expanded to consolidate democracy and markets in the East, not to defend them in the West.

From the early 1950s on, the embryonic democratic sentiments linking Great Britain and the United States grew to include a restored democracy in France, new and strong democracies in Italy and Germany, and eventually democratic governments in former fascist countries such as Spain, Portugal, and Greece. Then in 1999 and again in 2003, NATO enlarged to include new democracies in eastern Europe and parts of the old Soviet Union. Today the major countries of NATO and indeed most of the rest (Turkey and some of the newest members being exceptions) are strong, mature democracies, tied together less by imminent threat (indeed that is what they currently disagree about) than by common political values and unprecedented economic, social, and cultural interdependence.[11]

How did interests, institutions, interdependence, and ideas affect this evolution? We gain some leverage on this question by examining previous crises

---

11. See Freedom House indicators for the depth of democratic strength among NATO countries; http://www.freedomhouse.org/template.cfm?page=15&year=2006.

in the transatlantic community and asking counterfactual questions about how those crises might have come out if the stakes, threats, institutional and economic relationships, and value configurations had been different. We can then apply these insights to evaluate the new crisis that confronted NATO in Iraq.

Comparing Previous and Present Transatlantic Crises

I look briefly at what I judge to be the five most severe security crises that confronted the transatlantic community from 1950 to 1990: the Suez crisis in the 1950s, the combined Berlin crisis and Cuban missile crisis from 1958 through 1962, the withdrawal of France from the NATO military alliance in 1966, the Vietnam War and oil crises in the 1970s, and NATO deployment of intermediate-range ballistic missiles (INF) in the early 1980s.[12]

Grading Crises

I grade these crises using the following rules of thumb. A threat crisis is more severe the higher the geopolitical stakes involved (a structural measure) and the greater the divergence of threat perceptions among the allies (a classical foreign policy measure). Thus, if a dispute focuses on a threat in central Europe and perhaps outside Europe as well and allied threat perceptions diverge (e.g., INF deployment and Soviet invasion of Afghanistan), that crisis scores as more severe than a crisis in an out-of-area conflict only in which threat perceptions also diverge (e.g., Suez). An institutional crisis is more severe if it involves disruption of both formal institutions and economic interdependence (e.g., a breakdown of consultative mechanisms and imposition of economic sanctions, as in the Suez crisis), less severe if it involves disruption

---

12. I combine the Berlin (1958–61) and Cuban missile crises (1962) for reasons of space but also because they represent a continuous series of tensions during 1958–62, followed by a visible easing of tensions after 1962. In addition, some analysts conclude that the Cuban missile crisis was really another attempt by Khrushchev to resolve the Berlin problem. See Graham Alison and Philip Zelikow, *Essence of Decision: Explaining the Cuban Missile Crisis*, 2nd ed. (New York: Longman, 1999), chap. 2. Hitchcock, in his chapter in the present volume, excludes two of my cases (Berlin/Cuba and INF) and considers two others: the formative years of the alliance during 1950–55, which I cover in my discussion of the formation of the alliance; and the Bosnian crisis, an out-of-area crisis that occurred after the cold war at a time of significantly reduced stakes in transatlantic relations. Hitchcock's cases focus only on intra-alliance crises. My cases include crises that involved extra-alliance challenges that may have actually strengthened intra-alliance ties. For helpful overall accounts of these crises, see, among others, Marc Trachtenberg, *A Constructed Peace* (Princeton: Princeton University Press, 1999); Thomas Risse-Kappen, *Cooperation among Democracies: The European Influence on U.S. Foreign Policy* (Princeton: Princeton University Press, 1995); Dieter Mahncke, *Berlin im geteilten Deutschland* (Munich: R. Oldenbourg, 1973); Allison and Zelikow, *Essence of Decision*; and the Hitchcock chapter in this volume.

of only one set of relationships (e.g., economic ties, as in the oil crises), and least severe if both formal institutions and economic interdependence remain largely unaffected or are maybe even strengthened (e.g., the Berlin and Cuban crises). A value crisis is most severe if it involves a breach of fundamental political values (that is, a perception that another country cannot be trusted and must be balanced against militarily), moderately severe if it involves diverging foreign policies (e.g., the Iraq War) or different parties in power across the Atlantic countries (e.g., social democratic governments in power in most of Europe, while conservative Republicans hold power in the United States), and least severe if it involves differences over civil society issues, such as the death penalty, religion, or abortion, which citizens often disagree about as strongly within countries as between them.

A key threshold point is when foreign policy or civil society disputes escalate to threaten fundamental political community, in this case democratic solidarity among the NATO allies. Common democratic values restrain foreign policy, political party, and civil society disputes among liberal countries and help resolve these disputes peacefully without resort to balancing military power and the use or threat of use of force.[13] Social and cultural disputes are commonplace, but they do not lead to violence and breakup of the political community. Such a breakup would require that specific disputes take on broader significance. For example, legal disputes over detainees might grow into a broad consensus in Europe that the United States is no longer a fellow democratic "in-law" but an "outlaw" country that Europe can no longer trust to abide by shared democratic constraints. This distrust may start with disputes over detainees or the use of force toward third countries, such as Iraq, but it becomes lethal to a security community if it eventually escalates to disputes involving the use of force or threat of force (e.g., economic sanctions) among the member countries themselves. Once countries cease to see each other as law-abiding democracies, the use of force becomes less predictable in their relationships, and violence or at least the fear (threat) of violence may once again become an accepted tool of statecraft.[14]

Previous Crises

Table 4.1 compares the five crises (and the present crisis) in terms of the stakes involved (first column), the degree of divergence among threat perceptions (second column), the disruption of institutional and economic relationships

13. Bruce M. Russett, *Grasping the Democratic Peace* (Princeton: Princeton University Press, 1993). Dieter Fuchs and Hans-Dieter Klingemann, in their contribution to this volume, confirm the constraining role of political values in transatlantic relations when they find that the allies converge strongly on "support for democratic rule," even while they differ on religion, personal versus social responsibility, and other sociocultural values.

14. Identifying trip wires or thresholds where cumulative distrust eventually gives way to violence is exceedingly difficult. See Hellmann's chapter in this volume.

Table 4.1. Comparison of transatlantic crises

Crisis	Level of geopolitical interests at stake				Differences in threat perceptions				Disruption of institutional and economic relationships		Differences in common values		
	Highest (central and out-of-area threats)	High (central threat only)	Intermediate (out-of-area threat only)	Low (reduced overall threat)	Narrow	Inter-mediate	Wide	Widest	Formal institutions	Economic interdependence	Political distrust of respective domestic systems	Foreign policy/party differences	Civil society issues
Suez			X				X		Disrupted	Disrupted—sanctions			
Berlin/Cuba	X				X				Unaffected	Unaffected			
French withdrawal from NATO's military command				X				X	Disrupted	Disrupted by de Gaulle's economic challenge but partially offset by more U.S. direct investment in Europe		X (mostly foreign policy differences)	X
Vietnam and oil crises			X				X		Disrupted but held together by Harmel report and G-7 summit process	Disrupted by oil crises and stagflation; deepened by financial liberalization and integration	X (among younger generations)	X (significant party differences)	X

Table 4.1—cont.

Table 4.1. Comparison of transatlantic crises

Crisis	Level of geopolitical interests at stake				Differences in threat perceptions				Disruption of institutional and economic relationships		Differences in common values		
	Highest (central and out-of-area threats)	High (central threat only)	Intermediate (out-of-area threat only)	Low (reduced overall threat)	Narrow	Intermediate	Wide	Widest	Formal institutions	Economic interdependence	Political distrust of respective domestic systems	Foreign policy/party differences	Civil society issues
NATO missile deployments/ Afghanistan	X					X			Managed crisis successfully	Disrupted by high interest rates/ Soviet gas pipeline sanctions	X (among younger generations)		X
Iraq and war on terror			X				X		Disrupted at political levels only	Unaffected; increased investment and trade	X (accelerated anti-Americanism)	X (significant party differences)	X

(third column), and the differences in common values (fourth column). The Berlin and Cuban crises clearly involved the highest stakes. Both concerned the central nuclear balance and threats inside Europe, and the Cuban crisis involved a threat outside Europe as well. Differences in threat perceptions among the allies during these crises were relatively narrow. De Gaulle's response to Dean Acheson during the Cuban missile crisis showed that France accepted U.S. threat assessments. Acheson visited de Gaulle four hours before President Kennedy announced the crisis to the American people. He told de Gaulle: "I have come to inform you of a decision which has been taken" and offered to show de Gaulle Kennedy's speech and intelligence photos justifying the decision to quarantine Cuba. De Gaulle, a stickler for being consulted rather than informed, nevertheless replied: "Not now. These will only be evidence—a great nation like yours would not act if there were any doubts about the evidence. I accept what you tell me as fact, without any proof of any sort needed."[15] Gone, for the moment at least, were prickly Gaullist pride and unhappiness over U.S. hegemony and preferential ties to Great Britain (residues of the Suez crisis), even though during the Cuban missile crisis Britain played a much more intimate role in Washington decision making (through the British ambassador in Washington) than did France.[16]

NATO missile deployments also involved the highest stakes. Soviet deployment of intermediate-range missiles in Europe was compounded by the Soviet invasion of Afghanistan. However, differences in threat perception among the allies were now more severe than as in the Berlin and Cuba crises. Public perceptions of the missile issue diverged significantly. There were massive street protests in Europe. Nevertheless, European and U.S. leaders saw the Soviet threat in similar terms. Chancellor Helmut Schmidt of Germany initially called for NATO deployments in the late 1970s, and when massive public protests against NATO deployments confronted the new German government under Helmut Kohl in 1983, France under François Mitterrand played a crucial role in persuading Bonn to stay the course. The Suez and Vietnam crises involved disputes outside Europe and hence only intermediate stakes. Here, however, the divergence of threat perceptions was wide. As William Hitchcock explains in his contribution to this volume, the United States feared Soviet threats and opposed the deployment of British and French forces in the Suez Canal because it might alienate Arab nations and widen Soviet influence in the region. Britain and France, on the other hand, feared local threats and focused on settling grievances with Egypt's leader Gamal Nasser. Finally, the crisis caused by France's withdrawal from NATO's military command

---

15. Douglas Brinkley, *Dean Acheson: The Cold War Years, 1953–1971* (New Haven: Yale University Press, 1992), 167.

16. Allison and Zelikow, *Essence of Decision*, 233.

featured perhaps the widest divergence in threat perceptions. As Hitchcock notes, de Gaulle felt at the time that "the United States was the greatest danger in the world today to peace," not the Soviet Union.[17] But this crisis occurred at a time of U.S.-Soviet détente and reduced or low overall geopolitical stakes. Differences in threat perceptions mattered less.

In terms of disruption of institutional and economic ties (third column), the Suez crisis and France's withdrawal from NATO's military command posed the worst transatlantic crises. The Suez crisis entailed disruption of both formal institutions and economic ties. The United States accused its allies of failing to consult through NATO (the same charge that Europe throws at the United States today).[18] In response, the United States exerted economic pressure on Great Britain (withholding International Monetary Fund support for the pound until British forces were withdrawn from the canal) and excluded France from subsequent nuclear arrangements with Great Britain. In 1956, therefore, both transatlantic institutional cooperation and trade relations were under siege.

The Suez crisis did not shatter the young alliance because the Soviet Union escalated the threat both during (Hungary) and shortly after Suez. The Berlin and Cuban missile crises of 1958–62 refocused alliance threat perceptions on the Soviet Union.[19]

Once the Soviet threat receded, however, the alliance experienced its most severe institutional crisis. French withdrawal from NATO's military command weakened alliance institutions at their core. It shattered the credibility of coordinated deterrence strategies against the Soviet Union. The withdrawal crisis also coincided with a broad attack by de Gaulle against the dollar and U.S. economic hegemony. So this crisis involved significant disruptions in both diplomatic and economic ties. As noted earlier, however, it occurred at a time of détente and reduced geopolitical stakes in Europe. The Harmel report papered over the differences in threat perceptions, and the United States' direct investments in Europe accelerated and deepened transatlantic economic ties.[20]

In the early 1970s, out-of-area crises challenged transatlantic ties. American withdrawal from Vietnam shook Europe's confidence in the United States, and Secretary of State Henry Kissinger set aside 1973 as "the Year of Europe" to repair transatlantic relations. The oil crisis of 1973–74 exacerbated economic conditions. Threats now came from OPEC and stagflation rather than from the Soviet Union. The major transatlantic countries and Japan responded by deepening institutional and economic ties. The Group of

17. See Hitchcock's chapter in this volume.

18. Risse-Kappen, *Cooperation among Democracies*, chap. 4.

19. Trachtenberg, *Constructed Peace*, chaps. 7–9.

20. On alliance military and economic conflicts in the 1960s, see Alfred Grosser, *The Western Alliance: European-American Relations since 1945* (New York: Continuum, 1980); and David Calleo, *The Imperious Economy* (Cambridge: Harvard University Press, 1982).

Seven inaugurated the economic summit process to coordinate economic policies, complete the Tokyo Round of multilateral trade negotiations, and launch a radical program of global financial liberalization. Private banking, investment, and financial markets were opened up to accommodate the recycling of petrodollars. Currency and capital controls were reduced, and massive financial flows swiftly dwarfed trade flows ushering in the new era of intense globalization. Interdependence (and vulnerability) reached levels that sharply surpassed for the first time levels existing before World War I.[21]

The institutional and economic (interdependence) setting was thus different and probably stronger by the time the next security crisis struck the alliance. Soviet deployment of intermediate-range nuclear missiles in Europe and its invasion of Afghanistan raised once again the geopolitical stakes of transatlantic relations. This time, however, in contrast to citizen reactions to the Cuba and Berlin crises, mass public movements opposed military deployments. An economic recession, the worst since 1933 (including the more recent recessions of 1990–91 and 2001), also soured Atlantic relations. High U.S. interest rates squeezed European economies, France almost bolted European institutions by pulling the franc out of the European snake, and U.S. gas pipeline sanctions against the Soviet Union disrupted summit cooperation at Versailles in 1982.[22] Nevertheless, alliance solidarity held, both because the Soviet Union proved a "helpful" enemy by escalating the threat once again (as it did in the late 1940s and again in the late 1950s) and because economic interdependence was now substantially greater. In addition, the United States began to rebound impressively from the economic and military malaise of the Vietnam era.

In terms of differences over values, the Vietnam and missile deployment crises may have been the most severe. They initiated a process of political alienation between younger generations in Europe and the United States that may be a factor in the Iraq crisis.[23] Political alienation, as discussed earlier, is more serious than policy, party, and socioeconomic differences.

When do sociocultural differences lead to political alienation? In earlier NATO crises, transatlantic democratic political sentiments were weak. Weak democracies, or communities that include nondemocracies as well as

---

21. One measure of financial integration is total international reserves held by individual countries. From 1950 to 1970, international reserves of Organization for Economic Cooperation and Development (OECD) countries doubled. From 1970 to 1973 they tripled, and from 1973 to 1986 they quadrupled. See Angus Madison, *The World Economy in the 20th Century* (Paris: Development Centre, OECD, 1989), 146.

22. For a record of the Versailles Summit and its aftermath, see Henry R. Nau, *The Myth of America's Decline: Leading the World Economy into the 1990s* (New York: Oxford University Press, 1990), chap. 7. See also Robert D. Putnam and Nicholas Bayne, *Hanging Together: The Seven Power Summits* (Cambridge: Harvard University Press, 1984), chap. 10.

23. Ronald Inglehart, *Culture Shift in Advanced Industrial Society* (Princeton: Princeton University Press, 1990).

democracies, are vulnerable to significance differences in sociocultural values.[24] If such differences dominate, communities fracture and return to balance-of-power politics. Why didn't NATO break up during these early crises? To sort out the relative influence of threat, institutions, interdependence, and values in shaping NATO, it helps to ask some counterfactual questions. Is it likely that the alliance would have survived the Suez crisis if the Soviet Union had not subsequently escalated the threat in the Berlin and Cuban missile crises? Probably not. Without a greater Soviet threat, de Gaulle's withdrawal challenge might have come sooner and proved more disruptive. Or to put it another way, is it likely that NATO would have survived détente in 1952, when Stalin proposed the unification and neutralization of Germany? Remember that NATO's military structures did not even exist in 1952. Again, NATO's survival is doubtful, especially since, as Hitchcock notes, France in this period was extremely reluctant to rearm West Germany. Similarly, would NATO have continued, let alone expanded, in the mid-1950s had the Soviet Union broken up after Stalin's death, as the alliance expanded in the 1990s when the Soviet Union actually did break up? The answer again is probably not. Germany might have sought reunification outside NATO.

In these early crises, therefore, threat had more to do with sustaining the alliance than did common institutions, interdependence, and values. To be sure, as Risse points out in this volume, common institutions and values always frame or give meaning to material threats. But institutions and values were weaker then compared to today, and sometimes material dangers can be great enough to narrow threat perceptions even without common institutions and values. Nazi Germany drove the United States and Soviet Union together in World War II, and the Soviet Union, especially by its approval of aggression in Korea, probably did more to create the NATO alliance than did common allied institutions or values.

In later crises, however, strengthened institutions, economic interdependence, and values helped the alliance survive the ebb and flow of material threats. The alliance held together in the early 1970s despite détente and a significantly lower threat because, in the meantime, military institutions had been tested and adapted to meet de Gaulle's challenge, and economic and especially financial ties had become more and more significant. When the Soviet threat escalated once again in the late 1970s, alliance institutions, interdependence, and values were much stronger. The alliance went on to deploy intermediate-range nuclear missiles and eventually to bring the Soviet Union to the bargaining table that ended the cold war. Even more impressively, the alliance flourished after the disappearance of the Soviet threat.

---

24. Edward D. Mansfield and Jack Snyder, "Democratization and the Danger of War," *International Security* 20, no. 1 (Summer 1995): 5–38.

Present Transatlantic Crisis

On the basis of the character and outcome of previous crises, how would we score the Iraq crisis in transatlantic relations? Some analysts define the Iraq crisis primarily as a breakdown of institutions. U.S. unilateralism threatens or has already shattered the multilateral legacy of cold war institutions.[25] Evidence supports this view at the level of formal institutions. In the Iraq crisis, both France and the United States bolted NATO institutions. France turned to the UN Security Council to shape a counterbalancing alliance against the United States. The United States turned to Great Britain, Spain, Italy, Japan, Poland, and other nations to form a coalition of the willing operating outside both the UN and NATO. Institutionally, therefore, formal transatlantic institutions stood in greater disarray in 2003 than ever before.

This conclusion, however, ignores evidence at other levels of institutionalization. Although Iraq shattered NATO cooperation at the political level, unprecedented cooperation took place at lower operational levels. German and U.S. officials confirm that the military alliance functioned flawlessly to facilitate the transfer of U.S. forces from Germany to the Iraqi theater.[26] In addition, and perhaps even more impressively, economic cooperation between Europe and the United States flourished. As Kathleen McNamara shows in her contribution to this volume, trade and investment rose to historic levels even at the height of the Iraq conflict.[27] And U.S.-EU cooperation not only maintained G-7 coordination of economic policies despite a synchronized recession in 2001 but also launched the Doha Round of multilateral trade negotiations. It is true, as McNamara and also Jens van Scherpenberg in his contribution to this volume argue, that economic interdependence is no guarantee against political conflict. Nevertheless, it is impressive that while media pundits and governmental officials exchanged insults across the Atlantic, business and banking activities not only went on as usual but sharply accelerated. Markets pay a lot of attention to politics (think about how closely Wall Street follows Congress and world events), and transatlantic markets in 2003 seemed to be saying that there was no anticipation of a broad-scale crisis in transatlantic relations, despite the dustup over Iraq.

---

25. G. John Ikenberry, *After Victory: Institutions, Strategic Restraint, and the Rebuilding of Order after Major Wars* (Princeton: Princeton University Press, 2001).

26. German defense officials, interview by author, Germany, June 2003.

27. In 2003 U.S. foreign direct investment in Europe increased by 30 percent, and European investment in the United States went up 38 percent. See Dan Hamilton and Joseph Quinlan, *Partners in Prosperity: The Changing Economy of the Transatlantic Economy* (Washington, DC: Center for Transnational Relations, Johns Hopkins SAIS, 2004); and Dan Hamilton and Joseph Quinlan, *Protecting Our Prosperity: Ensuring Both National Security and the Benefits of Foreign Investments in the United States* (Washington, DC: National Foundation for American Policy, 2006).

On the dimensions of stakes involved and differences in threat perception, the Iraq crisis ranks at an intermediate-wide level. For Europe, the severity of the crisis falls toward the lower end of the spectrum. Europe, like the United States, sees terrorism as a threat (e.g., the train bombing in Madrid in 2004 and transit system bombings in London in 2005).[28] But Europe feels no need of outside assistance to cope with this threat inside Europe, unlike its view of the Soviet threat, for which it wanted help. And Europe still perceives no need for a high level of NATO military activity to deal with the threat of terrorism outside Europe but instead emphasizes soft or civilian power to fight it. The United States, on the other hand, sees the crisis as more severe, both inside and outside the United States. The threat of terrorism is not considered as severe as the cold war face-off against the Soviet Union, but unlike the cold war threat, which endangered European territory primarily, the terrorist threat targets U.S. territory. And it involves a threat of still unknown dimensions that could metastasize quickly, especially if terrorists or their supporters acquired weapons of mass destruction. Thus the United States prefers to fight the battle now in the Middle East (the Iraq front) rather than later in the United States. Europe likewise hopes to keep the battle as far away from the Continent as possible. For Europe, however, that means southwestern Asia, not the Middle East.

How serious is the Iraq crisis in terms of value differences? Value differences over issues such as gay rights, abortion, religion, and the death penalty exist within individual countries as well as between the United States and Europe.[29] Economic philosophies also differ within and between countries. In classical nineteenth-century terms, the United States is more liberal than Britain, but Britain is more liberal than France and Germany, and the new EU members appear to be more liberal than the old EU members. Social attitudes are more communal and welfare-oriented throughout Europe, whereas Americans emphasize personal responsibility and meritocratic advancement. Sociologists have long noted that feudalism and statism in Europe fostered more communitarianism, whereas the absence of these traditions in the United States fostered more individualistic freedom and federalism. Religion is taken more seriously in the United States than in almost all European countries, with the possible exception of Poland.[30] Yet average differences on most of these issues between the two parts of the Atlantic do not appear greater than before. Tocqueville referred to substantial religious differences more than 150 years ago, and the United States is undoubtedly more secular today than it was in the 1840s.

28. On perceptions of the terrorist threat in Europe, see Dieter Mahncke and Joerg Monar, eds., *International Terrorism: A European Response to a Global Threat?* College of Europe Studies No. 3 (Brussels: P.I.E. Peter Lang, 2006).

29. In Italy, for example, more than a third of the citizens favor the death penalty.

30. Seymour Martin Lipset, *American Exceptionalism: A Double-Edged Sword* (New York: Norton, 1996), chap. 2. See also the chapter in this volume by Fuchs and Klingemann.

Moreover, data suggest that differences between the United States and Europe in the partisan composition of government may matter more.[31] Individual political parties in Europe and the United States often have as much in common across the transatlantic divide as inside each region. Republicans in the United States and Free and Christian Democrats in Germany, for example, share similar economic philosophies, whereas Democrats in the United States and Social Democrats and Greens in Germany share similar social concerns. On foreign policy issues, conservative parties on both sides of the Atlantic stress military strength and nationalism, whereas liberal parties on both sides emphasize diplomacy and international institutions. Thus when center-right parties or, conversely, center-left parties hold power simultaneously across the major Atlantic countries, transatlantic relations tend to function more smoothly. From 1947 to 1967, when the transatlantic alliance was consolidated and grew steadily, center-right governments held power in all five largest Atlantic countries (the United States, the United Kingdom, France, Germany, and Italy) 75 percent of the time.[32] During the more tumultuous decade of the 1970s, center-right and center-left governments split time in office across the Atlantic countries and thus contributed to more frequent transatlantic party disputes. From 1983 to 1987, when alliance ties strengthened once again, center-right governments held office in the five countries 80 percent of the time.[33] In the 1990s, when NATO and interdependence robustly expanded, center-left parties dominated the five governments. Thus some evidence suggests that transatlantic disputes wax and wane depending on the congruence of political parties in power across the Atlantic region.

Tensions created by party differences become especially sharp when conservative as opposed to centrist Republicans (e.g., Richard Nixon or George H. W. Bush) hold power in the United States. This happened in the early 1980s under Ronald Reagan and became acute once again under George W. Bush. The reason is that conservative Republicans are the most classically liberal of the transatlantic parties.[34] They champion personal (rather than social) responsibility, freedom, free markets, deregulation, open trade, and minimalist but often unilateralist foreign policies. (Remember George W. Bush's more humble foreign policy when he took office in 2001—erased, to be sure, by

31. Hans-Dieter Klingemann, "The State of the Transatlantic Relationship: Explorations in Party Politics and Incumbency," paper prepared for the Transatlantic Study Group, sponsored by Free University of Berlin and Georgetown University, Berlin, 17–18 October 2003.

32. Here, for example, one might ask the interesting counterfactual question: what would have happened if center-left parties that opposed NATO had won the vote for Germany's first postwar parliamentary government in 1949 rather than center-right parties that supported NATO?

33. For these calculations during the period 1947–87, see Nau, *Myth of America's Decline*, 48.

34. As Lipset notes, the United States as a whole is a more classically liberal polity than is Canada or any states in Europe, and conservative Republicans are the most classically liberal Americans. Lipset, *American Exceptionalism*, 35–39. The analysis in this volume by Fuchs and Klingemann confirms these differences.

9/11 and now the need to rebuild defeated powers, but still undoubtedly his preference.) Classical liberal parties in Europe, such as the Liberal Party in Britain or Free Democrats in Germany, are much smaller (less than 10 percent of the vote) and almost never constitute a government on their own. Thus when conservative Republicans take office in the United States, their rhetoric and style of classical liberalism find little resonance or empathy in Europe.

That one-third to one-half of Americans embrace a political philosophy that only one-tenth or less of Europeans share is potentially disturbing, but classically liberal and socially democratic views are still both democratic. Neither philosophy is extreme like fascism or communism. Europe experienced both fascism and communism, and this experience destroyed the center parties. Europe operates today through a broad political consensus between left and right that spans a weak center. The United States experienced neither fascism nor communism, and it retains a large and vital center, although this center, some Europeans fear, may always drift toward the extremes. One can make the case that a more classically liberal America and a more social democratic Europe need each other just the way they are.

Compared to other authors in this volume, I see these political party differences as accounting for more of the current transatlantic tension than sociocultural value gaps such as the politicization of religion. As Risse emphasizes, value gaps change only slowly over long periods of time ("global warming" rather than "meteoric" phenomena—see Gunther Hellmann's contribution), and there is little evidence that U.S.-European sociocultural value differences today are any wider than they were in Tocqueville's time or during the cold war when much of Europe had strong communist parties. Indeed, fundamental political (that is, democratic) values are more convergent today than ever before. What widened in the first term of George W. Bush's administration was the partisan gap between a conservative Republican government in Washington and social democratic governments in Europe.

The preceding argument suggests that the tsunami of anti-Americanism triggered by the Iraq war needs to be put into perspective.[35] Anti-Americanism was always rampant in the fascist and communist parties that played a strong role in Germany's and Europe's past. In that context, anti-Americanism represented a fundamental political split in the transatlantic community. Today, with fascism and communism all but dead in Europe, anti-Americanism is less significant and may seem greater precisely because it is milder and less threatening to fundamental transatlantic political solidarity. Politicians and pundits on both sides of the Atlantic speak freely and personally, as they do in domestic politics, because paradoxically they feel closer to one another's

35. For a careful assessment of anti-Americanism, see Peter J. Katzenstein and Robert O. Keohane, eds., *Anti-Americanisms in World Politics* (Ithaca: Cornell University Press, 2007).

political systems and entitled to voice an opinion in the other's politics. Is transatlantic political rhetoric really more vitriolic than such rhetoric within individual Atlantic democracies?

If there were a significant divorce taking place today in transatlantic values, we would expect member countries, at a minimum, to reduce their willingness to rely on one another to deal with third-party threats such as Iraq and, at a maximum, to build up their independent military and intelligence capabilities to handle unknown threats in the future. Yet there is only modest evidence of such developments in today's transatlantic relations.[36] Europe, especially France, seeks a more independent military role, but it does not seem ready to persuade its citizens to spend significantly more on defense or to put European troops into combat, as opposed to peacekeeping, situations, where casualties would be higher. Instead, many Europeans argue that civilian (soft) not military (hard) power is a sufficient way to defuse foreign threats. Annoyingly, to the United States at least, Europe threatens to sell arms to China and may have done so to Iraq before the U.S. invasion. If these differences were to persist and escalate, they could increase alienation. But Europe tends not to follow through on its dissatisfaction with U.S. policies because real alienation would require a substantial increase in both military expenditures and potential combat casualties.

Thus the most significant disagreement between the United States and Europe at this point may not be about internal values or institutions. Instead it is about when and where the use of military force may still be necessary in the rest of the world, which is the crux of the Iraq crisis. The NATO partners do not agree on the nature and extent of the new terrorist threat, just as they did not agree initially in the late 1940s on the nature and extent of the Soviet threat. In the next section, I look more carefully at these diverging threat perceptions and assess the various ways they may affect outcomes of the current crisis.

Five Perceptions of the Terrorist Threat

Five different perceptions of the terrorist threat currently divide the transatlantic community. These divisions exist within as well as between transatlantic countries. How they sort themselves out will determine whether the current transatlantic crisis leads to breakdown, adaptation, or transformation of the alliance.

Each perception of the threat is both logical and legitimate given the nature and size of the adversary it assumes. Although each has shortcomings, I consider

36. For a thorough discussion and assessment of European initiatives to integrate foreign and security policies, see Roy H. Ginsberg, *Demystifying the European Union: The Enduring Logic of Regional Integration* (London: Routledge, 2007).

them all because no one really knows the full empirical dimensions of the terrorist adversary. Estimates vary widely from millions of fundamentalist militants (2.5 million in the tribal border regions of northwest Pakistan alone) ready to serve as suicide bombers against both regional and global adversaries to a few thousand fanatical leaders associated directly with specific organizations such as al-Qaeda and concerned mostly with regional grievances such as the Arab-Israeli dispute. The unknown (and perhaps unknowable) character of the threat makes the current NATO crisis very different and the assessment of threat perceptions especially relevant.

Imperial Perception

The imperial (or unipolar) perception of the terrorist threat is shared by Pentagon strategists, neoconservative Republicans in the United States, and perhaps old Tories in Great Britain. It defines the threat confronting the alliance as any state or nonstate challenge to U.S. power.[37] Long before 9/11, Donald Rumsfeld (later secretary of state) and other Pentagon strategists emphasized the threat of proliferation of weapons of mass destruction and advocated the need for missile defenses against rogue and perhaps also rising states (North Korea and China, respectively).[38] The experience of 9/11 confirmed their fears. Like Pearl Harbor, it started a war. In Bush's words, "the war on terror is not a figure of speech. It is an inescapable calling of our generation."[39]

According to this perception of threat, terrorism cannot be contained by standing alliances, as the Soviet threat was. Terrorism does not originate in stable states and manifest itself in visible armies and missiles that can strike within the hour at a specific spot (an "imminent" threat). Rather it grows out of unstable states, collaborates with rogue states and transnational arms networks to acquire weapons of mass destruction, and buries itself deeply into sleeper cells, from which it can strike at any hour in an undisclosed spot (an "immanent" threat). Such threats have to be fought aggressively and at times preemptively using intelligence gathered from captured combatants who cannot be afforded the same rights as prisoners of war.[40] From this assessment of

37. The Pentagon first articulated this view in 1992. See "Excerpts from Pentagon's Plan: 'Prevent the Re-Emergence of a New Rival'," *New York Times*, 8 March 1992, A14; and Patrick E. Tyler, "U.S. Strategy Plan Calls for Insuring No Rivals Develop," *New York Times*, 8 March 1992, A1.

38. See *Report of the Commission to Assess the Ballistic Missile Threat to the United States*, Washington, DC, 15 July 1998.

39. Richard W. Stevenson, "President, Marking Anniversary of War, Urges World to Unite to Combat Terrorism," *New York Times*, 20 March 2004, A7.

40. It does not mean that such detainees have no rights, just that their rights are not the same as those of prisoners of war. See John Yoo, "Terrorists Have No Geneva Rights," *Wall Street Journal*, 28 May 2004, A16.

threat, the distinction between preemptive and preventive war becomes increasingly meaningless because the distinction rests on being able to see a threat materializing in the present. But the terrorist threat, while potentially catastrophic, is almost always not visible or detectable beforehand.

The imperial perception of threat views international institutions as obstacles and even threats if they are used by lesser powers to thwart aggressive action against terrorism. France and other middle powers used the UN for this purpose in the run-up to the Iraq War and NATO for similar purposes in Kosovo. Fighting the air war in Kosovo by NATO committee exasperated U.S. commanders.[41] The imperial power does not need or receive significant material help from allies, and when it puts up most of the men and women to do the fighting, it is particularly reluctant, for obvious domestic reasons, to share decision-making power over the fate of those men and women. When 9/11 occurred, those holding an imperial perception of the terrorist threat were in no mood to fight another war under NATO constraints.

The imperial perception of threat is not automatically illegitimate because it is the view of the most powerful state. It depends on the character and values of that state. As Robert Cooper points out, American values are democratic. U.S. policies are restrained by domestic checks and balances, and U.S. objectives are broadly anti-imperialist, namely, to spread democracy. The United States "tells countries how they should be run" (that is, as democracies) but then "tells them they should do the running themselves."[42] Thus U.S. imperialism is often short-winded and light-footed. Already, despite the fact that some critics believe that the United States seeks permanent bases in Iraq, the United States is reconfiguring its military strategy to combat terrorism from offshore facilities (so-called lily pads) that reduce the footprint of U.S. bases and troops worldwide.[43]

The great advantage of the imperial perception of threat is that it does not risk underestimating the terrorist adversary. Although increasingly discredited in Iraq, this perception may be quickly resurrected if further serious terrorist attacks occur, especially on U.S. soil. By acting forcefully, it exploits the United States' relative power and invulnerability. Historically, however, this perception is unsustainable. No imperial country has preserved its power indefinitely. Inevitably it provokes counterbalancing. The multipolar perception of threat championed by France is the classic response to imperial definitions of threat.

41. See accounts by the then NATO supreme commander Wesley K. Clark, *Waging Modern War: Bosnia, Kosovo, and the Future of Combat* (New York: Public Affairs, 2001).

42. Robert Cooper, *The Breaking of Nations* (New York: Atlantic Monthly Press, 2003), 49.

43. Thomas P. M. Barnett, *The Pentagon's New Map* (New York: Putnam, 2004). Other analysts who do not share the imperial perception of threat see U.S. imperialism as relentless and permanent. Chalmers Johnson, *The Sorrows of Empire: Militarism, Secrecy, and the End of the Republic* (New York: Henry Holt, 2004).

Multipolar Perception

The multipolar perception of threat is popular among French elites and structural realists in the United States (and clearly in Russia and China outside the transatlantic community). It defines threat largely in terms of the United States' overweening power and the need to counterbalance that power. As then French president Jacques Chirac explained, "Inevitably in this new century, we will see a number of important powers assert themselves. China, India, Europe and South America are examples. This leads to what I call a "multipolar world.' "[44] "Europe is, and certainly will be in the future, here to stay as a major power. . . . So there are other poles."[45] He might have added Russia.[46]

The multipolar perception is classic balance-of-power politics. But because U.S. power is so overwhelming and may not be so threatening, France looks to the UN Security Council, not countervailing military muscle, to restrain U.S. power. The Security Council becomes the great power game played out by vetoes rather than military rivalries. As Chirac says, "all military action not backed by the U.N. is illegitimate and illegal."[47]

Because the threat of U.S. power is greater than that of terrorism, stalemate at the UN is preferred over decisive action. France never supported Iraq sanctions strongly and did not object in 1998 when UN inspectors were kicked out of Iraq. It backed inspections again only after U.S. and British deployments in the Persian Gulf forced inspectors back into Iraq. France may have never accepted the use of force against Iraq because the bigger worry was always the unilateral use of U.S. power. And any military action against Iraq was likely to be an essentially American show.

The multipolar vision checks unipolar power. All countries, especially democratic powers, favor that. Outside a democratic security community, however, counterbalancing power, as Europe's history suggests, often leads to military rivalries and war. Chirac's multipolar view is less threatening because it is less real. As he concedes, "there will be essentially two poles: Europe and the US, who share common values; and in this context I have no real worries."[48] He is not talking about real military counterweights between Europe and the United States but commercial and diplomatic rivals within a security

44. Chirac, as quoted in Jim Hoagland, "Chirac's Multipolar World," *Washington Post*, 4 February 2004, A23.

45. Chirac, as quoted in Robert Graham and Andrew Gowers, "Interview with Jacques Chirac," *Financial Times*, 26 May 2003, 9.

46. As President Vladimir Putin has said, "we believe here in Russia, just as French President Chirac believes, that the future international security architecture must be based on a multipolar world." As quoted in Steven M. Walt, *Taming American Power* (New York: Norton, 2005), 111.

47. Keith B. Richburg, "Chirac's Show, Bush's Agenda," *Washington Post*, 4 June 2003, A22.

48. Graham and Gowers, "Interview with Jacques Chirac."

community of common values. This model is essentially the looser, more competitive Atlantic community discussed below and favored by those who take a conservative internationalist view of the terrorist threat.

Multilateral Perception

The multilateral perception of threat is popular among more left-wing social democrats in Europe and liberal Democrats in the United States. It defines threats largely in terms of breaches of international law and institutions, not disparities in power. From this perception, military power is almost never useful. It is a past, not a last, resort. The civilian power of the EU, not the military power of NATO, is the model for the future. As Robert Kagan writes, "most Europeans believe that it was the transformation of European politics, the deliberate abandonment and rejection of centuries of *machtpolitik*, that in the end made possible the 'new order.' "[49]

The EU notion of multilateral diplomacy sets law above politics and power. The law is fixed. To the extent that terrorism threatens the law, it is a crime, not an occasion for war. As Robert Cooper explains, "if the world is going to be governed by law rather than force then those who break the law will be treated as criminals."[50] But the United States is also a threat to the law when it seeks to change that law (e.g., the rules for warfighting in NATO) by acting minilaterally through coalitions of the willing. The threat from the United States stems not from its military power, as in the multipolar perception of threat, but from its lawlessness. The United States sets itself above the law and acts in defiance of lawful organizations such as the United Nations, NATO, and the EU.

This notion of law above politics is a product of Europe's unique experience in which power politics abused the rule of law for so long that postwar Europe constructed a community of law without politics. The EU governs by law, but to this day no EU Commission official is elected, and the European Parliament, while gaining powers incrementally, is still a faint shadow of its national counterparts. The absence of democracy in making European law gives rise to the "democratic deficit." Jed Rubenfeld, who served as U.S. representative on the Council of Europe's committee to draft a constitution for Kosovo, contrasts this EU view of law as a check on democratic politics with the U.S. legal view that the law answers to democracy:

> Europeans have embraced international constitutionalism, according to which the whole point of constitutional law is to check democracy. For Americans, constitutional law cannot merely check democracy. It must answer to democracy—have its source and basis in a democratic constitutional politics

---

49. Robert Kagan, "Power and Weakness," *Policy Review*, no. 113 (June/July 2002): 9.
50. Cooper, *Breaking of Nations*, 31.

and always, somehow, be part of politics, even though it [politics] can invalidate the outcomes of the democratic process at any given moment.[51]

The multilateral perception of threat has worked astonishingly well in Europe. But it has worked only among democratic nations under the umbrella of U.S. military security. Whether it can work in the UN, which still has a majority of nondemocratic members, or even in Europe, if Europe one day has to provide for its own security, is open to question.[52]

Liberal Internationalist Perception

The liberal internationalist perception of threat is popular among centrist Democrats in the United States and centrist social democrats in Europe. It sees threat primarily in terms of the disruption of postwar Atlantic institutions and order. Unlike the multilateralist view, however, it acknowledges that institutions work best among democratic states that bind themselves through institutions to restrain power.[53] Democratic states use institutions to check and balance power at home and rely on the same dynamic to restrain unchecked power in international institutions among democracies.

In this view, therefore, the most severe form of threat is not lawlessness (substantive violation), as in the multilateral view, but unilateral breakout of institutional commitments among democracies (procedural violation). After 9/11 the United States did just that, turning its back on NATO and the post–World War II institutions that spawned the transatlantic and European communities. No outside threat is severe enough to warrant such behavior among democracies. In fact, if democracies cannot agree on the nature of the outside threat, the threat is probably not that serious. After all, no dominant minority at home can take a democratic country to war. Why should a dominant country or minority be able to do so among democratic countries abroad?

Unlike multilateralists, liberal internationalists see terrorism as more than a crime. But terrorist acts are mostly a consequence of nonstate factors, such as the A. Q. Kahn network (a Pakistani ring to acquire nuclear weapons and technology) and loose nukes (in places like Russia), not rogue states such as Iraq, Iran, or North Korea. Terrorism can be handled best through aggressive

---

51. Jed Rubenfeld, "The Two World Orders," *Wilson Quarterly* (Autumn 2003): 30.

52. The EU security strategy released in June 2003 says that "the fundamental framework for international relations is the United Nations Charter." By contrast, the U.S. strategy document released in September 2002 identifies NATO and EU as "the strongest and most able international institutions in the world." See, respectively, the European Council, *A Secure Europe in a Better World*, 20 June 2003, 9; and the White House, *The National Security Strategy of the United States*, September 2002, 25.

53. Ikenberry, *After Victory*. See also Ivo H. Daalder and James M. Lindsay, "An Alliance of Democracies," *Washington Post*, 23 May 2004, B7.

policies within democratic institutions such as NATO or functional universal agencies such as the International Atomic Energy Agency. Preserving institutions should take priority over fighting wars. And diplomacy and economic initiatives should lead the way in resolving international disputes.

The liberal internationalist perception of threat offers many advantages, not the least of which is preserving the sunk capital invested in democratic international institutions since World War II. These institutions are not just important because they include other nations, as the UN does, but because they help spread democratic values, as NATO does in eastern Europe. Two factors, however, weaken the liberal internationalist view. First, what is the fallback position if democracies cannot achieve consensus? No national democracy functions on the basis of unanimity. Why should an international association of democracies do so, especially on difficult questions of war and peace? Second, are formal institutions really that important in a community tied together by deep social, economic, and cultural interdependence? In the Iraq crisis, formal institutions were disrupted, but lower-level institutions functioned well and economic ties expanded significantly. Liberal internationalists stress institutions because institutions ensure equality. But centralized institutions also reduce diversity and by forcing one-size-fits-all solutions on participants may reduce economic interdependence. Recent no votes on the European constitution suggest that for many Europeans even EU institutions have gone too far. Americans are certainly not ready for this kind of institutional centralization in the Atlantic region, especially in the security area. If not, proponents of a conservative internationalist perception of threat have an alternative approach for dealing with terrorists.

Conservative Internationalist Perception

The conservative internationalist perception of threat is shared by conservative Republicans in the United States and small classical liberal parties in Great Britain and Europe. It sees threat more in terms of the disruption of markets and civil society than intergovernmental institutions. Indeed, excessively centralized institutions are part of the problem, not the solution. Tensions in formal institutions are necessary to protect freedom and initiate change. Unilateralism is often a requirement to lead, and coalitions of the willing are not a threat to existing institutions but a lever to change them. The United States' rejection of NATO's help in Afghanistan, for example, was a way to change rigid containment policies and committee structures in NATO that had hampered operations in Kosovo. Today NATO is fashioning a different, more flexible out-of-area force in Afghanistan. In time, a reformed, more flexible, and agile NATO may become, in the hot war against terrorism, what the old containment and relatively fixed NATO was in the cold war against communism.

The conservative internationalist perception sees threat more in terms of differences in underlying values and civil society relations than in institutional processes or power disparities. It worries that fundamentalist Islam constitutes a universalistic alternative to democracy and markets, much the way communism did under the Soviet Union. A clash of worldviews is at stake, and views opposed to freedom have to be defeated or aggressively held at bay until the other side reforms, as the Soviet Union eventually did. Dealing with terrorism therefore will take a long time and require moral courage to denounce Islamic fundamentalism and radically reform international institutions.

The conservative internationalist view prefers more flexible and decentralized processes of coordination. A heavier emphasis on nationally centered and bottom-up associations can accommodate greater differences in transatlantic conceptions of sovereignty and law, such as those analyzed by Jeffrey Anderson and Michael Byers in their contributions to this volume.[54] Decentralized mechanisms still derive from common democratic values (and are thus similar to liberal internationalist and different from multipolar or multilateral perceptions of threat), but these values are shaped more by informal and private civil society connections than by public institutions. Trade, investment, professional ties, tourism, immigration, competitive educational systems and exchanges, religious diversity, a pluralist media—activities that build a strong civil society at home—also generate more meaningful transnational associations abroad. This conservative internationalist perspective resonates with American traditions more than with European ones in that in Europe nationalism developed from the top down and the state retains a prominent role in many sectors of society (e.g., state churches). Nevertheless, as noted earlier, Chirac's notion of multipolarity within a framework of shared values comes close to this conservative internationalist vision.

The conservative internationalist view recognizes that the United States is not ready to join the liberal internationalist project of centralized national security decision-making within NATO. It also recognizes that, in the case of the invisible terrorist threat, it may be more difficult to reach a consensus. But the conservative view takes an awful lot for granted. It assumes that institutional tensions and indeed crises will not adversely affect the interdependent civil society relations, such as free trade, on which a looser security community relies. It also assumes that dealing more forthrightly with differences between Islamic and Western worldviews can ultimately attract and not alienate Islamic moderates. Although multilateralists and liberal internationalists believe that drawing moral lines in the sand alienates such moderates, conservative internationalists believe it emboldens them to fight harder against internal extremists.

---

54. Examples of nationally centered alternatives include, in the economic area, processes such as subsidiarity and mutual recognition. For differences between conservative nationally led (or inward-oriented) and liberal internationally led (outward-oriented) mechanisms of foreign economic policy coordination, see Robert L. Paarlberg, *Leadership Begins at Home: U.S. Foreign Economic Policy after the Cold War* (Washington, DC: Brookings Institution Press, 1995).

Conclusions

Which perception of threat is likely to prevail, and as a result, will the alliance break up, adapt, or be transformed by the Iraq crisis?

If the imperial or multipolar perceptions prevail, alliance disputes will gradually undermine transatlantic institutions and community values. The only exception would be if terrorism became an overwhelming threat, like that of the former Soviet Union, and drove the alliance back together again. If multilateral perceptions prevail (assuming the United States goes along), transatlantic ties might be transformed from an alliance into a regional version of the United Nations, addressing terrorism largely through collective diplomacy and development aid. If liberal internationalist perceptions prevail, the alliance may be transformed into a combat alliance to defend democracies against out-of-area threats. Europe accepts the need to use military force in such situations as long as the United States decides to use force only through common institutions (as would have been the case with Afghanistan if Washington had accepted NATO assistance). If conservative internationalist perceptions prevail, NATO will adapt short of transformation by becoming a looser institutional arrangement in which all members tolerate but do not necessarily participate in coalitions of the willing against specific terrorist threats (as has been occurring in Iraq).

Which perception is likely to prevail? First, the comparison of previous crises in table 4.1 suggests that when the level of geopolitical interests at stake is highest, differences in threat perceptions are narrowest. Without a heightened Soviet threat in the late 1940s, late 1950s, and again in the late 1970s, it is doubtful that NATO would have formed and persisted. Objective threat, however, became less important as the transatlantic community evolved. In the 1990s NATO survived and expanded without the presence of threat. Common institutions, interdependence, and values shaped cooperation and defined common tasks in political and economic rather than military terms (e.g., expand democracy). When threat reemerged on 9/11, the objective stakes were higher for the United States than for Europe. Accordingly, threat perceptions diverged, especially with respect to Iraq, but stronger institutions, deeper economic interdependence, and underlying values held the community together. If the terrorist threat escalates and Europe is attacked more significantly on a scale similar to that of 9/11, the increased stakes for all democracies may narrow threat perceptions, as they did on several occasions during the cold war. If the terrorist threat persists at present levels, however, and affects primarily the United States, Europe may decide, as the United States did with Britain in 1940, that the United States can fight the threat largely on its own (essentially what has happened in Iraq).

Second, when external stakes are weaker, national values and institutions play a more prominent role. The United States and Europe see the terrorist threat differently in part because their domestic systems have been diverging incrementally since Vietnam and the end of the cold war. As happened only rarely with the Soviet Union during the cold war, many in Europe in the post–cold war world see the United States as the bigger threat, not terrorism. Although such political alienation is not yet significantly greater than before, it could become worse. One consequence would be a weakening of the United States' willingness to defend Europe. With the reconfiguration of its forces to less vulnerable, offshore facilities, the United States may be more reluctant to step into situations that threaten Europe. A bad end to the U.S. intervention in Iraq would increase this tendency. Europe may then confront violence more on its own, as it did briefly and unsuccessfully in the Balkans in the early 1990s. In the Middle East, it will have a chance to see if the multilateralist approach, which emphasizes law without politics and soft power over hard power, can succeed against extremists.

Third, as unfortunate as a military separation of the United States and Europe might be, it will not necessarily end the transatlantic security community. Indeed, it may actually strengthen it. Europe will face more directly the unpopularity and costs of wielding significant military power, as France did in a small way in 2003 when its intervention in the Ivory Coast drew sharp criticism. Greater European military influence will weaken transatlantic solidarity only if Europe and the United States come to see one another again as political foes. For that to happen, the view would have to grow in Europe that the United States is a right-wing, religious (fascist) state or in the United States that the EU is an authoritarian institution that sets law above democratic politics (law as diktat, in Vladimir Putin's terms). Although such severe polarization is unlikely, it is one reason to reject imperial and multipolar perceptions of the terrorist threat. Both of these perceptions accept if not encourage political alienation between Europe and the United States. The multilateralist perception does as well. It lionizes a utopian view of European law while villainizing a more competitive political approach to law in the United States.

The most likely outcome, therefore, may be determined by whether the liberal or conservative internationalist perception prevails. If threat differences narrow, perhaps because of more severe terrorist attacks, new institutional initiatives may be possible. But if threat differences remain large, a looser, less-institutionalized transatlantic community may be preferable. The United States is the most classically liberal society in the transatlantic world and may not be ready for strong centralized Atlantic institutions. Even Europe, as we noted, is having second thoughts about excessive centralization in the EU. At the same time the United States needs Europe to avoid self-defeating institutional breakouts toward isolation (either geographic or diplomatic), while Europe needs the United States to avoid relapses into nondemocratic visions of law that stand above popular accountability. Even without a narrowing of threat perceptions, the United States and Europe have a lot to gain by sticking together.

5 THE ATLANTIC ORDER IN TRANSITION

The Nature of Change in U.S.-European Relations

CHARLES A. KUPCHAN

The Atlantic order is in the midst of a fundamental transition. The transatlantic discord that has emerged since the late 1990s marks a historical breakpoint; foundational principles of the Atlantic security order that emerged after World War II have been compromised. Mutual trust has eroded, institutionalized co-operation can no longer be taken for granted, and a shared Western identity has attenuated. To be sure, the Atlantic democracies continue to constitute a unique political grouping. But as scholars and policymakers alike struggle to di-agnose the troubles that have befallen the Atlantic community and to prescribe mechanisms for redressing the discord, they would be wise to recognize the scope of change that has been taking place in the Atlantic order.

In the first section of this chapter I identify three key periods in Atlantic rela-tions: the Revolutionary War through Anglo-American rapprochement in the early 1900s; the early 1900s through the United States' entry into World War II in 1941; and World War II through September 11. I provide a brief historical overview, identifying the key attributes of the order that prevailed during each of these periods. My analysis provides a comparative framework for evaluating the recent turmoil in U.S.-European relations, shedding light on whether the Atlantic community is experiencing marginal adjustments within a prevailing order or more profound challenges that are order changing in scope and nature.

In the second section of the chapter I examine transatlantic relations since September 11. Drawing on the framework developed in the historical section, I present a number of theoretical and empirical arguments to make the case that the Atlantic order is experiencing fundamental change and that the cur-rent discord does indeed mark a turning point.

In the third and final section I address alternative trajectories for the At-lantic relationship. The analysis is predicated on the assumption that the rela-tionship remains in flux; it is too soon to discern a stable resting point.

I therefore reflect on the different forms that the Atlantic partnership has taken in the past, and the conditions that gave rise to those forms, to address where it might be headed in the future. Is the recent discord a passing aberration, likely to give way to renewed solidarity? What drivers could trigger the further unraveling of the Atlantic community? Is it conceivable that transatlantic relations could again fall prey to militarized rivalry? What steps can be taken to avert the further erosion of Atlantic unity?

The Evolution of Transatlantic Relations

To shed light on how the Atlantic order has evolved over time, I break the historical record into three periods: 1776–1905, 1905–41, and 1941–2001. I identify the defining attributes of these periods along four dimensions: (1) the geopolitical logic governing relations; (2) the definition of interests; (3) the composition of identities; and (4) the character of order. Table 5.1 illustrates how these defining attributes have changed over the three historical periods in question. The narrative that follows provides empirical elaboration.

From the Revolutionary War to Anglo-American
Rapprochement: 1776–1905

During this first phase of interaction between the United States and Europe, transatlantic relations were guided by balance-of-power logic. The major players—the United States, Great Britain, France, and Spain—were regularly jockeying for territory, trade, and geopolitical influence. Each balanced against the power of the other, capitalizing on opportunities for individual gain. The United States fought two wars with Britain and one with Spain. From the 1790s until Napoleon's defeat in 1815, Britain and France were in a prolonged state of war, competing for position on the imperial periphery as well as in the European theater. For the most part, America steered clear of struggles among European powers. The United States did form an alliance with France during the revolutionary period, a pact that nominally lasted

Table 5.1. Atlantic orders, 1776–2001

	Logic of interaction	Interests	Identity	Character of order
1776–1905	Balance of power	Separate and divergent	Oppositional	Militarized rivalry
1905–1941	Balance of threat	Separate but contingently convergent	Compatible	Peaceful coexistence
1941–2001	Cooperative security	Common	Shared	Alliance / security community

until the 1790s. But the alliance was a marriage of convenience aimed at balancing British power, not a signal of U.S. engagement in European rivalries. The United States' founding fathers were adamant that the young republic avoid "entangling alliances" of a more enduring kind. Indeed, successive U.S. governments heeded these warnings: throughout the nineteenth century they kept the country out of Europe's wars and took advantage of America's natural isolation.

The European powers and the United States saw their respective interests as separate and divergent, embracing a zero-sum view of the security environment. To be sure, transatlantic commerce was beneficial to Americans and Europeans alike, with British dependence on imports of American agricultural products leading to the pursuit of joint gains. On matters of security, however, states sought absolute gains. The United States focused its sights on driving the European powers from North America and, ultimately, the Western Hemisphere. Britain, France, and Spain sought to protect their colonial possessions, with Britain also intent on maintaining naval hegemony in the western Atlantic.

The European powers were also collectively concerned about the potential challenge that America's rise would pose to Europe's broader primacy on the global stage. Indeed, during the American Civil War, Britain and France supported the South's effort to secede, calculating that disunion would keep North America divided and weak, and thus limit its ability to challenge European hegemony. Britain came close to intervening on behalf of the Confederacy, holding back only when threatened with the prospect of war with the North. William Seward, the U.S. secretary of state, urged Abraham Lincoln to take on France and Britain as well as the Confederacy. The president, however, demurred, replying, "Mr. Seward, one war at a time."[1] Nonetheless, Europe's interest in "disaggregating" the United States, coupled with the United States' effort to drive Europe from the Western Hemisphere, starkly revealed the degree to which balance-of-power logic guided policy on both sides of the Atlantic.

Identities of opposition prevailed. The United States and Britain saw each other as primary enemies. The narrative of hostility was in part about geopolitical rivalry. Americans saw Europe as the Old World, stuck in the illiberal politics and jealous rivalries of the past. When President James Monroe addressed Congress in 1823, he warned Europeans that any effort to arrest the spread of republicanism in the Western Hemisphere would be seen as "the manifestation of an unfriendly disposition towards the United States." So too should Europe refrain from exporting its geopolitical instabilities across the Atlantic, Monroe warned, as the United States saw Europe's balance-of-power

---

1. Lincoln, as quoted in Warren Bass, "Off Target," *Washington Post Book World*, 6 November 2005.

system "as dangerous to our peace and safety."[2] The concurrent articulation of the Monroe Doctrine made such admonitions somewhat disingenuous; the United States' approach to its neighborhood was hardly one of disinterested pacifism. Nonetheless, Americans saw themselves as charting a new course, leaving behind the antiquated politics and geopolitics of the Old World.

Oppositional identities also took shape with respect to how Americans and Europeans viewed each other's social characteristics. Americans tended to view Europeans as elitist and arrogant. In turn, Europeans saw Americans as boorish and unsophisticated. Alexander Hamilton summarized these mutual perceptions in *Federalist 11*: "The superiority she [Europe] has long maintained has tempted her to plume herself as the Mistress of the World, and to consider the rest of mankind as created for benefit. Men admired as profound philosophers have, in direct terms attributed to her inhabitants a physical superiority, and have gravely asserted that all animals, and with them the human species, degenerate in America—that even dogs cease to bark after having breathed awhile in our atmosphere."[3]

Balance-of-power logic, separate and divergent interests, and identities of opposition kept transatlantic relations in a state of militarized rivalry through the end of the nineteenth century. The United States' final war with Britain was in 1812, but the two powers almost came to blows at numerous times during the second half of the 1800s—and kept war plans at the ready. Indeed, when a dispute broke out between Washington and London over Alaska's boundary with Canada, President Theodore Roosevelt in 1902 dispatched a contingent of cavalry to the region. The Spanish-American War in 1898 was itself a demonstration of the United States' will to drive European powers from its neighborhood—through force if necessary. To the degree an Atlantic order existed during the nineteenth century, it was an order defined by power balancing and militarized rivalry.

From Anglo-American Rapprochement to Pearl Harbor: 1905–1941

During the first four decades of the twentieth century, the geopolitical logic guiding Atlantic relations was balance of threat rather than balance of power. The United States and Europe's democracies began to enjoy the benefits of pacified relations. States no longer balanced against any concentration of power but only against those nations that they deemed threatening. Regime type started to play an important role in distinguishing aggressor states from benign states, with liberal democracies no longer engaging in militarized rivalry with each other.

---

2. Monroe, as quoted in Dexter Perkins, *Hands Off: A History of the Monroe Doctrine* (Boston: Little, Brown, 1941), 28.

3. Alexander Hamilton, *Federalist 11*, in *The Federalist Papers*, by James Madison, Alexander Hamilton, and John Jay, ed. Isaac Kramnick (London: Penguin Books, 1987), 133.

The key driver of this transformation was Anglo-American rapprochement. The process of reconciliation began in the mid-1890s, when London and Washington peacefully resolved their differences over the boundary between Venezuela and British Guiana.[4] Soon thereafter, the two parties settled a series of other outstanding disputes over fishing rights and borders. A mutual sense of durable reconciliation set in by roughly 1905, by which time Britain had effectively ceded naval hegemony in the Western Hemisphere to the United States and dropped the U.S. Navy from consideration in calculating its global naval requirements. London and Washington were both coming to see the prospect of an Anglo-American war as remote, if not unthinkable. France was gradually integrated into this community as a result of the Entente Cordiale and the wartime alliance forged to defeat Wilhelmine Germany.

Officials on both sides of the Atlantic still conceived of their national interests as separate, but they were coming to see them as contingently convergent rather than divergent. The strategic environment was no longer zero sum, meaning that states began to pursue absolute rather than relative gains, even on matters of security. In this respect, the security dilemma ceased to operate among the Atlantic democracies; one state's gain was not necessarily another state's loss—and could even be of mutual benefit.

Great Britain, for example, supported the U.S. war against Spain in 1898, thereafter welcoming the United States' arrival in the Pacific, its colonization of the Philippines, and its effort to open China's market, believing that British interests would be furthered by U.S. expansion. As Kenneth Bourne summarizes elite opinion, "the British cabinet, including Salisbury, preferred American acquisition to that of any other power."[5] In similar fashion, Americans were intent on exercising hegemony over the Western Hemisphere, but they did not otherwise see British power as inimical to U.S. interests. As Henry Cabot Lodge wrote to Theodore Roosevelt in 1900, there was in Washington "a very general and solid sense of the fact that . . . the downfall of the British Empire is something which no rational American could regard as anything but a misfortune to the United States."[6]

Identities of opposition gradually gave way to narratives of compatibility. Britain and the United States were not simply countries with similar interests; they also shared ancestral, racial, and linguistic bonds. Accordingly, elites on

---

4. See Lionel Gelber, *The Rise of Anglo-American Friendship: A Study in World Politics, 1898–1906* (London: Oxford University Press, 1938); A. E. Campbell, *Great Britain and the United States, 1895–1903* (London: Longmans, Green, 1960); Charles S. Campbell, *Anglo-American Understanding, 1898–1903* (Baltimore: Johns Hopkins University Press, 1957); Kenneth Bourne, *Britain and the Balance of Power in North America, 1815–1908* (Berkeley: University of California Press, 1967); and Stephen Rock, *Appeasement in International Politics* (Lexington: University Press of Kentucky, 2000).

5. Bourne, *Britain and the Balance of Power*, 345.

6. Lodge, as quoted in Campbell, *Anglo-American Understanding*, 203.

both sides of the Atlantic began to view the prospect of an Anglo-American conflict as an act of fratricide. As early as 1896, Arthur Balfour, leader of the House of Commons, ventured that "the idea of war with the United States carries with it some of the unnatural horror of a civil war. . . . The time will come, the time must come, when some statesman of authority . . . will lay down the doctrine that between English-speaking peoples war is impossible."[7] In early 1898, soon after stepping down as secretary of state, Richard Olney referred to Britain as the United States' "best friend" and noted "the close community . . . in origin, speech, thought, literature, institutions, ideals—in the kind and degree of civilization enjoyed by both."[8] He proclaimed that the United States and Britain "may have such quarrels as only relatives and intimate neighbors indulge in," affirming that "England, our most formidable rival, is our most natural friend. There is such a thing as patriotism for race as well as for country."[9]

The logic of balance of threat, separate but contingently convergent interests, and compatible identities transformed transatlantic relations from a state of militarized rivalry into one of peaceful coexistence. The Atlantic democracies were not yet peacetime allies or members of a security community; they banded together only as necessary to respond to common threats. The United States did enter World War I and World War II, but only after its own forces had come under attack. Britain was similarly reluctant to fight alongside France. In both world wars, it took the prospect of German domination of western Europe to convince London to countenance a continental commitment.

In this sense, the Atlantic democracies worked together when they deemed their collective interests were at stake—and otherwise acted separately. It was precisely the contingent nature of collective interest that induced the United States to keep its distance from institutionalized commitments, preferring the independence that comes with autonomy. As the Senate's rejection of U.S. participation in the League of Nations made clear, the country was simply unwilling to take on binding obligations to collective action. According to one historian of the Senate debate, opponents of the League were in agreement that "Washington would stir uneasily in his tomb in Mount Vernon if he should learn that we were going to underwrite a League of Nations and keep an army of American boys ready to fight strange peoples in strange lands—all at the behest of some superbody."[10] Europe's democracies showed a greater willingness to take on such obligations in principle, but their reluctance to

---

7. Rock, *Appeasement*, 32.

8. Campbell, *Anglo-American Understanding*, 201.

9. "Olney Talks at Harvard," *New York Times*, 3 March 1898.

10. Thomas A. Bailey, *Woodrow Wilson and the Great Betrayal* (New York: Macmillan, 1947), 32.

follow through with action became all too apparent during the 1930s. The interwar period proved to be the era of fragile "coalitions of the willing," not collective security.

From Pearl Harbor to September 11: 1941–2001

The Atlantic alliance reached its apogee during the long decades between Pearl Harbor and the dissolution of the Soviet Union. During this era, the guiding geopolitical logic of transatlantic relations was cooperative security. The Atlantic democracies pooled their resources to defend against external aggression. They also pooled their sovereignty, agreeing to multilateral and consensual decision making and binding themselves to each other through integrated military commands, joint forces, and transatlantic institutions. Far from triggering balancing, material power within the Atlantic community wielded a magnetic attraction, "grouping" states around centers of power such as the United States and the Franco-German coalition.

During the cold war, the Atlantic democracies had common interests, not just contingently convergent ones, making their security indivisible. The security dilemma was not simply in abeyance but was actually working in reverse: each state's effort to increase its own security enhanced the security of all. Accordingly, the members of the Atlantic community persistently encouraged each other to increase their military capabilities. Because they operated in a world of common interests and joint gains, the Atlantic democracies were prepared to take on institutionalized obligations. Whereas the League of Nations foundered on the shoals of the United States' reluctance to formalize its foreign commitments, the United Nations enjoyed near-unanimous support in the U.S. Senate. Whereas the United States steered clear of Europe's troubles in the 1930s, during the cold war the United States deployed troops in Germany, bound itself to Europe through the North Atlantic Treaty, and took other steps to ensure that the two sides of the Atlantic would not be decoupled.

The compatible identities of the interwar period gave way to a shared Western identity during the cold war. The separate states maintained their own national institutions and symbols, but they also worked hard to build a transnational sense of unity and commonality. With the deepening of a shared identity came a new narrative of solidarity and partnership, not unlike the one that had emerged between Britain and the United States during the early years of the 1900s. Backed up by a discourse of community, common values and culture, and durable partnership, transatlantic cohesion took on a taken-for-granted quality during the cold war years.

The logic of cooperative security, common interests, and a shared identity led to the formation and maintenance not only of a formal alliance but also of a security community—an international society knit together by a sense of "weness," an agreed upon set of rules and norms governing behavior, and a shared belief that armed conflict among members of the grouping was unthinkable.

The Atlantic community maintained its coherence even after the collapse of the Soviet Union precisely because it enjoyed deeper social linkages, a shared Western identity, and common adherence to the principles of multilateralism and consensual governance.[11]

The Erosion of the Post–World War II Atlantic Order

The main purpose of this historical overview has been to identify the different forms that the Atlantic order has taken over time, specifying the principal attributes that define these different orders. I now turn to the more recent past, arguing that on the four key dimensions of order—the geopolitical logic governing relations, definition of interests, composition of identities, and character of order—the Atlantic community has experienced a striking and consequential degradation. Indeed, in important respects, today's Atlantic order more closely resembles that of the interwar period than of the cold war era. From this perspective, the Atlantic community has entered a historical switching point that constitutes a fundamental break with the patterns of deep cooperation that emerged after World War II.

The Atlantic order that prevailed during the cold war began to erode well before the election of George W. Bush and the tragedies of September 11. The strategic priorities of the United States and Europe started to diverge soon after the dissolution of the Soviet Union. In the absence of a common external threat, Europe and the United States no longer relied on each other to defend first-order security interests. The Atlantic allies eventually succeeded in bringing peace to the Balkans, but only after years of procrastination and political disarray. NATO has continued to exist as a military alliance only in name, its collective defense mandate essentially becoming defunct after its main focus moved to missions beyond its boundaries. Moreover, in those regions that became the focal point of transatlantic efforts at cooperation—such as the Middle East—the United States and Europe have historically parted company. During the cold war, those differences were muted and marginalized by the solidarity resulting from the Soviet threat. Absent a militarized inter-German border, the troublesome issues that used to be distractions have come to dominate the transatlantic agenda.

The evolution of the European Union (EU) has added to the transatlantic discord. A Europe at peace and a deeper and wider EU have diminished European dependence on U.S. power. Europeans have accordingly grown more ready to assert their autonomy and chart their own course, upon occasion breaking with the United States on key policy issues such as the Kyoto

11. See Daniel Deudney and G. John Ikenberry, "The Logic of the West," *World Policy Journal*, no. 10 (Winter 1993): 17–26.

Protocol and the International Criminal Court (ICC). Enlargement also extended Europe's sway eastward and southward, its influence coming at the expense of America's. In the Balkans, for example, Brussels has replaced Washington as the region's principal diplomatic arbiter.

The end of the cold war further contributed to transatlantic tension by expediting the erosion of liberal internationalism in the United States. The bipartisan coalition that supported liberal internationalism took shape under Franklin Roosevelt, who capitalized on the threats posed by Nazi Germany and Imperial Japan to prevail, for the first time in U.S. history, against the United States' unilateralist and isolationist proclivities. The cold war then sustained this moderate and centrist coalition; strategic imperatives engendered political discipline. With the collapse of the Soviet Union, however, the political foundations of liberal internationalism began to weaken. By the mid-1990s, President Bill Clinton already faced a recalcitrant Congress, one that regularly preferred partisan politics to the responsible conduct of foreign relations.[12] The consequent change in the substance and tone of U.S. foreign policy contributed substantially to transatlantic acrimony, perhaps ensuring that what might have been a mere drift in the relationship has evolved into an open rift.

Virtually all the geopolitical effects of the cold war's end were magnified by the combination of the Bush presidency and the terrorist attacks of September 11, 2001. An administration hostile to liberal internationalism took power, at once announcing its opposition to the Kyoto Protocol and the International Criminal Court. The strategic priorities of Europe and the United States, which were already diverging, grew further apart. The U.S. government and its European counterparts embraced different views of the sources of Islamic extremism and how best to combat it. Washington turned down NATO's offer of help in toppling the Taliban regime in Afghanistan, dealing a blow to the spirit and form of collective defense. When the United States, without UN authority, next turned its sights on Saddam Hussein's regime in Iraq, many Europeans viewed the war as an illegitimate and unilateralist act—even in those European countries whose governments supported the invasion. The tragedies of September 11 also dealt a further blow to liberal internationalism in the United States. The attacks stoked an angry nationalism, advantaged more extreme voices at the expense of moderate ones, and exacerbated partisan polarization.

How consequential is the transatlantic rift that has opened since 2001? Do the substantive disagreements and political acrimony amount only to politics as usual within a robust liberal order? Or are the two sides of the Atlantic

---

12. The Senate, for example, regularly refused to confirm Clinton's diplomatic appointments. It also voted down the Comprehensive Test Ban Treaty, despite Clinton's willingness to withdraw the treaty from consideration.

breaking out of normative boundaries, signaling the end of the post–World War II Atlantic order?

The framework developed here indicates that the Atlantic order is indeed experiencing systemic change, not just elevated levels of political conflict within preexisting boundaries. Erosion is taking place on each of the four key dimensions of order.

Cooperative security is no longer the exclusive geopolitical logic governing relations; balance-of-threat thinking is making a distinct comeback. Europe is not balancing against U.S. power but against U.S. behavior. Europe's effort to resist U.S. policy has for the most part taken the form of "soft balancing"— organizing efforts to isolate the United States diplomatically, as occurred over the Kyoto Protocol and the ICC. The attempt by France and Germany to block the invasion of Iraq constituted a far more serious form of resistance, however. France and Germany did not just opt out of the war—a move that would have been consistent with cooperative security—but they campaigned assiduously to deny the United States the backing of the UN Security Council. Their willingness to do so indicated that they were prepared to deny Washington the legal right to pursue a military operation that U.S. leaders deemed vital to the country's first-order security interests.

The implications went well beyond diplomatic symbolism. Had the UN Security Council passed a second resolution authorizing the war, the United States may have been able to amass a much larger military coalition from the outset. A larger force may well have made a considerable difference during the early phases of the occupation, enabling the United States to pacify the country and neutralize the insurgency. Perhaps Turkey would have agreed to allow U.S. forces to open a northern front. Had the operation enjoyed international legitimacy, the United Nations and other international organizations would have been much more involved in postwar governance and reconstruction. The war might also have enjoyed greater support within the Middle East, limiting its ability to stoke radicalism and attract new recruits to the extremist cause. In short, the diplomatic actions taken by France and Germany to block the war arguably imposed considerable costs on the United States in terms of both resources and lives.

The United States responded by following suit and embracing balance-of-threat logic. The Bush administration sought to drive a wedge between pro-war and antiwar members of the EU, rewarding its supporters with access and promises of lucrative contracts in Iraq while punishing its detractors with isolation. The U.S. government also embraced a decidedly negative view of the project of European integration, worried that a common foreign and security policy might deny Washington the ability, when needed, to secure the support of individual EU members—as it did in the case of the Iraq War. Just as Europe sought to preserve its global sway by hoping that the American Civil War would divide and weaken the United States, Washington sought to disaggregate Europe to counter the potential threat it posed to U.S. hegemony. Balance-of-threat thinking prevailed on both sides of the Atlantic.

The record of the past five years has also made clear that Europe and the United States no longer share the commonality of interest that they enjoyed during the cold war. Instead, their interests have returned to being separate, even if contingently convergent. To be sure, the two sides of the Atlantic still have many international objectives in common. Indeed, there are arguably more areas of agreement than disagreement.

With the rift over Iraq, however, the United States and key European allies—France and Germany in particular—disagreed on fundamental matters of war and peace. The Iraq War was not the first episode to come along since World War II in which differing positions emerged on the use of force; the Suez crisis and the Vietnam War certainly provoked sharp disagreements across the Atlantic. But as mentioned earlier, these disagreements occurred amid the cold war, meaning that the political impact of policy differences over third areas was muted by common interests and objectives in the core strategic theater. The split over Iraq, however, occurred in the absence of a disciplining threat in Europe. As a result, the contrasting strategic perspectives that emerged on Iraq constituted a fundamental break in transatlantic unity. It became readily apparent that U.S. and European security were no longer indivisible.

The transatlantic divide over Iraq may well prove to be a unique event, representing a particularly glaring and damaging instance of strategic divergence between the United States and Europe. In light of the troubles that have befallen the United States in Iraq, another similar invasion seems a remote prospect. On the other hand, the United States and Europe have consistently taken quite different approaches to the Israeli-Palestinian conflict. And they may well differ on how to deal with Iran should Tehran refuse to curb its nuclear ambitions. On these and other important strategic issues, the two sides of the Atlantic have different interests and have historically pursued different policies.

This divergence in U.S. and European interests explains why transatlantic security institutions have been strained to the breaking point. Washington now prefers coalitions of the willing precisely because it accurately perceives a more divided geopolitical environment in which individual countries whose interests are affected—rather than the Atlantic alliance as a collective—are likely to be the key participants in most conceivable military operations. Furthermore, with Atlantic security no longer indivisible, Washington prefers the flexibility of ad hoc decision making to the binding obligations of formal alliance. Europe, meanwhile, continues to prefer institutionalized multilateralism in large measure because binding obligations offer a means of taming U.S. power.

Consider the diminished centrality of NATO, whose limited role in Iraq is a testament to the scope of the change that has taken place in the Atlantic security order. NATO is ostensibly the mainstay of that security order, an institution meant to orchestrate common action to defend common interests. France, Germany, and other members of the antiwar coalition may well have been right that the threat posed by Saddam Hussein's Iraq did not warrant war. But amid the insurgency and accompanying chaos that ensued after the fall of Baghdad, they could hardly maintain that the United States' first-order security interests were not at stake. With U.S. soldiers dying on an almost daily basis and Iraq's integrity in the balance, it was evident that the United States was in need of help.

Seventeen individual members of NATO sent troops to Iraq, but many of the contingents were limited in size. Nine members, including France and Germany, refused to send troops. Furthermore, the institutional and symbolic centerpiece of the Atlantic order—NATO—kept its distance, limiting its contribution to the training of Iraqi security forces. That NATO became only tangentially involved in a crisis of the magnitude faced by the United States in Iraq speaks volumes about the erosion that has taken place in Atlantic solidarity. The Atlantic community is back in a world of separate interests and contingent commitments to collective action.

The Atlantic order has suffered similar setbacks on matters of identity. The sense of "we-ness" that emerged amid World War II and the cold war has dimmed considerably. Indeed, not only has a shared Western identity weakened, but it has to some extent been replaced by a narrative of opposition. It is not only the French who have been calling for the return of a multipolar world and the rise of an EU capable of serving as a counterweight to the United States. Even in Sweden, a country that long ago renounced power politics, the prime minister speaks about the EU as "one of the institutions we can develop as a balance to U.S. world domination."[13] In the United States, it is not only partisan advocates, such as Secretary of Defense Donald Rumsfeld, who denigrate "old Europe" and lament its challenge to Washington's leadership. Even more centrist individuals, such as columnist Thomas Friedman, have added their rhetorical contributions to transatlantic acrimony, in 2003 referring to France as an "enemy" of the United States.[14]

In important respects, the evolving discourse resonates with the oppositional narrative of the nineteenth century—except the tables have turned in step with the reversal of power asymmetries. During the nineteenth century, the United States was Venus and Europe, Mars. Now, Robert Kagan claims, it is the United States that understands and wields power and Europe that has embraced pacifism.[15] Then, Americans saw themselves as progressive, leaving

13. As quoted in Charles A. Kupchan, "The End of the West," *Atlantic Monthly*, November 2002, 42–45.

14. Thomas Friedman, "Our War with France," *New York Times*, 18 September 2003.

15. Robert Kagan, *Of Power and Paradise: America and Europe in the New World Order* (New York: Knopf, 2003).

behind Europe's social atavisms. Today, it is Europe that criticizes the United States' social atavisms—the death penalty, the underclass and the uninsured, the insensitivity to environmental change. When Europe enjoyed global hegemony, Americans criticized its arrogance. Now that the United States is the global hegemon, Europeans regularly complain about its "selfish superpower position," lamenting that their leaders must go to Washington "to appear at the throne of the freshly anointed American Caesar."[16]

Such statements represent a radical departure from the declarations of community and partnership that prevailed during the previous five decades. Moreover, the erosion of communal identity is not just an elite phenomenon; surveys reveal a sharp increase in the percentage of Europe's citizens holding an unfavorable view of the United States.[17] Should balance-of-threat thinking continue to gain ground at the expense of the logic of cooperative security, these attitudinal changes could well mean growing European efforts to oppose U.S. policy.

The return of balance-of-threat thinking, the divergence of interests, and the dilution of a shared identity have led to a consequential erosion of the Atlantic order. NATO still exists, but its members no longer enjoy the solidarity that they once did. The Atlantic democracies still constitute a security community in the sense that war among them remains unthinkable. However, a transatlantic sense of "we-ness" has diminished considerably. Indeed, for many Europeans, the United States has lost its allure as a model and magnet. An Atlantic order characterized by alliance and security community appears to be giving way to one characterized by peaceful coexistence.

The Next Phase: Repair, Stable Equilibrium, or Further Erosion?

The Atlantic order has experienced a dramatic setback. In important respects, the evolving relationship between the United States and Europe has begun to resemble that of the interwar period more than that of the cold war era. The progress toward deeper and more regularized cooperation made during the cold war has been significantly compromised.

Although a step backward in the sense that advances in international cooperation have been reversed, the new Atlantic order that is emerging is not necessarily cause for alarm. Peaceful coexistence and transatlantic cooperation that is contingent upon the identification of joint interests still provide the basis for a stable order in which militarized conflict remains unthinkable. The

---

16. Quotes from Charles A. Kupchan, *The End of the American Era: U.S. Foreign Policy and the Geopolitics of the Twenty-First Century* (New York: Vintage, 2003), 223.

17. Andrew Kohut, Jodie Allen, Carroll Doherty, Carolyn Funk, "American Character Gets Mixed Reviews: U.S. Image up Slightly, but Still Negative," Pew Global Attitudes Project, 2005; available at http://pewglobal.org/reports/display.php?ReportID=247.

security dilemma would not operate unless an aggressor were to reemerge within the Atlantic community; balance-of-threat logic produces geopolitical rivalry only in the presence of revisionism. Regularized cooperation promises to continue on many fronts, with the transatlantic area enjoying far deeper and wider networks and institutions than existed during the interwar period. The loosening of Atlantic ties may make consensus more difficult to reach at the UN, NATO, the WTO, and other global and Atlantic institutions. But these institutions nonetheless continue to facilitate international cooperation. And the United States and Europe share a commitment to the spread of liberal democracy and markets, meaning that their basic international objectives align more often than not. From this perspective, the Atlantic democracies may be finding their way to "normalcy," an order that lacks the unique affinity and cohesion of the cold war years but nonetheless enjoys the benefits of pacific relations, economic integration, and not infrequent instances of political collaboration.

It is of course conceivable that the recent erosion in transatlantic ties represents only a temporary departure from deeper cooperation. Advocates of this view would claim that the Iraq War was a unique event, not to be repeated. They would also contend that the election of George W. Bush led to a particularly hawkish and ideological brand of foreign policy, one not likely to last beyond his presidency. A Democratic victory, the argument runs, would restore previous levels of harmony and affinity to the transatlantic relationship.

Although the Iraq War and Bush's brand of international leadership may well prove to be the exception, not the rule, this argument fails to recognize the deeper structural changes that have compromised the Atlantic order. The end of the cold war, the maturation of Europe, the differential impact of 9/11 on strategic priorities—these are the underlying causes of the tensions that have emerged between the United States and Europe. Furthermore, the foreign policy proclivities of the Bush administration hardly appear to be a passing aberration. The unilateralist turn in policy was evident well before Bush was elected. Despite the Iraq War and the Atlantic turmoil of the first term, Bush was reelected. And the bipartisan coalition of moderate Democrats and Republicans that was the political foundation of liberal internationalism during the cold war appears to be gone for good. Bipartisanship has become a rare commodity, and generational change is dramatically thinning the ranks of the traditional internationalists, especially in the Republican Party. If Europeans are waiting for the United States' liberal internationalism to make a comeback, they may be waiting for a long time.

Rather than pining for yesterday's Atlantic order and seeking to reclaim it, a wiser investment would be to recognize that a new Atlantic order is taking shape, seek to understand more fully its attributes, and figure out how to make the most of its cooperative potential. Indeed, policymakers already seem to be doing so. During the first year of Bush's second term, governments on both sides of the Atlantic appeared ready to put aside Iraq and theoretical disputes about multilateralism, instead opting for ad hoc, case-by-case instances of cooperation. On a host of important issues—Iran, Syria, Afghani-stan, and the Palestinian-Israeli peace process among them—the United States and Europe found considerable common ground. This pragmatic ap-proach to cooperation may well represent a model for the future, a new stable equilibrium that promises to ameliorate the recent acrimony and capitalize on available opportunities for transatlantic partnership.

At the same time, it would be premature and unwarranted to be confident that the Atlantic relationship is fast heading toward a stable resting point. During the 1990s, few scholars foresaw the speed or scope of the erosion in Atlantic relations that was about to take place. Just as a rift of the type that opened over the Iraq War was unimaginable then, so too it is unimaginable today that the Atlantic community could backslide even further, perhaps to the point at which militarized rivalry again becomes plausible.

The past, however, makes clear that security communities are by no means durable political formations. The Concert of Europe after 1848, the United States in the 1860s, Yugoslavia in the 1990s—all are examples of security communities that unraveled, their constituent members ultimately falling prey to geopolitical rivalry and bloodshed. From this perspective, it is worth identifying the pathways that could potentially lead to the further dissolution of the Atlantic order. The Atlantic democracies could then take steps to im-munize themselves against such adverse developments.

Parties on both sides of the Atlantic should be mindful of the potent impli-cations of identity politics and narratives of opposition. The Concert of Europe was dealt a decisive blow by the nationalism awakened by the revolu-tions of 1848. The union of U.S. states descended into war as the North and South parted company over contrasting social orders and incompatible na-tional identities. Yugoslavia unraveled as the ethnic identities of its con-stituent peoples were awakened by opportunistic elites.

These cases suggest that elites on both sides of the Atlantic should guard against the inflated rhetoric of the recent past. When European commentators repeatedly refer to the United States as an imperial power bent on global dom-ination, popular attitudes change accordingly. When German politicians cam-paign for office by insisting that Berlin stand up to Washington and that the EU serve as a counterweight to the United States, they shift the terms of public de-bate, potentially diminishing their own room for maneuver in managing At-lantic relations. In similar fashion, when U.S. officials and commentators refer to European countries as enemies, denigrate Europe's role in global affairs, and call for a boycott against French goods, Atlanticism in the United States suffers a blow. The ongoing changes in discourse are particularly important inasmuch as younger Europeans and Americans do not bring to the table the default Atlanticism of the World War II generation. For the generation coming of age after the fall of the Berlin Wall, rhetoric portraying the United States and Europe as arch rivals has the potential to fuel a self-fulfilling prophecy.

The United States and Europe would also be well served to adjust transatlantic institutions to new realities. If coalitions of the willing, rather than a collective NATO, are likely to be the main vehicle for security cooperation, then it makes sense to loosen NATO's unanimity rule. Otherwise, future efforts to organize ad hoc coalitions will come off as affronts to multilateralism rather than episodes of pragmatic teamwork. Furthermore, assuming that the EU succeeds in centralizing decision making on matters of foreign policy, building new links between Washington and Brussels makes more sense than clinging to the NATO model, in which each European country has its own voice.

If transatlantic security is no longer indivisible, as I argued earlier in the chapter, then the members of the Atlantic community need to learn how to disagree more agreeably. The rift over Iraq was particularly damaging because divergent strategic perspectives led not only to opposing policies but also to an open political confrontation. France and Germany did not just opt out of the operation but actively sought to block it. The United States retaliated in kind, not just ignoring Europe's protestations but actively seeking to impede the project of European integration.

Europe and the United States are likely to face continuing disagreements over policy in the Middle East, East Asia, and other third areas. Such disagreement was the norm during the cold war; it is likely to be even more pronounced now that the cold war is over. The United States and Europe should confront this reality, seeking to cooperate when possible but also finding ways to contain and limit the impact of the disagreements that will inevitably emerge.

Finally, the European Union should strive to develop a more unified voice on matters of security policy and acquire the military capability needed to back it up. Progress on the defense front would enable Europe to capitalize more effectively on opportunities for concrete cooperation with the United States. Confronted with the drain on resources that Iraq has imposed on the United States, Washington has become well aware that it needs help on virtually every front. It would therefore be prepared to listen hard to European concerns if the EU had important assets that it could offer in return for U.S. compromise. The United States would get the help it needs. The Europeans would get the influence they want, forestalling European inclinations to balance against U.S. policy.

Atlantic relations are still in a transitional phase; it is far too soon to determine what type of order will constitute a stable and durable equilibrium. Nonetheless, scholars and policymakers alike should realize that the Atlantic community has already passed through a historical breakpoint and that the close-knit security partnership of the past five decades is in all likelihood gone for good. It is better to recognize that reality and seek to lock in a new type of cooperative order than to pretend otherwise, unwittingly contributing to the further erosion of the Atlantic community.

6 TRADE IS NO SUPERGLUE

The Changing Political Economy of Transatlantic Relations

JENS VAN SCHERPENBERG

Have transatlantic economic relations been negatively affected by U.S.-EU foreign policy tensions under the reign of the United States' forty-third president? Or have they, on the contrary, acted as the essential glue to an otherwise fraying alliance? Maybe the fact that these questions have been asked with growing urgency in recent years is an indicator in itself of the severe strains in the transatlantic alliance. The usual answer is reassuring. On the surface, there seems to be no evidence of negative effects of a transatlantic political crisis on economic relations. In their widely quoted publications on the state of transatlantic economic relations, Daniel Hamilton and Joseph Quinlan draw on a large body of data on trade, on direct investment, and especially on foreign affiliate sales, to show that bilateral trade and investment between the United States and Europe, as well as the business by transatlantic subsidiaries, far from having suffered from the transatlantic tension resulting from the United States' decision to go to war against Iraq, expanded in the year 2003, when political relations seemed to have arrived at rock bottom.[1]

Logically, this empirical evidence would not allow for any clear conclusion to be drawn about political relations. If we consider economic relations as the dependent variable to political-security relations—following the low politics–high

1. Daniel S. Hamilton and Joseph P. Quinlan, *Partners in Prosperity: The Changing Geography of the Transatlantic Economy* (Washington, DC: Center for Transatlantic Relations, Johns Hopkins University, 2004); Daniel S. Hamilton and Joseph P. Quinlan, eds., *Deep Integration: How Transatlantic Markets Are Leading Globalization* (Brussels: Centre for European Policy Studies, 2005). For an earlier version of their argument, see Joseph P. Quinlan, *Drifting Apart or Growing Together? The Primacy of the Transatlantic Economy* (Washington, DC: Center for Transatlantic Relations, Johns Hopkins University, 2003). I follow the widespread if imprecise use of language by employing the terms Europe and EU as synonyms for the *political* actor EU, encompassing too the legal entity European Communities (EC), if not otherwise indicated.

politics dichotomy—the evidence shows that whatever *political* crisis may have occurred in transatlantic relations, it is so far not reflected in trade and direct investment flows. The latter obviously are resilient in their reaction to political irritations or crises. Hence, the recent transatlantic political crisis has either been too shallow or too short-lived to affect the economy—or its economic impact has yet to materialize.

Nevertheless, it is tempting to invert the dependency function. To give substance to a widely held view, Hamilton and Quinlan draw the reverse conclusion from the absence of a crisis in U.S.-EU economic relations in recent years. They claim that the deep transatlantic economic interdependence between the United States and the EU has acted as an independent variable, mitigating the recent political crisis, and the more political leaders are made aware of the role interdependence plays, the more it will perform that task. The stakeholders in the Atlantic economy on both sides—the business communities, the trade unions, and local and state governments—can make their voices heard, Hamilton and Quinlan assume, to prevent political tensions from spilling over into the economy and to foster instead a beneficial reverse spillover of economic self-interest into politics. The strong commonality of economic interests, they argue, can be expected to act as glue for strained political relations[2]; it has already acted as such, paving the ground for the more moderate political climate in transatlantic relations since 2004.

Their argument thus conforms to the standard liberal paradigm of the conflict-preventing or moderating force of economic interdependence, as reflected in international political economy theories based on "liberal" (classical) trade theory.[3] In the transatlantic sphere, in analogy to—or even as a substitute for—Karl Deutsch's widely accepted concept of the transatlantic security community,[4] the deep integration of the Atlantic economy as emphasized by Hamilton and Quinlan would contribute to the shared identity that is a constituent of such community.

In this chapter I raise some doubts about the liberal glue hypothesis. Taking up one of the lead questions of the discussions from which this volume originated—how do we know a crisis in transatlantic relations when we see one?—I suggest going back beyond the two questions at the beginning of this

2. Johannes F. Linn, "Trends and Prospects of Transatlantic Economic Relations: The Glue That Cements a Fraying Partnership?" paper presented at the Transatlantic Editors' Roundtable, April 2004.

3. See Richard N. Rosecrance, *The Rise of the Trading State: Commerce and Coalitions in the Modern World* (New York: Basic Books, 1986); Robert Gilpin, *The Political Economy of International Relations* (Princeton: Princeton University Press, 1987), 31. See also Kathleen McNamara's thorough overview in this volume of the liberal theory concerning the linkages between economic and political relations.

4. See also Thomas Risse, *Beyond Iraq: Challenges to the Transatlantic Security Community* (Washington, DC: AICGS, 2003).

chapter. My point of departure is the same as that of the other contributors to this volume: Are we witnessing simply a temporary blip of animosity, similar to others we have observed in the history of the alliance? Or does this one represent a fundamental breakdown in the Atlantic security community? Or is it a transformation into a different kind of cooperative relationship? Thus the alternative is not one of war or peace in Atlantic relations, but whether a viable alliance with common interests and working institutions will continue to exist or not. The distinction matters greatly with regard to economic relations. Therefore, in this chapter I discuss where to look when inquiring whether there are economic indicators of a possibly deeper structural crisis of the Atlantic community.

I start with a few remarks on the cyclical nature of research on the relationship between foreign policy and economic interests. These are complemented by an overview of postwar European-U.S. economic and political relations, including a brief analysis of why the transatlantic integration policy initiatives of the 1990s essentially failed. In the following section, I look at the present state of transatlantic economic interdependence, criticizing the "glue view" and Hamilton and Quinlan's hypothesis of the "primacy of the transatlantic economy."

I argue that the high level of exchange and the low level of conflict in day-to-day trade and direct investment relations should not be taken as an indication of the health of the Atlantic alliance. Nor should the common interests of private stakeholders in the Atlantic economy be seen as representative of a continuing commonality of political and security interests. Usually day-to-day trade and investment activities are the last ones affected by a political crisis between two international actors before it evolves into open conflict. When trying to identify lead indicators for a more structural crisis or breakdown of the Atlantic community that might spill over into economic relations, resorting to the realists' or economic nationalists' worldview we might rather want to look at areas of trade, technology, investment, and international finance that both sides consider strategic with regard to their respective economy's competitiveness and to their foreign and defense policy capabilities.[5]

Such areas include economic sanctions; trade in goods deemed strategic; dual use technologies; and defense trade and defense industrial relations; direct investment in strategic industries; and macroeconomic and monetary adjustment. A nation might be willing to trade toys or underwear with its worst enemy or its strongest peer competitor, but it would not trade strategic technologies or corporate stakes in strategic industries except with trustworthy allies. Nor would it impose sanctions on such allies. Last but not least, the introduction of the euro and the deeper macroeconomic integration of the Eurozone countries that it inevitably entails have challenged the mechanisms

5. Gilpin, *Political Economy of International Relations*, 31ff., 180–83.

of macroeconomic burden sharing, which had been a core element of the post–World War II transatlantic security bargain. EU-U.S. macroeconomic policy coordination, as it successfully addressed U.S. current account and budgetary imbalances for the last time during the Reagan years, is unlikely to be resumed.

Is Europe a trustworthy ally to the United States? Do European countries consider the United States a trustworthy ally that can be relied on in the strategic areas indicated earlier? Is mutual trust nevertheless a politically relevant part of the common identity of the West? Although not quite a category of realist analysis of international relations, trust is well acknowledged in economics as an indispensable factor for containing transaction costs.[6]

Since the end of the cold war, a significant shift in perceptions seems to have taken place on both sides of the Atlantic. Europe has tried to maintain its industrial and technological autonomy toward the United States for fear of losing out economically and having to forego pursuing its own foreign policy interests. These very attempts have given rise in the United States to perceptions of Europe as a potential rival or "peer competitor" rather than an ally— an impression further reinforced by the EU's apparent lack of concern for U.S. security interests in its economic and technological relations with China. These issues are addressed in the subsequent section, which analyzes the character of current economic conflicts between the United States and the EU, with a special focus on the strategic ones.

I conclude by taking up the lead questions of this volume. My findings are not straightforward. Economic relations—even if we consider the dimension of strategic areas of economic activity as addressed here—are unlikely to be severely disrupted, much less to break down. In many fields they may continue to look much like—literally—business as usual. However, this appearance cannot mask the deep change that transatlantic relations have undergone in recent years. There may be ever less reason to consider the Atlantic relationship as something special, not least with regard to economic relations. Economic stakes may nevertheless act as superglue for the Atlantic alliance to the extent that, for both Europeans and Americans, the stakes in other areas of the world keep growing more dynamically. In their regional integration policy since 2001, the United States and the EU already have acted rather as rivals, not as partners in a joint institutional framework, competing for spheres of political, economic, and institutional influence.[7] Thus, the multipolar world is taking shape in the economic sphere before it really has become a reality in high politics. But the political choices have yet to be made on

6. See Luis M. B. Cabral, *The Economics of Trust and Reputation: A Primer* (New York: New York University, 2005), http://pages.stern.nyu.edu/~lcabral/reputation/Reputation_June05.pdf.

7. See Jens van Scherpenberg and Elke Thiel, eds., *Towards Rival Regionalism? U.S. and EU Regional Regulatory Regime Building* (Baden-Baden: Nomos, 1998).

whether transatlantic relations will be transformed into a different, more balanced institutional bargain, with a strong focus on economic integration, or whether the transatlantic relationship—political as well as economic—will gradually dissolve into a multipolar order.

Cycles of Ambivalence: The Complex Interaction of the American and European Projects

The interaction between political/security relations and economic relations among states as well as the relationship between economic and political (conflicts of) interests have been widely explored in international relations literature in the last decades, as Kathleen McNamara has succinctly outlined in her chapter. Corresponding to the political cycles of the real world, realist theories and liberal internationalist or "democratic peace" theories have experienced their ups and downs in the scholarly "business cycle."

The same applies to economics and to international political economy. Post-Ricardian liberal trade theory, corresponding to liberal internationalism, was increasingly challenged by theories of imperfect competition and especially by Paul Krugman's strategic trade theory.[8] Stimulated by the stunning success of Japan's export-promoting industrial policy, Krugman's theory corresponded well to the resurgence of realism in the study of international relations theory that occurred during the Reagan presidency.

In the 1990s, after the end of the cold war, the United States was rebounding to its former dominant if not hegemonic role in an ever more globalizing world economy, while Japan languished and Europe lost its 1980s single-market dynamic. Accordingly, liberal trade theory took the lead again, as expressed by the "Washington consensus," and liberal internationalism in foreign policy analysis felt vindicated, at the expense of realism, by the strengthening and expansion of U.S.-led Western security and economic institutions.[9]

Why, however, did the upsurge in global and, even more, regional institution-building essentially bypass economic relations between the United States and the EU, despite their high level of market integration and their apparent political closeness? Did realist counterbalancing with a view to potential strategic rivalry prevail over the transatlantic integration initiatives that were tabled in the 1990s?

8. See Paul R. Krugman, ed., *Strategic Trade Policy and the New International Economics* (Cambridge, MA: MIT Press, 1986). For a recent update and further empirical testing, see Joanne Gowa and Edward D. Mansfield, "Alliances, Imperfect Markets, and Major-Power Trade," *International Organization* 58 (Fall 2004): 775–805.

9. See G. John Ikenberry, *After Victory: Institutions, Strategic Restraint, and the Rebuilding of Order after Major Wars* (Princeton: Princeton University Press, 2001), esp. 216–18.

The almost dialectic ambivalence among both U.S. and European political leaders as to the relationship between the European integration project and transatlantic cooperation, from time to time leaning either to the negative or to the positive side, suggests there is no clear-cut answer to these questions. Referring to John Ikenberry's statement in the introduction to this volume about the European and U.S. projects traveling increasingly separate pathways, I argue that European ambivalence to the relationship between the two projects has not yet given way to indifference. The same may be true for the United States. This conclusion hints at a possible transformation of EU-U.S. relations.

Talk of conflict or crisis has accompanied transatlantic relations for most of the six decades since the end of World War II. The cold war, of course, was constitutive for the alliance, but trade conflicts and European animosity toward U.S. economic predominance, initially put aside in light of the strong supportive role the United States played in post–World War II reconstruction, reemerged as soon as the first phase of European reconstruction had come to an end in the early 1960s.

On the European side, the integration process was very much driven by the desire to keep up with U.S. economic performance, in order to maintain some degree of autonomy in shaping European affairs but also to be able to influence the agenda of the Atlantic alliance. For the United States, European integration was part of the "institutional bargain,"[10] the other part of which was NATO. It was mostly welcome, because it strengthened the alliance's European pillar and its self-sustaining capacity, but a degree of ambivalence remained. European economic integration at the expense of U.S. market access was less appreciated; U.S. concerns about a "fortress Europe" have accompanied EU integration policies throughout the last decades. By initiating consecutive General Agreement on Tariffs and Trade (GATT) rounds of trade liberalization, starting with the Kennedy Round in 1964, the United States reacted to progress in European integration—wider or deeper or both—in order to preserve the momentum and attractiveness of the liberal multilateral trade regime, and thus an element of U.S. global economic hegemony, against emerging regional blocks. The last completed trade round, the Uruguay Round, was initiated by the Reagan administration in part as a reaction to the European single-market project. The Reagan era also saw a final display of the postwar institutional bargain, as an assertion of the common security interests toward the Soviet Union overruled economic disputes. The international

10. See G. John Ikenberry, "State Power and the Institutional Bargain: America's Ambivalent Economic and Security Multilateralism," in *U.S. Hegemony and International Organizations: The United States and Multilateral Institutions*, ed. Rosemary Foot, S. Neil MacFarlane, and Michael Mastanduno, 49–70 (Oxford: Oxford University Press, 2003).

monetary adjustment conflict of the mid-1980s was the last one to be solved, although at some cost, by transatlantic policy coordination, leading to the Plaza and Louvre agreements of the Group of Seven (major industrialized countries) in 1985 and 1987.[11]

As the security logic of the Atlantic alliance receded with the end of the cold war, the security-based institutional bargain seemed to have lost its common currency. On the U.S. side, ambivalence toward a stronger but also more assertive European pillar in the alliance gave way to a more skeptical view of European deeper (as opposed to wider) integration, as the bargaining process with Europeans got increasingly tough. The more the EU achieved the status of an "equal power" in foreign economic policy, the more the United States was tempted to resort to its military and technological superiority as the sole superpower.[12] The Balkan War offered the Clinton administration a welcome opportunity for a stark reminder to Europeans that in European (as in any other) security affairs, the United States remained the "indispensable nation." And in the wake of the transatlantic crisis of 2003, U.S. Euro-skepticism culminated in more or less clear hints that a stronger and more deeply integrated Europe may no longer be in U.S. interests and should therefore be opposed.[13]

By his demonstrative rapprochement with the European Union at the beginning of his second term, George W. Bush has moved away again from that stance. However, the prospects for a structural transformation of European-U.S. relations cannot be inferred from diplomatic niceties. Nor will some transatlantic military operations involving NATO indicate more than an unwillingness by both parties to choose between breakdown and transformation.[14] The test case for a successful transformation will be institutionalized relations between the EU and the United States, at the core of which will be economic integration policy.

11. See C. Randall Henning, "Global Economic Adjustment, the Euro Area and the United States," in *Visions of the Atlantic: The United States, the European Union, and NATO,* ed. Simon Serfaty, 152–69, Significant Issues Series 27, no. 8 (Washington, DC: Center for Strategic and International Studies, 2005). Henning has counted five transatlantic adjustment crises since World War II: (1) the breakdown of Bretton Woods in the early 1970s, (2) the conflict over world reflation in 1978, (3) the mid-1980s adjustment crisis triggered by Reagan's "twin deficit," (4) the recession in the early 1990s, and (5) the adjustment dispute that emerged in 2005–6.

12. See C. Fred Bergsten, "America and Europe: Clash of the Titans?" *Foreign Affairs* 78, no. 2 (March–April 1999): 20–34. The military and technological linkage has been addressed already by Keohane, in Robert O. Keohane and Joseph S. Nye, *Power and Interdependence: World Politics in Transition* (Boston: Little, Brown, 1977), 47–49.

13. See Jeffrey L. Cimbalo, "Saving NATO from Europe," *Foreign Affairs* 83, no. 6 (November–December 2004), http://www.foreignaffairs.org/20041101faessay83610/jeffrey-l-cimbalo/saving-nato-from-europe.html?mode=print.

14. See John Ikenberry's introductory chapter in this volume.

Strengthening Transatlantic Economic Institutions: A Futile Endeavor?

There are two approaches to assessing the degree of economic integration be-tween states. Economists primarily look at the level of *market* integration, which can be quantified by the ratio of trade to GDP, the ratio of bilateral trade to overall trade, and the volume of bilateral direct investment and its share of each party's overall inward and outward direct investment. Deep market integration, in terms of trade and even more so of investment links, clearly is a characterizing feature of the Atlantic economic sphere, as McNa-mara shows in her chapter in this volume, referring, among others, to Hamil-ton and Quinlan.

Political scientists would rather focus on the degree of *institutional* integra-tion, which can be described by the number of bilateral economic agreements and by the institutional arrangements to implement those agreements. In this regard the Atlantic economic community has been remarkably deficient, de-spite the integration policy endeavors of the 1990s.

To mitigate the deep impact on transatlantic relations of the Iraq crisis, the United States and the EU leaders at their 2004 bilateral summit in the Irish castle of Dromoland agreed on a major initiative to revive the Atlantic com-munity by giving new impetus to enhanced economic integration. To this pur-pose, both sides resorted to an extensive stakeholder consultation—an idea that relied on Hamilton and Quinlan's adaptation of liberal internationalist theories about the way economic interdependence is influencing foreign pol-icy by stakeholders voicing their interests. That consultation duly produced a long wish list from business organizations and experts. As a result, the EU-U.S. summit of June 20, 2005, in Washington, D.C., endorsed several joint policy declarations. Their central piece is the EU-U.S. "Initiative to Enhance Transatlantic Economic Integration and Growth," supplemented by an ad-dendum on implementation and an inaugural annual report titled "2005 Roadmap for U.S.-EU Regulatory Cooperation."[15]

In substance, however, this new initiative is a modest one, essentially estab-lishing yet another transatlantic regulatory dialogue, the high-level Regula-tory Cooperation Forum, to overcome the barriers to trade in goods, services, and investment owing to the substantial differences in regulatory policies. Moreover, from a European point of view, these dialogues have to be seen in

15. Council of the European Union, EU-U.S. Declaration, "Initiative to Enhance Transat-lantic Economic Integration and Growth," Washington, DC, 20 June 2005, http://www.consilium .europa.eu/ueDocs/cms_Data/docs/pressData/en/er/85383.pdf. For the European position in preparation for the summit, see Commission of the European Communities, "A Stronger EU-U.S. Partnership and a More Open Market for the 21st Century: Communication from the Commission to the Council, the European Parliament and the European Economic and Social Committee," Brussels, 18 May 2005, COM (2005) 196 final.

perspective in that they are part of a wider network of similar dialogues that the EU maintains with Canada, Japan, China, and India. Rather than pointing the way toward a bold new vision for transatlantic relations, this modest approach seems to reflect the futility of earlier attempts to overcome the strong resistance by administrative and regulatory stakeholders on both sides against deeper U.S.-EU economic and regulatory integration.

Since the end of the cold war, deep market integration has encouraged politicians to attribute an ever-greater political role to transatlantic economic relations. The idea must have been that strengthening bilateral economic institutions might make up for the loss of coherence due to the weakening of Atlantic security institutions since 1990. In a way, the goal was nothing less than an attempt at recasting—or transforming—the Western institutional bargain that had shaped the cold war decades.

At first, the initiative came from the American side. Reacting to the then EC's successful single-market program, Robert A. Mosbacher, President George H. W. Bush's first secretary of commerce, in one of his first official speeches in February 1989, asked for a "seat at the table" of EC single-market rule making.[16] The same request was voiced more elegantly by Secretary of State James Baker, in his famous Berlin speech of December 12, 1989, one month after the fall of the Berlin wall.[17] His proposal for a new Atlantic architecture in which transatlantic relations would keep pace with European integration was substantiated by the joint U.S.-EC Transatlantic Declaration of February 27, 1990. Characteristically, at the end of the cold war it was the United States that demanded stronger institutional links for the transatlantic economy. When George H. W. Bush, for whom a strong Atlantic alliance transatlantic coalition was the very basis of a new world order, was voted out of office, that momentum died out on the U.S. side. His successor, Bill Clinton, was highly focused on reestablishing the predominance of the U.S. economy: getting the North American Free Trade Agreement (NAFTA) ratified in Congress, promoting Asian-Pacific economic integration through the Asia-Pacific Economic Cooperation (APEC) process as well as Pan-American regional economic integration through the Free Trade Area of the Americas (FTAA) initiative, and in the process getting the EU to agree to a strengthened multilateral trade order. In line with this position, contrary to the essentially bilateral institutional base of the security alliance, the multilateral WTO actually remained the United States' favored institution to deal with transatlantic economic relations.

16. Remarks of Secretary of Commerce Robert Mosbacher, Columbia Institute Conference on Europe 1992, Washington, DC, 24 February 1989, http://www.findarticles.com/p/articles/mi_m1052/is_n5_v110/ai_7430187/pg_1.

17. James Baker, "A New Europe, A New Atlanticism: Architecture for a New Era," U.S. Department of State, Current Policy, no. 1233, 12 December 1989.

The role of demandeur for stronger bilateral transatlantic economic institutional links, therefore, shifted to Europe.[18] In 1995, German foreign minister Klaus Kinkel, building on the mostly inconsequential Transatlantic Declaration and supported by his British colleague, adopted the idea of a Transatlantic Free Trade Area (TAFTA), which had initially been proposed by the Canadian minister of international trade, Roy MacLaren. This association would compensate for the loss of identity suffered by the alliance in issues of foreign and security policy and give Atlantic economic relations a new dynamic.[19]

Among most economists and economic policy actors, skepticism prevailed.[20] They understood that the attempts to significantly improve the conditions of market access by means of negative integration—simply and merely doing away with trade barriers—would inevitably lead to positive integration in Tinbergen's sense of the term, that is, to the development of shared political norms, standards, and other regulations governing the trade in goods and services.[21] To engage in the cumbersome effort of positive integration policies, in the North Atlantic economic area, with its highly diverse and entrenched regulatory cultures,[22] was seen by many as a fruitless political nightmare, the more so when compared to potential welfare gains from regional trade liberalization and integration with Asia or Latin America.

18. The account that follows is as short as possible, referring only to the important milestones, subject to developments in the Euro-American balance of power, in this dialogue process. For a full account, see most recently Rebecca Steffenson, *Managing EU-U.S. Relations: Actors, Institutions and the New Transatlantic Agenda* (Manchester: Manchester University Press, 2005).

19. See Brian Hindley, "New Institutions for Transatlantic Trade?" *International Affairs* 75, no. 1 (January 1999): 45–60, on the formation of the TAFTA recommendations. For an assessment of the TAFTA proposals in the context of trade ratios between the United States and the EU, see Youri Devuyst, *Transatlantic Trade Policy: U.S. Market Opening Strategies*, Policy Paper Series (Pittsburgh: University of Pittsburgh Press, 1995), http://www.ucis.pitt.edu/cwes/papers/poli<->series/transatl_trade_policy.pdf.

The TAFTA acronym, used to this day as a shorthand term for far-reaching transatlantic integration proposals, since 2005 has stood for an existing free trade agreement, the Thailand–Australia Free Trade Agreement, which became operational on 1 January 2005.

20. See Horst Siebert, Rolf J. Langhammer, and Daniel Piazolo, "The Transatlantic Free Trade Area: Fuelling Trade Discrimination or Global Liberalization?" *Journal of World Trade* 30, no. 3 (1996): 45–61. For a more recent economic assessment of the TAFTA concept, see Rolf J. Langhammer, Daniel Piazolo, and Horst Siebert, "Assessing Proposals for a Transatlantic Free Trade Area," *Aussenwirtschaft* 57, no. 2 (2002): 161–85; Horst Siebert, *TAFTA—A Dead Horse or an Attractive Open Club?* Kiel Working Paper No. 1240, Kiel Institute for World Economics, March 2005, http://www.uni<->kiel.de/ifw/pub/kap/2005/kap1240.pdf.

21. Jan Tinbergen, *International Economic Integration*, 2nd ed. (Amsterdam: Elsevier, 1965).

22. See Stephen Woolcock, "European and North American Approaches to Regulation: Continued Divergence?" in van Scherpenberg and Thiel, *Towards Rival Regionalism?* 257–76.

Accordingly, the glue-seeking process of the early 1990s resulted in little more than a diplomatic fig leaf to hide the failure to achieve consensus on a more far-reaching vision of transatlantic integration. The New Transatlantic Agenda (NTA) and the Joint EU-U.S. Action Plan of December 1995 provided for the setting up of a number of governmental and nongovernmental dialogues.[23] First among them was the biannual EU-U.S. summit, to facilitate the dismantling of trade and investment barriers and to strengthen cooperation in, among other things, government contracts, information services, and competition policy, and through mutual recognition of standards and certifications. A mutual recognition agreement (MRA), which covered six product groups, was signed in 1997 and came into force on December 1, 1998, but its implementation dragged on for many years.[24]

In March 1998, the EU Commission put forward a proposal for a comprehensive New Transatlantic Marketplace Agreement (NTMA), which was to facilitate the realization of the new transatlantic marketplace. It sought to draw on experiences made in the context of the single-market project and to transfer these to the transatlantic economic area,[25] but the agreement did not make it past the Council of Ministers. Interest in transatlantic integration, notably low among the Americans anyway, began to dwindle among EU members. A far more modest document for a Transatlantic Economic Partnership (TEP) was agreed upon in November 1998, and concrete outcomes have, as was to be expected, remained scant and limited to two more MRAs.[26]

23. New Transatlantic Agenda, http://www.eurunion.org/partner/agenda.htm; Joint EU-U.S. Action Plan, http://www.eurunion.org/partner/actplan.htm.

24. The agreements do not, as in the EU, envisage mutual recognition of each other's product norms and standards as equivalent. Rather, these agreements should allow officially accredited certification bodies in the exporting country to certify the conformity of goods with the standards of the country for which they are bound, making sure that the test procedures and certification of conformity be recognized and accepted by the importing country. In the MRA of 1997, it was agreed that this procedure be adopted for standards governing telecommunications, medical equipment, electromagnetic compatibility, electrical safety, pleasure boats, and pharmaceuticals. See the text of the agreement: http://trade-info.cec.eu.int/tbt/documents/oth _42_oth_40_1.pdf. For the significance and problems of the Euro-American MRA, see also Steffenson, *Managing EU-U.S. Relations*, 123.

25. "The New Transatlantic Marketplace," communication of Sir Leon Brittan, Mr. Bangemann, and Mr. Monti, 11 March 1998, http://www.eurunion.org/partner/ntm/contents.htm.

26. "Transatlantic Economic Partnership: Action Plan," 9 November 1998, http://ec.europa .eu/comm/external_relations/us/economic_partnership/trans_econ_partner_11_98.htm. For a generally highly positive and optimistic collection of analyses of the NTA and TEP processes, see Mark A. Pollack and Gregory C. Shaffer, eds., *Transatlantic Governance in a Global Economy* (Lanham, MD: Rowman and Littlefield, 2001). The agreements on marine equipment of 27 February 2004 and the agreement on the reciprocal recognition of the professional qualification of architects of 18 November 2005 have come into force. For a collection of predominantly favorable analyses of the NTA and TEP processes, see Pollack and Shaffer, *Transatlantic Governance*.

The fate of the most promising and well meaning of those glue institutions of the 1990s, the Transatlantic Business Dialogue (TABD), underscores this skeptical assessment. The TABD was established as a transatlantic forum of business leaders in which the EU Commission and the U.S. Department of Commerce were to participate. Modeled after the European Business Roundtable of the early 1980s, which contributed significantly toward the momentum for the "Europe 1992" single-market project, the TABD was to identify political and regulatory impediments to transatlantic business and make recommendations on how to address them. It did so in a number of remarkable reports.[27] In the end, however, the responsiveness of policymakers remained far below expectations, and the substantial momentum of the TABD process was allowed to peter out until it was revived in 2004.[28]

Indeed, for lack of economic or political incentives, the whole idea of transatlantic integration policy fell out of fashion in the boom years of the late 1990s. Ever-deeper transatlantic *market* integration was evolving, despite only scant progress of institutional integration, not least through tremendous increases of transatlantic investment flows, especially from East to West. This movement was to some degree supported by negative integration—that is, the removal of impediments to trade—as long as it took place in the GATT/WTO context. But when countries moved beyond the level of WTO agreements, agreement on positive integration—that is, on common policies needed to further facilitate transatlantic trade and investment, such as mutual recognition agreements on product standards—proved virtually impossible. Even at the global level and even in cases in which refusal to commit to positive integration carries long-term competitive disadvantages such as in the field of international norms and standards, the United States has been extremely hesitant.[29]

As of May 2006, the EU Council listed thirty-four bilateral U.S.-EU agreements, most of which fall into the category of negative integration. Only two of the thirty-four cover "strategic" areas of transatlantic trade and technology relations: the bilateral agreement of 1992, which, on the basis of the 1979 GATT agreement on trade in civil aircraft, regulated the trade in large civil aircraft between the only two GATT members manufacturing them, and the agreement reached in 2004 on satellite navigation systems dealing with certain conflicting aspects of the American Global Positioning System (GPS) and the

27. See Maria Green Cowles, "The Transatlantic Business Dialogue: Transforming the New Transatlantic Agenda," in Pollack and Shaffer, *Transatlantic Governance*, 213–33.

28. An analysis of the TABD declarations of Cincinnati (2000), Brussels (2001), and Chicago (2002) shows increasing resignation as a result of the inactivity and disinterest by government and in light of the implementation problems—problems that affected even agreements already concluded such as the MRA of 1997.

29. See Tim Büthe and Jan Martin Witte, *Product Standards in Transatlantic Trade and Investment*, AICGS Policy Report 13 (Washington, DC: American Institute for Contemporary German Studies, 2004).

European Galileo systems.[30] The first agreement was terminated by the United States in October 2004; the second is considered more of a preliminary ministerial consensus on a still contentious bilateral issue with significant conflict potential. All this is hardly an encouraging backdrop for the initiative of June 2005.

Deep Market Integration: Strong Enough Glue?

Should we then be content with transatlantic market integration as a sufficient glue, renouncing for good any attempts at "positive" policy integration? Or, on the contrary, is the United States' ambivalence about committing itself in transatlantic institutions[31]—by supporting security institutions, which it can dominate, and rejecting bilateral economic institutions, in which it would be one of two equal players—an essential structural weakness that allows for the buildup of conflict?

To underscore the primacy of the transatlantic economy, Hamilton and Quinlan assemble almost every piece of statistical evidence that somehow fits with their conclusion on the "glue" or "tie" role of economic relations.[32] Accordingly, politicians and government officials on both sides frequently quote them. But they have also become a point of referral for liberal internationalist writers on transatlantic economic interdependence.[33]

The authors' original approach consists in moving beyond the usual rehearsal of the substantial and essentially balanced bilateral trade or investment

30. "Bilateral Agreement of 1992: Agreements between the European Economic Community (EEC) and the United States Government on the Application of the GATT Rules on the Trade in Passenger Aircraft to the Trade in Large Passenger Aircraft," *Official Journal of the EU*, no. L 301, 17 October 1992, 31–39. The agreement bans production and marketing subsidies and caps direct development subsidies to 33 percent of the development costs. Indirect subsidies, e.g., through government-funded research programs, are capped at 3 percent of total turnover in passenger aircraft manufacturing. Satellite navigation systems agreement of 2004: Agreement on the Promotion, Provision, and Use of Galileo and GPS Satellite-Based Navigation Systems and Related Applications, 21 June 2004, http://ec.europa.eu/dgs/energy_transport/galileo/documents/doc/2004_06_21_summit_2004_en.pdf.

The remaining 32 bilateral U.S.-EU agreements listed by the EU Council include the NTA as well as the following: 3 are the MRA mentioned; 2 deal with market access to government contracts; 2 deal with cooperation on issues of economic policy; 13 deal with predominantly GATT-related trade issues; 6 with cooperation in the fields of science and technology as well as environmental and health issues; and 5 with cooperation in legal matters and questions of internal security.

31. See Ikenberry, "State Power and the Institutional Bargain."

32. "The ties that bind" is the metaphor preferred in Hamilton and Quinlan, *Partners in Prosperity*, 21ff. See also Johannes F. Linn, "Europe and America: The Economic Ties That Bind," *Current History*, November 2004, 370–75.

33. See Philip H. Gordon, "The Dog That Has Not Barked," *E! Sharp*, May–June 2005, http://www.brook.edu/dybdocroot/views/articles/gordon/20050504.pdf; Linn, "Trends and Prospects."

flows as such and their dominant role in each side's foreign trade and investment, compared to U.S. and EU trade with other countries or regions. They attempt to uncover the "deep structures" of economic relations by pointing at

- the high stock of transatlantic investment, which generates almost 50 percent of U.S. capital income from foreign direct investment (FDI);
- the massive transatlantic intrafirm or related-party trade, accounting for roughly half of bilateral trade, which is almost impervious to exchange rate changes; and
- the enormous amount of foreign affiliate sales—four times that of bilateral trade.

Their conclusion as to "deep structures," however, comes with a number of minor and a few major methodological flaws. From a business point of view, for instance, two of the main motives for FDI—gaining market access and ensuring against the impact of currency changes—relate to a lack of integration rather than being proof of deep integration. Regional integration areas such as the EU—and to a lesser degree also the NAFTA—reduce these incentives for FDI as they facilitate trade.

Moreover, FDI via mergers and acquisitions often meets with strong political objections, based on economic nationalist positions. Inward direct investment in certain industries, the proponents of such objections argue, may pillage financial assets (see the German "locust" debate) or hand over control of vital strategic industries and technologies to foreign ownership. Outward investment may easily face similar objections: it could lead to technology transfer into countries that may use it to challenge the home country's economic, technological, or even military superiority. These objections carry as much weight in the United States as they do in Europe.[34] The issue is addressed in the subsequent section.

Finally, with regard to foreign affiliate sales, Hamilton and Quinlan observe that "it remains largely invisible to policymakers on both sides of the Atlantic"[35]—something they want to change. But the "political invisibility" of foreign affiliate sales might as well relate to the fact that they really do not matter politically. Trade relations involve continuous policy choices, although mitigated by WTO rules that directly affect domestic constituencies. Even inward, FDI, although essentially a matter of property rights that are protected by the rule of

34. The U.S. government and Congress have given themselves wide discretion in ruling whether a specific foreign takeover of a U.S. firm violates U.S. national security interests. Most major European states, among them Britain, France, Italy, and most recently also Germany, have laws and procedures in place to preclude unwanted foreign control of core national technological assets, especially those with a potential defense use.

35. Hamilton and Quinlan, *Partners in Prosperity*, 22.

law, has more political visibility than foreign affiliate sales. Legally, politically, and publicly the latter are essentially treated the same as sales by locally owned firms, except for some rare protests and boycott calls against some major foreign brands that are deemed particularly representative of their home country.

There is, however, a more fundamental methodical flaw in applying the stakeholder argument to a bilateral economic relationship such as the transatlantic one in a time of ever more diversified global economic links. In doing so one must demonstrate the uniqueness or clear preponderance of that relationship as compared to the stakes, which the economic actors on each side are holding in other countries, such as, for example, China and India. Otherwise, the relative weight of the transatlantic stakes could diminish, resulting in possibly awkward political choices if major conflicts of interest arise between doing business in the United States and doing business elsewhere, due to foreign policy divergences.

Does the authors' assertion of the uniqueness or primacy of transatlantic economic relations hold? Looking at the trade figures, I have doubts. To support their argument the authors rely on selective use of data, mostly avoiding longer-term time series whose trends tell a different story.

Transatlantic trade relations, while strong, have evolved a lot less dynamically than have U.S. and EU trade with China, or U.S. trade with the other NAFTA countries, Canada and Mexico. In 1990 both EU and U.S. trade with China (i.e., imports as well as exports) were only roughly 10 percent of transatlantic trade. Transatlantic trade for both the United States and the EU was five times their respective trade with China.[36] In 2005, this ratio had risen to 58 percent for the United States and 50 percent for the EU. The share of U.S. exports to the EU declined from 26 percent (1990) to 21 percent (2005) of U.S. overall exports, while during the same period the export share going to NAFTA increased from 28 percent to 37 percent. EU exports to the United States increased slightly from 21 percent (1990) to 24 percent (2005) of overall extra-EU exports. The U.S. share of EU imports, however, fell from 20 percent (1990) to 14 percent (2004), while the EU share of the U.S. import market remained almost static at 18.4 percent (it had been 20 percent in 1990).

As the NAFTA data demonstrate—and data from other U.S. and EU regional integration agreements mostly confirm this point—it is not just the rise of China as a major trading power that shifts weights in the world economy. The story is also one of regionalism against multilateralism.

Both the EU and the United States have engaged in multiple regional trade agreements (RTAs), the latter with more vigor in recent years than the former. Whereas the multilateral trade system has increasingly moved away from a hegemonic regime under de facto co-leadership of the United States and the EU, RTAs involving the United States or the EU, by the sheer economic gravity

36. EU trade data presented here refer to the EU-15.

of the integrating power's domestic market,[37] still are essentially hegemonic, the more so when they are of the hub-and-spoke type: bilateral RTAs of a dominant integrator with several other countries. The hegemonic power, if it wants to, can use RTAs to promote positive integration on its own terms, thus expanding its own regulatory system beyond its borders. Even if they do not take into account the foreign policy impact, such regional spheres of positive integration can bring about rival regionalism among regional hegemons, as indeed has been happening to some extent between the United States and the EU in recent years, especially with regard to Western Hemisphere RTAs.[38]

In principle, of course, regional economic integration policies by the United States and the EU do not just promote rivalry. By bringing more modern and effective regulatory rules to other countries through positive integration, these policies can promote global regulatory convergence. However, as long as progress toward transatlantic regulatory convergence is as slow as it has been, prospects for such positive global effects of RTAs look dim.

Liberal internationalists, therefore, may want to have a more sober look at the underlying trends. They might take a cue from Princeton economist Peter Kenen, a skeptical liberal economist who simply looks at the dynamics of the numbers in a global context. To him, they do not look too auspicious for transatlantic economic relations to carry much weight in binding together the alliance.[39]

Strategic Economic Conflicts in European-U.S. Relations

Do transatlantic economic conflicts provide a hint as to the "deepness" of the transatlantic rift? Not easily. Trade policy disputes are mostly dealt with by the comprehensive set of rules embodied in the various WTO agreements.

37. Jens van Scherpenberg, "Whither Euro-American Leadership in the WTO, Intereconomics," *Review of European Economic Policy* 38, no. 5 (September–October 2003): 235–37. For the gravity approach to regional economic integration, see Jeffrey A. Frankel, *Regional Trading Blocs in the World Economic System* (Washington, DC: Institute for International Economics, 1997).

38. When the main protagonist of U.S. regional economic integration policy in recent years, former U.S. trade representative Robert Zoellick, adopted the phrase "competitive trade liberalization" from C. Fred Bergsten, "Globalizing Free Trade: The Ascent of Liberalism," *Foreign Affairs* 75, no. 3 (May–June 1996): 105–20, he made it clear that this policy was primarily aimed at supporting wider U.S. foreign policy goals. For an assessment, see Jeffrey J. Schott, "Assessing U.S. FTA Policy," in *Free Trade Agreements: U.S. Strategies and Priorities*, ed. J. Schott, 359–82 (Washington, DC: Institute for International Economics, 2004).

In the recent transatlantic foreign policy conflict over Iraq, however, regional integration or the prospects of an RTA have not prevented disagreement between the United States and some of its RTA partners (Canada, Mexico, Chile) as well as between the main continental European EU members and some new or aspiring members such as Poland or Bulgaria and Romania.

See the contributions in van Scherpenberg and Thiel, *Towards Rival Regionalism?*

39. Peter B. Kenen, "Transatlantic Relations and the Global Economy," *North American Journal of Economics and Finance* 15 (2004): 149–59.

Handling and settling them on the basis of existing trade law, therefore, is primarily a task for trade lawyers.[40] Actually, nearly 20 percent of all cases dealt with through the WTO dispute settlement mechanism originate in disputes between the United States and the EU. Adding up the major U.S.-EU trade disputes by value, economists Gary Hufbauer and Frederic Neumann estimate that these conflicts refer to 5.4 percent of U.S. exports to the EU and 5.1 percent of EU exports to the United States.[41] Keeping Philip Gordon's remark in mind that "margins can be pretty important," these percentages are not trivial.[42] But despite their high political visibility, these conflicts are no indicator of a fundamental crisis of economic relations, the more since neither side has questioned the legitimacy of WTO dispute settlement rulings.

There are, however, conflicts that fall outside WTO rules and thus have to be dealt with bilaterally. To assess the relevance of transatlantic economic conflicts as indicators of deeper structural ruptures in transatlantic relations, I suggest distinguishing two categories of conflicts derived from international political economy: commercial conflicts and strategic economic conflicts.

Commercial conflicts are the result of a domestic policy making process in which specific domestic special economic interest groups prevail over other groups. The conflicts' outcome, in an economic liberalist understanding, would be the result of a public choice decision based on domestic welfare maximization. Strategic economic conflicts are best explained by means of the economic nationalist or realist paradigm. Domestic economic interest groups play a minor role if any, while policy making is dominated by long-term strategic or national security considerations. Of course, the distinction between those two categories will never be clear-cut, because the political weighting will but gradually shift from one to the other. To illustrate, figure 6.1 depicts various transatlantic trade disputes of recent years as well as areas of economic conflict; the x axis represents the commercial value of the conflict, and the y axis represents the conflict's national security relevance. Commercial conflicts have their place in the lower half (quadrants II and III), whereas strategic economic conflicts are found in the upper half (quadrants I and IV). Conflicts in the left half carry less material (commercial) weight than do those in the right half, although they still may occupy a disproportionately high spot on the transatlantic political agenda for symbolical reasons.

40. See Ernst-Ulrich Petersmann and Mark E. Pollack, eds., *Transatlantic Economic Disputes: The EU, the U.S., and the WTO* (Oxford: Oxford University Press, 2004). Most of the contributors to the volume are indeed trade lawyers from government, academia, and private law firms.

41. Gary Clyde Hufbauer and Frederic Neumann, "U.S.-EU Trade and Investment: An American Perspective," paper presented at the conference Transatlantic Perspectives on the U.S. and European Economies: Convergence, Conflict and Cooperation, John F. Kennedy School of Government, Harvard University, 11–12 April 2002; http://www.iie.com/publications/papers/paper.cfm?ResearchID=460.

42. See Gordon, "Dog That Has Not Barked."

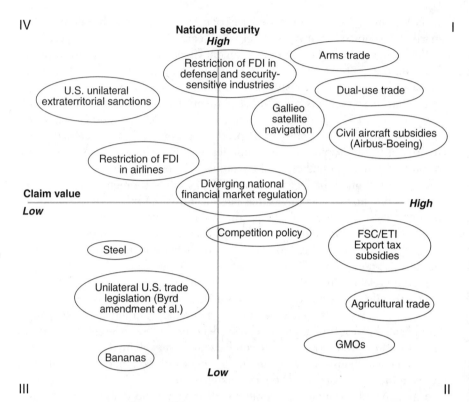

Figure 6.1. Recent transatlantic trade disputes and areas of economic conflict. FDI, foreign direct investment; FSC/ETI, U.S. export tax subsidies regime; GMO, genetically modified organism. Estimated dollar values determining the *x*-axis positions may be available in some cases; the values in this graph are a rough and mostly intuitive estimate. The *y* values (national security relevance) must remain intuitive ones based on the legal foundations of the respective issues and on their political profile, as estimated from the political attention they receive. Indicators may be, for instance, the involvement of the Department of Defense and the State Department, the invoking of the Exxon-Florio Act to assess the national security impact of inward foreign direct investment projects, the invoking of other vetting legislation, or the involvement of the U.S. Congress on national security grounds.

Typically, most conflicts in the lower half can be dealt with in the WTO context. If WTO rules do not apply (such as in competition policy), conflicts are dealt with bilaterally. Most of the conflicts in the upper half, because of their national security dimension, fall under the GATT article 21 exception.[43] Therefore they require bilateral solutions. These are the more difficult to reach, the higher the commercial stakes. It is therefore the quadrant I conflicts that I call

43. As to Helms-Burton, the EU initially decided to submit the case to the WTO's Dispute Settlement Body rule. The United States, however, warned that it would invoke the article 21 exception clause in that case, which probably would have put the WTO system under extreme

major strategic economic conflicts in transatlantic relations, whereas the high-profile commercial disputes are grouped in quadrant II.

Strategic conflicts, in this context, are defined as those conflicts that touch directly on matters of national security and defense, or that arise from economic nationalism as expressed through a mercantilist trade policy or through restrictions on foreign direct investment,[44] or that originate in industrial policies aimed at harnessing the positive externalities that are expected for the national economy, for example, from mastering certain advanced technologies of high commercial significance. In all three cases, the role played by domestic interest groups, though not unimportant, is a secondary one. Such conflicts confute the logic of institution building, as Steffenson admits: "no amount of dialogue will eliminate conflict rooted in deep political interest."[45]

The whole field of quadrant I strategic conflicts goes to the heart of what has increasingly strained transatlantic relations since the end of the cold war, as I show by briefly analyzing some major conflicts in this area: the Airbus-Boeing subsidies conflict, the dispute over satellite navigation, disagreements involving the technology trade with China, and economic sanctions disputes. A brief look at the one sector in which push comes to shove in European-U.S. economic relations—transatlantic defense relations—concludes this section.

Strategic Technologies

The Airbus-Boeing conflict over launch subsidies and government-backed loans to manufacturers of large civil aircraft—of which but two, the European Airbus SAS and the American Boeing Company, have remained in the Atlantic economy—straddles several conflict levels. At first sight, it looks like a normal trade dispute about distortion of competition through subsidies, similar—and indeed related[46]—to the dispute about the U.S. export tax subsidies regime (FSC/ETI). But the dispute also involves a core strategic industry that procures for a huge global market, with revenue estimated in trillions of dollars over the midterm. As such, it generates substantial technological as well as macroeconomic externalities for the respective economies. And finally,

---

stress since invoking article 21 with regard to Cuba would have opened the door to an inflationary use of the national security exception. Both sides, therefore, agreed on a face-saving compromise. For an analysis of the conflict and of how it was precariously defused, see Hugo Paemen, "Avoidance and Settlement of 'High Policy Disputes': Lessons from the Dispute over 'The Cuban Liberty and Democratic Solidarity Act,' " in Petersmann and Pollack, *Transatlantic Economic Disputes*, 361–70.

44. See Jens van Scherpenberg, *Economic Nationalism on the Rise: Foreign Direct Investment in the USA after the Dubai Fiasco*, SWP Comment 10 (March 2006) (Berlin: Stiftung Wissenschaft und Politik, 2006).

45. Steffenson, *Managing EU-U.S. Relations*, 63.

46. Boeing has been one of the major beneficiaries of export tax subsidies under Foreign Sales Corporation (FSC) legislation and subsequently Extraterritorial Income (ETI) legislation.

the dispute touches on the commercial profitability and technological performance of the aerospace industry in the United States and Europe as the most important segment of the defense industry. Therefore, any analysis focusing primarily on its trade aspects would miss the point, especially since it would fail to explain why in this particular conflict a working bilateral regime that was to deal with the trade distortion issue has broken down, making the dispute an exemplary case of a trade conflict that is about to be transformed into a high politics conflict.[47]

From its beginning in 1970, the Airbus project was at least as much driven by political motives as by commercial ones. When the then U.S. manufacturers of large passenger aircraft—Boeing, McDonnell Douglas, and Lockheed—introduced long-distance wide-bodied aircraft,[48] the remaining European firms faced being squeezed out of civil aircraft manufacturing. The huge investment costs required to enter the market combined with the enormous economies of scale and scope enjoyed by the U.S. aircraft industry, not least from its huge defense business,[49] acted as major impediments for any newcomer. The international market for passenger aircraft was about to become a U.S. monopoly. To prevent this from happening, the major European governments made available to Airbus the funds needed to overcome its initial competitive disadvantage, allowing it to catch up in static economies of scale and scope as well as to master the learning curve in aircraft manufacturing. Accordingly, during its first two decades, the Airbus venture was widely covered in the economic academic literature as "the world's largest example of strategic trade policy."[50] In strategic trade theory, the "strategic" objective of states is economic welfare maximization by industrial policy, especially with regard to high-technology industries, and in the process subsidizing domestic firms to become competitive in global markets. The economic rationale is to overcome market failure by paying high-technology firms for the positive externalities that they create—for example, through technology spillover and diffusion.[51]

47. The following analysis draws on my essay in Nicolas Hausséguy, *The Airbus-Boeing Dispute: Not for the WTO to Solve*, SWP Comment 30-2005 (Berlin: Stiftung Wissenschaft und Politik, 2005), http://www.swp-berlin.org/common/get_document.php?id=1327.

48. Boeing's B747 entered service in 1968, Lockheed's TriStar and McDonnell Douglas's DC10 in 1970.

49. See Philip K. Lawrence and Derek Braddon, *Aerospace Strategic Trade: How the U.S. Subsidizes the Large Commercial Aircraft Industry* (Aldershot, U.K.: Ashgate, 2001).

50. Paul R. Krugman and Maurice Obstfeld, *International Economics: Theory and Policy*, 5th ed. (Reading, MA: Addison-Wesley, 2000), 275–96, 291. See also Richard Baldwin and Paul Krugman, "Industrial Policy and International Competition in Wide-Bodied Jet Aircraft," in *Trade Policy Issues and Empirical Analysis*, ed. Richard Baldwin, 45–78 (Chicago: University of Chicago Press, 1988); Laura d'Andrea Tyson, *Who's Bashing Whom? Trade Conflict in High-Technology Industries* (Washington, DC: Institute for International Economics, 1992), 155–216.

51. See Krugman and Obstfeld, *International Economics*, 280ff.

In accordance with the cold war institutional bargain, the United States initially addressed the transatlantic civil aircraft subsidies conflict by means of traditional trade policy. A plurilateral Agreement on Trade in Civil Aircraft (ATCA), concluded within the GATT context in 1979, became a major success story in removing barriers to trade in civil aircraft and aircraft-related subsystems and components.[52] On the matter of subsidies, however, ATCA remained vague and unenforceable. In 1992, the bilateral U.S.-EU Agreement on Trade in Large Civil Aircraft (ATLCA) addressed these shortcomings, capping direct and indirect subsidies for both sides, and established a working bilateral regime, with which both sides complied.

In October 2004, however, the U.S. government terminated ATLCA and filed a case with the WTO for violation of the GATT/WTO Agreement on Subsidies and Countervailing Measures (SCM) of 1994; the EU responded by filing a reciprocal case against U.S. subsidies for Boeing on the same grounds. The obvious reason for the U.S. decision was the remarkable commercial success of Airbus in the years up to 2004. The European manufacturer not only gained market share at the expense of Boeing, but its new A380 superlarge aircraft ended the monopoly Boeing had enjoyed with the B747 in that market segment. The profitability of the U.S. firm's civilian business, therefore, hinged on the commercial success of its newest model, the B787. By terminating the agreement, the U.S. government aimed at preventing Airbus from endangering the latter project by bringing its competing model A350 early to market.

After failed bilateral consultations, in May 2005 both sides requested the establishment of dispute settlement panels with the WTO.[53] Although both may prevail in their respective cases, they will effectively neutralize one other if authorized to implement trade retaliations against each other.[54] The WTO dispute settlement, however, may not only be ineffective in solving this conflict. It may also be severely damaged by being used in a dispute that is essentially a bilateral one, reaching far beyond the WTO's institutional scope into transatlantic strategic competition of defense-related industries.[55]

A direct link to the defense sector has already been made, given that EADS, in a consortium led by Northrop Grumman, intends to submit a bid,

---

52. See Richard Aboulafia, "Commercial Aerospace and the Transatlantic Economy," in Hamilton and Quinlan, *Deep Integration*, 74–90.

53. The panels for the two cases, DS316 and DS317m, were established on 20 July 2005.

54. A precedent to such outcome has been set by the Canadian-Brazilian trade conflict over subsidies to their respective manufacturers of small regional passenger aircraft, Bombardier and Embraer. Both sides prevailed in their cases but refrained from imposing trade retaliation.

55. Philip K. Lawrence and Paul G. Dowdall, "Strategic Trade in Commercial-Class Aircraft: Europe v. America," Royal Institute for International Affairs Discussion Paper 78, London (RIIA), August 1998. Lawrence and Dowdall use the term "military industrial policy."

based on its A330 plane, for a refurbishing of the U.S. Air Force tanker fleet. The tender confronts the U.S. administration with a stark choice between competitive dual sourcing of its tanker fleet and strengthening transatlantic defense industrial relations on the one hand and exacerbating a major strategic trade conflict with the EU on the other. Given the paramount role of the defense sector in U.S. foreign and security policy, the second alternative is likely to prevail.

The paradigmatic character of the Airbus-Boeing conflict has been emphasized recently by another transatlantic dispute, in the area of industrial and technology policy, concerning high-precision satellite navigation.[56] The joint EU-ESA (European Space Agency) European satellite navigation venture, initially known by the acronym Galileo, was launched in 1999 and is projected to be operational by 2011, competing with the United States' Global Positioning System.[57] It reemphasizes European determination to achieve independent technology capabilities in areas deemed of major importance commercially as well as for defense. The Galileo system is expected to generate substantial direct revenues from licenses and services but also to spawn a whole range of new service industries. Galileo can also be used for military purposes that require precision location and navigation.[58] A U.S.-EU agreement at the bilateral Dromoland Castle summit of June 2004 has allayed some U.S. concerns about frequency overlap and interference.[59] But the dual-use characteristics of Galileo continue to act as an irritant in transatlantic relations, the more since, following an EU-Chinese agreement, Galileo is being developed with substantial Chinese financial and technical participation.[60]

---

56. For an analysis of the parallels between the Airbus and Galileo ventures and their transatlantic contentiousness, see Sorin Lungu, "Power, Techno-Economics and Transatlantic Relations in 1987–1999: The Case of Airbus Industry and Galileo," *Comparative Strategy* 23 (October–December 2004): 369–89.

57. ESA has seventeen members, consisting of the EU-15 plus Norway and Switzerland. The first approval of the program by the EU and ESA occurred in 1999. The formal launch of the development phase, including a first installment of funding, was approved by the European Council of Transport Ministers in March 2002. See Gustav Lindström with Giovanni Gasparini, "The Galileo Satellite System and Its Security Implications," Occasional Paper 44, European Union Institute for Security Studies, Paris, April 2003, http://www.iss-eu.org/occasion/occ44.pdf.

58. Ibid.

59. Agreement on the Promotion, Provision, and Use of Galileo and GPS Satellite-Based Navigation Systems and Related Applications, concluded 26 June 2004. The agreement mostly settles a dispute about frequencies used by GPS and Galileo. Although ratification is still pending in some EU countries at the time of this writing, the agreement is being applied provisionally.

60. See John J. Tkacik and Neil Gardiner, "Blair Could Make a Strategic Error on China," Backgrounder, no. 1768, Heritage Foundation, Washington, DC, 7 June 2004, http://www.heritage.org/Research/AsiaandthePacific/loader.cfm?url=/commonspot/security/getfile.cfm&PageID=64508.

The China Arms Embargo: Scope and Limits
of U.S. Leverage on Europe

The most recent strategic U.S.-EU conflict has erupted over EU relations with China. It was triggered in the second half of 2004 when, despite earlier concerns to which it had given voice, the United States realized that the EU was moving forward to lift its 1989 arms export embargo of China.

Although the Airbus-Boeing dispute at first sight looks like a normal trade conflict, which, as has been shown, it is not, the transatlantic conflict over the lifting of the EU arms embargo at first sight looks like a conflict between U.S. global security responsibilities and European greed-driven free riding, which it is not. There is a distinct wider foreign policy as well as an economic dimension to it. Moreover it has become an interesting test case for U.S. economic leverage over Europe in cases of conflict.

Should the EU eventually lift its arms embargo against China, it will do so not just to profit from business opportunities in the Chinese market but because it is implementing a distinct China policy of its own. After strong pressure from the United States, initial European willingness to lift the embargo on the cheap waned. Meanwhile, the EU has clearly spelled out the conditions China must meet for the embargo to be lifted: ratify the UN Covenant on Civil and Political Rights; release all Tiananmen protesters who are still imprisoned; and terminate the policy of confinement without trial in forced labor camps. Lacking among these, however, is the one condition that matters most to the United States—and the one that China is most unlikely to meet: become a responsible international actor by submitting to the U.S.-led international order. Indeed, at the core of the conflict lies the fact that Europe, because it does not share in the United States' role as the world's leading power, does not share the U.S. perception of China as a potential threat to that role.[61]

By doing away with the last elements of special treatment of China as a semirogue state that can claim less respect than "normal" responsible nations, Europe aims at engaging with China as a major actor in an increasingly multipolar world. Thus, on the occasion of the arms embargo dispute, and to the sudden irritation of many in the current U.S. policy establishment,[62] the United States has had to discover that Europe has started to pursue a distinct foreign policy of its own, diverging from U.S. interests, far beyond its hitherto regional limits.

Consequently, the economic dimension of the conflict equally points straight to core security policy issues. European trade with China is much more

61. See Bates Gill and Gudrun Wacker, eds., *China's Rise: Diverging U.S.-EU Perceptions and Approaches* (Berlin: Stiftung Wissenschaft und Politik, 2005), http://www.swp-berlin.org/common/get_document.php?id=1379.

62. See David Shambaugh, "The New Strategic Triangle: U.S. and European Reactions to China's Rise," *Washington Quarterly* 28, no. 3 (Summer 2005): 7–25.

balanced—in the textbook way that trade relations between a high-wage, highly developed country and an emerging industrial country with abundant cheap labor should be—than is U.S.-China trade. Between 1995 and 2005, roughly 65–70 percent on average of EU exports to China consisted of goods with high-technology content, whereas in the same period the percentage of total U.S. exports to China falling into the same class of goods has remained in the range of 45–55 percent.[63] Thus the European arms embargo has more symbolic than practical significance. EU-Chinese technology trade and technological cooperation, including dual-use technologies, is already well under way.

The underlying issue, therefore, is export control. Although the major EU countries are probably as little inclined as the United States is to transfer security-sensitive core technologies to third countries, their export control policy vis-à-vis China is less restrictive than is that of the United States, resulting in a competitive advantage over U.S. industry.[64] The United States, on the other hand, duly asserts its own security interests in its relationship with Europe. Clearly, the U.S. administration and Congress are concerned that Europe could increasingly export technology with military use to China, thus contributing to an erosion of the United States' technological edge over China as a potential peer competitor.[65] By pressing this point, however, the United States is also trying to prevent erosion of its commercial advantage over European competition. This intricate trade-security linkage is seldom fully addressed either by liberal internationalist proponents of transatlantic deep integration who emphasize business rivalry and normal competition among firms in an integrated market when addressing transatlantic economic conflicts, or by realist analyses, which tend to understate the role of commercial interests in the execution of national security policies.

Should the EU be expected to closely coordinate its arms export control policy with the United States, essentially in accordance with the U.S. Interna-

63. Data refer, as a very broad measure, to exports of goods in group 7 (machinery and transport equipment) of the Standard International Trade Classification (SITC). U.S. data: U.S. Census Bureau and U.S. International Trade Statistics; EU data: Eurostat.

64. For a critical assessment of U.S. export control policy toward China, see Jia Wen Yang, Hossein Askari, John Forrer, and Hildy Teegen, "U.S. Economic Sanctions against China: Who Gets Hurt?" *World Economy* 27, no. 7 (July 2004): 1047–81; and Adam Segal, "Practical Engagement: Drawing a Fine Line for U.S.-China Trade," *Washington Quarterly* 27, no. 3 (Summer 2004): 157–73.

65. "The People's Liberation Army (PLA) is in the process of long-term transformation from a mass army designed for protracted wars of attrition on its territory to a more modern force capable of fighting short duration, high intensity conflicts against high-tech adversaries. . . . as the 2006 Quadrennial Defense Review Report notes, 'China has the greatest potential to compete militarily with the United States and field disruptive military technologies that could over time offset traditional U.S. military advantages.'" Office of the Secretary of Defense, *Annual Report to Congress: Military Power of the People's Republic of China 2006*, http://www. defenselink .mil/pubs/pdfs/China%20Report%202006.pdf.

tional Traffic in Arms Regulations (ITAR), after the model of the common cold war export control regime?[66] The EU countries do not think so. They anxiously defend Europe's autonomy in controlling defense and dual-use exports. The EU intends to implement a revised, more transparent, and stricter code of conduct on defense exports to third countries, which will eventually replace or align different national export control regimes. The United States' ability to unilaterally influence European arms and dual-use export policies may significantly decrease under such common European regimes, yet it would certainly strengthen the European hand in any transatlantic negotiations on defense and dual-use export control.

Therefore, it is likely that the U.S. Congress will at some point take economic relations with Europe hostage to transatlantic security divergences on China by calling for sanctions against European firms that export defense or dual-use goods to China that the United States deems security sensitive. Calls for such measures already were part of the background noise accompanying U.S. diplomatic pressure during the embargo dispute. Should that happen, an interesting test of the liberal internationalist stakeholder principle could result. Would European firms renounce business opportunities in China for the sake of their transatlantic business? Would European governments risk a major transatlantic trade conflict over U.S. sanctions against European firms by granting export licenses for sensitive items bound for China? As I pointed out earlier, European trade with China, although still lower in absolute figures than trade with the United States, is growing much more dynamically than transatlantic trade. The stakes for maintaining and expanding high-technology exports, which will inevitably include dual-use items, are therefore most likely much higher on the European side than in the United States, the more so since such exports contribute substantially to keeping Europe's balance of trade with China from veering too deep into deficit.

Economic sanctions, however, have been a primary U.S. foreign policy instrument for many years, and Europe has not been spared. Increasingly targeting investment and financial transactions, such sanctions have become ever more sophisticated.[67] However, as previous conflicts over transatlantic sanctions have shown, unilateral U.S. sanctions are a double-edged sword if applied to transatlantic relations.[68]

---

66. Since the demise of the CoCom Agreement at the end of the cold war, and with its sequel, the Wassenaar Agreement, largely ineffective, no transatlantic defense technology export control regime is operational.

67. Benn Steil and Robert E. Litan, *Financial Statecraft: The Role of Financial Markets in American Foreign Policy* (New Haven: Yale University Press, 2006).

68. For an analysis of the conflict on the Helms-Burton legislation imposing extraterritorial sanctions against firms investing in Cuba and of how it was precariously defused, see Paemen, "Avoidance and Settlement."

From a more general perspective, it is ironic that the deepness of transatlantic integration—that is, the adhesive forces of economic interdependence as glue for the Atlantic alliance—may ultimately be measured not so much in terms of the positive influence that business can bring to bear on politics but rather by the EU's degree of vulnerability to U.S. sanctions.

Defense Industrial Relations

In every country that has a defense industry, no other industry is subject to economic nationalism to the same extent that the defense industry is.[69] Even in close alliances, the EU not excluded, the defense sector has been the great exception to economic integration. Until the late 1980s, however, the defense sector was fairly insulated from the civilian industrial sector. Thus defense and technology issues did not result in major U.S.-EU economic conflicts.

In the 1990s, things changed fundamentally on the technological as well as the economic level.[70] As a result of accelerated technology developments and growing mass markets in civilian high-technology products and applications, technology spillover intensified and increasingly worked both ways, from civilian to defense as much as from defense to civilian manufacturing. Accordingly, integration among defense, dual-use, and nondefense high-technology industries deepened,[71] which enhanced the competitiveness of the U.S. high-technology sector while further strengthening U.S. defense firms. The latter had undergone, from the early 1990s onward, a major restructuring and consolidation process, under pressure from defense budget reductions and actively encouraged by the Department of Defense,[72] which resulted in a much less fragmented array of a few formidably strong, integrated firms on the major systems level. Among them was Boeing, which acquired the then second largest aircraft manufacturer, McDonnell Douglas, in 1997.

When searching for the deep structures of transatlantic estrangement after the end of the cold war, I found that the alarm in Europe in the 1990s about the widening transatlantic defense technological gap and the ever-increasing dominance of the U.S. defense industry on major world armaments markets

69. Gilpin, *Political Economy of International Relations*, 183.

70. See Stephanie G. Neuman, "Defense Industries and Global Dependency," *Orbis* 50, no. 3 (Summer 2006): 429–51, 433.

71. See Jacques S. Gansler, *Defense Conversion: Transforming the Arsenal of Democracy* (Cambridge, MA: MIT Press, 1995).

72. The restructuring concept was developed, among others, by Jacques Gansler, who, after serving on the Defense Science Board, became undersecretary of defense for acquisition and technology in the second Clinton administration. The key event was the famous "last supper" of then secretary of defense William Perry with representatives of major U.S. defense firms in July 1993, at which he made clear that the Department of Defense was prepared to see major defense contractors go out of business.

was overwhelming.[73] Also, Europe's concern that its industry would be condemned to irrelevance or to second- and third-tier component production can hardly be overstated.[74]

Nevertheless, in the 1990s, under pressure to broaden the market despite defense downsizing and to maintain competition despite concentration among firms, the United States, employing a defense industrial policy as conceived in the Department of Defense under the intellectual stewardship of Jacques Gansler, took a remarkably positive stance with regard to transatlantic cooperation. Gansler envisioned an integrated Atlantic defense industrial base made up of competing transatlantic consortia serving both the U.S. and European defense markets. His concept would have amounted to nothing less than extending a renegotiated transatlantic institutional bargain to the defense industrial base.

Political resistance in the U.S. administration and Congress and reluctance to forego defense industrial autonomy in Europe proved to be insurmountable obstacles, preventing this model from coming even close to being considered for political implementation. However, a generally benign political climate on both sides favored transatlantic acquisitions of defense firms.[75] This climate has changed with the advent of the Bush administration and especially with the Iraq crisis, which has affected even established transatlantic defense industrial relations.

On the trade level, there is some exchange of defense-related goods and components. European governments continue to buy U.S. weapons systems for their armed forces. And for lack of suitable American suppliers, U.S. defense firms, despite the restrictions of U.S. federal "Buy American" legislation, have turned to foreign suppliers for components and materials,[76] which has met with eager willingness on the part of European suppliers to secure their niche in the huge U.S. market. The stark downside, however, is accepting wide-ranging U.S. technology-transfer constraints. As Stephanie Neuman states, for other countries the cost of entry into the U.S. market is increased dependence for them and greater political leverage for the United

73. See the provocative article by Ethan Kapstein, "Towards an American Arms Trade Monopoly," *Foreign Affairs* 73, no. 3 (May–June 1994): 13–19. See also Neuman, "Defense Industries and Global Dependency."

74. See Jens van Scherpenberg, "Transatlantic Competition and European Defence Industries: A New Look at the Trade-Defence Linkage," *International Affairs* 73, no. 1 (January 1997): 99–122. For a more recent analysis, see Lungu, "Power, Techno-Economics and Transatlantic Relations."

75. Burkhard Schmitt, ed., *Between Cooperation and Competition: The Transatlantic Defense Market*, Chaillot Paper no. 44 (Paris: Institute for Security Studies, 2001), http://www.iss-eu.org/chaillot/chai44e.pdf.

76. See "U.S. Weapons, Foreign Flavor," *New York Times*, 27 September 2005, http://www.nytimes.com/2005/09/27/business/27weapons.html.

States.[77] The same cost holds for European purchases of components. U.S. approval is required for exports by European firms to third countries of any product that contains components subject to U.S. export control legislation.

Moreover, growing suspicions on the European side about the noncommercial motives of U.S. investment in European defense firms have made such acquisitions more difficult if not impossible,[78] while on the U.S. side, procedures for control of foreign acquisitions of security-sensitive firms through the Committee on Foreign Investments in the United States (CFIUS) are being tightened.[79]

On balance, a paradox emerges. Although, from the perspective of governments, defense industrial relations have rendered the Atlantic wider and deeper in recent years, European defense firms scramble to bridge the growing divide in hopes of getting hold of a small share of the U.S. market in order to better survive commercially.

Conclusion

Transatlantic economic relations do not by themselves give useful hints about the direction of U.S.-European relations: toward a breakdown of the alliance, toward transformation by a new institutional bargain, or toward adaptation by muddling through. They serve neither as superglue for the alliance nor as an independent source of transatlantic crisis. They are but a mirror image of current transatlantic relations. A huge volume of transatlantic "low business" corresponds to the broad exchange of people that occurs through tourism, youth exchange, higher education, and business travel, and to the daily professional exchange at lower government levels on operational and technical issues. On these levels, deep integration exists, as does its main immaterial ingredient, mutual respect and trust. But an important area of "high" or strategic economic policy issues, including macroeconomic and currency issues, directly corresponds to high politics. On that level, relations are characterized by strategic competition and a mutual lack of trust. So far there is little evidence that at the end of the day the cooperative spirit of "low business" and "low politics" will prevail over strategic conflicts in shaping the overall relationship.

The real test for transatlantic relations is one of crises to come. These could well be economic ones, such as a major financial adjustment crisis that originates in the United States. Would Europeans be willing, as they were in the

---

77. Neuman, "Defense Industries and Global Dependency," 439.

78. Germany implemented legislation in 2004 that allows the federal government to veto foreign (i.e., primarily U.S.) acquisitions of German defense firms.

79. See Edward M. Graham and David M. Marchick, *U.S. National Security and Foreign Direct Investment* (Washington, DC: Institute for International Economics, 2006).

mid-1980s, to come forward and share the economic and financial burden of U.S. foreign policy? Or would such a crisis be exacerbated instead of alleviated by a Europe either weak and introspective or strong and uncooperative?

The euro has substantially changed the parameters for monetary policy coordination in transatlantic relations.[80] As Fred Bergsten, one of the foremost champions of transatlantic monetary cooperation, remarks, "there are no institutional arrangements through which Euroland and the United States meet to address these issues [the range of the dollar-euro rate, mechanisms for achieving or sustaining that rate, policy implications, and the like] together."[81] Of course the need for such coordination may not arise if the U.S. economy were to remain resilient to a large and rising current account deficit, as it continues to attract the world's savings.

If, however, we assume that the growing U.S. current account deficit will ultimately result in a major adjustment crisis—as indeed it has before—then a lack of policy coordination could deepen that crisis. A major adjustment crisis in the United States that is not addressed by transatlantic economic policy cooperation may erode domestic support for the WTO regime and substantially increase protectionist pressures in the United States. Such pressures could be directed toward Europe as well as toward China, provoked by a bilateral trade surplus that for the EU has been rising even faster than the Chinese-U.S. one, although in absolute terms China's surplus with the United States is still much higher. However, for political sentiment to be stirred up even on "normal" transatlantic trade conflicts to an extent that they would become unmanageable by WTO dispute settlement procedures, a spillover from the level of strategic conflicts would have to occur.

In such a scenario, not at all unlikely, transatlantic economic relations, far from having a stabilizing effect on the relationship, may be taken hostage and become instrumental to the underlying structural conflict. Obviously, a fundamental ingredient of closer transatlantic economic cooperation and integration is so far lacking or, worse, has been lost: the mutual awareness or perception of interdependence. Trying to raise this awareness is the merit of empirical research like that of Hamilton and Quinlan. However, such research fails to address two problems. First, the issue may not be unawareness of interdependence but rather taking *mutual* interdependence for granted. Second, perceptions of interdependence seem to be asymmetrical.[82]

80. For a definition of "policy coordination" in this regard, see Edwin M. Truman, "The Euro and Prospects for Policy Coordination," in *The Euro at Five: Ready for a Global Role?* ed. Adam S. Posen, 47–77 (Washington, DC: Institute for International Economics, 2005).

81. C. Fred Bergsten, "The Euro and the Dollar: Toward a 'Finance G-2'?" in *The Euro at Five: Ready for a Global Role?* ed. Adam S. Posen, 27–39 (Washington, DC: Institute for International Economics, 2005), 28.

82. On asymmetrical interdependence, see Keohane and Nye, *Power and Interdependence*, 16–19.

In transatlantic relations, these asymmetrical perceptions are reflected in mid- and long-term economic perspectives of each other that diverge greatly. Conservative American analysts see Europe in the midst of a long-term demographic and structural decline that will lead to its slow demise as a major international player, just like Japan in the 1990s, whereas, for the same reasons, the United States should remain the dominant economic power for the foreseeable future. Therefore, Europe should be more dependent on the United States rather than vice versa. The real problem may be that from the viewpoint of the Bush administration's economic policy, the transatlantic economic "balance of power" that was the basis for transatlantic monetary and trade cooperation in bilateral relations as well as on the multilateral level of international economic and financial institutions has shifted in the United States' favor. Europe, however, does not share this view. Therefore, if we define economic balance of power as the balance of mutual capabilities to inflict economic costs on each other in case of conflicts, these capabilities may have to be tested repeatedly before perceptions of interdependence converge—either toward balance or toward U.S. predominance.

It seems that the future of the transatlantic institutional bargain lies less in negotiating a settlement aimed at increasing benefits for both sides but rather in a more modest agreement to refrain from inflicting costs on each other, whether in economic terms or in terms of restrictions on each other's foreign and security policy.

7 THE TIES THAT BIND?

U.S.-EU Economic Relations and the Institutionalization of the Transatlantic Alliance

KATHLEEN R. MCNAMARA

In the autumn of 2003, at one of the lowest points in the history of the postwar transatlantic alliance, negotiators representing the European Union and the United States sat down in Washington to begin discussions on the Open Skies initiative—a radical liberalization of transatlantic air services. Through multiple rounds of talks and complex regulatory tangles, negotiators continued to work toward a comprehensive agreement. The goal was a radical one: to dismantle the web of regulations, pricing rules, and national preference programs that make the air industry a virtual cartel and reconstruct the transatlantic civil aviation system as a fully integrated market.

The deepening of cooperation between Europe and the United States on civil aviation issues is surprising at any time, given the extremely complex legal, social, and economic issues involved. But coming at a time when the United States and the EU had experienced several years of stark foreign policy disagreements, it raises a key question. Will the continuing deepening of economic ties keep the transatlantic relationship healthy, regardless of the severity of immediate political conflicts? To begin to answer this question, in this chapter I consider more broadly the role of economic exchange in the generation of political order. How do the low politics, of trade and finance, and the high politics, of foreign policy, influence each other? Do high levels of economic exchange ameliorate, have no effect on, or exacerbate broader political conflict? And what implications might the answers to these questions have for the future of U.S.-EU relations?

To get some leverage on these questions, I examine two historical cases in which economic partners experienced political conflict, namely, the pre–World War I period and the Suez crisis, and draw out the likely implications for the present-day transatlantic relationship. Against much of the conventional wisdom, I argue that high levels of underlying economic interdependence cannot by themselves serve as a panacea for political crises. Private-sector interests have a limited direct impact on high-politics decision making, and foreign policy elites are more likely to view the economy as a tool of statecraft and national interests rather than vice versa. Both analytic logic and existing empirical evidence point toward this conclusion and suggest that the deep economic interdependence enjoyed by the United States and the EU may not by itself provide a brake on political crisis.[1]

I suggest, however, that all is not lost: that is, more complex and intervening factors may build on economic interdependence to shape the path of political interactions. I conclude the chapter by proposing that economic ties are more likely to bind politically if they are embedded within specific kinds of social and political institutions that more subtly shape actors' calculations away from intense political conflict. These institutions are generated through incremental and path-dependent historical processes that are difficult to specify a priori but that are highly consequential for outcomes of political conflict.

To evaluate the potential role of economic ties in the current transatlantic relationship, I begin by assessing the prevailing theoretical models of interaction between high politics and low politics. I analyze the various schools of thought on how politics and markets interact, and I develop a series of hypotheses about the links between economic interdependence and foreign policy. I set out a causal argument about market exchange, institutions, and ideas, and compare U.S. engagement with Europe in two periods of interdependence and conflict—the years before World War I, and the Suez crisis. I conclude by discussing the contemporary period and offer some cautionary warnings about relying on economic ties alone to sustain the U.S.-EU relationship.

Economic Exchange and Political Conflict

The relationship between economic interdependence and political conflict is not only of academic interest but is a critical foundational question for contemporary policymakers. Many politicians seem to hold the view that nations tightly knit together by commerce have more peaceful relations. The notion that the spread of democracy will make the world safer has been a primary motivating assumption of U.S. foreign policy from Clinton through the second Bush administration, but the idea that capitalism and integration into the world economy will do the same has followed a close second.[2] What Thomas

---

1. This view is largely congruent with Jens van Scherpenberg's assessment, in this volume, of the implications of economic policy conflict and cooperation in the present era.

2. Michael Mastanduno surveys the postwar history of policy and thought on the relationship between economic and security policy in "Economics and Security in Statecraft and Scholarship," *International Organization* 52, no. 4 (Autumn, 1998): 825–54. An argument that economic interdependence is an important stabilizer in the contemporary transatlantic relationship is

Friedman has termed the Golden Arches theory of international politics[3]—
the assertion that no two countries that both have a McDonald's within their
territory have ever gone to war with each other—is largely, but not completely, true. The history of the European Union has likewise been driven by
postwar political elites' visions of economic exchange as a foundation for
peace and political stability.

Long before such real-world policy initiatives, the relationship between
economic interdependence and political conflict was the focus of political philosophers, as classical theorists pondered the causes of war and peace. It has
also been the subject of extensive quantitative study by contemporary scholars. In the following section, I review the main arguments about the relationship between economic interdependence and political conflict in the hope of
better understanding the nature of the contemporary U.S.-EU alliance.

Liberal Pluralist Arguments

The simplest potential argument about the causal linkages between international market integration and political conflict is that there is no causal link.
Perhaps there is a decisive separation between the low politics of economic
policy making and the high politics of geostrategy and alliances. This sort of
separate spheres argument would posit that the actors, motivations, and activities in the two arenas are sufficiently different such that variation in the level
of interdependence would have no impact on political conflict. In this view,
core national interests in either maintaining or expanding state power drive
political outcomes in the international system, whereas profit motives and
prices drive market interactions. Political relations among states only interact
with economic exchange in the event of a catastrophic breakdown in the
global political order, such as a world war. Proponents of this argument can
point to the fact that the level of economic interdependence in the first half of
the twentieth century was a poor predictor of political conflict: high levels of
market integration preceded World War I, whereas low levels preceded
World War II. During the cold war, the division of the world trading order
into two completely separate blocs also contributed to some scholars' view
that the two areas were separate spheres.[4]

In contrast, a set of arguments congruent with a liberal perspective on international politics offers causal stories that do link interdependence to political outcomes, namely, through mutual interest as expressed within a pluralist

Miles Kahler, "U.S. Politics and Transatlantic Relations: We Are All Europeans Now," in *The Alliance under Stress: The Atlantic Partnership after Iraq*, ed. David M. Andrews (Cambridge:
Cambridge University Press, 2005).

3. Thomas Friedman, *The Lexus and the Olive Tree* (New York: Farrar, Straus and Giroux,
1988), chap. 10.

4. Kenneth Waltz, *Theory of International Politics* (Reading, MA: Addison Wesley, 1979).

policy process.[5] The idea that economic exchange may promote peace through the mechanism of mutual interest has roots at least as far back as the early eighteenth century, when Montesquieu argued that "peace is the natural effect of trade."[6] From this perspective, commerce between states naturally leads to peace because both sides in international trade benefit from economic interactions. Over time, the states develop a mutual dependence on one another, as well as a set of strong common interests in avoiding war, because conflict would disrupt their mutually beneficial exchange relationship. As developed by Adam Smith and Joseph Schumpeter, what Albert Hirschman called the *doux commerce* (sweet commerce) theory implies that an international liberal economic regime that fosters trade and investment multilaterally also produces a more peaceful international system of states.[7] The key actors in this causal chain are state leaders who recognize the value of their exchange relationships and calculate it into their foreign policy, and politically powerful societal actors who stand to gain from international commerce while suffering from its loss, and who pressure governments to keep relations smooth among trade and investment partners.

Contemporary theorists have extended this logic and sometimes added other variables to enrich the analysis. For example, Christopher Gelpi and Joseph Grieco add in democracy and focus on the interaction effects between trade and a democratic system.[8] They use median-voter logic and the likely growth-producing effects of trade to argue that leaders of democracies are less likely to put their trade ties at risk in political conflict with their economic partners, because they depend on growth from trade for electoral advantage. There are several other lines of prominent argumentation in the newer literature, including the idea that trade produces peace because it can act as a substitute for conquest and territorial expansion.[9] In addition, Christopher Way offers an alternative theoretical extension of the liberal argument, which focuses on the informational role that commercial actors can play in strengthening or weakening the government's threats to potential adversaries.[10] Through

---

5. Edward Mansfield and Brian Pollins, eds., *Economic Interdependence and International Conflict: New Perspectives on an Enduring Debate* (Ann Arbor: University of Michigan Press, 2003), provides a "state of the art" overview.

6. As quoted in Michael Doyle, *Ways of War and Peace* (Princeton: Princeton University Press, 1997), 306.

7. Albert O. Hirschman, *The Passions and the Interests: Political Arguments for Capitalism before Its Triumph* (Princeton: Princeton University Press, 1977).

8. Christopher Gelpi and Joseph Grieco, "Economic Interdependence, the Democratic State, and the Liberal Peace," in Mansfield and Pollins, *Economic Interdependence*, 44–59.

9. Richard Rosecrance, *The Rise of the Trading State: Commerce and Conquest in the Modern World* (New York: Basic Books, 1986).

10. Christopher Way, *Manchester Revisited: Economic Interdependence and Conflict* (Ithaca: Cornell University Press, forthcoming).

careful quantitative and case study research, Way argues that the private sector plays a role in enhancing or detracting from the government's credibility in negotiations. Way's work convincingly demonstrates the shortcomings of a simple model of exchange and conflict, emphasizing instead the multiple mechanisms and nuanced causal paths between economic interdependence and conflict.

Although not as prominent in the classical *doux commerce* literature, these extensions of the pluralist model of the policy process often allow for the logical inference that powerful commercial interests may, in some cases, have an interest in war if it will result in profits to their industries. Winners might include defense contractors, or domestic producers who would gain back markets lost to imports from the adversary state. If commercial interests are pivotal in foreign policy making, then the balance of interests must be carefully understood before conclusions can be drawn about their pacifying effects.

Another set of authors has further enriched the pluralist story by situating it within an institutional context, arguing that it is not commercial interests alone but interests together with domestic and/or international institutions that truly bind states. Bruce Russett and John O'Neal argue that peace is most likely when the international political order is made up of democratic states, economic interdependence, and international institutions.[11] Surveying a dizzying array of theories and causal pathways, they posit these elements as reinforcing peaceful relations. Alternatively, Etel Solingen focuses on the interaction between shifting domestic coalitions, the internationalization of the economy, and the choice of grand strategy and regional institutions.[12] She depicts a complex and highly dependent reality in which coalitions can press for policies of backlash and aggression as well as peace, depending on the makeup of the coalition and the members' domestic strategic political environment. Considered together, these scholarly arguments lead us to be skeptical that the tight U.S.-EU economic relationship will lessen any political crises, but they provide clues about where we might look to see subtler impacts through a variety of different channels.

Empirical Findings in the Literature

These various strands of liberal argumentation have been subject to intensive statistical tests, yet a conclusive result remains elusive in that the findings

---

11. Bruce Russett and John O'Neal, *Triangulating Peace: Democracy, Interdependence, and International Organizations* (New York: Norton, 2001).

12. Etel Solingen, *Regional Orders at Century's Dawn: Global and Domestic Influences on Grand Strategy* (Princeton: Princeton University Press, 1998); Etel Solingen, "Internationalization, Coalitions, and Regional Conflict," in Mansfield and Pollins, *Economic Interdependence*, 60–88.

are often contradictory.[13] In assessing the state of our empirical knowledge, Edward Mansfield and Brian Pollins conclude that more attention should be paid to the microfoundations of the arguments, that greater appreciation is needed for the role of contingency, and that the conceptualization and measurement of the variables of interdependence and conflict need to be made more rigorous. When Russett and O'Neal undertake multiple tests of democracy, interdependence, and international organizations, they find that each of these elements contributes to more peaceful relations and that together they have complementary effects.[14] However, Russett and O'Neal's assessments are pitched at a high level of generality, the nature of the variables are not fully explored, and their ambitious work ends up being more suggestive than definitive.

The indeterminacy of quantitative analyses of the Golden Arches theory results in part from the threefold challenges of this area of study. First, the scope of the issues involved is potentially huge: interdependence and conflict are concepts with multiple definitions and many potential manifestations. Second, the causal direction of the relationship between interdependence and conflict is intuitively a reciprocal one and thus difficult to study effectively. Finally, the literature has more recently identified multiple pathways and complex contingency as critical in shaping outcomes of international conflict or harmony in the presence of high levels of exchange. However, the difficulties of sorting out exactly how these many intervening variables really matter has meant progress has been slow in the statistical realm. The obvious next step is to perform historical process tracing, but remarkably few systematic investigations have been conducted of the behavior of internationally oriented commercial interests in the face of political crisis, despite the pressing real-world importance of this question.

The extant literature includes several case study treatments, all of which tend to reinforce the complexity of the relationship between commerce and conflict. Norrin Ripsman and Jean-Marc Blanchard examined the pre–World War I and pre–World War II cases for evidence that commercial interests had in any way slowed the march to war, as I discuss further in the case study section.[15] Their research found no evidence that private actors' views influenced

13. The collection of essays in Mansfield and Pollins, *Economic Interdependence*, is a notable example; an overview of progress and gaps in the literature is provided in Jonathan Kirshner, "Political Economic in Security Studies after the Cold War," *Review of International Political Economy* 5:64–91.

14. Russett and O'Neal, *Triangulating Peace*.

15. Norrin M. Ripsman and Jean-Marc F. Blanchard, "Commercial Liberalism under Fire: Evidence from 1914 and 1936," *Security Studies* 6 (1996–97): 4–50. See also their review of the broader qualitative literature in Norrin M. Ripsman and Jean-Marc F. Blanchard, "Qualitative Research on Economic Interdependence and Conflict: Overcoming Methodological Hurdles," in Mansfield and Pollins, *Economic Interdependence*, 310–23.

the actions of the major powers in the two world wars. In contrast, Way's nuanced study of three cases of U.S.-U.K. disputes in the nineteenth century finds evidence to support his argument that throughout these political crises, internationally oriented economic interests promoted peace in their role as information providers in times of political confrontation.[16]

These case studies, along with the quantitative work, suggest that we should be wary of drawing a direct linkage between commercial exchange and outcome of conflict or peace, but rather indicate that there may be subtler and contingent relationships at work in the *doux commerce* dynamic. In the following section, I sketch an alternative argument, one less developed in the existing literature, that focuses on the social institutions surrounding market exchange as the source for effects on the broader foreign policy relationships across the Atlantic and elsewhere.

The Social Institutionalization of Low Politics

The theoretical logics sketched out earlier, and the sophisticated empirical tests of those logics, all suggest that economic exchange alone is indeterminate: deep market integration across borders may precede and coexist with outcomes of either political conflict or cooperation. A promising alternative theoretical logic worthy of more study focuses instead on the causal impact of the social institutionalization of market exchange.[17] Here, what makes the difference between conflict and cooperation is institutions, whether supranational, intergovernmental, or self-organized by private actors, and the ideas and social understandings embodied in them.

In this view, certain social institutions have the unique potential to translate the positive facets of mutual dependence and social interaction fostered by international economic exchanges into more stable and sticky political outcomes. Commercial exchange obviously increases social interactions. The more that private and public actors are involved in exchanges across borders, the more they come into contact with foreigners, either physically or virtually, and, as one line of argument goes, the more they communicate and develop shared understandings that can further both commerce and cooperation. This notion is congruent with some of Kant's ideas about the development of a cosmopolitan community of nations.[18] It also has affinities with the neofunctionalist

---

16. Way, *Manchester Revisited*.

17. On social institutions, see W. Richard Scott and John Meyer, *Institutional Environments and Organizations* (Thousand Oaks, CA: Sage, 1994), and Alexander Wendt, *A Social Theory of International Politics* (Cambridge: Cambridge University Press, 1999); Thomas Risse, "Collective Identity in a Democratic Community: The Case of NATO," in *The Culture of National Security*, ed. Peter Katzenstein (Ithaca: Cornell University Press, 1996); Martha Finnemore and Michael Barnett, *Rules for the World* (Ithaca: Cornell University Press, 2004).

18. Emmanuel Kant, "To the Perpetual Peace" (1795).

writings of EU scholars, who viewed the Common Market as an ideal context within which to transform European antipathy into a shared community in which actors develop interdependent identities that make war virtually unthinkable.[19]

Contemporary markets cannot function without an elaborate legal scaffolding to support them, and the more deeply we integrate across the Atlantic, the more tasks have to be taken on by transgovernmental actors to enable private actors to engage in trade, investment, and production abroad. What scholars from Robert Keohane and Joseph Nye to Anne-Marie Slaughter have termed "transgovernmentalism," today exists in an intricate network of relationships across national regulators, courts, legislatures, and executives.[20] This high degree of institutionalization is likely to be critically important to the fate of the U.S.-EU relationship, particularly because it shapes the impact that commercial exchange has on political relations.

As with the mutual dependence argument, however, it is possible to imagine that increased interactions could lead, under some circumstances, to more conflict, not less. Just as the right neighbors can become one's close friends, the wrong neighbors can become one's worst enemies. With closeness, there is more opportunity for discord, because there are more points of interaction, than in separate spheres. The question is, what tips the balance such that incentives to work out problems outweigh the drive to disagree.

A promising answer to the question of cooperation or conflict lies in the ideational or social content of this institutional web. The causal link between the incentives that market integration creates for broader foreign policy may be dependent on the creation of social institutions that construct actors' interests over time in ways that make extreme or violent political conflict less likely. Liberal ideas, particularly positive-sum views of the role of trade and investment and a faith in multilateralism and the rule of law, embedded within institutions, may channel and reinforce the impetus for *doux commerce*.[21]

Historically, many economic actors have viewed their market interlocutors as competitors, and trade and investment not in liberal terms but rather as a zero-sum game. In such mercantilist cultural contexts, economic ties are logically less likely to be pacific. Today, however, many private and public actors

19. Ernst Haas, *The Uniting of Europe* (Stanford: Stanford University Press, 1958).

20. Robert Keohane and Joseph Nye, *Power and Interdependence* (Boston: Little, Brown, 1977); Anne-Marie Slaughter, *A New World Order* (Princeton: Princeton University Press, 2004).

21. See John Ikenberry's larger characterization of the postwar liberal institutional order in G. John Ikenberry, *After Victory: Institutions, Strategic Restraint, and the Rebuilding of Order after Major Wars* (Princeton: Princeton University Press, 2001), and his discussion in the introduction to this volume. Also see Gary Bass, *Stay the Hand of Vengeance* (Princeton: Princeton University Press, 2000), for a discussion of how evolving liberal norms determined the nature of judicial institutions over time.

in the EU and the United States see economic exchange as a positive-sum relationship and have sought the creation of international institutions to safeguard these benefits: this view may lead them to lobby political actors to reduce tensions; it will also produce sets of institutional rules that encourage diffuse reciprocity and a willingness to play by the rules of the game, even if they do not always favor one's immediate interests. The rulings of the World Trade Organization (WTO), most prominently, are overwhelmingly complied with, despite a few high-profile exceptions.[22] And although commercial interests always try to get the most preferential treatment possible in trade deals, and partisan politics continues to make trade politically volatile, mainstream business in the United States has largely shunned protectionism as a strategy for the past decade.[23]

If these liberal economic ideas, rather than mercantilist norms, are the dominant culture among key commercial actors, institutions can help formalize networks of transgovernmental and private actors so that their social interactions are routinized and regularized in such a way as to promote the development of stable, cooperative relationships. As institutions channel interests and create locations of political authority, these positive effects of institutions are dependent on the shared social understandings that constitute them and motivate the actions of political actors. In this political process, material and ideational effects have the potential to work together to construct an institutional web promoting transnational stability.

The case studies in this chapter indicate that in earlier periods of globalization, such as the end of the nineteenth century, mercantilist ideas tended to be dominant among diplomats, and the institutional framework for market exchange was extremely limited. In contrast, interdependence in the twenty-first century is highly institutionalized, and liberal ideas are embedded within the formal and informal rules of the Bretton Woods institutions and beyond. These evolving liberal norms promote and make possible the nature of contemporary market integration. Trade in goods has given way to trade in services; complex production supply chains and the interaction of disparate regulatory regimes have all conspired to make the international system deeply and profoundly institutionalized. This institutionalization can be found in policy arenas that are less visible to the average citizen than are those of high politics, yet the arenas may be experienced on a regular basis by those same citizens. For example, international standard setting, an area that rarely makes

22. For current empirical data on WTO compliance, see the WTO Web site; a historical overview is provided in Kathleen R. McNamara, "The Institutional Dilemmas of Market Integration: Compliance and International Regimes for Trade and Finance," in *International Law and Organization: Closing the Compliance Gap*, ed. Michael Doyle and Edward Luck (Lanham, MD: Rowman and Littlefield, 2004), 41–60.

23. I. M. Destler, "The Decline of Traditional Protectionism," chap. 9 in *American Trade Politics*, 4th ed. (Washington, DC: Institute for International Economics, 2005).

the front page of the *New York Times*, comes into play every time a consumer uses a foreign-made product, such as a hair dryer or child's car seat, and determines the ease of use and compatibility of that product with other goods. Much of this sort of policy making is highly routinized, either formally in specific, ongoing organizations, such as the International Standards Organization, or in informal, customary, or ad hoc ways. Often such routines depend on interactions between policymakers not directly elected: for example, bureaucrats, functionaries, and lawyers engaged in regulatory cooperation to support opening markets across borders.

In sum, adding social institutionalization as an intervening variable in the relationship between economic interdependence and conflict gives us a stronger theoretical link between commercial exchange and interdependence, and posits important variation over time in the ways in which actors perceive their interests vis-à-vis their trading and investment partners. We can hypothesize that when key private actors share liberal ideas about the reciprocal benefits of trade and investment, institutions can act as binding agents by channeling societal interests in support of peaceful relations among close trading partners. New regulatory and other institutions created to manage today's complex trade and investment also facilitate the deepening of a network of transnational actors, with the potential for socialization through iterated interaction. Simply put, if this particular form and content of liberal institutionalization occurs in the context of economic independence, then the chances are higher that economic ties will be binding on the high politics of nation-states.

In the historical case study section that follows, I briefly examine the ways in which economic interdependence across the Atlantic has ebbed and flowed over the last century and discuss the role, if any, that private actors and social institutions have had on political conflict between the United States and Europe. My preliminary empirical overview presents a mixed record for the role of economic interdependence, defined simply as economic exchange, on conflict. It also suggests that history is only a reliable guide to the present transatlantic relationship in so much as it suggests what has changed over time, as well as what may remain the same. If, as I suggest, the social institutionalization of liberal ideas is the intervening variable between economic interdependence and political conflict, its absence in the earlier cases and its presence in the current context give us more reasons to be optimistic about the nature of the deep structure of the transatlantic relationship.

Evaluating Interdependence and Conflict

To illustrate how economic interdependence and market integration may or may not have a pacifying effect, I examine each variable in the context of the run-up to World War I, the 1956 Suez crisis, and the present transatlantic dis-agreements. The outcome, or dependent variable, I am interested in is political conflict. As Mansfield and Pollins have carefully detailed, the statistical empirical literature has used a wide variety of definitions of conflict, each with its own promises and pitfalls, which makes comparisons across scholars' findings sometimes difficult.[24] Here, I assume that political conflict occurs on a continuum ranging from no conflict to low- to moderate-intensity conflict to high-intensity conflict. On the "low-intensity political conflict" end of the scale, where the current U.S.-EU situation is located, political tension is indicated through a variety of policy actions and diplomatic, rhetorical, and symbolic indicators. Hostile or confrontational statements by leaders, diverging opinions and actions on key geopolitical issues, split votes and divisive debates in international forums such as the United Nations, and the imposition of penalties or sanctions by one state on another are all examples of low-intensity political conflict. Going up the scale to "moderate-intensity political conflict," indicators include more dramatic diplomatic actions such as the withdrawal of ambassadors, the expulsion of states from international organizations, and the nullification of cooperative treaties between states. Further along again, toward "higher-intensity conflict," would be the unilateral departure from or dissolution of alliances and overtly hostile actions involving diplomatic crises over spies, military postures, and so on. Finally, armed conflict involving a substantial number of casualties would represent the "highest-intensity political conflict." Obviously, World War I is the highest-intensity political conflict, whereas the present transatlantic rift is at the low-intensity level. The Suez crisis arguably bordered on moderate political conflict. During Suez, the remarkable willingness of France and the United Kingdom to mislead and contravene the U.S. government, and the resoluteness of President Eisenhower to bring all of the United States' economic and diplomatic power to bear to undermine the British position, created a level of immediate political conflict that was more intensive than the diplomatic rifts of present transatlantic situation.

Two broad independent, or causal, variables are important to the theoretical story I wish to tell: economic interdependence and institutions. The most widely used interdependence measure is the trade-to-GDP ratio, which essentially captures the openness of a country's economy to international trade in goods. This data set is the most readily available and the most straightforward.

Some scholars, however, argue that trade is no longer the most important type of interdependence knitting together today's world; rather, investment has become a crucial driver. I therefore also include foreign direct investment (FDI) as a measure of economic interdependence. Portfolio capital—or the movement of money in and out of more liquid assets, such as stocks, bonds, and other financial instruments, across borders—is also a key component of

---

24. Mansfield and Pollins, *Economic Interdependence*.

the global economy, so I also include measures of the level of capital mobility. Taken together, these various indicators give a reasonable picture of the level of interdependence at each time period of political conflict.

Finally, social institutions are the intervening variable that, I argue, may better explain the degree and direction of impact that interdependence has on political conflict. Broadly understood, international institutions can be formal or informal, and those included in the category for assessment in the cases comprise supranational organizations, intergovernmental organizations, and regimes more loosely organized in tandem with nongovernmental actors. All of these formal institutions are understood to embody sets of shared understandings or ideas, forming a certain historically bounded culture. Most of the discussion in the sections that follow concerns more formal intergovernmental institutions, because they can be quantified more readily: I offer only a suggestive sketch of what might be the social understandings providing the foundation for these institutions. In all three instances—World War I, Suez, and the present—two key historical questions intrude. First, to what degree were private and public actors with an interest in maintaining good economic relations between the United States and Europe both active and influential in mediating the political tensions at the foreign policy level? And second, what were the basic precepts held by actors about the nature of trade and investment, and what role did institutions play in channeling and shaping those interests? With only three select cases, I do not claim, of course, that this test of the theories discussed earlier is a conclusive test but rather view it as a suggestive overview for understanding today's transatlantic relationship.

Trends in Interdependence over the Past Century

Our first task in understanding the potential role of interdependence in political conflict is to examine levels of economic interaction. Figures 7.1–7.6 depict the general trends in trade interdependence between the United States and the major powers of Europe (the United Kingdom, France, Germany, and Italy) from the late nineteenth century to the present. Data are also provided on trends in foreign direct investment and investment capital.

The first set of figures, generated from Katherine Barbieri's International Trade Database, supplemented with International Monetary Fund (IMF) trade data from 1992 onward, examines levels of trade interdependence in each salient time period (World War I, Suez, and today) between the major European powers (United Kingdom, France, Germany, and Italy combined) and the United States (fig. 7.1) and breaks down the data into bilateral trade flows between the United States and the individual states (fig. 7.2). The most striking result is the level of high trade interdependence in the first

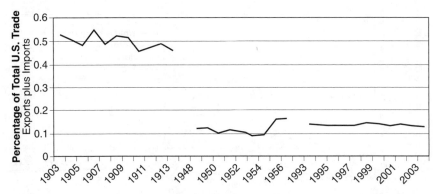

Figure 7.1. U.S. trade with Europe during three critical periods, 1903–19, 1948–56, 1993–2003. Trade between the United States and Europe (United Kingdom, Germany, Italy, and France combined) as a percentage of total U.S. trade. *Sources:* Katherine Barbieri, International Trade Database, 1870–1992; IMF Direction of Trade Statistics, 1993–2003.

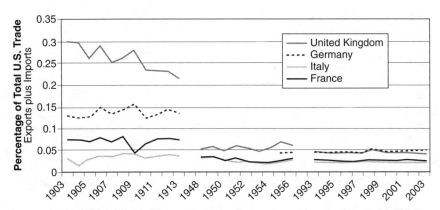

Figure 7.2. U.S. bilateral trade with individual European states during three critical periods, 1903–19, 1948–56, 1993–2003. Bilateral trade between the United States and the United Kingdom, Germany, Italy, and France as a percentage of total U.S. trade. *Sources:* Barbieri, International Trade Database, 1870–1992; IMF Direction of Trade Statistics, 1993–2003.

period compared with that of the second and third. I also present the data in terms of a rolling ten-year average, which conveys a similar picture (figs. 7.3 and 7.4). Figures 7.5 and 7.6 depict trade with Europe as a percentage of total U.S. trade, showing that this relationship represents over half of U.S. trade in the early period but is dramatically less important to U.S. trade in the postwar period.

An alternative way of measuring economic interdependence across goods markets is simply to look at price differentials for commodity goods instead of

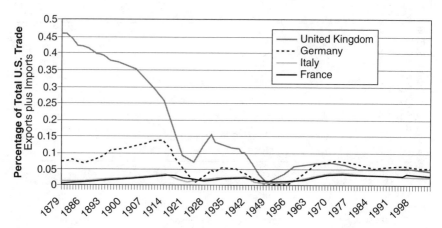

Figure 7.3. U.S. bilateral trade with individual European states, 1870–2003. Bilateral exports and imports as a percentage of total U.S. trade (rolling ten-year average). *Sources:* Barbieri, International Trade Database, 1870–1992; IMF Direction of Trade Statistics, 1993–2003.

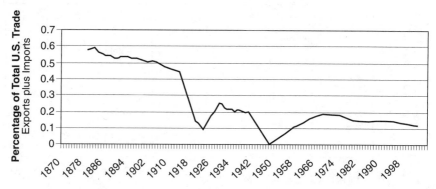

Figure 7.4. U.S. trade with Europe, 1870–2003. Trade between the United States and Europe (United Kingdom, Germany, Italy, and France combined) as a percentage of total U.S. trade (rolling ten-year average). *Sources:* Barbieri, International Trade Database, 1870–1992; IMF Direction of Trade Statistics, 1993–2003.

actual trade flows. Large differences in the cost of similar goods imply that markets are not closely integrated and that barriers are driving a wedge between national prices. Kevin O'Rourke and Jeffrey Williamson surveyed price convergence in the pre–World War I Atlantic economy and found that although prices for wheat and other tradable foodstuffs such as pork diverged by over 50 percent in 1870, by 1913 the differences were as low as 15 percent.[25]

25. Kevin H. O'Rourke and Jeffrey G. Williamson, *Globalization and History: The Evolution of a Nineteenth-Century Atlantic Economy* (Cambridge: MA: MIT Press, 1999), 43.

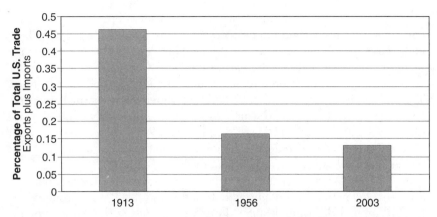

Figure 7.5. U.S. trade with Europe at three historic points, 1913, 1956, and 2003. Trade between the United States and Europe (United Kingdom, Germany, Italy, and France combined) as a percentage of total U.S. trade (rolling ten-year average). *Sources:* Barbieri, International Trade Database, 1870–1992; IMF Direction of Trade Statistics, 1993–2003.

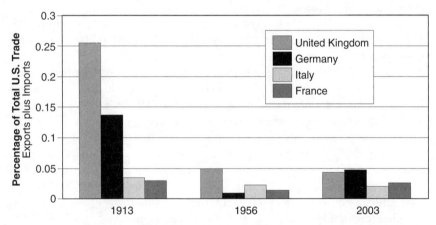

Figure 7.6. U.S. trade with individual European states at three historic points, 1913, 1956, and 2003. Trade between the United States and the United Kingdom, Germany, Italy, and France as a percentage of total U.S. trade. *Sources:* Barbieri, International Trade Database, 1870–1992; IMF Direction of Trade Statistics, 1993–2003.

O'Rourke and Williamson argue that dramatically falling transportation costs were the impetus for dramatic increases in market integration across the Atlantic, as well as within Europe itself, but note that this intensive globalization process also engendered a political backlash and a turn toward protectionism that preceded World War I.

Trade is not necessarily the best measure of interdependence, however, particularly in the current era of deep cross-border integration within firms and sectors, which may account for the seeming decrease of relative engagement in European trade on the part of the United States. Foreign direct investment may better capture the nature of economic interdependence today. The data on FDI for the earlier periods are scarce, however, making FDI a less useful cross-temporal measure. Most analysts generally agree that the level of FDI at the turn of the last century was low compared to the level of trade and financial integration; it then fell during the interwar period, began to rise in the 1950s, and today is at historically high levels.

Several scholars have calculated outward foreign investment as a percentage of overall national economic activity and found that it was substantial for the Britain and the United States, in particular, during the decades before World War I. Britain's economic empire expressed itself in investments abroad, particularly in its colonies, such that these investments made up a significant portion of British GDP at the turn of the century. The stock of U.S. investment abroad was $2.65 billion in 1914, or 7 percent of GNP,[26] about what it was in 1966. Nonetheless, the level of FDI is higher today, and the nature of FDI has also changed.

Data are readily available demonstrating the investment ties between the United States and Europe in the present era. Daniel Hamilton and Joseph Quinlan provide a comprehensive dataset on transatlantic FDI in the current context, documenting the deep commercial engagement of U.S. firms in Europe, and European firms in the United States. Using Bureau of Economic Analysis data, they note that during 1999–2003, including the post-2001 period of increasing political tensions, Europe continued to be the United States' most important partner for foreign direct investment. U.S. FDI compared with that of Europe as a percentage of annual totals ranged from 52.2 percent in 1999 to 55.1 percent in 2003, with a dip in 2001 to 43.1 percent and a peak in 2003 at 64.1 percent (see fig. 7.7). Moreover, profits from foreign affiliate corporations, both U.S. companies in Europe and vice versa, have been booming from the late 1990s into 2003, with a dip only in 2001.[27] On the European side as well, there has been a rapid increase in the amount of euros flowing into the United States in the form of direct investment, so that Europe now accounts for nearly 75 percent of all foreign investment in the United States.

26. M. Wilkins, *The Emergence of Multinational Enterprise: American Business Abroad from the Colonial Era to 1914* (Cambridge: Harvard University Press, 1970), 201–2, as cited in O'Rourke and Williamson, *Globalization and History*, 217.

27. Daniel S. Hamilton and Joseph P. Quinlan, *Partners in Prosperity: The Changing Geography of the Transatlantic Economy* (Washington, DC: Center for Transatlantic Relations, 2004), 17.

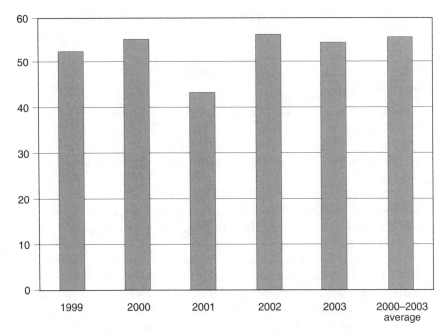

Figure 7.7. U.S. FDI outflows to Europe as a percentage of total U.S. FDI

Finally, transatlantic capital market integration is also an important part of the picture of economic interdependence in the three time periods of interest to us. There is general empirical agreement on the outlines of the story of financial market integration: well-integrated markets and subsequently high international capital flows were established by the turn of the nineteenth century, fell dramatically during the period of the world wars, and were gradually rebuilt until, in the 1990s, they reached their previously high levels.[28] There is less agreement on how to measure capital mobility than in the trade and FDI area; scholars use a variety of proxies and different yardsticks to capture financial market integration. One such measurement is interest rate differentials, which works on the assumption that the better the convergence in the price of borrowing money, the more closely are financial markets integrated. Maurice Obstfeld and Alan Taylor have explored the degree of international interest rate (real and nominal) convergence since 1870s, demonstrating that transatlantic rates for a sample of ten countries were relatively low between 1870 and 1914, widened during World War I, and converged again in the late 1920s. Rates then diverged in the 1930s and stayed

28. O'Rourke and Williamson, *Globalization and History*, 1999.

relatively spread until the late 1980s, except for some variability in the 1960s until 1973.[29]

Political Conflict, Commercial Interests, and Institutions

Having presented illustrative data on economic interdependence that chart the rise, fall, and reemergence of transatlantic market integration, I now briefly survey the three periods of crisis for indications of commercial interests' role in shaping the path of political conflict between Europe and the United States.

The three cases under consideration are the period before World War I, the Suez crisis of 1956, and the present transatlantic crisis over the Iraq War. In the first and third cases, the level of economic interdependence was historically extremely high, and societal interests might be expected to effectively voice their preferences for political stability and the maintenance of peace (and thus their personal prosperity). In the second case, the transatlantic economy was in the process of being rebuilt and thus was at a relatively low level of economic engagement. More recently, transatlantic interdependence has been at a historical peak. My overview suggests that the political activity and effectiveness of commercial interests have varied in ways that do not fit the *doux commerce* expectation, and that interdependence does not map systematically onto the outcomes of the conflicts. Although a straightforward liberal pluralist theory seems not to work in these cases, a discussion of the various time periods suggests how institutions, formal and informal, may act as an important intervening variable in shaping outcomes of political conflict.

Prelude to World War I: Angell's Paradox

The period before World War I was one of deep commercial linkages across Europe and between Europe and the United States, leading author Norman Angell in 1913 to argue "not that war is impossible, but that it is futile— useless, even when completely victorious, as a means of securing those moral or material ends which represent the needs of modern, civilized peoples." Angell built his case by arguing, in tune with much conventional wisdom today, that globalization qua market integration challenged traditional notions of statecraft as resting on war and territorial expansion. Angell saw instead the

29. Maurice Obstfeld and Alan M. Taylor, "The Great Depression as a Watershed: International Capital Mobility in the Long Run," in *The Defining Moment: The Great Depression and the American Economy in the Twentieth Century*, ed. M. D. Bordo, C. D. Goldin, and E. N. White (Chicago: University of Chicago Press, 1998).

likely result of globalization as the replacement of national interests that rely on borders with interests rooted in international interactions and exchange. In addition to the importance of changing sources of wealth, globalization and modernization were, for Angell, reducing the success of brute military power, because "the forces which have brought about the economic futility of military power have also rendered it futile as a means of enforcing a nation's moral ideals or imposing social institutions upon a conquered people."[30]

What is remarkable about Angell's book today is that it is so modern: he argues both that a material interest–based mechanism of commerce reduces the benefits and increases the costs of war, as well as that the mechanism of social interactions across a broad multiplicity of actors, private and public, produces common understandings of need for a new mode of foreign policy.[31] The futility of war, for Angell, was summed up in his view that the consequence of interdependence is that the use of force against another state is tantamount to the use of force against one's self.[32]

Angell's motivation for writing *The Great Illusion* was to challenge what he saw as the incorrect assumptions behind "the present rivalry of armaments in Europe" at the beginning of the twentieth century, particularly the Anglo-German naval buildup. Although he understood that his view of the futility of war, given interdependence, was a "little recognized fact," he believed that it would be embraced by publics if given the chance, and that mass opinion would then reformulate political elites' postures. Angell states that his discussions with both international financiers and labor leaders provided evidence of a similar "attitude of internationalization" and that these private economic actors embodied the complex interdependence that was for him the reality of states at the time.[33] The book spends little time providing evidence, however, of the views of commercial actors; rather, Angell reports on the debates and rebuttals that his views sparked among political leaders and journalists. Nonetheless, Angell's book became infamous for its argument that rational economic interests should carry the day, as Europe sank into a brutal grinding war that destroyed a generation.

More recently, one careful and systematic empirical case study of the World War I period examined the impact of economic interdependence on decision making during the July crisis of 1914. Ripsman and Blanchard assess the degree to which Germany was materially interdependent on other states, whether national decision makers were aware of that interdependence, and

---

30. Normal Angell, *The Great Illusion: A Study of Military Power to National Advantage* (New York: G. P. Putnam's Sons, 1913), 10, xi.

31. Ibid., chaps. 3 and 6, respectively. Socialization is particularly highlighted in Norman Angell, *Arms and Industry: A Study in the Foundations of International Polity* (New York: G. P. Putnam's Sons, 1914), xxxvff.

32. Angell, introduction to *Arms and Industry*.

33. Angell, *Great Illusion*, ix, 318–19.

"the relative weight they gave to economic, strategic, and domestic political factors in deciding whether or not to risk war."[34] Their historical analysis concluded that the German leaders were well aware of their dependence on the British for key food stuffs and raw materials, and they had clear signals that the British might oppose them in the event that a European war resulted from the Serbian affair. Despite this, of course, the Germans ran the risk of war and a trade blockage in pursuit of their strategic goals.

Although Ripsman and Blanchard offer a deeply skeptical view of the role of commercial interests in "high politics" in the case of Germany and Britain before World War I, Peter Trubowitz has found correlations in the U.S. historical record between different regional economic interests in global trade and regional conflicts over U.S. foreign policy. Certainly various regions of the United States had different material stakes in the transatlantic relationship before World War I, and Trubowitz, in a nuanced historical study, has documented the variation over time in this difference, and the ways this sectionalism has translated into different postures vis-à-vis foreign policy.[35] He argues that in United States, the Northeast had a significant stake in transatlantic exchange at the turn of the century, as did the South in its agrarian (most importantly cotton) export-based economy. In contrast, the West was more inwardly focused during the pre–World War I time period.[36] Trubowitz shows that these patterns of economic engagement correlated with the positions of regional congressional representatives on whether the United States should pursue a more aggressive, expansionist foreign policy, and if so, what form it should take. Important regional commercial interests were deeply engaged with Europe, and they were able to express their political beliefs to some degree in the U.S. case. However, Trubowitz focuses more on patterns of political conflict over U.S. grand strategy, as opposed to decision making over military conflict, so his account does not directly demonstrate the role of interdependent commercial interests in dampening political conflict in the first World War.

Even if there was decisive evidence about the role of commercial interests in promoting peaceful relations, pre–World War I private actors did not have a network of international institutions based on liberal norms of reciprocity and the positive-sum nature of trade. Such institutions, I have suggested, might have formed a sturdy framework for channeling economic actors'

---

34. Ripsman and Blanchard, "Commercial Liberalism under Fire," 6.

35. Peter Trubowitz, *Defining the National Interest: Conflict and Change in American Foreign Policy* (Chicago: University of Chicago Press, 1998). On British, French, and U.S. class interests and foreign policy stances, see Kevin Narizny, "Both Guns and Butter, or Neither: Class Interests in the Political Economy of Rearmament," *American Political Science Review* 97 (May 2003): 203–20. Narizny finds that right-wing governments tend to be more pacifistic, in part because they represent commercial elites whose interests would be harmed by military expansion.

36. Trubowitz, *Defining the National Interest*, chap. 2.

interests and socializing participants into viewing their national interests as interdependent and mutually reinforcing. There were, however, no generalized, multipurpose international organizations like we have today; there was no liberal economic order made up of multilateral organizations governing the international economy.

The most prominent international system in place, the gold standard, established a set of rules for the stabilization of exchange rates and international monetary affairs, but the formal rules were not joined to a concrete organization; rather, they operated automatically within the foundation of Britain's monetary hegemony.[37] On the trade side, countries engaged in bilateral treaties directly with other states, in a manner far different that of the deeply multilateral institutions of the General Agreement on Tariffs and Trade (GATT) and the WTO. The dominant thinking of the time did not embrace the positive-sum trade ideas of classical economics or the notion of "most-favored nation" but rather viewed trade agreements in a much narrower, competitive light.[38]

There was a series of more narrow functional and regional organizations, such as the Central Commission for the Navigation of the Rhine, established in 1815, and the Universal Postal Union.[39] There were only thirty-seven intergovernmental organizations on record in 1909, whereas after World War II that number quickly rose into the hundreds. Russett and O'Neal calculate that before World War I, intergovernmental organizations were less than 10 percent as numerous as they would be in the 1980s.

In sum, the pre–World War I case combines extremely high interdependence on trade and capital market integration between Europe and the United States, but low international institutionalization of these relationships into a liberal, multilateral regime. Although Norman Angell's arguments about how economic linkages across states make war a losing proposition made him a best-selling author whose infamous book was translated into two dozen languages, interdependence did not keep war at bay. The main foreign policy actors seem to have been relatively insulated from commercial actors' concerns, and the empirical literature cites little evidence that strategic considerations included the impact of military actions on trade and investment relations.

The Suez Crisis

Renewal of economic interdependence had only just begun between Europe and the United States after World War II when the Suez crisis erupted in 1956 into a serious challenge to transatlantic relations. As William Hitchcock

---

37. Barry Eichengreen, *Golden Fetters: The Gold Standard and the Great Depression, 1919–1939* (New York: Oxford University Press, 1992).

38. Douglas A. Irwin, *Against the Tide: An Intellectual History of Free Trade* (Princeton: Princeton University Press, 1997).

39. Russett and O'Neal, *Triangulating Peace*, 176.

recounts in this volume, the clash between, on the one hand, Britain and France, both of which hoped to stop Egyptian nationalization of the Suez Canal, and the United States, on the other hand, where President Eisenhower refused to support military intervention by U.S. allies to stop the nationalization, brought the crisis to a head. Figures 7.1–7.6 illustrate the reduced nature of trade relations between the United States and the European powers in 1956. However, economic statecraft still proved an effective tool for the United States, and the dramatic economic penalty that the United States demanded of Britain in terms of the decline of the pound sterling and financial instability was a major issue on both sides of the Atlantic.

The seminal historical literature on the Suez crisis does not address the question of how commercial interests viewed the dramatic political rift that it caused between Britain and France, on one hand, and the United States on the other. Eisenhower seems to have had a relatively free rein in bringing the weight of the United States to bear on its European allies, and in the process dealing the British in particular a damaging economic blow by refusing to support the pound sterling. Much of the responsibility for developing and carrying out U.S. policy lay with Secretary of State John Foster Dulles, with direct oversight by Eisenhower, and societal interests seem to have played a marginal role. Typically, one prominent and detailed account of the crisis does not include any information in its nearly six hundred pages about political elites' concerns regarding the impact of the transatlantic rift on commercial relations; rather, it focuses solely on the various "high politics" involved.[40]

Economic issues do come into play in the story—on the British side in concerns by the Treasury that the pound sterling could not sustain its losses, as well as on the U.S. side as a tool of statecraft to punish the British until a Suez withdrawal.[41] Historian Diane Kunz's account of the economic diplomacy of the Suez crisis details the uses and limitations of economic power in the crisis, but her analysis paints a picture at odds with the liberal pluralist story of engaged commercial interests seeking to smooth diplomatic relations. Instead, her account highlights a more realpolitik understanding of the motivation of actors, in which government officials focused on using economic resources solely to shore up national security.

In addition, Kunz interestingly argues that the period before the Suez crisis was marked by a sense of competition between the United States and the

---

40. Keith Kyle, *Suez: Britain's End of Empire in the Middle East* (London: I. B. Tauris, 1991). Herman Finer, "Dulles over Suez: The Theory and Practice of His Diplomacy"; Kennett Love, "Suez; The Twice-Fought War"; Terence Robertson, "Crisis: The Inside Story of the Suez Conspiracy"; and Robert R. Bowie, "Eisenhower, Dulles, and the Suez Crisis," in *Suez 1956: The Crisis and Its Consequences*, ed. William Roger Louis and Roger Owen (Oxford: Oxford University Press, 1989).

41. Kyle, *Suez*, 357, 500–502, 505 (on economic considerations); 404–7 (on the divided public opinion more broadly over the legitimacy of Britain's role in the crisis).

Britain, and finds that both key policymakers and U.S. commercial interests favored harsh policies toward the British, seeing the transatlantic economic relationship in stark zero-sum terms after World War II. Harry Dexter White, one of the chief architects of the postwar settlement, "feared that Britain, using the sterling monetary and tariff areas as a base, would develop a network of trade through the world from which the United states would be excluded," although he and others eventually recognized the dire British financial situation and concluded that it would be in the United States' interest to help stabilize Britain.[42] Selling the loan program (the Anglo-American Financial Agreement) in Congress was made difficult, according to Kunz, because "in this case many American companies did not support aid to Britain, which had been their most significant prewar rival. Bankers, eager to expand American financial networks, also opposed such aid. Prewar isolationists and fiscal conservatives also joined the fray, making the battle for legislative approval a close one."[43]

On the other side of the Atlantic, many British criticized the U.S. loan program as unfavorable to their interests, with one leading Conservative backbencher, Robert Boothby, calling it an "economic Munich."[44] The Marshall Plan aid that began flowing to Britain and the rest of Europe in 1948 represented recognition by some in the United States that, as the most robust economy and creditor to the world, the United States had a responsibility to aid in reconstruction, but the U.S. view of Britain as a potential economic competitor continued to inform policy in American circles. For his part, Eisenhower, according to Kunz, was constrained in his economic diplomacy by conservative Republicans, who clung to their party's traditional high-tariff positions.[45]

In the period immediately surrounding the Suez crisis, there is remarkably little record in the historical accounts of the representation of transatlantic commercial interests in the motivations and strategies of both the United States and Britain. On the British side, the ill-advised decisions about Suez were made by the highest security and foreign policy political elites—the prime minister, foreign secretary, and upper reaches of the Treasury department. As events unfolded, and the economic repercussions were evident, a concern with retaining British sterling as an international reserve currency, both for reasons of political prestige and for the benefit of certain segments of the City of London, was the guiding economic concern, not the overall health of the transatlantic relationship.

---

42. Diane B. Kunz, *The Economic Diplomacy of the Suez Crisis* (Chapel Hill: University of North Carolina Press, 1991), 8; see also Diane B. Kunz, "The Importance of Having Money: The Economic Diplomacy of the Suez Crisis," in Louis and Owen, *Suez 1956*, 215–32.

43. Kunz, *Economic Diplomacy of Suez*, 10.

44. Ibid., 9.

45. Ibid., 12.

Kunz writes that, on the U.S. side, "the administration's victorious campaign against Britain illustrated the executive branch's virtually untrammeled power to mobilize negative economic power in the field of foreign relations. While congressional leaders were kept informed of the administration's actions, the president had no need to obtain legislative approval to withhold financial assistance. He and his colleagues had almost complete freedom to conduct their crusade against American's allies as they saw fit."[46]

The Suez case demonstrates the power of economic statecraft in that the United States used both carrots and sticks to force British compliance in getting out of Egypt and following U.S. wishes. When the Brits retreated, the United States granted massive currency support and credits, and promoted IMF loans as well. Commercial interests were involved in that U.S. oil companies worked with the British to make contingency plans regarding oil supply continuity in the event of the closure of the canal. Within the Eisenhower administration, several key officials had held leadership positions in the private sector, but consistently seem to have used those backgrounds in support of the overall expressed national security interests of the administration rather than shaping policy to deepen economic interdependence. It is thus difficult to draw a direct link between private actors and the unfolding of the Suez crisis and its aftermath.

Finally, what of the role of international institutions in providing a subtler, intervening effect on the path of transatlantic politics? Most observers agree that international institutionalization was significantly higher in the 1950s than in the period before World War I. Whereas the number of intergovernmental organizations was 39 in 1909, it rose to 132 in 1956. The United Nations had been established, and other key common institutions of the Bretton Woods regime had begun and were expanding their memberships and activities. However, the institutionalization of the interests of commercial actors and the embedding of liberal norms within that institutional framework were relatively undeveloped compared to the current period. The GATT and pre-GATT rounds of trade talks focused on reducing the high tariff levels established in the interwar period, a much more rudimentary task requiring much less bureaucratization on the international and domestic levels to carry out than do the complex nontariff barrier negotiations of today. The diffuse reciprocity of the future WTO regime was still far away as countries scrambled to restore their economies. The IMF, as well, was in its formative stages. This relatively low level of institutionalization, both formal and informal, suggests a weaker potential for institutionalization to have a pacifying effect on the unfolding of political conflict between the United States and its European allies in the Suez period.

46. Ibid., 143.

The U.S.-EU Relationship Today

My final task is to report on the relative degree of economic independence in the contemporary era between the United States and the EU, probe the level of political conflict demonstrated between them, and discuss the potential for deeper and qualitatively different institutionalization to promote more cooperative outcomes than those of the World War I or Suez periods.

The data I presented in the first section of this chapter (figs. 7.1–7.6) illustrate that trade with Europe is surprisingly less important to the U.S. economy than it was at the turn of the century, as other regions of the world, particularly Latin America and Asia, have gained in economic prominence and engagement with the United States. However, trade levels alone do not necessarily provide the best measure of economic engagement. As Hamilton and Quinlan extensively document in their 2004 study, the transatlantic relationship has reached historic levels of foreign direct investment as U.S. and European corporations invest in each other's countries and engage in complex commercial interactions (see fig. 7.7). These economic stakes have been apparent in the expression of concern by private actors over the ratcheting up of transatlantic tensions. For example, the CEO of Daimler-Chrysler was the first European to meet with President Bush after the events of September 11, 2001. Policymakers such as Pascal Lamy, then EU trade commissioner, have voiced the view that commercial relations constitute the cement of the alliance: "Trade is the stabiliser in the transatlantic relationship—a billion euros a day of stabiliser."[47]

How have these levels of economic interdependence translated into political concern and action? A survey of U.S. congressional hearings from 1995 to 2004 gives us a picture of the political concerns of members of Congress and their constituents in the area of the transatlantic relationship and some insights into the public representation of economic interests in this area (table 7.1). The data are as follows. Ninety hearings were coded as engaging with some aspect of the transatlantic relationship over this nine-year time period.[48] Almost half of the hearings were evenly divided between those focused on the general relationship (a mix of security, economic, and other concerns) and those on economic matters (for example, regulatory standards, financial integration, and the effects of the euro on the dollar). A significant minority was specifically about military concerns (fifteen), with other more specific hearings concerned with the perennial sticking points of agriculture and the Foreign Sales Corporation (FSC) tax.

47. Pascal Lamy, EU trade commissioner, "Where Next for EU Trade Policy?" speech delivered at Deutsche Gesellschaft für Auswärtige Politik, Berlin, 11 June 2004.
48. All cases are from the Lexis-Nexis Congressional Database for this time period. The following keywords were used: European Union, United States, Europe, foreign economic relations, foreign trade, Subcommittee on the European Union, Subcommittee on Europe, and Subcommittee on European Affairs.

Table 7. 1. Congressional hearings on transatlantic topics, 1995–2004

U.S.-EU general relationship	25
U.S.-EU economic (general and misc. specific)	26
U.S.-EU military	15
U.S.-EU terrorism / war on terror	5
U.S.-EU regulatory framework	3
U.S.-EU visa issues	1
U.S.-EU agriculture issues	8
U.S.-EU FSC/extraterritorial income regime	7
TOTAL	90

In addition to considering what issues concerned Congress, it is useful to consider the changing frequency of these hearings over time. Over the past decade, the number of hearings on some aspect of the U.S.-EU relationship has varied year to year, but there was a dramatic rise in the number of hearings after the Bush administration decided to pursue a war in Iraq. Whereas the number of hearings before 2001 had never exceed 10 in a given year, there were 12 in 2002, and the total expanded to 21 in 2003 before falling to 10 again in 2004. Clearly, the U.S. Congress was feeling political pressure to investigate the relationship, and the hearings on the nature of the alliance were taking up broader issues than the usual diet of trade-related squabbles. The main speakers testifying at these hearings, however, were academic and think tank experts on the transatlantic alliance rather than private economic actors voicing their views, as might be predicted by the liberal pluralist argument.

The liberal pluralist argument is also put into doubt when we examine accounts of the decision making surrounding the diplomacy of the Iraq War. There is little evidence that the growing concern in some parts over the potentially deteriorating U.S.-EU relationship penetrated the inner circles of decision making on foreign policy and the war in Iraq. Accounts of the decision-making processes surrounding the run-up to and prosecution of the war stress the small circle of officials involved in the decisions regarding diplomacy and strategy. For example, Ron Suskind's carefully researched account of Paul O'Neill's tenure as secretary of the treasury makes it clear that O'Neill had little input or even knowledge of what was being discussed and planned after 9/11.[49] If concerns on the part of important commercial interests are to have an impact on major decisions about what level and type of political conflict the United States should engage in, it seems likely that the secretary of the treasury might be a key conduit for expressing those views. Suskind as-

49. Ron Suskind, *The Price of Loyalty: George W. Bush, the White House, and the Education of Paul O'Neill* (New York: Simon and Schuster, 2004).

sembles a portrait of the administration's decision-making process that in many ways echoes the historical narrative of the Suez crisis: a small group of insiders making policy driven by their own narrowly but decisively constructed view of the national interest and strategy. In addition, electoral politics did not seem to force officials to focus on maintaining good relations with trade and investment partners in the way that some theorists of the pacifying effects of interdependence would posit. Because the U.S. national elections of 2004 were framed as a contest more about national security and values issues rather than the traditional "bread and butter" economic ones, this channel also seems to have been closed off. The straightforward effects of high levels of economic interdependence do not seem to have had much of a brake on the escalation of political crisis in the transatlantic relationship in the current era.

Perhaps these outcomes are not so surprising when put in the context of our survey of previous episodes of transatlantic conflict and the limited role of trade and investment in generating pacifism. More convincing, but not likely to show immediate effects that we can report on, might be the argument I outlined in the theoretical section, but that is less explored by the literature on economic interdependence and war. If the "socialization of low politics" within institutional frameworks might have a causal impact on conflict outcomes, might we see the maintenance of strong transatlantic ties into the future? Although levels of economic interdependence are similar today in many respects to those at the turn of the century, the nature of that interdependence is different in that it involves much more complex, domestically entrenched linkages via foreign direct investment. For this market integration to be sustained, actors have worked to embed these relationships within a broad array of formal international institutions.

During the 1990s, the number of intergovernmental organizations reached nearly three hundred.[50] They span an array of functions and geographic configurations. Most pertinent to the dynamics of the transatlantic relationship are the vast number of institutional linkages that have been established between the United States and the EU in the past decades. If the content and working of these institutions are on the whole cooperative, they will most likely strengthen and reinforce the relationship. Reacting to an op-ed piece stating that the U.S.-EU rift would not easily be bridged, Niall FitzGerald, the chairman of Unilever, wrote that the economic links are prospering, and

> we can do more still if we try. . . . According to some studies, removing remaining tariff and non-tariff barriers to transatlantic trade and commerce could produce gross domestic product gains of 1–2 per cent. That is the reason why chief executives on both sides of the Atlantic have agreed to join forces in

50 . Union of International Associations, *Yearbook of International Organizations* (Brussels, Belgium, 1992–93), 1610–11.

a revived Transatlantic Business Dialogue—to work with the EU and US authorities to encourage mutual prosperity and to remind the pessimists of the permanent ties that continue to bind the transatlantic relationship.[51]

These subtler effects of interdependence on political outcomes may end up being decisive as the transatlantic alliance weathers the years following the stresses and strains of the diplomatic rifts around the Iraq War.

Conclusion

The United States and Europe have much in common across a wide range of foreign policy issues, not the least of which is their deep economic interdependence. The persistence of negotiators working on the current Open Skies negotiations, despite tensions in the realm of high foreign policy across the Atlantic, reflects those common economic interests. However, my evaluation of the theoretical and empirical arguments for the *doux commerce* thesis and my survey of the World War I, Suez, and present-day periods give us little reason to believe that economic interdependence alone can bind together the United States and the EU. Historically, decision making during perceived crises in the transatlantic alliance has been driven much more by direct national security concerns than the liberal pluralist arguments might suggest. In the case of the Suez in particular, economic exchange relations were more likely to be viewed as a tool of statecraft that leaders could use to gain their desired geopolitical ends, rather than being ends in themselves. From this perspective, trade and investment do not inevitably produce equal benefits to all transacting nations but rather can both reflect and shape future power asymmetries.

Instead of the straightforward causal links assumed by some observers, it may be more likely that complex and intervening factors build on interdependence to shape the path of political interactions. Future research should investigate the argument that economic ties are more likely to bind politically if they are embedded within specific kinds of social and political institutions, ones that may subtly shape actors' calculations away from intense political conflict. Most importantly, if economic ties are knit into a political order that privileges diffusive reciprocity and universal rules over mercantilist winner-take-all competition and zero-sum thinking, intensive trade and investment may be more likely to have a pacifying effect. Today's trade and investment exchanges are largely viewed by economic elites in a positive-sum light, as providing reciprocal benefits, and this social understanding is institutionalized into multilateralism of the Atlantic order. This view was far from the case in the pre–World War I or Suez periods. The combination of market integration

---

51. As quoted in the Letters section, *Financial Times*, 15 June 2004.

and deeply institutionalized comity between the United States and the EU is likely to smooth the transatlantic relationship—with the caveat that the "high politics" of national security strategy will always trump commercial interests in situations of extreme conflict. Future researchers and policymakers might do well to focus more on the socially constructed, institutional aspects of the transatlantic relationship if they want them to yield benefits in promoting peace and stability.

8 CRISIS, WHAT CRISIS?

Transatlantic Differences and the Foundations of International Law

MICHAEL BYERS

International law was at the center of the political conflict that consumed the Atlantic community in 2002–3. Between September and November 2002, U.S. secretary of state Colin Powell spent eight weeks negotiating UN Security Council Resolution 1441.[1] In February 2003, British prime minister Tony Blair fought for, but failed to obtain, a so-called second resolution to bolster the legal case for war. In the end, both the U.S. and British governments retreated to an argument that Resolution 1441, by finding Iraq in "material breach" of its disarmament obligations, had implicitly reactivated the authorization to use force provided twelve years earlier on the eve of the Gulf War. Spain, Italy, and Poland went along with this argument; other members of the Atlantic community, including France, Germany, and Canada, did not.

International law's central position in the transatlantic conflict makes the international legal system an ideal focal point for considering whether relations between the United States and Europe have changed fundamentally during recent years. An analysis of international law before, during, and after the conflict can help us answer the question that motivates this book: Are the recent tensions and disputes between the United States and Europe a reflection of deep problems, contradictions, and dysfunctions of the Atlantic political system or part of the healthy functioning of a stable political order?[2]

In particular, an analysis of international law can help to determine whether the recent conflict has led to a crisis, defined by John Ikenberry in the

I am grateful for incisive comments from the editors and contributors to this volume as well as from Nico Krisch, Richard Price, and Adriana Sinclair. In parts of this chapter I draw on Michael Byers, *War Law* (London: Atlantic Books, 2005/New York: Grove/Atlantic, 2006).

1. S/Res/1441, 8 November 2002, http://www.un.org/documents/scres.htm.
2. The question is asked by John Ikenberry in the introduction to this volume.

introduction to this volume as "a situation in which one or more of four circumstances obtains: (1) a fundamental disagreement breaks out over what at least one side believes is a core interest; (2) a sharp break occurs in market and social interdependence; (3) an institutional breakdown occurs regarding the rules and norms of process; (4) and/or a breakdown occurs in a sense of community." In this chapter I am concerned with the third of these indicia, the rules and norms of process that regulate the transatlantic relationship, many of which will be rules of international law.

International law is distinct from other phenomena in international relations in that it is created consensually by states for the purpose of constraining or shaping their own behavior (although its rules sometimes take on a life of their own, for example, by altering state identities and interests). International law is not immutable—indeed, the international legal system continually evolves—but rules, in order to constrain or shape behavior, must possess a degree of resistance to change. In other words, a norm or standard cannot be considered a rule if it may be altered at the whim of those whom it supposedly constrains.

Some rules of international law are more resistant to change than others.[3] In the case of customary international law, this resistance to change develops through the gradual accretion of state practice and *opinio juris* (a subjective belief in the existence of obligation). In the case of a treaty, resistance develops through widespread ratifications, which render renegotiation difficult, or through the inclusion of a supermajority requirement or veto in the treaty's amendment provisions. Not surprisingly, some of international law's most resistant rules concern foundational aspects of state sovereignty, such as the right of self-defense, or process rules (what H. L. A. Hart famously called "secondary rules")[4] that govern how rules are made, interpreted, or changed.

In this chapter I focus on two of these relatively more resistant rules, namely, the right of self-defense and the general rule of interpretation, and follow their course through the geopolitical transformations of the last two decades. These particular rules are selected for two reasons. First, the content of both rules has repeatedly been the subject of prominent contestation, and it seems likely that divergence on foundational aspects of international law, if it occurs, will appear first with respect to rules that are repeatedly and prominently disputed. The right of self-defense was at issue during the 1981 Israeli bombing of an Iraqi nuclear reactor, the 1986 U.S. bombing of Tripoli, Libya, the 1984–86 *Nicaragua* case in the International Court of Justice, the 1998 cruise missile strikes in Afghanistan and Sudan, the 2001 invasion of Afghanistan, and the subsequent articulation of the Bush doctrine of preventive self-defense. For its part, the

---

3. See generally Michael Byers, *Custom, Power and the Power of Rules* (Cambridge: Cambridge University Press, 1999).
4. H. L. A. Hart, *The Concept of Law* (Oxford: Oxford University Press, 1961), 77–96.

general rule of interpretation figured prominently in debates over the 1972 Anti-Ballistic Missile Treaty (and its compatibility with the U.S. Strategic Defense Initiative as well as, later, ballistic missile defense), Security Council Resolutions 1199 and 1203 before and during the 1999 Kosovo War, Security Council Resolutions 678, 687, and 1441 in the lead up to the 2003 Iraq War, and various provisions of the 1949 Geneva Conventions and 1984 Torture Convention during the so-called global war on terrorism.

The second reason for examining the right of self-defense and the general rule of interpretation is that these are longstanding, deeply rooted rules of customary international law that are more resistant to change than any treaty. The United States and European countries have disagreed in recent years over the 1997 Kyoto Protocol, the 1997 Landmines Convention, the 1998 Rome Statute of the International Criminal Court, and other treaties. These differences are clearly important, but it is unclear whether they reflect fundamental divergences over the international legal system as a whole, rather than different policies on fairly specific issues.

In this chapter I dig deeper by examining two foundational rules of more general importance. and find that the approaches taken by the United States and European countries to these rules have remained remarkably constant. This discovery in turn suggests an absence of breakdown concerning "the rules and norms of process that regulate the transatlantic relationship." With respect to at least one of the four indicia identified in this book, there is no apparent crisis—notwithstanding the very public controversies over international law that have recently occurred.

Right of Self-Defense

The right of self-defense in contemporary international law dates back to 1837, when the British were crushing a rebellion in Upper Canada (now Ontario). The United States, while unwilling to antagonize a superpower by supporting the rebels directly, did not prevent a private militia from being formed in upstate New York. The "volunteers" used a steamboat, the *Caroline*, to transport arms and men to the rebel headquarters on Navy Island, on the Canadian side of the Niagara River. The British responded with a night raid, capturing the vessel while it was docked at Fort Schlosser, New York. They set the boat on fire and sent it over Niagara Falls. Two men were killed as they fled the steamer, and two prisoners were taken back to Canada but later released.

The incident caused disquiet in Washington, D.C. British forces, having torched the White House and Capitol in 1814, were again intervening on U.S. territory. Some careful diplomacy ensued, with U.S. secretary of state Daniel Webster conceding that the use of force in self-defense could be justified when "the necessity of that self-defense is instant, overwhelming, leaving no choice of means, and no moment of deliberation," and provided that nothing "unreasonable or excessive" was done.[5] The British accepted Webster's criteria. Over time, as other countries expressed the same view of the law in other disputes, the *Caroline* criteria—often referred to simply as "necessity and proportionality"—were transformed into the parameters of a new right of self-defense in customary international law.

In 1945, the drafters of the UN Charter included self-defense as an exception to their new, general prohibition on the use of military force. In addition to the existing customary criteria, three further restrictions were introduced: (1) a state could act in self-defense only if subject to an "armed attack"; (2) acts of self-defense had to be reported immediately to the Security Council; and (3) the right to respond would terminate as soon as the council took action.[6]

Despite this careful attempt at definition, the precise limits of self-defense still depend greatly on customary international law, in part because the UN Charter refers explicitly to the "inherent" character of the right. And so, although the right of self-defense is codified in an almost universally ratified treaty, its parameters have evolved gradually—or at least become more easily discernable—as the result of the behavior of states since 1945. And as with all rules of customary international law, the relevant behavior includes not only the action and claims of the state proponents of legal change but also the responses—or lack of responses—of other countries.[7] This broad compass of behavior (state practice and *opinio juris*) should be borne in mind as we turn to our first transatlantic dispute over this rule.

Self-Defense against Terrorism

In April 1986, a terrorist bomb exploded in a West Berlin nightclub crowded with U.S. servicemen. One soldier and a Turkish woman were killed and 230 people were wounded, including 50 U.S. military personnel. Two weeks later, the United States responded by bombing a number of targets in Tripoli. Thirty-six people were killed, including an adopted daughter of Libyan leader Muammar Gadaffi.

Washington claimed that the strike on Libya was an act of self-defense— notwithstanding that the right of self-defense, as traditionally conceived, did not extend to acts committed by nonstate actors outside the territory of the responding state. As then secretary of state George P. Shultz said, "the Charter's restrictions on the use or threat of force in international relations include a specific exception for the right of self-defense. It is absurd to argue that international law prohibits us from capturing terrorists in international waters or airspace; from attacking them on the soil of other nations, even for

5. See R. Y. Jennings, "The *Caroline* and *McLeod* Cases," *American Journal of International Law* 32 (1938): 82.

6. Article 51, UN Charter, http://www.un.org/aboutun/charter/index.html.

7. See generally Byers, *Custom, Power and the Power of Rules*.

the purpose of rescuing hostages; or from using force against states that support, train, and harbor terrorists or guerrillas."[8]

The claim was widely rejected, with many governments also expressing doubt about whether the strike—with its two-week delay and use of heavy munitions—met the "necessity and proportionality" criteria for self-defense. The most significant evidence of the lack of support was the refusal of France and Spain—both NATO allies of the United States—to allow their airspace to be used by the bombers that conducted the raid. As a result, the pilots, who began their mission at a U.S. airbase in Britain, had to fly westward around the Iberian Peninsula. The widespread negative reactions from other countries meant that the legal claim and associated military action failed to change international law, at least at the time. Yet the United States continued to hold fast to the claimed right to use force in self-defense "against states that support, train, and harbor terrorists or guerrillas."

For instance, when Nicaragua filed suit against the United States in the International Court of Justice in 1984, Washington justified its actions in support of the Contras as collective self-defense—on the basis that Nicaragua's supply of arms, and its financial and logistical support of rebel groups in surrounding countries, amounted to an armed attack on those countries, to whose assistance the United States could then come. The United States also argued that the Court lacked jurisdiction to hear the case; when the majority of the judges ruled otherwise in a preliminary judgment, Washington refused to participate in further hearings. In 1986, the Court held that Nicaragua's combined actions did not amount to an armed attack. It also decided that collective self-defense may only be exercised if the country under attack requests assistance, and this Nicaragua's neighbors had not done. The United States publicly rejected the judgment in the strongest terms.[9]

Twelve years later, in August 1998, two bombs exploded outside the U.S. embassies in Nairobi, Kenya, and Dar es Salaam, Tanzania. Twelve Americans and almost three hundred Kenyans and Tanzanians were killed; thousands more were injured. U.S. intelligence sources indicated that Osama bin Laden and his al-Qaeda organization were behind the attacks. Two weeks later, the United States fired seventy-nine cruise missiles at six terrorist training camps around Khowst, Afghanistan, and at a pharmaceutical plant on the outskirts of Khartoum, Sudan. At the time, the Central Intelligence Agency believed that the plant was producing precursors to chemical weapons; subsequently it emerged that the intelligence was flawed.

---

8. "Address by Secretary of State George P. Shultz, Low-Intensity Warfare Conference, National Defense University, Washington, D.C., January 15, 1986," reprinted in *International Legal Materials* 25 (1986): 204.

9. See Paul Lewis, "World Court Supports Nicaragua after U.S. Rejected Judges' Role," *New York Times*, 28 June 1986, 1.

The United States again sought to justify its actions on the basis of self-defense. As then national security adviser Sandy Berger said: "I think it is appropriate, under Article 51 of the UN Charter, for protecting the self-defense of the United States . . . for us to try and disrupt and destroy those kinds of military terrorist targets."[10] The continuity between this claim and that used to justify the 1986 bombing of Libya is apparent, although the United States did a better job of promoting its position the second time around. For example, President Bill Clinton telephoned Tony Blair, Jacques Chirac, and German chancellor Helmut Kohl shortly before the cruise missile strikes and asked for their support. Without time to consult their lawyers, all three leaders agreed—and subsequently made concurring public statements immediately following the U.S. action. As a result of the timely expressions of support, other countries were more restrained in their response than they might have been. The muted response was probably not sufficient to change a relatively resistant rule of international law, but it contributed to obfuscating the limits of self-defense, making that rule more susceptible to change in a subsequent situation.

That situation arose on September 11, 2001, when nineteen al-Qaeda operatives seized four passenger jets, crashing two of them into the World Trade Center and another into the Pentagon; the fourth plane was brought down in a Pennsylvania field after the passengers revolted against the hijackers. Nearly three thousand people were killed in the attacks. Almost immediately, the U.S. government declared that it would respond militarily on the basis of self-defense. The following statement by John Negroponte, then U.S. permanent representative to the United Nations, advanced a claim that, at its core, was nearly identical to the one asserted by George Shultz in 1986:

> The United States of America, together with other States, has initiated actions in the exercise of its inherent right of individual and collective self-defense following armed attacks that were carried out against the United States on September 11, 2001. . . . Since September 11, my Government has obtained clear and compelling information that the Al-Qaeda organization, which is supported by the Taliban regime in Afghanistan, had a central role in the attacks. . . . The attacks on September 11, 2001, and the ongoing threat to the United States and its nationals posed by the Al-Qaeda organization have been made possible by the decision of the Taliban regime to allow the parts of Afghanistan that it controls to be used by this organization as a base of operation.[11]

10. Secretary of State Madeline Albright and National Security Adviser Samuel Berger, "News Briefing," FDCH Political Transcripts, 20 August 1998.

11. John Negroponte, "Letter Dated 7 October 2001 from the Permanent Representative of the United States of America to the United Nations Addressed to the President of the Security Council," UN Doc. S/2001/946, 7 October 2001, http://www.un.int/usa/s-2001–946.htm.

The reappearance of the Shultz doctrine in 2001 demonstrates significant continuity in an international legal position adopted by the United States. This continuity is likely based on a multiplicity of factors, including continuity of personnel—even within a system in which periodic alternations between Republican and Democratic administrations result in significant management turnover. For example, William Taft IV was the general counsel to the Department of Defense who crafted the legal response to the terrorist attack on the West Berlin nightclub in 1986. Fifteen years later, the same Taft was the State Department legal adviser who crafted the international legal response to the terrorist attacks of September 11, 2001.

Despite the continuity, the Shultz doctrine was modified somewhat in its 2001 expression so as to better enable the United States to comply with the *Caroline* criteria of necessity and proportionality and, through this compliance, build and maintain the coalition of countries willing to use force in Afghanistan. To meet the criteria, the military action had to focus on those individuals believed responsible for the three thousand deaths. If, however, the United States had singled out bin Laden and al-Qaeda as its targets, it would have run up against the widely held view that terrorist attacks, in and of themselves, do not justify military responses within the territory of sovereign countries. Even today, most countries are wary of a rule that could expose them to attack whenever terrorists were thought to operate from within their borders. Consider, for instance, the position of Germany after September 11, 2001: although the city of Hamburg unwittingly harbored several of the terrorists, few persons would maintain that this fact alone could have justified a U.S. attack.

The dilemma was overcome when the United States implicated the Taliban. By giving refuge to bin Laden and al-Qaeda and refusing to hand them over, the Taliban was alleged to have directly facilitated and endorsed their actions. The United States even gave the Taliban a deadline for surrendering bin Laden, a move that served to ensure their complicity. Moreover, the Taliban's continued control over Afghanistan was portrayed as a threat, in and of itself, of continued terrorism.[12]

In this way, the United States framed its claim in a manner that encompassed action against the state of Afghanistan, but without asserting the right to use force against terrorists regardless of their location. Although still contentious, this claim was much less of a stretch from preexisting international law than a claimed right to attack terrorists who simply happened to be within another country. Subsequent statements by the Taliban that endorsed the terrorist acts further raised the level of their alleged responsibility. For these reasons, the claim to be acting in self-defense in Afghanistan—and the modification of customary international law that that

12. Ibid.

claim entailed—had a much better chance of securing the expressed or tacit support of other countries.

The United States also deployed its considerable influence to secure widespread support in advance of military action. The collective self-defense provisions of the 1949 North Atlantic Treaty and the 1947 Inter-American Treaty of Reciprocal Assistance were engaged, and both NATO and the Organization of American States formally deemed the events of September 11, 2001, an "armed attack"—legally relevant language under the self-defense provision of the UN Charter. Similarly, UN Security Council resolutions adopted on September 12 and 28, 2001, were carefully worded to affirm the right of self-defense in customary international law, within the context of the terrorist attacks on New York and Washington, D.C.[13]

As a result of the events of September 11, 2001, the consequential worldwide concern about terrorism, widespread sympathy for the United States, and the strategic lawmaking approach adopted by U.S. government lawyers, the right of self-defense now includes military responses against countries that willingly harbor or support terrorist groups, provided that the terrorists have already struck the responding state. The Shultz doctrine, in its more narrowly articulated form, is now part of customary international law, after a nearly two-decade-long effort involving the maintenance of a remarkably consistent U.S. legal position—and despite, in the first decade, determined opposition from countries such as France and Spain. Instead of transatlantic divergence on this sensitive issue, we see consistency by the United States and convergence, toward the U.S. position, by European countries. Much the same can be said about the even more sensitive issue of preemptive self-defense.

Preemptive Self-Defense

In June 1981, nine Israeli air force pilots conducted a bold and dangerous raid deep into hostile territory. Hugging the ground to avoid detection, they flew more than six hundred miles before dropping their bombs on a nuclear reactor under construction at Osirak, near Baghdad. The reactor was badly damaged, Iraq's nuclear program was impaired, and none of the attacking planes was lost. Israel claimed preemptive self-defense on the basis that a nuclear-armed Iraq would constitute an unacceptable threat, especially given Saddam Hussein's overt hostility toward the Jewish state. The UN Security Council immediately and unanimously condemned the action as illegal.[14] The condemnation was all the stronger because the United States joined in the vote rather than abstaining.

13. S/Res/1368, UN Doc SC/7143; S/Res/1373, UN Doc SC/7158; both at http://www.un.org/documents/scres.htm.

14. S/Res/487, 19 June 1981, http://www.un.org/documents/scres.htm.

More than customary international law was at issue, since the UN Charter sets out a general prohibition on the use of force before recognizing the right of self-defense "if an armed attack occurs." Interpreting the self-defense provision of the charter requires that we look to the customary international law rules of treaty interpretation, which are codified in the 1969 Vienna Convention on the Law of Treaties and stipulate that treaties must be interpreted in accordance with the "ordinary meaning of the terms."[15] When this approach is applied, any preexisting right of preemptive self-defense is apparently superseded by the "if an armed attack occurs" language—particularly since the right of self-defense is codified as an exception to the general prohibition on the use of force.

The UN Charter also refers to the "inherent" character of the right of self-defense, however. This reference complicates the analysis by implicitly incorporating the preexisting customary international law of self-defense into the treaty. Consequently, it is sometimes argued that preemptive action is justified if there is a "necessity of self-defense, instant, overwhelming, leaving no choice of means, and no moment of deliberation"—the *Caroline* criteria in their original, full expression.[16] Until the adoption of the UN Charter in 1945, these criteria were widely accepted as delimiting a narrow right of preemptive self-defense in customary international law. Today, even a narrow right of preemption can only exist if the language of the charter is ignored, re-read, or viewed as having been modified by subsequent state practice. Yet during the latter half of the twentieth century, most of the state practice cut the other way.[17]

After 1945, most governments refrained from claiming preemptive self-defense.[18] The United States, concerned about establishing a precedent that other countries might employ, implausibly justified its 1962 blockade of Cuba as "regional peacekeeping." Israel, concerned not to be seen as an aggressor state, justified the strikes that initiated the 1967 Six-Day War on the basis that Egypt's blocking of the Straits of Tiran constituted a prior act of aggression. And in 1988, the United States argued that the shooting down of an Iranian civilian Airbus by the USS *Vincennes*, although mistaken, had been in response to an ongoing attack by Iranian military helicopters and patrol boats. Even the most hawkish leaders baulked at a right of preemptive action during the cold war, at a time when both of the world's principal disputants possessed armadas of nuclear missile submarines designed to survive first strikes and ensure "mutually assured destruction." The unanimous vote in

15. Article 31, Vienna Convention on the Law of Treaties, http://untreaty.un.org/ilc/texts/instruments/english/conventions/1_1_1969.pdf.

16. See Jennings, "*Caroline* and *McLeod* Cases," 82.

17. See generally Christine Gray, *International Law and the Use of Force*, 2nd ed. (Oxford: Oxford University Press, 2004), 129–33.

18. See Michael Byers, "Preemptive Self-Defense: Hegemony, Equality and Strategies of Legal Change," *Journal of Political Philosophy* 11 (2003): 171.

the Security Council to condemn the Osirak bombing was but the clearest indication of this thinking. That said, during the cold war there was widespread acceptance of what could be considered a narrow right of preemption in one very particular context, namely, the right to launch missiles as soon as it became clear that enemy missiles were incoming, without having to wait for them to strike.

Today, as seen from the White House, the situation looks quite different. Relations with Russia have improved, no other potential enemy has submarine-based nuclear missiles (although China may eventually acquire some), and the first phase of a missile defense system has been initiated. When President George W. Bush announced an expansive new policy of preemptive military action on June 1, 2002, he clearly did not feel deterred by the prospect of Armageddon.

During a commencement speech at West Point, President Bush addressed the threat of weapons of mass destruction in association with international terrorism. He advocated a degree of preemption that extended toward the preventive or even precautionary use of force: "We must take the battle to the enemy, disrupt his plans, and confront the worst threats before they emerge." Even if the threats are not imminent, "if we wait for threats to fully materialize, we will have waited too long."[19] The new policy—now widely referred to as the Bush doctrine—made no attempt to satisfy the *Caroline* criteria. There was no suggestion of waiting for a "necessity of self-defense" that was "instant, overwhelming, leaving no choice of means, and no moment of deliberation." As a policy statement, the Bush doctrine was a radical departure from the U.S. position during the cold war.

Although the president was articulating a new policy and not a legal claim, some hard legal thinking was required. That task was left to State Department lawyers who were aware that the policy—as articulated—had little chance of achieving the widespread international support necessary to change customary international law. Relatively few countries possess enough of a military deterrence to be able to contemplate a world without the combined protections of the UN Charter and the *Caroline* criteria.

The State Department lawyers had at least two reasons for wanting to keep the U.S. legal position within the sphere of widely accepted international law. First, legal criteria for self-defense can sometimes usefully be deployed, by the United States, to deter and constrain the actions of other countries. Second, acting within the scope of the law can facilitate efforts to persuade others to support and join those actions, while avoiding such penalties (such as the refusal of most countries to deploy forces to postwar

---

19. Remarks by President George W. Bush at the 2002 graduation exercise of the United States Military Academy West Point, New York, http://www.whitehouse.gov/news/releases/2002/06/20020601-3.html.

Iraq) as can be imposed on the single superpower when it acts outside the rules.

Accordingly, the Bush doctrine was reformulated into a legal claim that would be more acceptable to other countries, and therefore more effective in promoting legal change. In September 2002, the national security strategy of the United States explicitly adopted—and then sought to extend—the criteria for self-defense articulated by Daniel Webster following the *Caroline* incident:

> For centuries, international law recognized that nations need not suffer an attack before they can lawfully take action to defend themselves against forces that present an imminent danger of attack. Legal scholars and international jurists often conditioned the legitimacy of preemption on the existence of an imminent threat—most often a visible mobilization of armies, navies, and air forces preparing to attack.
>
> We must adapt the concept of imminent threat to the capabilities and objectives of today's adversaries.[20]

In other words, the national security strategy took George W. Bush's newly articulated policy of prevention or precaution and recast it within the widely accepted, preexisting framework of preemptive self-defense. It did so, first, by omitting any mention of the UN Charter, thus implicitly asserting that the pre-1945 customary right of self-defense remained the applicable law. By glossing over the problematic relationship between the *Caroline* criteria and the charter, the document strategically sought to establish a new baseline for the legal discussion of self-defense. Only then did it go further, asserting that the criterion of imminence now extends beyond threats that are "instant, overwhelming, leaving no choice of means, and no moment of deliberation," to include more distant and uncertain challenges.

This claim was made within a context that at least suggested the need for legal change. Few would contest that terrorism and weapons of mass destruction are serious problems. But more significantly, other governments were not actually asked to agree on a change in the rule. Instead, all the national security strategy proposed was an adaptation of how the (supposed) existing rule is applied in practice. As a result, the subsequent debate over the U.S. legal position has revolved not around radically different understandings of what the law is or should be, but around where and when the changing character of weaponry and warfare justifies recourse to that law. In short, the existence of an imminent threat, in any specific context, is a factual rather than a legal determination.

20. National security strategy of the United States, 20 September 2002, 19, http://www.whitehouse.gov/nsc/nss.html.

Admittedly, by seeking to stretch the concept of imminence to encompass new facts, the U.S. approach would render the law more flexible and thus allow power, influence, and assertions of secret intelligence to play a greater role in its application. Other countries have properly opposed the reformulated Bush doctrine on this basis. However, the important point for the purposes of this chapter is that the Bush administration, in its legal claim, has neither sought to radically change the status quo nor caused any significant change inadvertently.

The only legally related change noticeable as a result of the Bush doctrine is a marked decline in assertions, by states and scholars, that the UN Charter precludes any right whatsoever of preemptive self-defense. Even the UN secretary-general's High-Level Panel on Threats, Challenges and Change assumed, without question, that "a threatened State, according to long established international law, can take military action as long as the threatened attack is *imminent*, no other means would deflect it and the action is proportionate."[21] However, this shift in opinion represents the final resolution of a debate over the continued existence of a tightly limited right of preemptive self-defense and does not constitute acceptance of the more extended right currently sought by the U.S. government.

Ironically, the fact that no further legal change has occurred may be attributable, in part, to the successful U.S. effort to negotiate UN Security Council Resolution 1441.[22] Although the resolution did not expressly authorize the use of force against Iraq, it provided some support for an argument that a previous authorization, accorded in 1990, had been revived as a result of Iraq's "material breaches" of the 1991 cease-fire resolution and, later, Resolution 1441 itself. In its statements outside the Security Council, the Bush administration relied on both this argument and an extended claim of preemptive self-defense to justify the 2003 Iraq War; inside the council, it invoked the resolutions-based argument only. Its two principal allies, Britain and Australia, relied solely on the Security Council resolutions in both contexts. The advancement of two distinct arguments, with the one focused on the resolutions being given primacy and receiving broader support, reduced any effect that the extended claim to preemptive self-defense might have had on customary international law.

For our purposes, what matters is that the United States remains committed to the customary international law criteria that it helped craft following the *Caroline* incident more than a century and a half ago. Notwithstanding the new policy position known as the Bush doctrine, the U.S. legal position on preemptive self-defense has remained more or less consistent, as indeed have

21. *A More Secure World: Our Shared Responsibility*, report of the secretary-general's High-Level Panel on Threats, Challenges and Change, December 2004, p. 54, para. 188, http://www.un.org/secureworld/report.pdf.

22. S/Res/1441, 8 November 2002, http://www.un.org/Docs/scres.htm.

the positions of European states. Much the same can be said about the next area of international law under consideration, namely, the general rule of interpretation—as applied to treaties and UN Security Council resolutions.

General Rule of Interpretation

Treaties

Compared to most other countries, the United States tends to place more weight on the "object and purpose" of international documents and less weight on the actual language used. This tendency dates back to at least 1968 when the U.S. delegation to the Vienna Conference on the Law of Treaties proposed a purposive approach to treaty interpretation. The proposed approach emphasized a comprehensive examination of the context of any particular treaty in order to ascertain the common will of the parties. But it was rejected overwhelmingly by the other delegations, and accordingly, article 31(1) of the Vienna Convention stipulates: "A treaty shall be interpreted in good faith in accordance with the ordinary meaning to be given to the terms of the treaty in their context and in the light of its object and purpose."[23] Thus, the emphasis is on the actual text of the treaty. As importantly, article 32 of the Vienna Convention restricts consideration of the "preparatory work of the treaty . . . to determine the meaning" to situations in which "the interpretation according to article 31" has left the meaning "ambiguous or obscure" or led to a result "which is manifestly absurd or unreasonable." In other words, preparatory documents, records of negotiations, and other evidence of the will of the parties cannot generally be used for interpretative purposes. In 1971, the United States changed its position and acknowledged that the Vienna Convention was an accurate codification of customary international law.[24]

More recently, the U.S. government has occasionally reasserted a preference for a more purposive approach to treaty interpretation. For example, in June 2000, lawyers from the State Department, the Defense Department, and the National Security Council concluded that the 1972 Anti-Ballistic Missile Treaty between the United States and Russia (as the successor to the Soviet Union's treaty obligations) could be interpreted so as to allow construction work, including the pouring of concrete, for a new ballistic missile defense radar station in Alaska.[25] They came to this conclusion notwithstanding articles 1(2) and 2(2)(b) of the ABM treaty, which read:

23. Vienna Convention on the Law of Treaties, http://www.un.org/law/ilc/texts/treatfra.htm.

24. President Richard Nixon, "Letter Submitting the Vienna Convention on the Law of Treaties to the U.S. Senate for Advice and Consent to Ratification," Senate Executive Document L, 92nd Cong., 1st sess., 1971, 1.

25. Eric Schmitt and Steven Lee Myers, "Clinton Lawyers Give a Go-Ahead to Missile Shield," *New York Times*, 15 June 2000, A1.

1(2) Each Party undertakes not to deploy ABM systems for a defense of the territory of its country and not to provide a base for such a defense, and not to deploy ABM systems for defense of an individual region. . . .

2(2) The ABM system components . . . include those which are: (b) undergoing construction.[26]

When we apply article 31 of the Vienna Convention on the Law of Treaties, the ordinary meaning of the term "under construction" seems to include the pouring of concrete.[27] Yet a White House spokesman felt able to assert that "the treaty, itself, does not provide a definition of what constitutes a so-called 'breach,' but it's prudent for us to examine what the possible interpretations of the ABM Treaty would be as we continue with our development effort. There are a range of interpretations available, but we have made no decision."[28] In other words, the U.S. government focused on the purpose of the ABM treaty—to prohibit antiballistic missile systems—and the fact that its terms did not specifically and categorically prohibit work preparatory to the installation of such a system.

Another example of a possible move back to a more purposive approach can be seen in the efforts of U.S. government lawyers, after September 11, 2001, to reinterpret fundamental provisions of the 1949 Geneva Conventions and the 1984 Torture Convention. They have done so in at least three respects. First, they asserted that the Third Geneva Convention does not apply to al-Qaeda and the Taliban, because its drafters had not foreseen armed conflicts involving terrorist and other nonstate groups and could not therefore have intended that the convention extend to them.[29] This interpretation is directly contrary to the language of the convention, which provides no scope for a category of individuals between civilians and prisoners of war.

Second, a U.S. government lawyer argued—in an internal memorandum—that article 49 of the Fourth Geneva Convention could be read in a manner that allows "protected persons" (i.e., individuals in a country or territory under occupation) to be transferred out of the country for interrogation,

26. Anti-Ballistic Missile Treaty, http://www.state.gov/www/global/arms/treaties/abmpage.html.

27. See *Shorter Oxford English Dictionary*, 5th ed., updated, on CD-ROM (Oxford: Oxford University Press, 2002), which defines the verb "construct" as "make by fitting parts together; build, erect."

28. Press briefing by Jake Siewert and P. J. Crowley, 15 June 2000, http://clinton6 .nara.gov/2000/06/2000–06–15–press-briefing-by-jake-siewert-and-pj-crowley.html.

29. Thom Shanker and Katharine Q. Seelye, "Behind-the-Scenes Clash Led Bush to Reverse Himself on Applying Geneva Conventions," *New York Times*, 22 February 2002, A12; "Memorandum for the President from Alberto R. Gonzales: Decision Re. Application of the Geneva Convention on Prisoners of War to the Conflict with al-Qaeda and the Taliban," in *The Torture Papers*, ed. Karen Greenberg and Joshua Dratel (New York: Cambridge University Press, 2005), 118.

because such transfers, if temporary, would promote rather than undermine the purposes of the convention.[30] This interpretation is directly contrary to the clear language of article 49, which prohibits "individual or mass forcible transfers, as well as deportations of protected persons from occupied territory . . . regardless of their motive."[31]

Third, U.S. government lawyers argued that the Torture Convention is aimed at prohibiting severe forms of interrogation and therefore only bars techniques that cause suffering "equivalent in intensity to the pain accompanying serious physical injury, such as organ failure, impairment of bodily function, or even death."[32] This argument is plainly inconsistent with article 1 of the convention, which defines torture as "*any* act by which severe pain or suffering, *whether physical or mental*, is intentionally inflicted" (emphasis added).[33] Various courts, tribunals, and commissions, both before and after the adoption of the Torture Convention, have held that the prohibition on torture extends to acts causing only mental suffering.[34]

One could regard these various examples of purposive interpretation as evidence of consistency between the U.S. approach at the 1968 Vienna Conference on the Law of Treaties and its approach today. However, only one of these efforts at reinterpretation has been sustained by the United States. Attempts to reinterpret the ABM treaty were abandoned in favor of renouncing the treaty itself in December 2001, in a manner perfectly consistent with the treaty's provision on renunciation. Efforts to reinterpret the Torture Convention were disowned by the U.S. government as soon as the memoranda setting out the arguments were leaked to the press. Only the efforts to reinterpret the Geneva Convention were maintained, although even here the U.S. government was quick to assert that standards set out in the Geneva Conventions would still be applied to al-Qaeda and Taliban detainees—while maintaining that this was not legally required. Later, after the U.S. Supreme Court decided that the jurisdiction of U.S. federal courts extended to detainees held outside U.S. territory, the Pentagon belatedly

30. Dana Priest, "Memo Lets CIA Take Detainees Out of Iraq; Practice Is Called Serious Breach of Geneva Conventions," *Washington Post*, 24 October 2004, A1; "Memorandum for William Taft IV et al. from Jack Goldsmith: Permissibility of Relocating Certain 'Protected Persons' from Occupied Iraq," in Greenberg and Dratel, *Torture Papers*, 366.

31. Geneva Convention (IV) Relative to the Protection of Civilian Persons in Time of War, http://www.icrc.org/Web/Eng/siteeng0.nsf/html/genevaconventions.

32. Dana Priest and R. Jeffrey Smith, "Memo Offered Justification for Use of Torture; Justice Dept. Gave Advice in 2002," *Washington Post*, 8 June 2004, A1; "Memorandum for Alberto Gonzales from Jay Bybee: Standards of Conduct for Interrogation under 18 U.S.C. §§ 2340–2340A," in Greenberg and Dratel, *Torture Papers*, 172n.

33. Convention against Torture and Other Cruel, Inhuman or Degrading Treatment or Punishment, http://www.ohchr.org/english/law/cat.htm.

34. See generally Nigel Rodley, *The Treatment of Prisoners under International Law*, 2nd ed. (Oxford: Oxford University Press, 1999), 85–100.

established the "status review tribunals" required by the Third Geneva Convention to determine whether any of the detainees were, in fact, prisoners of war. In short, the purposive approach to interpretation has not decisively and consistently been reasserted by the United States with respect to treaties. It has, however, reappeared strongly in U.S. arguments concerning UN Security Council resolutions.

Security Council Resolutions

Only some UN Security Council resolutions clearly and unequivocally authorize the use of force. Resolution 678, adopted in November 1990 following the Iraqi invasion of Kuwait, was one such resolution, authorizing UN member states "to use all necessary means . . . to restore international peace and security to the area."[35] Many other resolutions are considerably less clear and therefore open to several different interpretations—which are sometimes arrived at through the application of differing interpretive approaches.

Unlike the UN Charter, Security Council resolutions are not treaties. Treaties resemble contracts (where obligations are consensually assumed), whereas Security Council resolutions resemble executive orders (where obligations are imposed from above). As a result, the interpretive rules applicable to the two kinds of documents may differ somewhat. It is important to note that while the rules governing the interpretation of treaties are set out in the Vienna Convention on the Law of Treaties, neither that convention nor any other treaty indicates which interpretive approach should be taken to Security Council resolutions. Relatively little academic writing has been directed to the issue of how to interpret Security Council resolutions—perhaps because the council was inactive during much of the cold war—but two distinct approaches have been advanced in the literature. These approaches more or less accord with governmental positions: a British-U.S. position on the one hand and a continental European approach on the other.

Michael Wood, before he became legal adviser to the British Foreign and Commonwealth Office, advanced an approach to interpreting UN Security Council resolutions that mirrors the approach advanced by the U.S. delegation at the Vienna Conference on the Law of Treaties. Wood argued that one should examine the full background of the Security Council's involvement with an issue in order to determine the result the council was seeking to achieve. As it happens, such a purposive approach leads relatively easily to a presumption in favor of an authorization to use force when (1) a resolution is adopted; (2) the council identifies the situation as a threat to international peace and security; (3) strict conditions are placed on the threatening state;

35. S/Res/678, 29 November 1990, http://www.un.org/Docs/scres.htm.

and (4) that state conspicuously fails to meet the conditions. Although the presumption may be countered by clear evidence to the contrary, textual ambiguities are read, where possible, in a manner consistent with the view that the Security Council intends its demands to be obeyed and enforced. The use of force by states tends to be facilitated rather than constrained by this purposive approach to interpretation.

In contrast, Jochen Frowein, the former director of the Max Planck Institute for International Law in Heidelberg, Germany, has advocated an approach to interpreting Security Council resolutions that is even more restrictive than the approach taken to interpreting treaties under the Vienna Convention on the Law of Treaties.[36] Instead of attempting to discern the subjective intentions of Security Council members, Frowein insists that we focus on the resolution's text. Such a focus, he argues, is necessary because the country against which the resolution is directed will not have participated in its drafting; in other words, the resolution is imposed rather than consensually agreed upon. Frowein also argues that a strictly textual approach is needed because Security Council resolutions frequently interfere with sovereign rights and that the centrality of sovereignty in international law creates a presumption that such rights have neither been surrendered nor removed. The strictly textually oriented approach to the interpretation of Security Council resolutions tends to limit the occasions on which force may be used.

The following examples demonstrate how this divergence of views is replicated in the positions adopted by national governments, with Britain and the United States favoring the purposive approach and continental European countries favoring (though not always consistently) the textual approach.

Resolution 688 (Northern Iraq)   In April 1991, following an attempted Kurdish uprising during the Gulf War, Saddam Hussein's forces began a campaign of retribution in northern Iraq. In response, the United States, Britain, France, Italy, and the Netherlands deployed forces and established so-called safe havens for civilians in the region. The five intervening countries justified their action on the basis of UN Security Council Resolution 688.[37] That resolution, adopted on April 5, 1991, expressed grave concern at "the repression of the Iraqi civilian population . . . including most recently in Kurdish-populated areas, which led to a massive flow of refugees towards and across international frontiers and to cross-border incursions, which threaten international peace

36. See Jochen A. Frowein, "Unilateral Interpretation of Security Council Resolutions—A Threat to Collective Security?" in *Liber amicorum Günther Jaenicke—zum 85. Geburtstag*, ed. Volkmar Götz (Berlin: Springer, 1998), 98.

37. S/Res/687, 3 April 1991, http://www.un.org/Docs/scres.htm.

and security." It also called on countries to aid UN-led humanitarian relief efforts.

Resolution 688 did not expressly authorize the use of force. China, concerned about the Security Council reaching into the domestic affairs of sovereign states, had reportedly threatened to veto any resolution that authorized military action to protect the Kurds. Within a few weeks, more than a million refugees had either crossed, or were attempting to cross, from Iraq into Turkey and Iran. Television footage of hundreds of thousands of desperate people trapped in frigid mountain passes resonated with the Western public, and this in turn prompted the U.S., British, Dutch, French, and Italian governments to declare all Iraqi territory north of the 36th parallel out of bounds to Iraqi armed forces. They argued that this move was "in support of " Resolution 688.

Later, the United States, Britain, and France transformed the northern exclusion zone into two no-fly zones: one north of the 36th parallel, the other south of the 32nd parallel. The southern no-fly zone was created to protect Shiites who had similarly attempted an uprising against Saddam Hussein. Both no-fly zones were again justified on the basis of Resolution 688, despite the apparent absence of any words of authorization in the text. This purposive approach to interpretation was questioned by other countries—some of them European—and in 1996 France pulled out of the operation after the United States and Britain extended the southern zone northward to just south of Baghdad.

Resolutions 1199 and 1203 (Kosovo) In 1997, the Federal Republic of Yugoslavia, headed by Slobodan Milosevic, launched a brutal crackdown on a rebel militia army and its supporters in the primarily Muslim province of Kosovo. Within a year, UN secretary general Kofi Annan reported that force was being used in an "indiscriminate and disproportionate" manner against civilians and that "appalling atrocities" were being committed.

The UN Security Council responded on September 23, 1998, by adopting Resolution 1199.[38] Acting expressly under chapter VII—the section of the UN Charter that grants the council the capacity to authorize force—the council demanded that the Milosevic government cease its "repressive actions against the peaceful population" of Kosovo and resolve the situation by nonforceful means. The council also warned that, if the government failed to comply, it would "consider further action and additional measures to maintain or restore peace and security in the region."

One month later, the Security Council adopted Resolution 1203 in which it welcomed an agreement between Belgrade and the Organization for Security and Cooperation in Europe (OSCE), which provided for the establishment of a peace verification mission in Kosovo.[39] The Security Council emphasized

38. S/Res/1199, 23 September 1998, http://www.un.org/Docs/scres.htm.
39. S/Res/1203, 24 October 1998, http://www.un.org/Docs/scres.htm.

the need to ensure the safety and security of the members of the OSCE mission and affirmed that the situation in Kosovo remained a threat to peace and security. Then, again acting expressly under chapter VII, the council stated that "in the event of an emergency, action may be needed to ensure their [the members of the mission's] safety and freedom of movement." The council hinted at a possible need to intervene to rescue the OSCE personnel but said nothing more that could ordinarily be construed as authorizing military action. The council also decided to "remain seized of the matter."

On March 24, 1999, without the adoption of a further Security Council resolution, the United States and its NATO allies began an air campaign against targets in Kosovo and Serbia. To the degree the intervening powers provided a legal justification at all, they argued that once the Security Council had identified a threat and demanded action from a "problem" state—as it did in Resolutions 1199 and 1203—countries are implicitly entitled to ensure that the council's will is carried out. Even then, some European governments were hesitant about the argument. Germany, for instance, acknowledged that the intervention was illegal but justified it as morally legitimate.

Resolutions 678, 687, and 1441 (Iraq)   In March 2003, the United States led a second intervention in Iraq—this time capturing Baghdad, occupying the country, and ousting Saddam Hussein. The principal justification for the invasion harkened back to Resolution 678, adopted by the Security Council following Iraq's invasion of Kuwait in 1990, whereby it had authorized UN member states to "use all necessary means . . . to restore peace and security to the area."[40] The argument claimed, essentially, that the authorization provided by Resolution 678 was suspended—not terminated—by the cease-fire imposed in April 1991 by Resolution 687.[41] This suspended authorization could be reactivated—so the argument went—if and when Iraq engaged in a "material breach" of its cease-fire and disarmament obligations. The concept of material breach, drawn from the law of treaties, had been expressly endorsed by the Security Council in the context of Iraq, most notably in the unanimously adopted Resolution 1441 of November 2002, which found Iraq in material breach of Resolution 687.[42] Resolution 1441 also gave Iraq "a final opportunity to comply with its disarmament obligations" and warned that noncompliance would have "serious consequences." Iraq's failure to cooperate fully, including during February and March 2003, when it had refused to allow weapons scientists to be interviewed outside the country, was argued to constitute a further material breach of Resolution 687, and of Resolution 1441, thereby permitting countries to unilaterally carry out the

40. S/Res/678, 29 November 1990, http://www.un.org/Docs/scres.htm.
41. S/Res/687, 3 April 1991, http://www.un.org/Docs/scres.htm.
42. S/Res/1441, 8 November 2002, http://www.un.org/Docs/scres.htm.

council's will. The argument concluded with the assertion that, had the Security Council thought that an additional resolution was necessary before military action could be taken, it would have spelled out this requirement in Resolution 1441.

This approach, coupling a purposive approach to interpretation with the concept of material breach, was countered by arguments based on a more textually oriented approach to interpretation. First, the 1991 cease-fire resolution was clearly worded to terminate—not suspend—the previous year's authorization of military force. Second, because the parties to the cease-fire were the UN Security Council and Iraq, the coalition countries involved in the ejection of the Iraqis from Kuwait were not parties to the cease-fire (although they were bound by it); any material breach could not have reactivated a right for the coalition members to use force independently. Third, Resolution 1441 neither specified the legal consequences of material breach nor expressly authorized military action. Indeed, following its adoption, all the Security Council's members, including the United States and Britain, confirmed publicly that the resolution provided no "automaticity"—by which they presumably meant that states could not use force until a further resolution was adopted.

The fact of the matter is that the members of the UN Security Council had agreed to disagree when they adopted Resolution 1441.[43] Different provisions of that resolution provided support to both sides of the debate over the legality of going to war against Iraq in 2003—as long as both sides applied different approaches to interpretation. In other words, the debate over the legality of the 2003 Iraq War went deeper than contesting political positions supported by an intentionally ambiguous UN Security Council resolution. At a more fundamental level, it concerned competing approaches to the interpretation of Security Council resolutions. The United States, Britain, and several continental European countries, including Italy, Poland, and Spain, applied the purposive approach articulated by Wood whereby the identification of a threat to international peace and security, the imposition of strict conditions, and the failure of the target state to meet those conditions lead to a presumption in favor of military action when interpreting an ambiguous resolution. In contrast, most European countries held to the more textually oriented approach advanced by Frowein whereby force must be authorized by clear language before it can be deployed against a sovereign state.

The clash between these two approaches to interpreting Security Council resolutions has not been resolved. Subsequent to the Iraq War, the reluctance

---

43. See Jane E. Stromseth, "Law and Force after Iraq: A Transitional Moment," *American Journal of International Law* 97 (2003): 629–31, 628; Michael Byers, "Agreeing to Disagree: Security Council Resolution 1441 and Intentional Ambiguity," *Global Governance* 10 (2004): 165.

of many countries to support the U.S.-led occupation and reconstruction confirmed that Washington and London's purposive approach to the interpretation of Resolution 1441 lacked widespread support. Moreover, in the last several years governments have exercised greater caution when negotiating and adopting UN Security Council resolutions. Resolution 1483 on Iraq, adopted in May 2003, was worded tightly in order to leave little room for arguments that it provided retroactive authorization for the war.[44] The same is true of Resolution 1511, adopted in October 2003, even though this resolution authorized a U.S.-led multilateral force to provide "security and stability" in Iraq.[45] One can thus conclude that the attempt to advance a purposive approach to the interpretation of Security Council resolutions has not achieved sufficient support to become the approach required under international law. At the same time, there is little indication of the approach being abandoned by Britain and the United States. On the issue of the interpretative approach to be applied to Security Council resolutions, there is as yet no clear rule of international law, and a relatively consistent divergence in views between Britain and the United States, on the one hand, and many continental European countries on the other.

Conclusion

Despite the significant geopolitical shifts of the past two decades and the controversy over the 2003 Iraq War, remarkably little has changed at the level of deeply rooted international rules, either in the law itself or in the positions taken on the law by the United States and European countries. A combination of factors seems to promote consistency in the legal positions asserted by governments. Continuity of personnel is one factor: staff diplomats and lawyers tend to outlast their political masters and to cleave closely to analysis and conclusions arrived at previously. Another factor involves the fact that professional diplomats and lawyers are part of a transnational "epistemic community" in that they share a conceptual universe—of training, source materials, methodology, and terminology—that extends beyond the interests and policies of the countries they represent. A third factor involves the ability of lawyers to reformulate policy decisions in a manner that helps bring them within the scope—or at least the penumbra—of preexisting rules and legal positions. Indeed, part of the role of lawyers involves the development and application of analogies: taking the seemingly novel and relating it to what has transpired before. As a result, apparently significant differences in the legally related positions adopted on opposite sides of the Atlantic are frequently brought back into the sphere of widely accepted international law through the

44. S/Res/1483, 22 May 2003, http://www.un.org/Docs/scres.htm.
45. S/Res/1511, 16 October 2003, http://www.un.org/Docs/scres.htm.

efforts of professional lawyers and diplomats operating within a common framework of concepts, institutions and deeply rooted rules. Too often, commentators and scholars focus on the greatly simplified, widely reported policy statements of political leaders and ignore the more nuanced legal positions conveyed in diplomatic correspondence and presented in official venues such as the UN Security Council.

The professionals who inhabit foreign ministries and embassies are also likely to believe that their countries have a strong interest in adhering to foundational rules of international law. Even the United States relies heavily on allies, including those periods when it is fighting wars abroad. Access to airspace, bases, foreign troops, and financial assistance is often contingent on showing a modicum of respect for widely accepted, deeply rooted rules. Countries do, of course, differ on their interpretations of the rules and even on the appropriate means by which to interpret them, but they rarely denigrate the rules or deny their existence. Instead, they seek to modify the rules by making claims and engaging in action designed to persuade other countries of the need for legal change, or they renounce or simply do not ratify treaties they oppose.

This consistency and commonality are particularly evident in the Atlantic community, where the similarities in identities and interests greatly outweigh the differences. Indeed, the contemporary international legal system is predominantly a joint creation of western Europe and the United States, and these countries therefore have a strong interest in maintaining, strengthening, and only occasionally—and cautiously—altering the rules.[46] If one wished to see true divergence or even crisis, the most likely place to find it would be in the positions and approaches adopted by countries in the southern hemisphere and Asia as compared to those of the North Atlantic region.

Yet the considerable power and influence of the United States have prompted some change with respect to foundational rules. European countries have recently accepted the Shultz doctrine of self-defense against state sponsors of terrorism, and some of them (particularly Britain) support a purposive approach to the interpretation of Security Council resolutions. On other issues, such as the Bush doctrine of preemptive self-defense and the treatment of detainees, it was the United States that moved toward divergence and then fell back in line. Some of these changes in position—for example, of European countries on the Shultz doctrine—are partly the result of changed factual circumstances, or at least changed appreciations of the facts. Others, such as the U.S. government's efforts to distance itself from the torture memoranda, are partly the result of a realization that the opinions of

46. See generally Wilhelm G. Grewe, *The Epochs of International Law*, trans. and rev. by Michael Byers (Berlin: Walter de Gruyter, 2000).

other countries do matter—that even the single superpower operates within a community of states, that communities exist on the basis of deeply rooted rules, and that ignoring such rules can be detrimental to cooperative efforts that advance national interests. Finally, on some issues that international law has yet to crystallize—such as on the approach that should be taken to the interpretation of Security Council resolutions—countries have, at the diplomatic level, simply agreed to disagree. What is of most interest for our purposes is that their legal positions, even in disagreement, have remained more or less consistent over time.

When it comes to international law, there is contestation, controversy, and compromise across the Atlantic as well as within Europe and North America. But these are the signs of a healthy, fundamentally stable, but continually evolving system. There is no transatlantic crisis, at least not with respect to foundational rules.

There are, however, ample signs of divergence on less deeply rooted aspects of the international legal system. Since coming into office in January 2001, President George W. Bush and his administration have renounced the 1972 Anti-Ballistic Missile Treaty, refused to ratify the 1996 Comprehensive Test Ban Treaty and the 1997 Kyoto Protocol, and "unsigned" the 1998 Rome Statute of the International Criminal Court. They have opposed other multilateral treaty initiatives, such as an inspection protocol for the 1972 Biological Weapons Convention, and undermined existing treaties such as the 1970 Nuclear Non-Proliferation Treaty—at least insofar as it imposes disarmament obligations on the five declared nuclear-weapon states. Yet these renunciations, refusals, withdrawals, and efforts in opposition are not illegal, nor indeed is the Bush administration consistently opposed to multilateral lawmaking. President Bush has sent the 1982 United Nations Law of the Sea Convention to the U.S. Senate for its advice and consent to ratification. He has also championed the Proliferation Security Initiative—a U.S.-led, multilateral effort to apply existing international law and develop new treaties to prevent the international trafficking of weapons of mass destruction and missile components on the high seas. Bush and some of his most senior advisers may be openly skeptical of international rules, but in this sphere as elsewhere, actions sometimes speak louder than words. The United States' approach to international law is considerably more complex than it first appears.

For a crisis to occur in the legal dimension of the transatlantic relationship, one or the other side would have to reject outright widely accepted, foundational rules such as the right of self-defense or the general rule of treaty interpretation. A crisis in the legal dimension might also result if one or the other side withdrew from an international law-based institution of quasi-constitutional importance, such as the United Nations, the World Trade Organization, or perhaps the international human rights regime. But again, there is no realistic prospect of this happening. The United States remains the single largest financial supporter of the UN, the most active litigant in the WTO, and a frequent critic of the human rights records of other countries. The surface of the international legal system may have been ruffled of late, but the currents of transatlantic international law run deep. Crisis, what crisis?

9 THE SOVEREIGN FOUNDATIONS OF TRANSATLANTIC CRISIS IN THE POST-9/11 ERA

Jeffrey Anderson

One of the objectives of this volume is to establish whether the increased tensions and strains that have beset the transatlantic relationship since September 11, 2001, constitute a true crisis. Put another way, are we witnessing a worsening in degree or in kind of relations between the United States and Europe? U.S.-European relations have experienced significant highs and lows since the end of the Second World War, and the term "crisis" has been bandied about far too easily on both sides of the Atlantic throughout this period. It is therefore a worthy exercise to establish criteria for evaluating the state of the relationship, ones that can distinguish between ordinary tensions and disagreements within the existing institutional order on the one hand, and profound ruptures or crises that may lead to the disintegration of said order or to significant adaptation or transformation other.

The question of whether we are experiencing a crisis in transatlantic relations is addressed more centrally in other chapters, particularly those that consider the current situation from a broad theoretical or historical position, as well as those that explore substantive issue areas such as security and economics. In the introduction to this volume, John Ikenberry offers the following definition of a crisis: "an extraordinary moment when the existence and viability of the political order are called into question. . . . It is a historical juncture when conflict within the political order has risen to the point that the interests, institutions, and shared identities that define and undergird the political system are put in jeopardy." Thus, a crisis in international relations can result from the emergence of sharp differences among partners in one or more of three areas: the content and relative priorities of the *interests* held by national governments; the value and purpose attached to international *institutions* that heretofore have linked the partners in common endeavors; and finally, the *ideas*, or cognitive frameworks broadly conceived, that national elites employ

in conducting relations with foreign powers. Put another way, if we are searching for the root causes of new tensions—and perhaps even full-blown crisis—
in U.S.-European relations after 9/11, we should examine the shared interests,
institutions, and ideas for signs of stress, deterioration, and even rupture.

In this chapter, I delve into the realm of ideas—specifically, the differing
meanings attached by U.S. and European policymakers to the concept of sovereignty, and any resulting differences in foreign policy strategy and behavior.
Regardless of how one characterizes the transatlantic relationship after
9/11—crisis or no crisis—the issues taken up in this chapter can be cast in
terms of the following question: Can the recent deterioration in U.S.-Europe-
an relations be traced back to noticeably different conceptions of sovereignty
reigning on either side of the Atlantic?

Even a quick glance at the popular literature on the newest installment of
the transatlantic divide suggests that fundamental differences in the meaning
and significance of sovereignty exist between the United States and Europe,
and that these differences are a source of conflict and discord in the relationship. To be sure, one has to read between the lines to tap the sovereignty dimension of the discussion, but it is real, as the following excerpt from Robert
Kagan's celebrated *Policy Review* piece demonstrates:

> It is time to stop pretending that Europeans and Americans share a common
> view of the world, or even that they occupy the same world. On the all-
> important question of power . . . American and European perspectives are di-
> verging. Europe . . . is moving beyond power into a self-contained world of laws
> and rules and transnational negotiation and cooperation. It is entering a post-
> historical paradise of peace and relative prosperity. . . . The United States,
> meanwhile, remains mired in history, exercising power in the anarchic Hobbe-
> sian world where international law and rules are unreliable and where true se-
> curity and the defense and promotion of a liberal order still depend on the
> possession and use of military might. That is why, on major strategic and inter-
> national questions today, Americans are from Mars and Europeans from Venus.[1]

As I outline in subsequent sections, embedded in this mythological metaphor
is the assumption of divergent approaches to sovereignty.

In this chapter my first task is to present a basic definition of sovereignty and
then outline the main elements of the American and European approaches to
it, paying particular attention to the points of overlap and departure between
the two, as well as to the likely origins of both the similarities and differences.
Finally, I examine the role of sovereignty conceptions in shaping and driving
the tenor of U.S.-European relations after 9/11. I conclude that although there

---

1. Robert Kagan, "Power and Weakness," *Policy Review Online* 113 (June 2002), http://www
.hoover.org/publications/policyreview/3460246.html.

are long-standing and tangible differences in the way American and (at least some) European foreign policymakers conceptualize sovereignty, these differences are not at the heart of the current transatlantic disorder. To the extent that these differences have mattered, the effects have been felt on the margins, and only then as loose cognitive frames that appear to rule in certain strategies while ruling out others. For the most part, though, the differences in the goals pursued by American and European foreign policymakers since 9/11, as well as the strategies they have employed to achieve their objectives, can be traced back to divergent assessments of threat, interest, and power capabilities.

What Is Sovereignty?

Sovereignty is an attribute, or more precisely stated a set of attributes, of the state. It has both an internal and an external dimension, and can be summarized in the following terms: a sovereign state is one that "is subject to no other state and has full and exclusive powers within its jurisdiction without prejudice to the limits set by applicable law."[2] A sovereign state, in other words, is both internally supreme and externally independent.[3]

One can trace the conceptual roots of sovereignty back to the sixteenth-century political philosopher Jean Bodin, considered the father of the notion of "unitary" sovereignty. Bodin maintained that the state's authority is indivisible and cannot be shared, delegated, or otherwise parsed.[4] Sovereignty must reside in one place—the national state—or it does not exist at all. Put another way, sovereignty à la Bodin is an all or nothing proposition. This conception of sovereignty, which was advanced as an intellectual foundation of European absolutism, achieved hegemonic status with the emergence of the state system in Europe after the Treaty of Westphalia in 1648—hence the term "Westphalian sovereignty."

The contemporary scholarly debate about sovereignty has revolved not around the notion that there is both an internal and an external dimension to this condition. This is generally uncontested. Rather, differences have arisen over the unitary characteristic of sovereignty: specifically, whether sovereignty can be divided; if so, whether it has been divided empirically; and (again) if so, how much, to what end, and with what consequences.[5]

---

2. Stanley Hoffman, *Janus and Minerva: Essays in the Theory and Practice of International Politics* (Boulder: Westview Press, 1987), 172–73.

3. Robert Keohane, "Ironies of Sovereignty: The European Union and the United States," *Journal of Common Market Studies* 40 (2002): 746.

4. The conventional reference is Jean Bodin, *Les six livres de la République* (Paris, 1577).

5. A comprehensive overview of this debate is found in Thomas Biersteker, "Locating the Emerging European Polity: Beyond States or State?" in *Regional Integration and Democracy: Expanding on the European Experience*, ed. Jeffrey Anderson, 21–43 (Lanham, MD: Rowman and Littlefield, 1999).

Few scholars challenge the proposition that state sovereignty in the late twentieth–early twenty-first century is not what it used to be. Internally, many states have become less "supreme" in their authority and control over citizens, groups, and the market. Externally, states have grown less independent and are now subject to the authoritative influences of a vast array of nongovernmental actors (NGOs), international institutions, and other actors. What is at issue are the implications of these shifts in the terms with which states relate to their internal and external environments. Those who insist on a unitary conception of sovereignty fall into one of two groups. One maintains that state sovereignty is now a thing of the past—challenges from within and from without have resulted in the complete dissolution of state sovereignty. The other, far less convincingly, argues that whatever appearances might suggest to the contrary, states remain sovereign within their domestic and international domains, and any apparent loss or delegation of sovereignty is illusory—tolerated by the sovereign state that remains capable of clawing back its prerogatives at a time and place of its choosing. Although forcefully stated and reassuring in tone, the claims on behalf of indivisibly sovereign states are rarely accompanied by empirical evidence. Such arguments are akin to whistling in the dark.

A useful challenge to this perspective on the contemporary state of sovereignty is advanced by those who challenge its unitary nature on theoretical and empirical grounds. Drawing on constructivist theoretical perspectives, for example, Thomas Biersteker offers a provisional definition of sovereignty: "the external recognition (by states) of claims of final authority by states." He goes on to argue that these claims are not absolute: "States' authority claims vary from one issue area to another and are not fixed over time, which is the key to understanding the changing meaning of sovereignty. The question is not whether sovereignty exists as a unitary condition or state of being, but how claims of authority are issue specific and change over time."[6] Pointing to the emergence of new "locations of authority" in the international system—the EU, the UN, the International Court of Justice, transnational issue networks, even global society—Biersteker maintains that the range of authority claims made by states has shifted and even narrowed at the end of the twentieth century, but this alteration does not signal the demise of state sovereignty. Its meaning has changed, not its existence.

The constructivist insight—that sovereignty, like anarchy, is what states make of it—also hints at an important empirical insight of great significance to our exploration of the contemporary nexus between sovereignty and the transatlantic relationship. In short, not only do states' authority claims vary from one issue to another and over time, but at any given point in time there may exist significant differences in one state's authority claims from issue area

6. Ibid., 28.

to issue area as compared to others. That is, states attach difference meanings to sovereignty, rendering the concept a variable not only longitudinally but also cross-sectionally. This conception opens up the possibility that before, on, or after 9/11, the meanings attached to state sovereignty by the United States and its European allies diverged. Why this should be the case, if in fact it is, and if so with what implications are key questions that must be addressed. The following section takes up the empirical question of whether the U.S. and European operational conceptions of sovereignty differ in significant and substantial ways.

Although constructivism's insights are significant, they cannot be readily operationalized into an analytical framework for evaluating and comparing differing conceptions of sovereignty at work in the contemporary international system. Instead, I turn to Stephen Krasner's recent work on the concept. Krasner argues that the term "sovereignty" has been employed in four distinctive ways:

> *domestic sovereignty*, referring to the organization of public authority within a state and to the level of effective control exercised by those holding authority; *interdependence sovereignty*, referring to the ability of public authorities to control transborder movements; *international legal sovereignty*, referring to the mutual recognition of states or other entities; and *Westphalian sovereignty*, referring to the exclusion of external actors from domestic authority configurations.[7]

In an exhaustive and methodical analysis, Krasner demonstrates that these four meanings of sovereignty are not linked in any logical or deterministic sense and that they have not covaried in any predictable manner over time. There are, however, two common threads running through sovereignty's varied meanings: authority and control. Authority entails the mutual recognition of an actor's right to act in certain ways. Control, on the other hand, involves the ability, but not necessarily the acknowledged right, to engage in certain kinds of activities. Thus, actors may find themselves in four distinct situations: possessing both authority and control; possessing authority but not control; possessing control but not authority; and possessing neither authority nor control.

Krasner points out that the threads of authority and control weave a varied course through the four meanings of sovereignty.

> Westphalian sovereignty and international legal sovereignty exclusively refer to issues of authority: does the state have the right to exclude external actors, and is a state recognized as having the authority to engage in international

7. Stephen Krasner, *Sovereignty: Organized Hypocrisy* (Princeton: Princeton University Press, 1999), 9.

agreements? Interdependence sovereignty exclusively refers to control: can a state control movements across its own borders? Domestic sovereignty is used in ways that refer to both authority and control: what authority structures are recognized within a state, and how effective is their level of control?[8]

Krasner notes that rulers historically have attached a great deal of rhetorical weight to international legal sovereignty and Westphalian sovereignty. That said, there have always been tensions between the rules as outlined in theory and the way they have been observed in practice. Violations of Westphalian and international legal sovereignty—most often imposed on others, on occasion self-inflicted—have been and continue to be commonplace and typically flow from hardheaded calculations of costs and benefits shaped by self-interest and relative capabilities. All this leads Krasner to describe the institutions of sovereignty in all its manifestations as a system of organized hypocrisy.

Krasner goes on to identify at least four ways in which sovereignty has been limited or violated in practice.

> Rulers can join international *conventions* in which they agree to abide by certain standards regardless of what others do. Rulers can enter into *contracts* in which they agree to specific policies in return for explicit benefits. Rulers can be subject to *coercion*, which leaves them worse off, although they do have some bargaining leverage. Finally, rulers or would-be rulers can suffer *imposition*, a situation that occurs when the target ruler cannot effectively resist.[9]

Krasner presents a deep, rich analysis of sovereignty based on his classification scheme; I can only scratch its surface here. This brief outline, however, is useful for addressing the question of whether there are significant sovereignty underpinnings of the transatlantic crisis that broke out shortly after September 11, 2001. What I show in the following pages is that although there are differences between the United States and European countries—and at times "Europe"—in their approaches to international legal and Westphalian sovereignty, these differences are long-standing (in other words, they have not increased or sharpened since 9/11), and in the grand scheme of things they do not amount to much at all in terms of shaping or driving the state of transatlantic relations.

Sovereignty Roots of Crisis?

Even a casual reader of newspapers and foreign affairs journals over the past several years will have noticed the markedly different positions occupied by the United States and its European partners dating from well before the end

8. Ibid., 10.
9. Ibid., 26.

of the cold war.[10] The United States is perceived to be and is in key respects the lone superpower on the planet—the sole country at the present time with a credible claim to hegemonic status. Particularly—but not only—since George W. Bush became president in 2001, the United States has blocked or abstained from a string of significant international efforts, many of them spearheaded by European countries, at collective hand-tying: the Kyoto Protocol to the United Nations Convention on Climate Change; the creation of the International Criminal Court; and the Ottawa Treaty to ban land mines, to name just a few.

When the United States is described as worried about the loss of its sovereignty, or willing to encroach upon or violate the sovereign rights of other states in the international system, then what is implied is a point of comparison or benchmark. Clearly, this appraisal cannot be an objective exercise; we currently have no cardinal "scale of sovereignty" against which a state's preferences and actions can be measured. Rather, such statements land in the realm of the subjective and utilize other actors as points of comparison. In most instances, the subjective reference point for statements about U.S. approaches to sovereignty has been the European Union. Thus, in some sense a transatlantic fault line is built in to the discussion about sovereignty and what states make of it in the contemporary era.

The standard narrative of postwar European integration is cast in terms of the cumulative and progressive "pooling" of national sovereignty in a collective, supranational order. This storyline is implied in the very definition of integration; for example, Paul Taylor defines integration as "the process whereby an international organization acquires responsibility for taking an increasing number of decisions in areas which were previously reserved to the state."[11] From the nascent and limited steps toward sectoral integration in the 1950s to the more ambitious (but ultimately faltering) constitutional project of the 2000s, integration has come to be synonymous with a bold and permanent redefinition of national prerogatives and capacities in Europe. Although the process is by no means complete—indeed, on the basis of recent developments there is good reason to believe that integration will remain in a state of "coming into being" for the foreseeable future—traditional conceptions of sovereignty have been recast in Europe since 1945.

What this change means in practical terms is the subject of a rich literature, which describes not a uniform European tapestry but a patchwork quilt in which authority relations among actors and institutions at the national and supranational levels vary from policy sector to policy sector. In some areas, such as trade and agriculture, strong supranational frameworks

10. Keohane, "Ironies of Sovereignty."

11. Paul Taylor, *The Limits of European Integration* (New York: Columbia University Press, 1983), 26.

with authoritative decision-making powers exist, and the potential for autonomous national action and initiative is effectively nil. In others, such as foreign policy, a more balanced situation prevails. In still others, like social welfare policy and labor market policy, the nation-state continues to reign alone.

Cast in terms of Krasner's typology, European integration involves two distinct yet related processes. Within the member states (and one could even argue, within aspiring member states), integration has resulted in a dramatic reduction in the degree of authority and control that states may exercise over transborder movements. The gradual yet inexorable implementation of the barrier-free market, which permits the virtually unrestricted flow of goods, services, capital, and even people, represents a marked change in interdependence sovereignty for members of the European Union. Perhaps even more significant, decades of integration have limited or, in some instances, eliminated completely the ability and the right of the member states to exclude external actors (e.g., the European Commission, the European Court of Justice) from domestic authority configurations. It is this dramatic transformation of Westphalian sovereignty that has received the most attention in the literature. Integration has also had a more modest impact on the domestic sovereignty of the members states—that is, the way in which public authority is organized domestically, and the level of effective control exercised by those holding authority.[12]

At the supranational level, a more complex pattern is visible. EU institutions appear to have absorbed, in a relatively straightforward manner, the interdependence sovereignty that has been pooled or otherwise given away by the member states. It is now the EU that exercises authority and control over movements of goods, services, capital, and people across its outer borders—that is, vis-à-vis the non-EU world. This is true despite the fact that the EU must rely on national agents—border police, customs officials, and the like. The key issue is not who is carrying out orders and actions but who is authorizing the orders and actions.

The virtually zero-sum transfer of interdependence sovereignty from national to supranational level is not replicated along the other dimensions of sovereignty defined by Krasner. Significant—and ultimately telling—is the fact that integration has not (yet) had an appreciable impact on the international legal sovereignty of the member states, which continue to retain and

12. This is the subject of the "Europeanization" literature; see, for example, Adrienne Héritier, Dieter Kerwer, Christoph Knill, Dirk Lehmkuhl, Michael Teutsch, and Anne-Cécile Douillet, *Differential Europe: The European Union Impact on National Policymaking* (Lanham, MD: Rowman and Littlefield, 2001); Johan Olsen, "The Many Faces of Europeanization," *Journal of Common Market Studies* 40 (2002): 921–52; and Jeffrey Anderson, "Europeanization in Context: Concept and Theory," in *Germany, Europe, and the Politics of Constraint*, ed. K. Dyson and K. Goetz, 37–53 (Oxford: Oxford University Press, 2003).

exercise their sovereign prerogatives when it comes to the mutual recognition of states and other entities. To be sure, on many foreign policy and especially foreign economic issues, the EU members coordinate closely, achieving truly joint or common policies in some instances, but the fundamentals of international legal sovereignty continue to reside at the national, not the supranational, level. This resilience of international legal sovereignty was clearly evident, for example, in the discussions among EC members in the early 1990s about whether and when to recognize the newly independent states in the Balkans. Although, for better or worse, the Europeans sought to achieve a coordinated response, in the end the recognizing was done by each member state and not the EC as a collective, supranational entity.[13]

How did Europe arrive at this juncture? A comprehensive answer would take one deep into the heart of theoretical debates about the motivations, engines, and drivers of the integration process. Suffice it to say that the process, and its far-reaching implications for sovereignty, unfolded incrementally, without regard to a final blueprint or design, and took the form of countless decisions, some momentous and highly public, others much more modest, even subterranean. The pooling of sovereignty sprang from differing yet ultimately reinforcing calculations of interest and expressions of core values. For many smaller states in Europe, integration promised technical solutions to policy challenges that appeared to be beyond the capacity of the nation-state acting alone to address.[14] Larger states like France envisioned tangible material benefits for key economic sectors like agriculture and also hoped to create a ready collective vehicle for the projection of foreign policy influence consistent with—indeed, driven by—French national interests. The case of the Federal Republic of Germany is distinctive. To be sure, European integration was seen as securing specific policy objectives German leaders considered vital to economic success, such as protecting domestic agriculture, securing access to neighboring markets for manufacturing industry, and promoting free trade with countries outside Europe. To West German political elites, however, the main motivation to promote a Europe committed to multilateral cooperation and democratic principles sprang from their desire to rebuild democracy at home and to rehabilitate the country's ruined international credentials.

It is easy to construct a narrative that casts integration—and the attendant effects on national sovereignty —as the outcome of a conscious sequence of incremental decisions by the member states. There would be much to recommend such a narrative; after all, the major milestones in integration—the Treaty of

13. Beverly Crawford, "Explaining Defection from International Cooperation: Germany's Unilateral Recognition of Croatia," *World Politics* 48 (July 1996): 482–521; Richard Caplan, "Conditional Recognition as an Instrument of Ethnic Conflict Regulation: The European Community and Yugoslavia," *Nations and Nationalism* 8 (April 2002): 157–77.

14. Alan Milward, *The European Rescue of the Nation-State*, 2nd ed. (New York: Routledge, 2000).

Rome, Single European Act, Maastricht—have been "grand bargains" entered into by the member governments with eyes wide open. Yet such a narrative would overlook many key dynamics, particularly emanating from the European Court of Justice, that have pushed along integration and radically redefined the boundaries and limits of national sovereignty, yet at the same time cannot be traced back to the express desires and intents of the member states. Integration is at least partially the product of unintended consequences.[15] Be that as it may, the European approach to foreign policymaking had evolved out of and in many ways was a natural extension of the norms, mores, and practices of state interaction within the framework of European integration. The willingness to consider constraints on sovereignty in pursuit of European objectives translated into a parallel willingness to entertain constraints on sovereignty in pursuit of international goals.

Flowing from their very different experience with sovereignty, European countries have behaved very differently from the United States, and these differences have become more visible since the end of the cold war. Bolstered by the hope that the decade after 1990 had opened up the possibility of the construction of a new and peaceful world order and by the certain knowledge that nearly a half century of integration had produced a radically different mode of interstate cooperation, the Europeans set about exporting their supranational model of pooled sovereignty to the international level. Kyoto, the International Criminal Court (ICC), conflict management and prevention through UN mechanisms: these initiatives and objectives addressed serious problems that could only be solved through deep forms of international cooperation that necessarily entailed a transformed approach to national sovereignty. This vision appears to have set the stage for a major falling out after the terrorist attacks of September 11, 2001.

The Sovereign Underpinnings of Post-9/11 Transatlantic Relations

It would be relatively straightforward to conclude that differences in the meaning attached to core principles like international law and sovereignty lie at the heart of the post-9/11 crisis enveloping the United States and its European partners. The refrain "Americans are Martians, Europeans are Venusians" conjures up an image of two diametrically opposed, even clashing worldviews that in turn lead to conflictual behavior and action on the international stage. Yet as Michael Beyer argues persuasively elsewhere in this volume, there is far less to this conventional wisdom than meets the eye in the realm

15. Paul Pierson, "The Path to European Integration: A Historical-Institutionalist Analysis," in *European Integration and Supranational Governance*, ed. W. Sandholtz and A. Stone Sweet, 27–58 (New York: Oxford University Press, 1998).

of international law. Much the same can be said for conceptions of sovereignty within the transatlantic community. In this section, I outline the case for a strong, sovereignty-based dimension to the post-9/11 crisis and then move to show how this view is ultimately superficial and in some ways misleading.

Without too much effort, one can spin a tale about the post-9/11 period that places differences over the meaning and significance of sovereignty at the heart of the transatlantic conflict. The Bush administration took office in January 2001 committed to acting the part of the world's lone superpower and immediately sought to uphold and defend the country's traditional sovereign prerogatives in ways that inevitably ruled out any form of international cooperation on greenhouse gases (Kyoto) and the International Criminal Court, and led to a much less constructive approach to a range of issues normally dealt with through the United Nations.

After the terrorist attacks of September 11, 2001, the United States marshaled a response that accorded top priority to preserving the country's sovereign rights and prerogatives, leading it to eschew any international entanglements—be they formal arrangements like the UN and NATO, or informal condominiums like the transatlantic relationship—that threatened to undermine its ability to protect and defend American interests, and to act resolutely and with a minimum of constraints. The "war on terror," embracing the invasions of Afghanistan and Iraq as well as nonmilitary intelligence operations around the globe and significant legal and institutional reforms on the home front, has been waged with the protection of sovereignty uppermost in the minds of U.S. foreign policymakers. The overarching concept for this manifold response is contained in a new national security strategy document released by the White House a year after the 9/11 attacks; this document is perhaps best known for the doctrine of preemption boldly outlined within.[16]

In one way or another, each of these instances of muscular international action appears to raise profound questions about the U.S. approach to sovereignty. In the immediate aftermaths of the campaigns launched against the Taliban and al-Qaeda in Afghanistan and Saddam Hussein in Iraq, the United States stood accused of having flouted United Nations process and, by extension, international law. The implication, unstated to be sure, was that U.S. policymakers had acted in ways that contravened the rights of sovereign nations. Similarly, the fallout from U.S. rejections of the Kyoto treaty, the land mines ban, and the ICC often portrayed the United States as subscribing to an extreme, even antiquated, conception of what Krasner would describe as Westphalian sovereignty. U.S. policymakers were easily cast as wholly intolerant of any initiatives that would result in actual or even potential infringements on the United States' sovereign prerogatives.

---

16. President of the United States, *The National Security Strategy of the United States of America* (Washington, DC: White House, 2002).

According to this narrative, the European response to 9/11 was markedly different, which in some ways was to be expected given that Europe was not the direct target of the terrorist attacks. As other chapters in this volume document in vivid detail, the Europeans, after professing solidarity with the people of the United States and invoking article 5 of the NATO treaty as a precursor to a concerted, joint campaign against international terrorism, soon began to express profound concerns about the U.S. response. Many accused the United States of acting in ways that placed primary emphasis on American interests, capabilities, and objectives, with little or no consideration given to the interests, capabilities, and objectives of other states, to say nothing of standing alliances like NATO or international organizations like the UN. Putting the U.S. agenda first, and going it alone to achieve it, were described as the hallmark not of a wise foreign policy but of a reckless adventurism. As the U.S. administration's attention shifted increasingly to Iraq over the course of 2002, Europeans implored their American counterparts to act multilaterally, with particular emphasis on the United Nations. For Europeans, the coalition determined the mission, and not the other way around.

To supporters of a multilateral approach to the war on terror, the European position was representative of a highly evolved approach to foreign affairs; to detractors, this was pure naïveté, or a cynical effort to block U.S. initiatives. The contrasts between U.S. unilateralism and European multilateralism were starkly drawn; defenders and detractors of these diametrically opposed approaches put forward their arguments passionately and with conviction. At the core of the rhetorical exchanges, two different conceptions of sovereignty appeared to be operating: a strapping defense of traditional national sovereignty voiced by U.S. policymakers and a postmodern challenge advanced by the Europeans. In other words, the debate can be interpreted as a proxy for imputed differences over the meaning and significance of state sovereignty. Unilateralists like the United States are said to behave that way because they fear constraints on their sovereign autonomy and are reluctant to enter into joint commitments, especially formal ones, that will limit their options and establish uncomfortable precedents (and expectations). Multilateralists, on the other hand, because they have no—or at least fewer—compunctions about losing sovereignty, are apparently willing to enter formal and informal covenants with other like-minded countries; over time, this conduct becomes the preferred way of dealing with the vagaries of the international system and even seems to be worn as a badge of honor.

So the question becomes: does the rhetoric match the reality? Put another way, do the terms "unilateralism" and "multilateralism" adequately capture the character of the strategic choices made by the United States and Europe, respectively? And if there is some truth to these monikers, do the differences in foreign policy behavior stem largely from differences in beliefs (e.g., the meaning and significance attached to sovereignty) or from differences in interest, power, and capability? As we shall see, the answers to the first question shed light on the second.

In a penetrating analysis of the unilateralism versus multilateralism debate, John Van Oudenaren lays bare some of the misconceptions and obfuscations generated by this dichotomization of complex reality.[17] His focus is more on the conceptual slippage that often occurs when the term "multilateralism" is employed in the transatlantic dialogue of late. He notes that in recent disputes over international treaties like Kyoto, the ICC, and the Comprehensive Test Ban Treaty, there has been a tendency for proponents of multilateralism (or, put another way, detractors of U.S. unilateralism) to equate large numbers of like-minded states with multilateralism and small numbers—with a limiting case of one—with unilateralism. Subtly and perhaps deceptively, a normative benchmark creeps in; large numbers equates with a kind of democratic legitimacy—majority rules—whereas the lone holdout, especially one capable by virtue of its power of determining the outcome, assumes an autocratic and illegitimate caste, even if the holdout (not always the United States) appeals to a broader norm to justify its course of action. Van Oudenaren suggests that there is in fact a more established tradition that regards multilateralism in terms of norms, not numbers. The numbers approach grows even more problematic as a justification for multilateralism in instances where the coalition of the like-minded and willing falls well short of universality—Van Oudenaren points out by way of example the ICC initiative, which brought together 27 states, 16 of which were European. He notes:

> While such self-defined leadership groups can play pioneering roles in international diplomacy, it is not clear on what basis they lay claim to multilateralist legitimacy and ascribe unilateralist illegitimacy to states that refuse to follow their lead. This is particularly the case when members of the like-minded group are disproportionately from a single region, are less affected than non-like-minded states by the proposed agreements under discussion . . . , or when the claim to moral leadership of a like-minded state is open to question.[18]

What emerges from Van Oudenaren's analysis is that there are no clear standards for identifying multilateralism and unilateralism in international affairs; the designations are inherently subjective and increasingly polemical. Moreover, because of the conceptual fuzziness that plagues both terms, neither is of much use descriptively or analytically. Fashioning a narrative in which multilateral Europe faces off against unilateral United States is easy enough,

17. John Van Oudenaren, "What Is Multilateral?" *Policy Review* 117 (February–March 2003), http://hooover.org/publications/policyreview/3449941.html; John Van Oudenaren, "Unipolar vs. Unilateral," *Policy Review* 124 (April–May 2004), http://www.hoover.org/publications/policyreview/3438956.html.

18. Van Oudenaren, "What Is Multilateral?" 4.

but it ignores important features of the empirical record—for example, the presence and role of European countries that joined or shared the U.S. position on the key disputes in question; or the at times uncompromising stance of the Europeans in international negotiations, which is typically held up as a trademark characteristic of unilateralism. The issue here is not which side holds the moral or rational high ground. Rather, the issue is whether the unilateral/multilateral distinction gets us very far in understanding the essential features of these disputes—how they arose, and whether they are capable of being resolved. The answer appears to be no.

There is something simply unconvincing at the core of this face-off between unilateralism and multilateralism, at least as it relates to putative differences in the way states define and use sovereignty. It suggests that specific state actions are usually if not always motivated first and foremost by principles ("protect and conserve sovereignty!") and strategic considerations ("act in concert with other states!"). That this often implied assertion is occasionally true is beyond dispute; for example, U.S. objections to the ICC have turned wholly on arguments of principle.[19] When one surveys the broad contours of the post-9/11 transatlantic dispute, however, differences in interests, objectives, vulnerabilities, and capabilities (and not the procedural or strategic accents) that give rise to conflicts and agreements among states in the international system appear to be of far greater significance. By implication, differences in the meaning and significance attached to sovereignty are not driving forces behind the emergence of these cleavage lines. This is especially clear in the chapters by William Hitchcock and Henry Nau in this volume; at best, sovereignty conceptions can be said to lurk behind the scenes of the narrative, but they are not central factors. A few examples taken from the period after 9/11 show that sovereignty truly is what states make of it, and depending on the context, the same state may make something very different of it.

Much can and has been made of European efforts to prevail on the United States to pursue its war on terrorism through multilateral channels—specifically, the NATO alliance and, more prominently, the United Nations. The conventional subtext—that U.S. reluctance to engage in multilateral responses stemmed from a desire to protect sovereignty, whereas European eagerness to embrace multilateralism sprang from a conviction about the benefits of pooled sovereignty—is hard to sustain, however, in light of the facts. Two in particular must be kept in mind.

---

19. U.S. objections to the ICC that call up questions of national sovereignty revolve around concerns that the court might limit the use of U.S. military power and that the court could be used as a venue for politically motivated attacks on U.S. leaders and members of the U.S. armed forces. Richard Goldstone and Janine Simpson, "Evaluating the Role of the International Criminal Court as a Legal Response to Terrorism," *Harvard Human Rights Journal* 16 (Spring 2003); Jamie Mayerfeld, "Who Shall Be Judge?: The United States, the International Criminal Court, and the Global Enforcement of Human Rights," *Human Rights Quarterly* 25 (2003): 93–129.

First, to speak of a European initiative to cajole the United States onto a multilateral track, with all that might entail for national sovereignty, is to ignore hard realities on the ground. Europe was very much divided on the question of how best to deal with Iraq, a split that crystallized in January 2003 with the publication of a letter signed by eight European countries in support of the U.S. stance. The characterizations of the U.S. secretary of defense to the contrary notwithstanding, this split was not one between "old" and "new" Europe, unless one wished to count the United Kingdom, Spain, Italy, Denmark, and Portugal as newly baptized Europeans. More important, it was a deep split, running haphazardly both across the EU space and within individual member countries.[20] Thus, even if one were to assume that conceptions of sovereignty were the root cause of foreign policy strategy and objectives, then the inescapable conclusion from the recent European past is that there is no monolithic conception of sovereignty at work within the European Union or within its constituent member states.

Second, in the case of NATO and Iraq, both France and Germany signaled that the military option was off the table well before alliance decision-making mechanisms had been activated. Similarly, the French had made it clear by late 2002 that they would use their veto in the UN Security Council to kill any resolution authorizing the use of force against Iraq. The point is not that these actions or threats were somehow improper or even extraordinary—in fact, a tough-minded approach to agenda setting and a stated willingness to block initiatives that are not to one's liking are typical of interstate behavior. That said, these actions smack more of classic diplomacy, and a desire to balance or check the power advantages of an adversary, than a postmodern, postsovereign approach to foreign relations.

Germany is the locus of two of the more startling departures of state action from multilateral rhetoric. As other chapters in this volume have relayed, the fall 2002 federal elections in Germany turned on foreign policy issues—Chancellor Gerhard Schröder, who had been fighting for his political life just a few months before, made a conscious decision in the late summer to put U.S. foreign policy front and center in the election campaign. Schröder presented himself and, by extension, Germany as resolutely opposed to the invasion of Iraq and cast the Bush administration and the United States as a reckless aggressor. Whether Schröder played the anti-American card in the election, or whether he presented nothing more (or less) than a vigorous and unvarnished critique of an ally, is the subject of a long and unresolved debate, and getting to the bottom of it does not really concern us here. Rather, two points are especially significant. First, Schröder's decision to emphasize this issue in the campaign paid strong electoral dividends, whether or not it

---

20. The gulf between the government position and public opinion was especially pronounced in both the United Kingdom and Spain.

sprang from deeply rooted anti-Americanism, pure political opportunism, or principled policy objections. Second—and far more central to the argument developed in this chapter—in making the case against the war option, Schröder effectively stood fifty years of German multilateral foreign policy on its head by stating categorically at an early point in the campaign that even in the event of a UN resolution sanctioning the use of military force against Iraq, Germany would not participate in any military actions directed against Iraq. A more resolute defense of Westphalian sovereignty is difficult to imagine.

The second German example that points up the dangers and difficulties of sketching stark contrasts between U.S. and European approaches to sovereignty involves the recent initiative by the Berlin government to secure a permanent seat on the UN Security Council. As part and parcel of a broader, UN-launched discussion of institutional reform, the German campaign picked up steam in 2004. The official rationale put forward by the Berlin government, which has met with strong opposition from the United States, China, and several African countries, casts Germany's claim to permanent membership on the council as just and proper acknowledgment of the scale of its financial contributions to the UN and of its more active international role, particularly in the area of international peacekeeping, since unification in 1990. In short, Germany is demanding full rights of nation-state representation in exchange for the larger stake and greater responsibilities. Germany is not demanding a single, permanent seat in the Security Council for the EU—an option that would be far more consistent with the postmodern, postsovereign ethos typically ascribed to members of the European Union. Neither, for that matter, is France or the United Kingdom; indeed, both countries have lent quiet support to the German drive for a Security Council seat because they do not wish to call into question their own long-standing places on this key UN decision-making body. All of which suggests that for these large and therefore consequential European states, multilateralism as a preferred method of operation in the international arena is more a matter of instrumental utility than one of high principle. Embedded within this realist conception is a traditional notion of state sovereignty that is very much alive and kicking.

Just to show how murky things become when one delves inside the often facile debate over unilateralism versus multilateralism (and what it implies about differences in sovereignty conceptions), a case can be made that U.S. and European views of sovereignty are not even rhetorically that far apart in the post-9/11 era. Take, for example, the security strategy documents issued by the Bush administration and the EU in the post-9/11 period. The national security strategy document issued by the Bush administration in September 2002 reads in many ways like a primer on classic principles of national sovereignty. "America is now threatened," it argues, "less by conquering states than we are by failing ones." The country will counter this threat by "defending the United States, the American people, and our interests at home and abroad by identifying and destroying the threat before it reaches our borders. . . . [We] will not hesitate to act alone, if necessary, to exercise our right of self-defense by acting preemptively." Moreover, sovereignty is held up as part of the solution to the problem—the United States will seek to "[deny] further sponsorship, support, and sanctuary to terrorists by convincing or compelling states to accept their sovereign responsibilities."[21] Here, the U.S. administration is expressing an interest in helping to restore and preserve three of the four types of national sovereignty that Krasner identifies: domestic, interdependence, and Westphalian.

The European response to the U.S. national security strategy arrived a little over a year later. Those expecting a *Weltanschauung* diametrically opposed to that of the Americans were surely disappointed; in fact, the extent of the common ground, rhetorically and conceptually, was surprising. State failure— intimately bound up, however implicitly, with sovereignty—was identified as a key problem: "Collapse of the State can be associated with obvious threats, such as organized crime or terrorism. State failure is an alarming phenomenon, that undermines global governance, and adds to regional instability."[22] Although not as expansive as its American counterpart, a European doctrine of preemption, or rather "preventive engagement," is also outlined, which would seem to undermine the notion that the European approach, to the extent there is one, entails an ironclad respect for *Westphalian* sovereignty. And perhaps of greatest interest, there is an acknowledgment that part of the problem, stemming from the fact that it is simultaneously part of the threat, involves a loss of *domestic* sovereignty within the European space: "Europe is both a target and a base for such terrorism: European countries are targets and have been attacked. Logistical bases for Al Qaeda cells have been uncovered in the UK, Italy, Germany, Spain, and Belgium. Concerted European action is indispensable."[23] It would be rash to push the point too far, but there may well be developing *within* Europe a newfound concern with the attributes and legal-institutional prerequisites for traditional conceptions of sovereignty.

Conclusion

On the basis of the preceding analysis, are we in a position to offer up plausible answers to the questions about sovereignty posed at the beginning of the chapter? Is there a gap between the American and the European approaches to sovereignty? If so, has this gap widened in recent years, in response to the

21. President of the United States, *National Security Strategy*, 1, 6.

22. European Council, *A Secure Europe in a Better World: European Security Strategy* (Brussels: European Council, 2003), 4.

23. Ibid., 3.

end of the cold war or the attacks of September 11, 2001? If so, has the widening gap come about because of simultaneous changes in both the United States and Europe or in just one of the transatlantic partners? And most important, did the gap—whatever its current size and direction of change—play a significant role in the strains that have beset the transatlantic relationship since 1991?

In line with earlier scholarly contributions to this area of inquiry,[24] there are in fact significant differences between the conceptions of sovereignty at work in U.S. foreign policy circles, on the one hand, and those held by Europeans on the other, *at least insofar as European states relate to each other within the supranational EU treaty framework*. And this point is key; it is one that Krasner's framework allows us to see more clearly. In the realms of domestic, interdependence, and Westphalian sovereignty, European elites accept and strive for very different outcomes *when dealing with each other* than their American counterparts do when dealing with the outside world.

These differences, however, are not replicated in nearly as stark terms when it comes to international legal sovereignty: individual EU member states have been in many ways as protective of their authority and control in this area as the United States has been. Moreover, when EU member states have dealt with the external world on their own or through the EU in areas in which supranational competences are not particularly well developed (e.g., foreign and security policy), they have frequently behaved in ways that suggest a sensitivity to encroachments on authority and control over the other forms of sovereignty, especially Westphalian.

Viewed from this more refined perspective, the terrorist attacks of 9/11 did not usher in a transatlantic crisis whose roots are based in changing or widening differences in American and European conceptions of sovereignty. The U.S. response, as other chapters in this volume have amply documented, has followed from a hard-bitten assessment of the new threat and a calculation as to which strategic options would be most effective in dealing with the new threat. If concerns about limitations on this or that form of sovereignty have played a part in these decisions, by ruling in certain courses of action and ruling out others, then the influence has been at best on the margins. Key European countries, on the other hand, have sought to channel the disagreements with the United States into multilateral venues like the UN in order to slow down, deflect, or even block American actions they see as unwise or otherwise undesirable. Clashes of interest, not of principle, have driven the rhythm of this latest crisis in the transatlantic relationship. And often as not, European countries have acted in ways that are entirely consistent with traditional conceptions of sovereignty in all its Krasnerian manifestations. To summarize, the recent and at times sharp political conflicts over threat definition, the doctrine

24. Keohane, "Ironies of Sovereignty."

of preemption, the use of military force versus diplomacy, and other bones of contention in the transatlantic relationship have not flowed from differing conceptions of the proper scope and validity of national sovereignty.

All of which brings us back to Krasner. The subtitle of his book on sovereignty—*Organized Hypocrisy*—speaks to the rationalist, even realist underpinnings of all states' approaches to issues involving or implicating prevailing conceptions of sovereignty. As Krasner states in the opening chapter, "outcomes in the international system are determined by rulers whose violation of, or adherence to, international principles or rules is based on calculations of material and ideational interests, not taken-for-granted practices derived from some overarching institutional structures or deeply embedded generative grammars. Organized hypocrisy is the normal state of affairs."[25] According to Krasner, this has always been so. Evidence gleaned from the post-9/11 period suggests that it remains so for all state actors participating in the transatlantic relationship.

25. Krasner, *Sovereignty*, 9.

10 PASSIONS WITHIN REASON

John A. Hall

The most sustained treatment of Atlantic relations remains the volume *Political Community in the North Atlantic Area: International Organization in the Light of Historical Experience*.[1] The team of scholars led by Karl Deutsch considered key historical cases—Austro-Hungary, Great Britain, America in the colonial and early national periods—to produce generalizations about the North Atlantic area. These case studies suggested a distinction between alliances, essentially ad hoc and often temporary, and security communities—and more particularly between amalgamated and pluralistic versions of the latter. Much of the theoretical apparatus that emerged applied to both types of security community. Emphasis was placed on a leading power's need to help construct a security community, habitually in the midst of a shared sense of threat. Maintenance of community depended, however, upon some sense of shared values, and a firm commitment to talk and bargain rather than to polarize and fight. Pluralism necessarily meant the presence of greater levels of conflict, but Deutsch's team saw this tension in a most sophisticated manner. Where difference was great, amalgamation could all too easily be a mistake. Conflict was not catastrophe; indeed it could be seen as a safety valve. The flexibility of pluralism was to be preferred, in circumstances of difference, to the brittleness likely to result from amalgamation. More than one member of Deutsch's team knew this preference as the result of visceral experience, namely, the collapse of Austro-Hungary. The argument about the Atlantic

---

1. Karl W. Deutsch, Sidney A. Burrell, Robert A. Kann, Maurice Lee, Martin Lichterman, Lindgren Raymond, Francis L. Loewenheim, and Richard van Wagenen, *Political Community in the North Atlantic Area: International Organization in the Light of Historical Experience* (Princeton: Princeton University Press, 1957). Cf. Emanuel Adler and Michael Barnett, eds., *Security Communities* (Cambridge: Cambridge University Press, 1998).

community was accordingly almost wholly optimistic: in its pluralistic form it was seen as having both strength and resilience.

This brilliant theoretical construct greatly helps us to understand the Atlantic community in the initial decades after the end of the Second World War. But we need to add to this construct if we are to understand how things have changed and to make an informed guess about the future state of relations in the North Atlantic area. My argument can be seen as a piece of counterpunching, a response to the meritorious plea of Gunther Hellmann in this volume for resistance to either/or thinking, that is, in this case, to the binary opposition of marriage and divorce so often present in the minds of scholars and pundits concerned with the state of transatlantic relations.[2] My main purpose in this chapter is to advance theory, that is, to provide the conceptual tools necessary to understand community. One necessary element to that end is appreciation of the full range of emotional states that can exist with any relationship. But we need to theorize something else as well, namely, the fact that emotional states are not always stable—as is certainly the case, in my view, within the relationship considered in this volume. I seek not just to describe but to explain the oscillation between passion and reason, between outbursts of feeling and cooler second thoughts, so very characteristic of Europe. My account rests firmly on an appreciation of the relations between structure and identity, between, as Max Weber had it, material and ideal interests. Understanding the structural conditions faced by Europe necessitates mentioning banal and slightly unpalatable facts.

I begin this chapter by addressing these theoretical issues so as to demonstrate the relevance of the concepts developed to transatlantic relations; in the remainder I turn to the historical record. In the second section I consider key historical conjunctures, identifying basic changes in senses of transatlantic belonging over the *longue durée*. A particular claim I make is that much discontent within Europe predates the divisions caused by the invasion of Iraq. In the third section I analyze the contemporary situation, noting some novelty while emphasizing still more factors suggesting continuity. In the conclusion I contrast the situation discovered with alternative accounts on offer, including those provided by some of the authors in this volume.

2. Robert Kagan, *Of Paradise and Power: America and Europe in the New World Order* (New York: Knopf, 2003); Elizabeth Pond, *Friendly Fire: The Near-Death of the Transatlantic Alliance* (Washington, DC: Brookings Institution Press, 2004); Thomas Mowle, *Allies at Odds: The United States and the European Union* (Basingstoke, U.K.: Palgrave Macmillan, 2004); David M. Andrews, ed., *The Atlantic Alliance under Stress: U.S.-European Relations after Iraq* (Cambridge: Cambridge University Press, 2005); Nikos Kotzias and Petros Liacouras, eds., *EU-U.S. Relations: Repairing the Transatlantic Drift* (Basingstoke, U.K.: Palgrave Macmillan, 2006). The titles of these books demonstrate that there is, understandably, some confusion as to the participants of the European side of the transatlantic community—that is, whether relations within NATO are now trumped by the greater size and putatively greater integration of the European Union.

Bundles of Sensations, Intermittences of the Heart

It is scarcely revealing a secret to admit that the editors of this volume turned to a sociologist in the hope that specialized expertise on the nature of community and identity—not traditionally at the core of international relations theory—may help cast light on the problems addressed in this volume.[3] For once, this is indeed the case. Sociological theory has ideas that deserve attention. The work of Michael Mann can be considered first for a simple reason: the most distinguished historical sociologist of the contemporary scene is essentially at one with Deutsch, thereby lending reinforcement to his argument and allowing us to see better the nature of the great Sudeten Czech's thought.

Mann distinguishes a range of social identities. The vast majority of social interaction in the historical record has been *local*. The creation of *national* patterns of interaction is accordingly quintessentially modern. If an obvious element of the rise of the national is that of the increasing power of states to extract resources from their societies, quite as significant an indicator is the emergence of national patterns of fertility in the late nineteenth century.[4] Where national identity is passive, *nationalist* identity is active—especially because it has ideas about the proper conduct of geopolitics. The insistence that a nation has its proper "place in the sun" can and has led to conflict with those with *internationalist* identities. In late nineteenth-century Europe, nationalists sought to control and cage foreign-policy-making elites whose behavior was held to be altogether too internationally responsible. Finally, international interaction and identity are, although this distinction is not always appreciated, different from the truly *transnational*.[5]

These categories overlap with Deutsch's work as a whole, especially given that the distinction between pluralistic and amalgamated forms of community is so similar to Mann's last two categories. But Mann makes explicit what is implicit in Deutsch, namely, that foreign policy making tends to be an elite affair, with key counsels being essentially private. Nationalism is an exception to this general rule since it often involves domestic forces, although these are likely to be middle class and intellectual rather than popular or capitalist. The pluralism of a security community is likely to be international—that is, it is likely to involve negotiations between heads of state. Accordingly, concentration

3. I write as much as a European, trying in large part to explain to Americans how the exercise of its power feels to many in a world that has lost its leading edge.

4. Susan Cott Watkins, *From Provinces into Nations: Demographic Integration in Western Europe, 1870–1960* (Princeton: Princeton University Press, 1991).

5. Michael Mann, *The Sources of Social Power*, vol. 2, *The Rise of Classes and Nation-States, 1760–1914* (Cambridge: Cambridge University Press, 1993).

hereafter is on elite matters; broader-based social pressures are mentioned when appropriate.

Although these ideas are important and helpful, we can go further—and can do so best by reflecting on the ideas of David Hume. The elegance and power of the great Scottish moralist's thought cannot hide the fact that he is a poor guide to questions of identity. One critical consideration is well known and obvious from the experience of most human beings. Hume's sensationalism—the doctrine that we build up a picture of the world from the accumulation of sensory data—is ridiculous as a descriptive account of our inner lives. It simply is not the case that every experience is equal and that we judge each one as if we were some weird combination of a gourmet and an accountant. Nietzsche was right: we learn in situations of trauma, with much boredom in between such dramatic moments. An appreciation of the importance of trauma is, as noted earlier, clearly present in *Political Community in the North Atlantic Area*.

What matters here, however, is a different negative criticism, namely, that of complacency. The first volume of *A Treatise of Human Nature* becomes distraught and despairing toward its end. If we are but the product of sensations, bereft of any belief in causation or the continuity of nature, then surely we are indeed "inviron'd with the deepest darkness, and utterly depriv'd of the use of every member and faculty."[6] In the next paragraph, however, Hume escapes despair. The formal reason is that custom fills the vacuum left by philosophy with a game of backgammon or dinner with friends, producing merriness sufficient to make speculation seem ridiculous and strained. But what is even more important than this facile argument is the taken-for-granted view that a human being is *a* bundle of sensations. It seems that there is a self after all, single and solidary, lending unity and coherence to a booming series of disconnected impressions. This view most certainly does not hold at all times. Some humans are blessed with a clear personality in which different passions fit together in a unified manner. This model does not apply to schizophrenics, but equally it does not apply to many of us who are pulled by passions in such a way as to ignore our best interests. This simple consideration opens the door to analysis of the varied emotions that can characterize community. Nor is social life as simple as Hume suggests, as we see if we consider the range of positions that are possible in marital relations—before then returning to the instabilities that can characterize the self.

A brilliant essay by Peter Berger and Hansfried Kellner argues that marriage is the creation of a shared reality.[7] At its most extreme we have absolute

---

6. David Hume, *A Treatise of Human Nature* (1739 and 1741; rept., London: Penguin, 1969), 316.

7. Peter Berger and Hansfried Kellner, "Marriage and the Social Construction of Reality," *Diogenes* 46:1–24.

love, perhaps best expressed by John Donne's phrase that "we two being one are it." But most marriages are not quite like that, being instead constant sources of bargaining—along the lines of "if you do this for me, I will do that for you." Such bargaining in no way undermines the notion of a shared reality, of a common frame of understanding. Sociological research on marriage in fact tends to stress that such bargaining is likely to lead to the strengthening of a relationship—and certainly to an avoidance of the brittleness involved in pretending that "we two are it" at every moment of every day. This finding of course supports Georg Simmel's view that conflict integrates and solidifies, and it has an obvious resonance with the claim of Deutsch's team that a pluralistic security community may have greater resilience than an amalgamated security community.[8]

There are, however, positions other than love and bargaining that should concern us. Consider the fate of women within all too many marriages. Inequality in gender relations can mean that women are unhappily caged within a relationship, bereft of opportunities for exit, forced to stay but filled with resentments. Complexities lurk here. On the one hand, there are those who would escape if they could but are prevented from so doing because of the presence of children and the knowledge that divorced men all too often refuse to pay for the support of their children. On the other hand stands the psychology dramatized in *Who's Afraid of Virginia Woolf*. The mental state so well portrayed in that play fully justifies the technical term "co-dependency." In that world, resentments are nourished and maintained, a situation of endless complaint bereft of any real determination to change, let alone to leave. I am not claiming that this position is somehow the most prevalent one in modern marriage. But it is present at times, and without question it exists as a logical possibility. Divorce is indeed the opposite of absolute love. But matters are far from simple at this end of the scale. There can be trial separations, continued life within the same house, separations that do not lead to divorce—and of course both messy and amicable divorces. And it is not merely licentious to let one's imagination go further. People live double lives; affairs occur. Perhaps readers have imaginations that take them still further. However, enough has been said to make the key analytic point, namely, that of the sheer variety of human experience.

It is crucial to note two different ways in which people live within what seems to be a singular institution. Up to now what I've had to say involves the complexity of a world in which there are several positions within a single institution. This complexity is not really so frightening, however: the holders of those positions may themselves be solidary selves, united bundles of sensation. But if Hume's psychology is wrong, then it is necessary to move beyond

8. Georg Simmel, *Conflict and the Web of Group Affiliations* (Glencoe, IL: Free Press, 1955).

stressing that the institution of marriage contains varied possibilities. Bluntly, it is not always the case that people occupy one place along the scale in a consistent manner. Resentment is in itself unstable, at once filled with complaint yet stalled in terms of action. Much more importantly, human beings suffer from what Marcel Proust termed "the intermittences of the heart." It is well known, for instance, that the breakdown of a marriage tends to be easier to deal with than the death of a spouse. In the latter case, memories remain intact, and so does one's sense of self; the former situation raises doubts, habitually insoluble, and tends to mandate reconstruction of identity. And this case is but an extreme example of something much more common. How often we wobble back and forth, trying again and again, to give another example, to bargain before finally slipping into resentment.

A whole series of suggestive if staccato points about the state of transatlantic relations rises to the surface immediately, all components pointing to the falsity of the binary opposition between absolute love set against complete divorce. First, different countries occupy different places in such relations.[9] For the Poles the situation is close to one of pure love, given the feeling that the United States helped end the cold war and assure the freedom of their nation—a feeling of course massively reinforced by links to Polish-Americans. France is complicated. This great republican rival to the United States, now bereft of its empire, has always longed for some way to sustain grandeur—often assuaged by doing much to design the European Union but prone on that very ground to call for separation from the United States.[10] Second, the affections of states are often as inconstant as those within marriage. France is a classic example. De Gaulle's withdrawal from the NATO command structure stands as a supremely complex move—in the end, a separation without consequence rather than a genuine divorce. German reunification ended French withdrawal, for the strengthening of NATO was instantly seen as a way of maintaining the U.S. presence and thereby limiting the potential of German power. Perhaps this example is one of a solitary self, calculating national interest in different circumstances. But France is not immune to the intermittences of the heart, reacting emotionally to the invasion of Iraq before retreating from a moment of romanticism. Many more positions can be easily conjured up, making it clear that Pandora's box is now open. Still further complexity derives from the presence of multiple units within Europe, most notably the European Union (itself internally divided in defense and foreign policy matters), the Western European Union (WEU), and NATO itself (whose membership contains some countries from all these groups but joins to them Turkey).

9. Andrews, *Atlantic Alliance under Stress*, is particularly useful in identifying differences within Europe.

10. Robert Jackson, "Non, Merci," *Times Literary Supplement*, 3 June 2005.

There are equal complexities within the United States. Historically, Americans have undergone considerable changes in attitude toward particular countries. Admiration for Germany before the First World War was extensive, reflecting of course massive immigration from central Europe. Two world wars changed admiration to distaste. In contrast, Americans' visceral dislike of Great Britain—at the popular level sustained in part by Irish-Americans, at the elite level driven by a desire to take over as hegemon—has now been all but forgotten, astonishingly so given its importance in U.S. foreign policy for such an extended period. Particularly noticeable in the most recent years, of course, has been the ascendancy, perhaps now terminated, of a group of intellectuals driven by romantic ideals far more than by any traditional sense of national interest.[11] But what matters most here is the fact that the United States has an ever-present choice within the Atlantic community. On the one hand is the demand, articulated by elite and popular forces, that Europe stand up for itself. The continuing presence of U.S. troops in Europe was certainly not planned, and there is much to be said for the view that this presence is historically idiosyncratic—making the occasional call for burden sharing, at times insistent, entirely comprehensible. On the other hand are the pleasure and benefit of being number one. Pleasure derives from the ability to set the agenda of world politics and thereby to establish a predictable environment. Benefit has derived from the extraction of seigniorage, seen most clearly in the past in European financing of the twin deficits and always present in varied ways for a country that provides the world's top currency. In a nutshell, the United States in this matter is prone to its own intermittence of the heart, that is, to wobble between asking for European independence and not liking for a moment what it sees when such a process seems to be under way.

It is well known that passions can run amok, thereby making rational calculation impossible. But if this is true of the moments of oscillation noted earlier, quite as important are those moments when sober second thoughts return. Such thoughts arise fundamentally because attention returns to structural constraints that cannot be avoided. In this matter there is a measure of difference between the United States and Europe.

It would be possible for the United States to turn its back on Europe. This move would be unusual historically, given the desire of great powers for a predictable political environment—it being probable that retreat from a leading role would lead to a more complex multipolar world. There may be economic risks attached to such a move. Further, a multipolar world may well diminish

11. There is a vast literature here. An early contribution from the outside was made by Michael Mann, *Incoherent Empire* (London: Verso, 2004). Francis Fukuyama, *America at the Crossroads: Democracy, Power and the Neoconservative Legacy* (New Haven: Yale University Press, 2006), is an autocritique from the inside, written after the difficulties of the Iraqi situation had become generally apparent.

the privileges of seigniorage that the United States enjoys, given that Europe still holds a vast amount of dollars.

In contrast, Europeans face severe constraints that have to this point curtailed momentary thoughts of greater autonomy. The most obvious historical constraint has been that of geopolitical fear, that is, awareness of the fact that defense has in the last analysis been guaranteed by the United States—with U.S. soldiers being less important as a fighting force than as hostages guaranteeing that the United States would come to Europe's defense if need arose. Geopolitical fears have now diminished greatly, although the historical experience of central European countries gives them a continuing appreciation of the United States' geopolitical role—an appreciation vastly enhanced by Putin's threats to cut off supplies of natural gas first to Ukraine and then to Belarus. But appreciation of objective facts needs to be complemented by awareness of the subjective situation. The presence of the United States in NATO has been of immense importance to Europeans for the simplest of reasons: two world wars have made it clear that Europeans do not trust each other and so consider themselves best served by having an external power able to enforce decent rules of behavior. The presence of competing visions within Europe remains a contemporary fact, as we have seen both at the time of the last Balkan wars and in the generalized desire to maintain U.S. troops in Europe so as to limit the power of reunified Germany. These considerations are supported by a further brute fact. A greater measure of European autonomy would necessitate increasing military capacity. There is every reason to believe that any sustained move in this direction will be massively unpopular. By and large, the majority of Europeans—more or less consciously at elite levels, somewhat unconsciously at the level of popular forces—have come to live with an odd, slightly schizophrenic mixture of complaint at U.S. power in combination with a lack of will to change the situation.

Context and Conjuncture

The concepts developed can help outline changes in identity across the North Atlantic over the *longue durée*. The key argument that emerges can be highlighted immediately by commenting on the position put forward by William Hitchcock. On the one hand stands much agreement: crises within the Atlantic community have been perennial, as have the limits to which estrangement between the parties can be taken. Limits of space rule out any complete history of the Atlantic community in the postwar period, but I doubt that Hitchcock would object to taking into account the varied positions and oscillations noted to this point. On the other hand stands an important difference. Although variations in position and mood make generalization difficult, it *is* possible to draw a real if imperfect distinction between two periods within the postwar pluralistic community of the North Atlantic—the first of relative consensus, the second of resentment. This second period was clearly in place before the recent crisis centering on the invasion of Iraq. Much can be said for the historic importance of the mechanisms of community repair identified by Hitchcock, but the repairs in question necessarily concern the reestablishment of the stability of the period of resentment, given that relative consensus has long gone. But perhaps more can be achieved, as I discuss in the conclusion.

The Atlantic arena as a whole has seen a retreat from a genuine transnational or amalgamated transatlantic community. Historians now pay much attention to the Atlantic society and economy of the early eighteenth century.[12] The first British Empire was, unlike its later successor, very profitable, and the inhabitants of the colonies were distinctively British. Nonetheless, the amalgamated community failed. Let us consider first the strongest case, that of Canada from confederation in 1867, before turning to British-U.S. relations.

Canada for most of its history has had a state that lacks its own national identity. This is not for a moment to say that there was no sense of identity present within Canada. If Quebecois identity was in large part inward looking, the same is not true for what is now known as the Rest of Canada. Here identity had a predominantly transatlantic character. The proof of loyalty was of course paid in blood, in the Boer War and still more so in two world wars. Three points can be made about this transatlantic entity.[13] First, the economic development of Canada, the shipping lines and the railways, depended on capital provided by London. More than 70 percent of the £500 million absorbed between 1900 and 1914 came from Britain. Second, Canada provided job opportunities for the highest level of the metropolitan aristocracy. One governor-general, Lord Lorne, was Queen Victoria's son-in-law; another, the Duke of Connaught, was her favorite son. Third, the imperial connection allowed for remarkable social mobility for colonials within the metropolis. Two examples make this point. Let us consider first Donald Alexander Smith, who arrived in Canada as a penniless Scot in 1838. For twenty-six years he worked for the Hudson's Bay Company. He then moved to Montreal and became a major figure in the Canadian Pacific Railway and in national politics. In 1895, when already long past seventy, he became the official representative of Canada in London, where he died in 1914—to the considerable irritation of Sir Frederick Borden, the famous minister of militia and defence, who had sought to succeed him.[14] Smith piled up colossal wealth, was ennobled as

12. David Langley, *The Americas in the Age of Revolution, 1750–1850* (New Haven: Yale University Press, 1996).

13. David Cannadine, "Imperial Canada: Old History, New Problems," in *Imperial Canada, 1867–1917*, ed. C. Coates, 1–19 (Edinburgh: Centre for Canadian Studies, 1997).

14. Carman Miller, "Sir Frederick Goes to London: Money, Militia and Gentlemen Capitalists," in Coates, *Imperial Canada*, 155–65.

Lord Strathcona and Mount Royal, and lived in great state on both sides of the Atlantic. He was chancellor of McGill University; he equipped at his own cost a troop of horses during the Boer War; he presided in London at an annual banquet each July 1 to celebrate Canadian confederation; and he spent £40,000 to celebrate his lord rectorship of Aberdeen University.

A second case is that of William Maxwell Aitken. Within a decade of his arrival in Britain, Aitken was a member of Parliament, a baronet, a peer, the owner of *Express* newspapers, and the friend and confidant of that other son of the Canadian manse, Andrew Bonar Law—who became prime minister (in contrast to Aitken himself, whose highest political post was that of minister of aircraft production in 1940). The causes to which Aitken was attracted—empire free trade in the 1930s, deep antipathy to Lord Mountbatten on the grounds that he gave away India, opposition to entry in the Common Market—were characteristic of this transatlantic world. Bluntly, he loved the British Empire more than the British themselves did.

This transatlantic entity has by and large come to an end. There is at least a Canadian national anthem (or rather two of them), the constitution has (at least for every province except Quebec) been repatriated, and it would not surprise me were a republican movement to arise in the future to echo the one that is now making inroads in Australia. Conrad Black, the owner of Britain's *Daily Telegraph*, illuminates matters by sheer contrast. His status as Aitken's presumptive heir seemed assured in 1999 when the British government offered him a peerage. But the Canadian government (whose prime minister had reason to dislike the newspaper tycoon) refused to allow him, as a Canadian citizen, to accept this honor. National identity has trumped this transatlantic political entity.

Initially, the cultural patterning of the thirteen American colonies was equally transnational. Bernard Bailyn has demonstrated ideological continuity, while David Hackett Fischer, in his monumental work, shows the recreation in the New World of varied social patterns, from architecture and familial life to political attitudes and leadership styles.[15] More importantly, rebellion occurred in large part because of colonial loyalty to the ideals of the homeland. The move from being the best Englishmen to becoming Americans took place as the result of a conflict; it was consequence rather than cause. The precise cause of the end of amalgamation does not matter here. What is particularly interesting, however, is that elements of an informal shared identity were revived at a later time—a development that adds yet another position to those already sketched. International relations scholars like to point to the transfer of power between Britain and the United States at the end of the nineteenth century as perhaps the sole example of a peaceful hegemonic transition within the

15. Bernard Bailyn, *The Origins of American Politics* (New York: Vintage, 1968); David Hackett Fischer, *Albion's Seed* (Oxford: Oxford University Press, 1989).

history of the world polity. This transition was certainly eased by geography, but it depended upon shared liberal norms—and perhaps still more on shared Anglo-Saxon habit.[16] Kipling lived in Vermont for a long period, knew Mahan and Teddy Roosevelt, and eventually felt as at home with the key figures in Great Britain's military apparatus, Lords Fisher and Esher.[17] The resulting division of military labor meant in particular that Britain could concentrate on designing plans to bottle up the German fleet so as to starve the German population into submission.[18]

The "special relationship" has received enormous attention, not surprisingly since it is with us still. One of its earliest architects was Winston Churchill. The fact that his mother was American lends authenticity to the notion of a transatlantic identity. Still, Churchill's behavior as first lord of the admiralty and as prime minister had at its core the pragmatic desire to extend *British* power by means of the American connection.[19] Calculation seems stronger still in Harold Macmillan's celebrated words to Richard Crossman while attached to Eisenhower's headquarters in Algiers in 1942: "[We] are the Greeks in this American empire. You will find the Americans much as the Greeks found the Romans—great big, bustling people, more vigorous than we are and also more idle, with more unspoiled virtues but also more corrupt. We must run [this HQ] as the Greek slaves ran the operations of the Emperor Claudius."[20] This same vein was struck by Keynes, when commenting to his staff before beginning meetings about the British loan: "they may have all the money, but we've got all the brains."[21] The experiences of Keynes at this time, however, point to fundamental limits to the special relationship. Bluntly, the hopes that Britain has rested upon the relationship have tended to be illusory, as was so dramatically apparent when Mrs. Thatcher was told of the bombing of Libya only when U.S. planes were airborne. America has always tended to listen only on occasions when it suited its own interest so to do.

Although these informal American-British understandings helped to defeat Imperial Germany, they were insufficient to establish a successful reordering of the world in 1919. The formal treaty that ended the war lacked the backing of power, due to the exhaustion of France and Britain and the withdrawal of

16. Shared liberal norms: Michael Doyle, "Kant, Liberal Legacies and Foreign Affairs," *Philosophy and Public Affairs* 12, nos. 3 and 4 (1983): 205–35, 323–53; shared Anglo-Saxon habit: Mann, *Sources of Social Power*, 2: 740–99.

17. Christopher Hitchens, *Blood, Class and Nostalgia: Anglo-American Ironies* (New York: Farrar, Straus and Giroux, 1990).

18. Avner Offer, *The First World War: An Agrarian Interpretation* (Oxford: Oxford University Press, 1990).

19. Henry Butterfield Ryan, *The Vision of Anglo-America: The U.S.-UK Alliance and the Emerging Cold War, 1943–1946* (Cambridge: Cambridge University Press, 1987).

20. Alistair Horne, *Harold Macmillan*, vol. 1, *1894–1956* (New York: Viking, 1988), 160.

21. This story was told to me in 1983 by the late James Meade, who worked closely with Keynes in these years.

the United States. The absence of a geopolitical order was always likely to lead to conflict, with chaos in fact ensuing from the actions of bolshevism and Nazism, the two great revolutionary forces of European modernity. Catastrophes undergone made for the far more settled—although informal—situation of the warlike peace that followed from the ending of the Second World War. One factor making for stability was that the U.S. elite blamed itself for the withdrawal from Europe in the interwar years—and anyway wished to use its newfound power to promote new architecture for the world polity. Crucially, Wilson's attempt to make a world safe for democracy by utilizing the principle of national self-determination was replaced by the brute but utterly comprehensible realism enshrined in the division of the world. All parties were prepared to enforce this division. What mattered for the Atlantic community, as both Deutsch's team and Henry Nau in this volume stress, was a shared sense of threat.[22] Unity was established through an "empire by invitation"—that is, NATO resulted from the famous calculation, coined by Lord Ismay, that it was necessary "to keep the Russians out, the Americans in and the Germans down"[23]—from which the United States could never escape. The community that resulted was very much a product of joint effort. If the European Union (or rather its varied forebears) was most of all the work of brilliant French bureaucrats insistent on finding a new relationship with Germany, their plans may well not have succeeded without pressure from Washington.[24] Equally, we now know that European economic recovery depended far more upon European efforts than upon the Marshall Plan.[25] Nonetheless, European investors would never have acted had not the United States solved Europe's security dilemma. And Europe benefited very much from the differential understanding of the interwar crisis. The United States tended to believe that the breakdown of trade brought war in its wake, whereas Europeans, more accurately, reversed the equation. This meant that U.S. hegemony was exercised in the most benign way, notably in allowing Europeans varied types of corporatist arrangements that did much to ensure social peace.[26]

What was the character of the early postwar Atlantic community? Genuine attempts were made to turn this situation into one of absolute love, that is,

22. Charles Maier, "The Two Postwar Eras and the Conditions for Political Stability in Twentieth Century Western Europe," *American Historical Review* 86 (1981): 327–52.

23. Geir Lundestad, "Empire by Invitation? The United States and Western Europe, 1945–1952," *Journal of Peace Research* 23, no. 3 (1986): 263–77.

24. Alan Milward, *The European Rescue of the Nation-State* (Berkeley: University of California Press, 1992).

25. Alan Milward, *The Reconstruction of Western Europe, 1945–1951* (Berkeley: University of California Press, 1984).

26. John G. Ruggie, "International Regimes, Transactions, and Change: Embedded Liberalism in the Postwar Economic Order," *International Organization* 36, no. 2 (Spring 1982): 379–415.

into a community in which both sides of the Atlantic, especially members at the elite level, saw the world in exactly the same way.[27] All those CIA-funded Congresses for Cultural Freedom sought to cement a shared identity, an enterprise in a sense personified in the vigorous figure of Edward Shils— resident for most of his life half a year in Chicago and half a year at the University of Cambridge. Still, how extensive and deep was transatlantic identity in practice? It is worth keeping at the center of one's mind that identities habitually involve some sort of mix between interest and affect. If we now revert to continental European cases, the air of calculation rather than of shared identity comes to the fore. As an intellectual, Raymond Aron, despite his fabulous intelligence and carefully nurtured American relationships, was first and foremost French. He is the perfect exemplar of what the community was in practice—a community, for sure, but one based on bargaining, calculation, and a combination of shared and dissimilar values. There was a clear understanding that the key transatlantic institutions were dominated in the last resort by the leading power. This ascendancy was obviously true of NATO, whose commanding officer was, is, and always will be an American. Still, the pretense was that of a complete community of equals, and there was considerable irritation—especially in London—when the United States acted unilaterally, as it did at times even in this period.

Something of a sea change occurred in the late 1960s and early 1970s. Many Europeans—even the British—were deeply opposed to U.S. actions in Vietnam. In a sense, these were the business of the United States alone, although the consequences of U.S. actions were not. Lyndon Johnson famously could not decide between guns and butter; rather than using U.S. dollars for its massively increased war spending, the United States used its hegemonic powers in a predatory manner. Seigniorage became a serious matter, as when, during Johnson's presidency, the United States extracted loans from Germany at below-market rates.[28] Nixon's closing of the gold window in 1971 was felt acutely, less for the change it brought than for the unilateralism so much enjoyed by John Connally. What mattered most of all was that the printing of money to finance the U.S. deficit set off the great inflation of the postwar period.[29] A striking symbol of the change at an intellectual level was the fact that the thinker most loyal to the United States, perhaps the leading intellect of the postwar community, Raymond Aron, wrote a powerful treatise titled *The*

27. Thomas Schaeper and Kathleen Schaeper, *Cowboys into Gentlemen: Rhodes Scholars, Oxford, and the Creation of an American Elite* (New York: Berghahn Books, 1998); Kees van der Pijl, *The Making of an Atlantic Ruling Class* (London: New Left Books, 1984); Volker Berghahn, *America and the Intellectual Cold Wars in Europe* (Princeton: Princeton University Press, 2001).

28. Gregory F. Treverton, *The Dollar Drain and American Forces in Germany: Managing the Political Economics of Alliances* (Columbus: Ohio University Press, 1978).

29. Michael Smith, *Power, Norms and Inflation* (New York: Aldine de Gruyter, 1992).

Imperial Republic.[30] Of course the great French thinker did not suggest turning away from the United States, but a tone of irritation, perhaps even of resentment, was present in his elegant treatise. The less sophisticated were more emotional. But what was established in general was the stability of oscillation between resentment suggesting action and the reversion to sullen compliance once realization set in that the costs of change were too great. Europeans had learned to whine while remaining supine.

Change and Continuity

Academics should resist being clearer than the truth. Given that predicting the past is hard, it is mere foolishness to offer certainty about the future. Some structural conditions of the Atlantic community have changed, but it is clear that particular personalities—above all, the neoconservative entourage with which Bush surrounded himself during his first term in office—have lent a flavor to transatlantic relations that may change rapidly should new leaders come to the fore. But if caution is called for, so too is there need for recognizing the types of variables that might matter. Let us begin with the forces of change, seen from both sides of the Atlantic, before considering other factors that suggest continuity.

The most striking recent portrait of U.S.-European relations, that of Stephen Walt's "The Ties That Fray," was written before the accession to the presidency of the younger Bush.[31] The key factor behind Walt's analysis was the end of the cold war, which he felt had provided glue for a community in which diverging interests—in geopolitical vision, value orientation, styles of political economy, and matters of trade—had been increasing in range and depth. Walt predicted the emergence of a multipolar world in which the euro would eventually challenge the continuing supremacy of the dollar. Divergences have certainly increased in recent years. Most striking in European eyes is the character of nationalism within the United States, revived and exacerbated by the terrorist attacks on New York and Washington. Anatol Lieven is surely correct when arguing that the behavior of the United States has been idiosyncratic in historical terms.[32] The United States had the possibility of cooperating with its allies, of behaving as a conservative, satisfied power, but this collaboration most certainly has not happened. The radicalism of intellectuals driven by geopolitical dreams has marked U.S. policy, to which can be added both a popular politics that favors a particular attitude toward Israel and the extreme confidence resulting from military success. Europeans listened in

30. Raymond Aron, *The Imperial Republic* (London: Weidenfeld and Nicolson, 1979).

31. Steven Walt, "The Ties That Fray: Why Europe and America Are Drifting Apart," *National Interest*, no. 54 (1988–89): 3–11.

32. Anatol Lieven, *America Right or Wrong: An Anatomy of American Nationalism* (Oxford: Oxford University Press, 2004).

some awe to Donald Rumsfeld, feeling his pleasure in the exercise of naked power. Perhaps as important—at least, should it continue—is the lessening of the economic salience of Europe for the United States. The twin deficits are no longer financed by Europeans—and no longer by petrodollars as well. East Asia has provided formal and informal financing, that is, through the purchase of U.S. Treasury bonds and stocks, which have kept the dollar strong and the market on which they depend open. The United States is less constrained by Europe than was once the case. From this situation derives the United States' unprecedented politics of trying to create a divide within Europe between the old and the new, so as better to exert hegemonic influence.

The European situation represents the other side of the coin. Particularly noticeable has been the spectacular unleashing of resentments and feelings of difference as the result of the U.S. decision to invade Iraq with the intent of toppling the regime of Saddam Hussein. European anti-Americanism has always existed, but it has gained new intensity in recent years, especially after the revelations that British and American troops in Iraq have tortured detainees.[33] There is noticeable irritation over U.S. pressure on Europe to allow Turkey to enter the European Union—a matter on which this author cannot restrain himself from wholly endorsing the U.S. position. Although arguments between the United States and Europe have existed over the years, near daily perusal of American and European newspapers in recent years sometimes reveals nothing less than different mentalities, at least in the perceptions of the problems of the Middle East. At the extreme have been interesting calls for a completely novel and wholly European policy. The absence of an external threat, so the argument goes, should lessen dependence on the United States, with confidence resulting from the realization that the exercise of soft European power—above all, in the postcommunist world—has been exceptionally effective.

Despite the cogency of these points, the weight of evidence still tilts, in my view, toward the likelihood of continuity. What was noticeable in response to the ending of the cold war was the desire to maintain the U.S. presence so as to balance Germany. The emotional exuberance of recent years has now been contained on both sides of the Atlantic; reasons have again dictated stepping back from the unknown abysses of a new world. German leadership within Europe currently seeks to repair transatlantic relations, and an attempt is being made to revive the failed Doha talks. More important than the to-and-fro of events, however, are structural conditions. Does anyone really think it likely that Europe's status as economic giant and military worm will change? A huge shock was administered to Europe by its failure to act cohesively in the face of

---

33. Jean-François Revel, *L'obsession anti-américaine: Son fonctionnement, ses causes, ses inconsequences* (Paris: Plon, 2002); Philippe Roger, *The American Enemy: A Story of French Anti-Americanism* (Chicago: Chicago University Press, 2005); Andrei S. Markovits, *Uncouth Nation: Why Europe Dislikes America* (Princeton: Princeton University Press, 2007).

ethnic cleansing in the Balkans during the last years of the Clinton administration. The promises to produce greater unity at that time have borne no
fruit. Europe remains divided, as manifested in the failure to pass a fairly
bland constitution. Accordingly, foreign policy coordination has not taken
place. The European Rapid Reaction Force has so far been a disappointment,
not least perhaps because it is effectively in conflict with NATO's Response
Force. Divisions between France and Britain remain great in military matters, and the lack of willingness of Europeans at the NATO meeting in Riga in
late 2005 to increase the number of troops in Afghanistan and to revise the
terms under which they operate was very striking. The United States has
increased—and will further increase—its defense spending; Europe shows no
sign of following this example. There is not the remotest sign that Europe
imagines its weapons systems working in an autonomous manner: differently
put, the sunk capital of shared technologies really looks to create a dependent
path. Further, most macroeconomic matters remain in the hands of national
governments. "These governments will not voluntarily give up their over-
representation in the G8 or the IMF in favour of a common EU stance."[34] Is
it likely that the euro can triumph over the dollar, when the United States remains the provider of geopolitical security—a vital need still in the eyes of the
new member states of central Europe? The interpenetration of American and
European economies is great, with perhaps fully 50 percent of U.S. foreign
direct investment being made in Europe; this interpenetration matters more
than trade because it gives direct access of each others' markets. Many other
considerations reinforce skepticism. Beneath the surface there remains a
good deal of commonality in value, as was evident in the initial European response to the terrorist attacks—and which is ever more reinforced by the expansion of the vibrant American consumer culture.[35] Further, against the
crisis over Iraq should be set the successful cooperation of France and the
United States in getting Syria out of Lebanon, the very fact of the NATO role
in Afghanistan, and the somewhat greater coordination of policy toward Iran.
A final general point can be made, usefully returning us to the concepts created at the start of this chapter. Getting married requires real decisiveness;
staying together has the force of habit and inertia on its side.

Conclusion

The argument made here can, as a first element of conclusion, be distinguished from two other positions prominent in current debate. The first has
just been noted. Europe will soon stand on its own, so it goes, free of U.S.

---

34. Charlemagne, "The Puny Economic Powerhouse," *Economist*, 10 December 2005.
35. Victoria de Grazia, *Irresistible Empire: America's Advance through Twentieth Century
Europe* (Cambridge: Harvard University Press, 2005).

tutelage. This position has been descriptively advanced by Charles Kupchan, who is convinced that the elites and peoples of Europe have the capacity and determination to become masters of their own fate.[36] Jürgen Habermas could be cited by Kupchan as evidence for his position, for the German philosopher has recently urged Europe—that is, he has issued a prescriptive polemic—to stand apart from the United States, suggesting that the invasion of Iraq can serve as a rallying call for the united federal Europe for which he so longs.[37] There are powerful reasons to doubt this view.[38] Europeans may have the means, but they most certainly lack the will to challenge U.S. power. Divisions between European countries remain endemic, and there is no sign of any general willingness to increase defense spending—nor any indication that a common foreign policy is possible.

The second position is one that expects or longs for—here too, authors can be either prescriptive or descriptive—a return to a unified voice for the West.[39] This position deserves nearly as much criticism. There has not been a unified West since 1945, in the sense identified at the start of this chapter, that is, as a transnational or amalgamated community of absolute love. The benign exercise of U.S. hegemony allowed for a consensual atmosphere within the Atlantic community in the quarter century after the end of the Second World War, but that atmosphere has not existed, for most of Europe for most of the time, for a further quarter century. The events of the last years make it unlikely that any taken-for-granted cordiality and civility will be restored. Once trust has gone, it is hard to restore it. We live somehow in the middle: the increase in U.S. power leads to less consultation, and so to greater European resentment—with neither side really prepared to change the rules of the game.

This situation is far from optimal. Power is always increased when it is based on a measure of legitimacy, making it necessary to say that the United States would be still more powerful if it joined to the amazing increase in its material capabilities an increase in legitimacy.[40] It is possible that greater power within the Atlantic community, derived from agreement, may even have made Saddam Hussein aware of the futility of his divide-and-rule tactics. This is not to contradict what I've just said: neither absolute love nor the

---

36. Charles Kupchan, *The End of the American Era* (New York: Vintage, 2002). Kupchan restates his position in the present volume, but in a slightly more nuanced form.

37. Jürgen Habermas, *Time of Transitions* (Cambridge, MA: Polity Press, 2005).

38. John A. Hall, "Plaidoyer pour l'Europe des patries," in *The European Union: Benign Imperial Power or Superstate*, ed. Ralf Rogowski and Charles Turner, 107–24 (Cambridge: Cambridge University Press, 2007).

39. Timothy Garton Ash, *Free World: America, Europe and the Surprising Future of the West* (New York: Random House, 2004); G. John Ikenberry, *After Victory* (Princeton: Princeton University Press, 2002); Ikenberry reiterates this position with still more force in his introduction to the present volume.

40. Steven Walt, *Taming American Power: The Global Response to U.S. Primacy* (New York: Norton, 2005).

straightforward and cordial bargaining of the immediate postwar period can be restored. What may work is something completely different, the character of which can be highlighted by reflecting on the nature of civil society. That popular concept is often seen in terms of difference. But what really matters is the *agreement* to differ. I concur with the conclusion drawn by Henry Nau in this volume: the Atlantic community would now be best served by a measure of separation in some areas so as to allow for greater harmony in others. Doubtless this change would require some restraint both within the United States and within Europe, but that may well already be in the cards. It would also require sophistication. For there are new challenges to order within international society, and liberal societies need to think, very hard, about how to manage them. At times this change may require the transatlantic community to act forcefully outside its own area; on other occasions, however, there may be much to be said for a division of labor.[41] It is as well to remember that successful marriages survive both through the division of labor and through the application of intelligence.

41. For the United States' desire for an expansion of NATO's role, see "How to Go Global," *Economist*, 25 March 2006; for a cautionary word from Europe, see Francois Heisbourg, "Why NATO Needs to Be Less Ambitious," *Financial Times*, 22 November 2006.

11 AMERICAN EXCEPTIONALISM OR WESTERN CIVILIZATION?

DIETER FUCHS AND HANS-DIETER KLINGEMANN

Are the current conflicts between the United States and Europe a "temporary irritation or [an] enduring crisis"? This question lies at the heart of this book. If those conflicts are rooted in the "deep structure of the transatlantic relationship," we can assume that it is indeed an enduring crisis. John Ikenberry has elaborated on some dimensions of this deep structure in his introduction to this volume.

Ikenberry proposes that differences in political value orientations and different political identities based on these values could be possible sources of fundamental and enduring conflicts. In this chapter we take up his proposition and ask two questions. First, is there any empirical evidence for pronounced differences in political value orientations of the people in the United States and Europe? The second question is contingent on the answer to the first. If there are differences in political value orientations, can they be regarded a source of fundamental conflicts between the United States and Europe?

It is remarkable that these questions are at the top of the political agenda at all. Some explanation is certainly needed. In his introduction, Ikenberry argues that for several decades the United States and Europe cooperated in a joint Atlantic political order. This Atlantic political order was supported and legitimized by shared political values and a common political identity. Representative democracy, market economy, and plural society were core elements of this shared political identity. This belief is also reflected in Samuel P. Huntington's thesis of a Western civilization that includes both the value communities of northern America and Europe.[1] This viewpoint is in contrast to that of Seymour Martin Lipset, who has developed the thesis of American

---

1. Samuel P. Huntington, *The Clash of Civilizations and the Remaking of World Order* (London: Simon and Schuster, 1996).

exceptionalism.[2] Lipset argues that the American and European value systems are based on different traditions and experiences. Despite the commonalities of some general convictions, like the value of democracy and human rights, these different cultural traditions will lead to considerable differences in the evaluation of political issues and differences about how to design and institutionalize a democratic regime. However, both positions can be plausibly reconciled. In the mid-twentieth century, when liberal democracy had to be defended against the fascist regimes and later on against communism, commonalities of political value orientations were emphasized on a more abstract level. Differences that existed at lower levels of abstraction tended to be deemphasized or neglected altogether. However, after the defeat of the autocratic regimes and the collapse of communism, this strategy, which aimed at integration, has lost its function. Subsequently, political value differences at a lower level of abstraction have gained in importance. It is not by accident that some prominent voices have called for a European identity that can and should be built in opposition to the United States.[3]

Our analysis unfolds in three steps. First, we briefly sketch major characteristics of the national identity of the United States and its corresponding value system. In the process, we highlight differences with Europe. This discussion structures the empirical analysis, which we carry out in the second step. Here we suggest theoretically defined value dimensions and link them to available indicators. Subsequently, we perform a factor analysis to confront theoretical expectations about the dimensionality of the value space and empirical data. These dimensions are used to establish the degree to which the value systems of Americans and Europeans differ empirically. Specifically, we discuss differences between the United States and Europe, as well as between the United States and the core European countries of France, Germany, and Poland. In the third and final step, we present a summary of the most important results and then draw conclusions.

America's National Identity

The American national identity emerged in the eighteenth century. It is a product of the American Revolution and the culture of Protestant sects whose members came to America as the founding settlers; both have decisively shaped several aspects of national identity.[4] The American Revolution, in contrast to the European revolutions, created a new collective—"the first new

2. Seymour M. Lipset, *American Exceptionalism: A Double-Edged Sword* (New York: Norton, 1996).

3. Jürgen Habermas, *Der gespaltene Westen* (Frankfurt: Suhrkamp, 2004).

4. Richard Hofstadter, *The Age of Reform: From Bryan to F.D.R.* (New York: Knopf, 1972); Robert N. Bellah, *The Broken Covenant* (New York: Seabury Press, 1975); Samuel N. Eisenstadt, *Die Vielfalt der Moderne* (Weilerswist: Velbrück Wissenschaft, 2000); Samuel P.

nation."[5] The consciousness of this collective was influenced by two beliefs: first, and this was promoted particularly by the Protestant sects, the belief that Americans are a "chosen people" and that America is God's country, the site of a " 'new Heaven' and a new earth, the home of justice"; and second, the belief that Americans had created a unique political order—the constitutional democracy, which is institutionalized through the U.S. constitution and happens to be an "innovation of universal importance."[6] This composition of two singularities, the "chosen people" and the unique constitutional order, formed the basis of a messianic credo and a missionary attitude that justified foreign policies such as the Spanish-American War.

Protestant sects in the United States differed from European churches in several respects. First, they derived their strength from a voluntary commitment of their members. They were not connected to governmental institutions and received no state funding. Second, their structure was not hierarchical. Their members' relation to God did not need the intermediation of priests and bishops. Rather, it was personal and direct. Third, these sects cultivated strict moral conduct by stressing the ethical principles of self-responsibility, a strong work ethic, and a meritocratic orientation. Alexis de Tocqueville has convincingly argued that these aspects led to the development of a particular type of individualism, which is regarded as one of the most striking features of American society to this very day.[7]

Originally American society was comprised of settlers, and the Protestant sects left a major imprint on its culture. Europe's political culture, in contrast, was mainly influenced by aristocratic and hierarchically structured, state-centered institutions. These differences were highlighted particularly by the American Revolution.[8] The value system that emerged among the American populace was influenced by the liberal thought of the eighteenth century, which in its essence was "the anti-thesis of Socialism. It was anti-state."[9]

The European value system proved itself to be antithetical to the American value system in several significant respects.[10] In Europe, the decisive influence was provided by the hierarchical structures of European societies (aristo-

Huntington, *Who Are We? The Challenges to America's National Identity* (New York: Simon and Schuster, 2004); see Lipset, *American Exceptionalism*.

5. Seymour M. Lipset, *The First New Nation: The United States in Historical and Comparative Perspectives* (New York: Basic Books, 1963).

6. "Chosen people": see Huntington, *Who Are We?* 64; unique political order: see Eisenstadt, *Die Vielfalt der Moderne*, 57.

7. Alexis de Tocqueville, *Democracy in America* (Garden City, NY: Anchor Books, 1969).

8. Lipset, *American Exceptionalism*.

9. Ibid., 32.

10. Herbert McClosky and John Zaller, *The American Ethos: Public Attitudes toward Capitalism and Democracy* (Cambridge: Harvard University Press, 1984); Richard Münch, *Die Kultur der Moderne* (Frankfurt: Suhrkamp, 1986); see Lipset, *American Exceptionalism*.

cratic and monarchic) and its institutions (church and state), which dated from the beginning of the Middle Ages. Finally, on this basis, conservative Toryism (Disraeli and Bismarck) emerged in the nineteenth century to shape the history of European society. The social status of the European aristocracies was based on land ownership, and as a consequence this aristocracy had a strong anticapitalist and antimarket orientation. Conservative Toryism was based on the belief that governing was the responsibility of an aristocratic state. The desolate situation of the lower classes ranked highest among the societal problems that needed to be solved in the nineteenth century. Disraeli and Bismarck favored solving this "social question" by stressing the role of the state, which finally led to the establishment of the European welfare states. The upper classes, by way of state-centered welfare policies, hoped to preserve their privileges and their belief in the norms of noblesse oblige.[11] These paternalistic ideas did not particularly encourage self-responsibility, nor did they support the idea of solving societal problems through voluntary associations or the idea of competition among individuals in free markets.

At this point in our analysis, we are confronted with a fundamental problem. Our description of the cultural traditions of America and Europe is in some ways limited to the time span up to World War I. It remains an open question how the dramatic political events and societal changes of the twentieth century have altered this picture. Lipset deals with this question explicitly: "American values were modified sharply by forces stemming from the Great Depression and World War II. These led to a much greater reliance on the state and acceptance of welfare and planning policies, the growth of trade unions and class divisions in voting."[12] Especially the social problems of the 1920s and 1930s fundamentally changed American politics and led to a certain Europeanization, to a "social democratic tinge."[13] The Europeanization of American politics left its mark on the American ethos and led to a moderation of the extremely individualistic and antistate value orientations.[14] However, Lipset emphasizes that America's convergence toward European patterns was merely relative. In fact, the lasting economic prosperity after World War II led to a revitalization of classic liberal ideology, which entails a profound distrust of welfare state policies. He summarizes this revitalization of classic liberal ideology as follows: "America remains more individualistic, meritocratic-oriented, and anti-statist than other peoples elsewhere."[15]

In the empirical analysis that follows, we test a series of expectations based on the description of differences and similarities between the cultural traditions of Americans and Europeans.

11. Lipset, *American Exceptionalism*, 31.
12. Ibid., 22.
13. Hofstadter, *Age of Reform*, 37.
14. McClosky and Zaller, *American Ethos*.
15. Lipset, *American Exceptionalism*, 38.

Empirical Analysis

Assumptions and Expectations

Our analysis is confined as far as possible to political value orientations. It corresponds with Ikenberry's characterization of the Atlantic political community and with the point of view that the contemporary conflicts between America and Europe are mainly political conflicts. Additionally, America's national identity and the value orientations associated with it are primarily political.

For the empirical description of the collective identity of Americans and Europeans, we rely on the concept of the political community.[16] This concept assumes that an individual's subjective awareness of membership in such a community is formed through shared historical experiences and value orientations. The historical experiences are not the subject of detailed empirical analysis here; the analysis is restricted to a comparison of value orientations. The analysis of value orientations relies on some theoretically reasonable dimensions (see table 11.1).

Table 11.1. Dimensions and indicators of a political community

Dimensions	Indicators
I. Form of government	1. Support of democratic rule
	2. Rejection of autocratic rule
II. Relationship self-state	3. Self-responsibility/state responsibility
III. Self as political actor	4. Political motivation
	5. Political participation (noninstitutionalized)
	6. Civic engagement (voluntary associations)
IV. Relationship to the others	7. Recognition of others as equal (equality of women)
	8. Trust in others
	9. Social tolerance
	10. Ethical tolerance
V. National identification	11. National pride
VI. Religion	12. Importance of God
	13. Attendance at religious services

16. David Easton, *A Systems Analysis of Political Life* (Chicago: Chicago University Press, 1965); Robert A. Nisbet, *The Sociological Tradition* (New York: Basic Books, 1966); Dieter Fuchs, "Demos und Nation in der Europäischen Union," in *Zur Zukunft der Demokratie: Herausforderungen im Zeitalter der Globalisierung*, ed. Hans-Dieter Klingemann and Friedhelm Neidhard (BerlinEdition Sigma, 2000).

Six dimensions of a political community are distinguished in table 11.1. Indicators available in the surveys at our disposal are allocated to each dimension. The guideline for the selection of these dimensions is the concept of democracy, with its two components of *kratos* (rule) and *demos* (people). The dimension "form of government" refers to the *kratos* component. In a democratic community, support of democratic rule as well as rejection of autocratic rule must be assumed by definition. The same is not so clear-cut for self-responsibility. This indicator contrasts self-responsibility for one's own life with the responsibility of the state to provide for its citizens. Even though a democracy is inconceivable without a certain degree of self-responsibility, there are divergent normative ideas about how strong this degree can and should be. A libertarian model of democracy emphasizes self-responsibility, whereas a social democratic one shifts responsibility to the state.[17]

Value dimensions III–V relate to the *demos* component in different ways. Dimension III refers to how the individual citizen sees himself or herself as a political actor, and dimension IV refers to the relationship of the individual citizen to the political community as a whole. The indicators of both dimensions touch on main characteristics of civil society or civic community as discussed by Robert D. Putnam.[18] Dimension V refers to attitudes toward the political community as a collective subject or "national identification."

The dimension "religion," which is operationalized by the items "importance of God" and "attendance at religious services," is probably the most problematic. Although religiosity is not a political trait and above all not a democratic value orientation, there are three reasons why it should be considered. First, there seems to be agreement among the authors cited earlier that religion is an essential component of the American value system. Second, religion directly affects some important political value orientations, such as social and ethical tolerance. Third, religious orientation may interact with political attitudes in various ways and thus take on a new meaning. The latter possibility we discuss later in the chapter.

We can specify a number of expectations based on the American and European cultural traditions we described earlier. On the assumption that democratic communities exist in both the United States and European countries (at least in the EU countries), we expect to find that citizens prefer democratic over autocratic rule. In fact, the United States was the first country to establish and institutionalize a constitutional democracy. In the course of history,

17. Dieter Fuchs, "Die demokratische Gemeinschaft in den USA und in Deutschland," in *Die Vermessung kultureller Unterschiede: USA und Deutschland im Vergleich*, ed. Jürgen Gerhards (Wiesbaden: Westdeutscher Verlag, 2000).

18. Robert D. Putnam, *Making Democracy Work: Civic Traditions in Modern Italy* (Princeton: Princeton University Press, 1993).

democracy has also become the only legitimate way to rule in Europe. Hence, our first hypothesis:

Hypothesis 1. There are no significant differences between Americans and Europeans in terms of their support for democracy as a form of government.

Conversely, we expect substantial differences in the relation of citizens and the state. The individualistic and antistate orientation of U.S. citizens should differ from the state orientation of Europeans. This state orientation has been a correlate of the formation of the welfare state and the resulting attitude of solidarity with the underprivileged. The orientation leads to two further hypotheses:

Hypothesis 2. Self-responsibility of individuals in contrast to state responsibility is significantly higher in the United States than in Europe.
Hypothesis 3. Solidarity with the underprivileged (enforced by welfare state policies) is significantly lower in the United States than in Europe.

Since Tocqueville, political participation as well as active membership in voluntary organizations have been regarded as a core difference between the American and European political communities. This difference can also be linked to the antistate orientation and the ethos of the Protestant sects in the United States. Thus, we have the following:

Hypothesis 4. Generally, political participation is significantly higher in the United States than in Europe.
Hypothesis 5. Civic engagement in voluntary associations is significantly higher in the United States than in Europe.

It is difficult—a priori—to formulate an expectation about the norms governing each country's relationships to the other members of the political community. There are two opposing traditions in the United States. The first tradition is represented by the Enlightenment, with its emphasis on tolerance and natural equality of all humans. The second tradition is the religious tradition, which affects the definition of the role of women as well as the evaluation of certain deviant norms and related behaviors (e.g., homosexuality, divorce, suicide, and abortion).

Citizens' identification with their own nation should be stronger in the United States than in Europe. This expectation can plausibly be related to the creation of a democratic constitution by the American people during the American Revolution and the myth of the Founding Fathers that goes with it. National identification is also supported by Americans' religious belief in themselves as a "chosen people."

Hypothesis 6. National identification is significantly higher in the United States than in Europe.

The final hypothesis refers to the dimension of religion. Tocqueville had observed that the United States is the most religious country in Christendom. This observation is still valid and, during the last few decades, has been empirically demonstrated through comparative studies.

Hypothesis 7. Religion is significantly more important in the United States than in Europe.

Dimensional Analysis

The European Values Study/World Values Survey of 1999–2002 is a database containing information about the United States and all European countries that were members of the European Union at the time of the survey, except for Cyprus and Malta. Central and eastern European countries that have since joined the EU are also included. In the following analysis, any references to the attitudes and value orientations of Europeans are based on the pooled random samples of the EU member countries, giving each country the same weight.

First we performed a dimensional (factor) analysis on the surveys fielded in twenty-three European Union countries and the United States, using the indicators listed in table 11.1. The results are presented in table 11.2.

Using principal component analysis, we empirically extracted six factors or components. These components correspond exactly to the theoretical dimensions postulated in table 11.1. Indicators load on principal components as theoretically expected. Only civic engagement in voluntary associations and ethical tolerance have relatively high secondary loadings on the religion dimension. In both cases there seems a plausible explanation. Strong religious orientation may serve as a motivation to participate in religious associations or related charities. As mentioned earlier, religious orientation may be connected to a rejection of certain ethical norms such as homosexuality, divorce, abortion, or suicide. All in all, the factor analysis unambiguously shows that the theoretical dimensions postulated for a political community can be found empirically.

In the following section, differences and similarities in value orientations between America and Europe are analyzed and described according these dimensions.

Difference between Value Orientations in the United States and Europe

For a systematic comparison of value orientations in the United States and Europe, the discriminant analysis is used as a methodological tool. Before discussing the results of this analysis, we briefly describe the distribution of our indicators for value orientations (see table 11.3).

Table 11.2. Factor analysis of the indicators of a political community

Indicators	1 (Religion)	2 (Relationship to others)	3 (Self as political actor)	4 (Form of government)	5 (National identification)	6 (Relationship self-state)
1. Support of democratic rule				.770		
2. Rejection of autocratic rule				.806		
3. Self-responsibility/state responsibility						.968
4. Political motivation			.761			
5. Political participation (noninstitutionalized)		.276	.630			
6. Civic engagement (voluntary associations)	.352		.585			
7. Recognition of others as equal (equality of women)	−.300	.612				
8. Trust in others		.505	.256			
9. Social tolerance		.719				
10. Ethical tolerance	−.379	.598				
11. National pride					.915	
12. Importance of God	.848					
13. Attendance at religious services	.866					

Source: European Values Study/World Values Survey, 1999–2002.

Notes: This pooled analysis includes 23 EU countries and the United States. The results are based on a principal component analysis with varimax rotation and six criteria factors; the explained variance is 65 percent.

Table 11.3 shows results not only for the EU as a unit (equally weighted average for twenty-three member nations) but also for France, Germany, and Poland. These three countries are singled out for two reasons. First, the EU is not a homogenous entity. Rather, there are considerable differences among the individual member states. Second, France and Germany have been selected because they are considered to be the core countries of the EU and because they were the relevant actors in the most recent conflict between the United States and Europe. Poland has been chosen because it is by far the biggest country of central and eastern Europe that has joined the EU in the latest accession wave and because its policy positions—especially with respect to the war in Iraq—differ from those of Germany and France.

The most important findings regarding our core question can be summarized as follows. The biggest differences (that is, those items for which there is

Table 11.3. Distribution of value orientations (%)

	United States	EU	France	Germany	Poland
I. Form of government					
1. Support of democratic rule	84.2	90.1	89.1	95.3	83.1
2. Rejection of autocratic rule	76.9	83.8	79.5	91.7	73.8
II. Relationship self-state					
3. Self-responsibility (instead of responsibility of the state)	46.8	31.5	46.1	46.5	18.3
III. Self as political actor					
4. Political motivation	23.9	17.5	13.8	24.3	22.8
5. Political participation (noninstitutionalized)	62.6	36.1	52.0	42.0	14.3
6. Civic engagement	64.7	27.7	21.9	19.5	12.1
IV. Relationship to the others					
7. Recognition of others as equal (equality of women)	50.3	51.3	55.1	49.7	45.2
8. Trust in others	35.8	31.1	22.2	34.8	18.9
9. Social tolerance	51.8	59.8	72.4	73.7	30.7
10. Ethical tolerance	50.3	47.0	51.5	55.7	26.0
V. National identification					
11. National pride	72.1	42.7	39.8	16.8	71.6
VI. Religion					
12. Importance of God	76.9	37.8	19.6	28.2	72.9
13. Attendance at religious services	45.2	22.2	7.5	13.6	26.7

Source: European Values Study/World Values Survey, 1999–2002.

a difference of 15 percentage points or more) between the United States and the EU occur in the areas of self-responsibility, political participation, civic engagement, national identification, importance of God, and attendance at religious services. These findings correspond largely to our theoretical expectations. As for the three single countries, we observe interesting differences between France and Germany on the one hand and Poland on the other. There is only one difference between France and Germany that meets our criterion of 15 percentage points: national identification. In all other respects the value orientations of these two EU core countries are relatively similar. The differences between Poland on the one hand and France and Germany on the other hand are much more pronounced. They are manifest in areas such as self-responsibility, political participation, social and ethical tolerance, and the importance of God. We interpret these differences after considering the results of the discriminant analyses.

The analytic strategy relies on discriminant analysis, which requires the definition of a benchmark "group." Considering our core question, we select the United States as the benchmark country. We assume that the pattern of political value orientations in the United States is adequately described by the thirteen indicators listed in table 11.1. The benchmark country provides the reference point for comparison with the so-called undefined groups. The undefined groups consist of the EU as a whole as well as the three core countries of the EU. Discriminant analysis is suited to answer two questions. First, how important are the thirteen indicators for discriminating between the benchmark country and the undefined groups? Second, discriminant analysis assigns for each respondent in the undefined group the probability of belonging to the defined group.

Table 11.4 shows the discriminatory power of the thirteen characteristics of a political community with respect to the benchmark country, the United States.

In technical terms, the coefficients in table 11.4 are pooled within-group correlations between discriminating variables and the canonical discriminant function. In substantive terms, the correlations show the relevance of each individual indicator when it comes to separating the predefined group from the undefined group. The higher the correlation, the more important this indicator is for discriminating between the benchmark country, on the one hand, and the EU and France, Germany, and Poland on the other.

First, we address the comparison between the United States and the EU as well as France and Germany. Second, we discuss the case of Poland, which we argue is a special case in many respects.

As the highest coefficients show, the most important differences between the United States and the EU, France, and Germany appear with regard to the indicators "importance of God" and "national pride," and two indicators of civil society—"political participation" and "civic engagement." These results confirm hypotheses 4–7 impressively. Tocqueville had already mentioned these characteristics as outstanding differences between the United States and Europe.

Table 11.4. Differentiation between the United States (benchmark country) and Europe (r)

	EU	France	Germany	Poland
I. Form of government				
1. Support of democratic rule	−.089	−.085	−.184	.194
2. Rejection of autocratic rule	−.203	−.069	−.296	.056[a]
II. Relationship self-state				
3. Self-responsibility/state responsibility	.156	−.048[a]	−.010[a]	.256
III. Self as political actor				
4. Political motivation	.141	.221	−.015[a]	.051[a]
5. Political participation (noninstitutionalized)	.331	.122	.216	.724
6. Civic engagement	.663	.474	.429	.477
IV. Relationship to the others				
7. Recognition of others as equal (equality of women)	.073	−.008[a]	.138	.111
8. Trust in others	.040[a]	.167	.018[a]	.184
9. Social tolerance	−.043[a]	−.174	−.173	.312
10. Ethical tolerance	−.018[a]	−.089	−.068	.302
V. National identification				
11. National pride	.338	.345	.542	.012[a]
VI. Religion				
12. Importance of God	.510	.753	.520	.031[a]
13. Attendance at religious services	.324	.658	.258	−.205
Eigenvalue	.133	.949	1.404	.900
Canonical correlation	.343	.698	.764	.688
Correctly classified	82.1%	83.6%	89.0%	83.4%
Mean	.276	.232	.166	.231
Mean United States	.680	.777	.836	.765

Source: European Values Study/World Values Survey, 1999–2002.
Note: The coefficients (r) are pooled within-group correlations between discriminating variables and the canonical discriminant function.
[a]Not significant at the .001 level.

"Support of democratic rule" is barely significant and does not contribute much to our discrimination between the United States and Europe. This finding supports hypothesis 1. In contrast, "rejection of autocratic rule" provides more discriminatory power. The coefficient for Germany is −.296, and for the EU −.203. The minus sign indicates that the degree of "rejection of autocratic rule" is much higher in Germany and Europe than in the United States (see also table 11.3). This surprising result can probably be explained by the European countries' experience with fascism. All in all, however, democracy is supported by citizens in both the United States and Europe. As a matter of fact, acceptance is slightly higher in Europe than in the United States.

A further finding that is surprising concerns "self-responsibility" versus "state responsibility." Here the correlations are almost insignificant, which disproves hypothesis 2. This result could also be affected by question formulation, however, which refers to a country's status quo. Respondents demand a higher level of self-responsibility or a lower level of state responsibility relative to the situation in their own country. Thus, in the United States, where self-responsibility enjoys widespread support, citizens don't want more of it; a similar logic applies to an increase in the level of state interventions in Germany and France.

The current data set provides no indicator to test hypothesis 3, which concerns solidarity with the underprivileged. However, we know from a previous analysis, using a different data set, that results support the hypothesis that the degree of solidarity is clearly lower in the United States than in Europe.[19]

An adequate hypothesis for the dimension "relationship to the others" could not be formulated. The respective indicators do not contribute to a systematic discrimination between the EU and the United States. However, "social tolerance" constitutes a significant difference between France and Germany on the one hand and the United States on the other, and "trust in others" differentiates only between France and the United States (see table 11.3).

For indicators discriminating between the United States and Poland, the findings strongly deviate from those for France and Germany. Unlike France and Germany, "self-responsibility" has a significant weight for Poland. This result can be readily interpreted, in light of the percentages in table 11.3. In Poland, only 18 percent of the respondents want a higher degree of self-responsibility. This proportion is considerably lower compared with that of France, Germany, and the United States, where about 46 percent favor higher self-responsibility. This finding is remarkable because in Poland the state has a considerably stronger role in shaping and governing society than it does in the United States, France, and Germany. A similarly low proportion of citizens favoring self-responsibility and a correspondingly high proportion

19. Dieter Fuchs and Hans-Dieter Klingemann, "Eastward Enlargement of the European Union and the Identity of Europe," *West European Politics* 25, no. 2 (2002): 19–55.

supporting state responsibility have been reported in other central and eastern European countries. With the accession of these countries to the EU, a reinforcement of state orientation among the citizenry of the enlarged EU can be expected. If true, this would contribute to a widening of the gap between value orientations of citizens of Europe and America.

The indicators "national pride" and "importance of God" do *not* discriminate between Poland and the United States, in contrast to France and Germany. The reason for this finding can be seen in table 11.3. Both Poland and the United States share almost identical distributions of these value orientations. One has to keep in mind, however, that in these two countries, belief in God is connected to entirely different denominations. In the United States, a little more than 50 percent of citizens claim to be Protestant, whereas almost 90 percent of Poles are Roman Catholic. Despite this difference, Poles are closer to the Americans both in terms of national identification and religiosity,.

So far we have differentiated between the United States and Europe through the importance of each of the thirteen indicators of a political community. Now we turn to some statistics that speak to the problem of the effectiveness of the discrimination effort. Table 11.4 lists the respective measures, and we discuss two measures in further detail. The first is the canonical correlation, and the second is the amount of correctly classified respondents. High canonical correlations mean that the two groups are well separated by the given set of variables. The canonical correlation is relatively high in terms of the differentiation of the benchmark country the United States and the three European countries of France, Germany, and Poland, whereas it is relatively low for the EU. The latter can be traced back to the heterogeneity of the value orientations of the citizens of the EU, as mentioned previously. Now, on the basis of a combination of the thirteen indicators (discrimination function), we have classified all respondents into one of two groups. In the four discriminant analyses that have been conducted, between 82 percent to 89 percent of these respondents were correctly classified. This good measure of fit shows that Europe and the United States differ indeed systematically in terms of political value orientations.

To identify the degree of difference among the United States, the EU, and the three single European states more precisely, we have aggregated the results obtained at the individual level. The mean in table 11.4 refers to this aggregation and indicates the mean probability for the respondents of any of the four European polities to belong to the benchmark country, the United States. The stronger the difference between the mean for the United States and that for the European countries, the stronger the difference between the value orientations. In general the lowest difference has been found to exist between the United States and the European Union as a whole. For Germany, this overall difference is largest; that is, Germany differs more from the United States than France, Poland, and the EU as a whole differ from the United States.

Conclusions

Is there any empirical evidence for di͡
tions of citizens of the United States and
to be answered in our analysis. The answe͡
ences in results regarding the EU, France, G͡
indeed, systematic differences in value orientati͡
the United States. They are even larger for the
EU—France and Germany—which have been the n͡
recent policy disputes with the United States and Euro͡
second question was related to the seriousness of these d͡
of a fundamental nature and thus constitute a long-lasting
political conflict, or do they reflect a temporary irritation? O͡
answering this question can be provided by relating the empiric͡
the title of this chapter: American Exceptionalism or Western Civi͡

Support of democratic rule and the corresponding values, such as ͡
for basic human rights, political equality, and tolerance toward others,
been chosen as criteria for Western civilization. Regarding these values, ͡
differences are so small that it is justified to count both the EU and the Unite͡
States as belonging to Western civilization. However, major differences between the United States and Europe arise in terms of how to institutionalize
democracy. Citizens of the United States predominantly support libertarian
ideas such as a minimal state, self-responsibility, and competition of citizens in
the market place. In contrast, European citizens support social democratic
ideas and institutions, such as an interventionist welfare state providing social
equality and solidarity. This value pattern is likely to gain even more widespread support by integrating central and eastern European countries in the
EU. Contrasting a social democratic Europe and a market-oriented, libertarian United States would speak in favor of American exceptionalism. This difference can affect the design of the future economic world order and other
issues high on the foreign policy agenda in the long run. Whether this development will lead to a *fundamental* conflict is another question.

The most exceptional position of the United States, compared to that of
Europe and probably also the rest of the world, presumably originates from
the unique constitution of the U.S. political community. As a result of the
American Revolution, individuals have simultaneously declared themselves a
people, given themselves a constitution, and thereby paved the way to a constitutional democracy. In those days, this event was exceptional, and this ex-
ceptionality has surely influenced American self-esteem. This self-esteem has
probably also been nourished by the beliefs of the Protestant sects that—in
the biblical sense—Americans are a chosen people.

To this day, the historical roots of the American people and their constitution
are expressed through an outstandingly high national identification. Beyond

ssianic or missionary creed is connected to the national identity—and
intries must come to grips with it. This creed has the potential to legit-
"just" war with political regimes that severely contradict fundamental
rientations of Americans—for example, the American-Spanish War, the
gainst Nazi dictatorship, and the war in Iraq. As with the Iraq War, how-
this facet of American exceptionalism can also develop into a serious
rce of foreign policy conflict between the United States and Europe.

We have discussed whether the differences in value orientations of Ameri-
ans and Europeans can become a source of fundamental political conflicts
and a basis for an enduring crisis. In this discussion, we have held constant
such important factors as different economic interests or power resources.
Answers to this question cannot be directly deduced from the empirical findings. For this reason, these findings merely provide a framework for interpretations of the empirical results based on the cultural traditions of Americans
and Europeans.

We finish the analysis by briefly turning to a problem that has already been
mentioned. Value orientations are conceptualized as stable attitudes; however, it has been shown in the literature that they can also be transformed. In
his analysis, Lipset assumes that at least a core of value orientations, which
evolved in the eighteenth century in America, had not changed until the early
1990s.[20] In contrast to Lipset, Huntington claims that since the 1960s a fundamental transformation of the value orientations has been taking place, and
he concludes that "challenges to America's national identity" arise from this
change.[21] According to Huntington, the reason for this transformation stems
from the increased immigration of Asians and especially Hispanics, who are
unwilling or unable to assimilate into the dominant Anglo-Protestant culture.
Further empirical studies are needed to clarify the controversy. So far, the
empirical findings of our analysis can merely corroborate the persistence of
value orientations that emerged in the eighteenth century. According to
Lipset, these value orientations have adapted to changes in society but have
not lost their substantial content. Nonetheless, it is possible to argue, along
the lines of Huntington, that the transformation of the American value system
is a long-term matter. Yet even if more recent waves of immigration leave
their mark, one can barely assume that they will lead to a decline in the differences between the value orientations of Americans and Europeans.

20. Lipset, *American Exceptionalism*.
21. Huntington, *Who Are We?*

12 THE END OF THE WEST?

Conclusions

THOMAS RISSE

One of the advantages of a scholarly project is that it takes time to develop and come to fruition. In the meantime, however, history and politics do not stop.[1] In fall 2003, when we started thinking about a book on the crisis of the transatlantic relationship, memories of the events of early 2003 were still fresh. At the time, French and German diplomats at the United Nations Security Council successfully cobbled together a coalition against the United States and Britain that was able to deny passage of another UN resolution legitimizing the invasion of Iraq.[2] This rebuff was extraordinary, and one must go back to the Suez crisis in 1956 to find a similar display of open and public transatlantic conflict (see William Hitchcock's chapter in this volume). A little more than three years later, in the summer of 2006, we watched U.S. president Bush and German chancellor Merkel enjoying themselves at a wild boar barbecue in Mecklenburg-Vorpommern. The contrast between the two events could not have been more pronounced.

The two instances tell us that a longer perspective is probably needed to evaluate the state of the transatlantic relationship. Although much has been

1. I thank the contributors to this volume and Ingo Peters for their insights into the transatlantic relationship. I am also grateful to Helga Haftendorn, Wagaki Mwangi, Henry Nau, Keven Ruby, and two anonymous reviewers for comments on the draft of this chapter. I thank audiences at Syracuse University, at Yale University, and particularly at the University of Chicago's Program on International Politics, Economics, and Security (PIPES) for their critical comments. Last not least, I thank Gisela Hirschmann for research assistance.

2. For details, see Elizabeth Pond, *Friendly Fire: The Near-Death of the Transatlantic Alliance* (Pittsburgh, PA/Washington, DC: European Union Studies Association/Brookings Institution Press, 2004); Stephen F. Szabo, *Parting Ways: The Crisis in German-American Relations* (Washington, DC: Brookings Institution Press, 2004); Philip Gordon and Jeremy Shapiro, *Allies at War: America, Europe, and the Crisis over Iraq* (New York: McGraw-Hill, 2004).

written about the Iraq crisis in the meantime, a thorough and comprehensive stock-taking of the state of the Western alliance is still rare.[3] This book is intended as just such a stock taking. Its authors explore the deep structure and long-term developments in the Western community—the West, in short. What is underneath the recent conflicts between the United States and Europe? Is it all about the Bush administration, post-9/11 U.S. foreign policy, or the rupture over the Iraq War? Alternatively, are we witnessing the beginning of the end of a happy transatlantic relationship, the gradual withering away of NATO, as some scholars predicted after the end of the cold war?[4]

Unfortunately, even a thorough look at the state of the West from the perspectives of political scientists, economists, historians, sociologists, and legal scholars does not provide ready-made answers easy to digest. Rather, this volume shows some remarkable agreements, many disagreements, and some counterintuitive findings. Among the agreements, two stick out. First, most authors agree (but see the chapter by Michael Byers) that the transatlantic relationship is in a serious crisis defined as one of those "extraordinary moment[s] when the existence and viability of the political order are called into question" (see John Ikenberry's introduction). Second, however, most contributors equally agree that it is far too soon to spell the end of the West. Not even Charles Kupchan, in his chapter, predicts the breakdown scenario spelled out in the introduction. Rather, the authors are divided among a transformation scenario in which the rules have to be renegotiated, an adaptation of some sort by the community to the new international environment, and a much looser and far less institutionalized transatlantic community.

Disagreements among the authors of this volume mostly concern the underlying sources and causes of the crisis, which is not surprising given their different theoretical orientations and disciplinary backgrounds. Yet in this area we also come across some significant counterintuitive findings and arguments that are rarely seen in the wider literature. First, many argue that

3. See, however, David M. Andrews, ed., *The Atlantic Alliance under Stress: U.S.–European Relations after Iraq* (Cambridge: Cambridge University Press, 2005); Ingo Peters, ed., *Transatlantic Tug-of-War: Prospects for EU-US Cooperation. In Honor of Helga Haftendorn* (Münster-Hamburg: Lit.-Verlag, 2006); Roland Dannreuther and John Peterson, eds., *Security Strategy and Transatlantic Relations* (London: Routledge, 2006); David Held and Mathias Koenig-Archibugi, eds., *American Power in the 21st Century* (Cambridge, MA: Polity Press, 2004); Michael Cox, "Death of the West? Terrors in Transatlantia," *European Journal of International Relations* 11, no. 2 (2005): 203–33.

4. See, e.g., John J. Mearsheimer, "Back to the Future: Instability in Europe after the Cold War," *International Security* 15, no. 1 (1990): 5–56; Stephen Walt, "The Ties That Fray: Why Europe and America Are Drifting Apart," *National Interest* 54 (Winter 1998–99): 3–11; Kenneth N. Waltz, "The Emerging Structure of International Politics," *International Security* 18, no. 2 (1993): 44–79.

different understandings of sovereignty and diverging approaches to international law explain why the Atlantic rift has deepened.[5] The chapters by Jeffrey Anderson and Michael Byers demonstrate that this narrative does not hold up, however. Neither has the United States left the foundations of international law in recent years, nor do enduring transatlantic divergences about understandings of sovereignty have much to do with the ongoing U.S.-European disputes.

Second, it is frequently argued that transatlantic economic interdependence will effectively prevent the political and security relationships from breaking down.[6] Yet both Kathleen McNamara and Jens van Scherpenberg convincingly argue in this book that "trade is no superglue" and that the jury is still out on the question of whether economic interdependence leads to more or to less conflict.

Third, there is much debate on either side of the Atlantic about the underlying value basis of the Western community. This debate ranges from Robert Kagan's famous Venus-Mars comparison to arguments that Europeans and Americans disagree fundamentally over the role of religion in political life.[7] The chapters by John Hall and by Dieter Fuchs and Hans-Dieter Klingemann show from both a historical sociological perspective and a macroquantitative statistical approach that at least some differences (as well as similarities) in value orientations have always been with us in the transatlantic community. As a result, they cannot explain the recent crises.

In this chapter I do not attempt to comprehensively summarize the rich and complex findings of the individual authors represented in this volume. Rather, I highlight some of the arguments and controversies—both in this volume as well as from the wider literature on transatlantic relations—and draw my own conclusions. I start with a few remarks on the nature of the Western order. Second, I comment on the degree to which the contributors to this volume see the transatlantic relationship in crisis. Third, I address what we can learn about the sources and causes of the current crisis. And fourth, I discuss the various scenarios for the future of the Western order.

---

5. See, e.g., Georg Nolte, "Die USA und das Völkerrecht," *Die Friedens-Warte* 78, nos. 2–3 (2003): 119–40; Christian Tomuschat, "Iraq—Demise of International Law?" *Die Friedens-Warte* 78, nos. 2–3 (2003): 141–60; Robert O. Keohane, "Ironies of Sovereignty: The European Union and the United States," *Journal of Common Market Studies* 40, no. 4 (2002): 743–65.

6. See, e.g., Daniel S. Hamilton and Joseph P. Quinlan, eds., *Deep Integration: How Transatlantic Markets Are Leading Globalization* (Brussels: Centre for European Policy Studies, 2005).

7. See, e.g., Robert Kagan, *Of Paradise and Power: America and Europe in the New World Order* (New York: Knopf, 2003); Josef Braml, *Amerika, Gott und die Welt: George W. Bushs Außenpolitik auf christlich-rechter Basis* (Berlin: Matthes und Seitz, 2005).

What Constitutes the West? The Nature
of the Atlantic Order

The authors of this volume agree that the transatlantic order—the West—constitutes more than just a traditional security alliance. As Ikenberry points out in the introduction, the Atlantic order is certainly more than NATO, which constitutes just one of the institutional expressions of the order. "The West" rests on a specific configuration of interests, institutions, and identities that resembles what Karl W. Deutsch, in the late 1950s, called a "pluralistic security community."[8] As a result, the transatlantic security community ensures "dependable expectations of peaceful change,"[9] so that war among the transatlantic partners has become unthinkable and the security dilemma has been mitigated. This notion is what we intend by "the West" in the title of this book.[10] The "end of the West" then implies a breakdown of the transatlantic security community.

This agreement among our authors about the character of the Western order is remarkable insofar as they do not share the same ground in international relations theory. Charles Kupchan and Henry Nau, who deeply disagree about the fate of the Western community, probably come closest to realpolitik thinking in this volume (but see also Anderson's chapter and van Scherpenberg's from a political economy perspective). In fact, Nau offers an interesting perspective integrating realist and constructivist thinking.[11] Ikenberry argues from a liberal institutionalist perspective, whereas my own work is usually identified as moderately social constructivist. But we all seem to share the view that the transatlantic order constitutes a security community. In other words, the transatlantic order is viewed as a particular social structure based on interests, institutions, norms, and collective identities. This

8. See Karl W. Deutsch, Sidney A. Burrell, Robert A. Kann, Maurice Lee Jr., Martin Lichterman, Raymond E. Lindgren, Francis L. Loewenheim, and Richard W. Van Wagenen, *Political Community and the North Atlantic Area: International Organization in the Light of Historical Experience* (Princeton: Princeton University Press, 1957); also Emanuel Adler and Michael Barnett, eds., *Security Communities* (Cambridge: Cambridge University Press, 1998); Thomas Risse-Kappen, *Cooperation among Democracies: The European Influence on U.S. Foreign Policy* (Princeton: Princeton University Press, 1995); and John Hall's chapter in the present volume for a discussion.

9. Deutsch et al., *Political Community and the North Atlantic Area*, 9.

10. Of course an even broader understanding of the term "West" encompasses the Bretton Woods institutions, including the World Trade Organization (WTO). Although the origins of the Bretton Woods institutions were certainly part of the Western, above all the U.S., attempt to shape the post–World War II order, they have become part of a globalized world economy today that can no longer be claimed exclusively as Western.

11. See also Henry R. Nau, *At Home Abroad: Identity and Power in American Foreign Policy* (Ithaca: Cornell University Press, 2002); Henry R. Nau, *Perspectives on International Relations: Power, Institutions, and Ideas* (Washington, DC: CQ Press, 2006).

outlook is a far cry from standard neorealist international relations theory that would consider the Atlantic order as just another security alliance.[12] It shows a collective attempt at theoretical synthesis that tries to overcome the paradigmatic warfare in international relations theory of the 1980s and 1990s, in particular binary oppositions between material interests, on the one hand, and ideas and norms, on the other (see also Gunther Hellmann's chapter on this point).

If we identify the Atlantic order as a security community with a particular configuration of interests, institutions, and identities, it is a matter of degree to what extent material power shapes or is itself shaped by the social structure of the Western world. This has substantial consequences for the way in which we analyze the current crisis and predict possible outcomes. First, material power and shifts in the Euro-Atlantic power balance matter, of course (see particularly the chapters by Kupchan and Nau, but also by van Scherpenberg). But the more we theorize the transatlantic relationship as a security community, the more changes in the material power balance are mitigated by institutional and ideational factors. (Social constructivists would add, of course, that the meaning of "material power" depends on their discursive construction.) As a result, one must analyze separately changes in the institutional fabric of the transatlantic order and in the realm of ideational meaning construction (identities, values, norms, etc.) and determine their contribution to the current crisis of the relationship as well as to possible outcomes. One cannot simply read the institutional and ideational components off the material factors that also shape the community.

Second, conceptualizing the Western relationship as a security community does not preclude the possibility that it will break apart or wither away. Earlier work, including my own,[13] assumed to some extent that security communities are unlikely to break apart and are more stable than mere security alliances held together by a common threat perception. (For a critical discussion of moderate social constructivist assumptions about stability, see Hellmann's chapter.)

There is no theoretical reason, though, why security communities should survive longer than traditional alliances. If the underlying sources of a security community start shifting, a security community undergoes crisis as well. The main point is here that conceptualizing the Western order as a security community rather than a traditional alliance directs our attention toward different causes for the survival or demise of such orders (see table 12.1). A decline in

---

12. See, e.g., Mearsheimer, "Back to the Future"; Waltz, "Emerging Structure of International Politics."

13. See, e.g., Thomas Risse, "U.S. Power in a Liberal Security Community," in *America Unrivaled: U.S. Unipolarity and the Future of the Balance of Power*, ed. G. John Ikenberry (Ithaca: Cornell University Press, 2002); Risse-Kappen, *Cooperation among Democracies*.

Table 12.1. Security communities versus traditional alliances

Elements	Security community	Traditional alliance
Power and security interests	Interaction with degree of collective identity/ shared values	Most important
Economic interdependence	Important	Less important
Institutions and law	Important	Significance depends on degree of shared interests
Identities and values	Important	Irrelevant

the degree of interdependence, in the institutional underpinnings, or in collective identities can trigger a crisis of a security community as much as a decline in the common threat that leads to the breakdown of traditional alliances.[14] In other words, if we witness a crisis of a security community, we have to look at the whole range of indicators and potential causes—which is precisely what the authors in this volume have done.

Crisis, What Crisis?

In this volume, Ikenberry defines a crisis as "an extraordinary moment when the existence and viability of the political order are called into question." At such a critical juncture, the four elements that constitute a security community are put in jeopardy: (1) power and security interests, (2) economic interdependence and market relations, (3) institutions and law, and (4) values and political identity. This volume assumes that the transatlantic community is in crisis when at least one of the four elements is in serious trouble. Note that these four elements of a security community are used in this volume both as indicators and as causes for the crisis, in the following sense. Because they are constitutive for the community, the degrees of common interests, of interdependence, of shared norms, and of collective identification indicate the strength of the relationship. At the same time, a reduction in the strength of these four elements causes the relationship, and as a result the security community, to weaken.[15]

Most authors in this volume (but see the chapter by Byers) share the view also predominant in the literature—that at least one of the conditions for a

14. One could argue, though, that security communities are ultimately more stable than traditional alliances because they rest on more than one underlying source. As a result, a change in one of the ingredients may not trigger an all-out crisis, as is the case with a declining threat that affects a traditional alliance.

15. See also Ingo Peters, "Introduction: Contending Versions and Competing Visions of Transatlantic Relations," in Peters, *Transatlantic Tug-of-War*, 5–51.

transatlantic crisis is fulfilled.[16] Although this finding is not particularly excit-
ing per se, nevertheless it is significant to specify precisely which one or more
of the components of the Western community are in crisis.

Power and Security Interests

In a certain sense, conflicts of interests are an enduring feature of security
communities as well as alliances. In fact, cooperative arrangements are meant
to deal with conflicts of interests almost by definition. In harmony, there is no
need for active cooperation.[17] Thus, conflicts of interest between the United
States and its European partners are a common feature of the transatlantic
partnership, and their peaceful resolution is a daily routine in a security community (see Hitchcock's chapter). When conflicts of interest develop into a
crisis, something more must be happening. I suggest that conflicts of interest
have escalated into a crisis when either of two conditions are met:

1. The various—and "normal"—policy disputes cover such a broad range
   of issues that the existing institutions are overloaded and unable to handle them.
2. The policy conflicts increasingly touch upon what either side believes to
   be a core interest.

Concerning the first point, few would probably disagree that the sheer
range of transatlantic policy disputes is almost without precedent in the history of the alliance. To be sure, the history of the transatlantic order is a history of enduring conflicts and crises, but we have rarely seen times when the
transatlantic policy disputes covered such a wide spectrum of issues.[18] For
years—and predating the Bush administration—Europeans and Americans
have disagreed over questions such as climate change and other environmental issues. Human rights issues such as creation of the International Criminal

16. See Pond, *Friendly Fire*; Szabo, *Parting Ways*; Gordon and Shapiro, *Allies at War*; Andrews, *Atlantic Alliance under Stress*; Peters, *Transatlantic Tug-of-War*; Dannreuther and Peterson, *Security Strategy*; Held and Koenig-Archibugi, *American Power in the 21st Century*;
and Cox, "Death of the West?"

17. In the language of rationalist institutionalism, mixed-motive games require institutions
to deal with them, which implies at least some degree of underlying conflict of interests. See,
e.g., Robert O. Keohane, *International Institutions and State Power* (Boulder: Westview, 1989).
For an application to NATO, see Helga Haftendorn, Robert O. Keohane, and Celeste A. Wallander, *Imperfect Unions: Security Institutions over Time and Space* (Oxford: Oxford University
Press, 1999).

18. See Gert Krell, *Arroganz der Macht, Arroganz der Ohnmacht: Der Irak, die Weltord-
nungspolitik der USA und die transatlantischen Beziehungen, HSFK-Report* (Frankfurt: Hessische
Stiftung Friedens- und Konfliktforschung, 2003); Andrews, *Atlantic Alliance under Stress*;
Peters, *Transatlantic Tug-of-War*.

Court (ICC), imposition of the death penalty, and—most recently—even the definition of torture and appropriate treatment of transnational terrorists have also become questions of transatlantic tension. The United States and its European allies do not see eye to eye on most arms control agreements, from the treaty to ban landmines to the Comprehensive Test Ban Treaty and the future of the nuclear nonproliferation regime. No transatlantic agreement exists on how to reform the United Nations in general and the UN Security Council in particular. Differences over the UN Millenium Development goals have been papered over rather than solved. The same holds true for the question of "preemptive self-defense" (see Byers's chapter on this question). Europeans continuously complain about what they see as increasing U.S. unilateralism in international affairs. And as van Scherpenberg points out in his chapter, a whole range of transatlantic economic disputes looms in the background. Given this range of conflicts, it is hard not to conclude that the transatlantic partnership faces a crisis.

Moreover, some authors in this volume go further and argue that the transatlantic conflicts have reached the level of core security interests. Kupchan suggests that the strategic priorities of Europe and the United States started to diverge after the end of the cold war. And Nau argues that the current crisis is rooted in serious and sharp differences in the perception of threats after September 11, 2001. The events of 9/11 have dramatically changed America's worldview: transnational terrorism is now considered a "clear and present danger" to the country's national security and must be countered by—among other things—military means. In contrast, most Europeans perceive terrorism as one threat among others and as mostly an internal rather than an external/military security issue.[19] Even the attacks in Madrid and London have not changed this perception. Europe does not feel "at war."

One should not overlook the solid degree of transatlantic security cooperation that remains, however. The United States, NATO, the EU, and the Organization for Security and Cooperation in Europe (OSCE) are all active together in various postconflict peace-building and institution-building efforts in, for example, Afghanistan and the western Balkans. Nau reminds us that the United States had no trouble using its military facilities in Germany before, during, and after the Iraq War. The United States and its European allies still cooperate closely, despite clearly diverging viewpoints on questions such as the Israeli-Palestinian conflict, Lebanon, and Iran's nuclear ambitions. Last but not least, and despite diverging threat perceptions concerning the nature of the terrorist threat, transatlantic police and intelligence cooperation remain largely intact.

---

19. On the different social constructions of the terrorist threat, see also Peter J. Katzenstein, "Same War—Different Views: Germany, Japan, and Counterterrorism," *International Organization* 57, no. 4 (2003): 731–60.

In sum, there is, of course, a wide range of transatlantic conflicts of interests, some of which touch on core security interests in ways that qualify as a transatlantic crisis. At the same time, many remaining core security interests lead to continuing and even enhanced transatlantic security cooperation. Thus, the real question concerns the crisis outcome. Can the various conflicts of interest be solved within the existing transatlantic institutional framework, or will they lead to the breakdown of these institutions? And what if there is a spillover from differences in threat perceptions to disagreement over values, as some have argued.[20]

Economic Interdependence and Market Relations

If there is one area in which many observers still paint a happy picture of the transatlantic community, it concerns the economic relationship.[21] These authors then conclude that economic interdependence can help overcome a period of policy crisis in the transatlantic relationship. After all, it was no coincidence that the first German to see President Bush after the Iraq turmoil was Jürgen Schrempp, then CEO of Daimler Chrysler, then a truly transatlantic company.

Two questions must be asked when it comes to transatlantic economic relations:

1. How deeply integrated is the transatlantic economy, both in historical comparison as well as in comparison with other interregional relations?
2. Can economic interdependence provide the "superglue" that keeps a political relationship together?

On both questions, McNamara and van Scherpenberg, in their chapters, depart from the literature's conventional wisdom. Although there is indeed continuing economic interdependence across the Atlantic,[22] U.S. dependence on transatlantic trade was much higher before World War I than in this "age of globalization." And the growth rates for transatlantic trade pale in comparison with both the United States' and the EU's trade with China and East Asia. In contrast, mutual foreign direct investment (FDI) has reached unprecedented high levels, and the same holds true for capital flows. But FDI constitutes an ambiguous indicator for interdependence. On the one hand, deep commercial engagements of U.S. firms in Europe and of European firms in the United States increase the mutual stakes in each other's well-being. On the other

---

20. See, e.g., Kagan, *Paradise and Power*.

21. See particularly Hamilton and Quinlan, *Deep Integration*.

22. In the classic formulation by Keohane and Nye, interdependent relationships are "costly to break" for either side and characterized by mutual high sensitivity and vulnerability. See Robert O. Keohane and Joseph S. Nye Jr., *Power and Interdependence* (Boston: Little, Brown, 1977).

hand, the motives for FDI—gaining market access and ensuring against currency changes—indicate a lack of economic integration rather than proving it (see van Scherpenberg's chapter). In a single and deeply integrated market such as the EU and increasingly NAFTA, foreign direct investment is less necessary. In sum, transatlantic economic interdependence continues, but it has not led to deep economic integration.

As to the second question, McNamara and van Scherpenberg are skeptical about the superglue vision, albeit for different reasons. Van Scherpenberg points to a whole range of transatlantic economic conflicts that can easily overwhelm the transatlantic political agenda too. Moreover, conflicts over security interests have recently spilled over into the economic area (and vice versa). Thus, van Scherpenberg's view is in line with a realist perspective that is also shared by economic nationalists.

McNamara comes to a similar conclusion, but from an institutionalist perspective. The old battle between interdependence theorists and (neo)realists is still being waged over whether economic interdependence leads to peace or is irrelevant for security.[23] But we can draw few conclusions from this debate for our superglue question. First, "interdependence" and "level of conflict" are such macrovariables that the statistical results are highly dependent on the precise indicators.[24] Second, and more important, the superglue question is not really about war and peace but about whether a tight economic relationship can prevent a political crisis from leading to the breakdown of a security community. It is vital to specify the dependent variable here. The functionalist interdependence argument concerns war and peace, whereas our dependent variable concerns the future of a much tighter cooperative relationship, namely, a security community. Not even those who predict the breakdown of the Western order expect the United States and Europe to go to war against each other.

In sum, and contrary to the conventional wisdom, the answer to the second question is negative, irrespective of whether one shares a realist or an institutionalist outlook on international affairs. "Trade is no superglue," as van Scherpenberg puts it. Yet McNamara's institutionalist perspective also offers a somewhat more hopeful outlook. It is not the economic relationship as such

23. See Edward D. Mansfield and Brian M. Pollins, eds., *Economic Interdependence and International Conflict: New Perspectives on an Enduring Debate* (Ann Arbor: University of Michigan Press, 2003); Bruce Russett and John R. O'Neal, *Triangulating Peace: Democracy, Interdependence, and International Organizations* (New York: Norton, 2001); Katherine Barbieri, *The Liberal Illusion: Does Trade Promote Peace?* (Ann Arbor: University of Michigan Press, 2002); Kenneth Waltz, *Theory of International Politics* (Reading, MA: Addison-Wesley, 1979).

24. This is in contrast to the "democratic peace" thesis, which has been proven empirically so robust that different indicators do not lead to different outcomes. See the review in Jack S. Levy, "War and Peace," in *Handbook of International Relations*, ed. Walter Carlsnaes, Thomas Risse, and Beth A. Simmons, 350–68 (London: Sage, 2002).

that might prevent the security community from breaking apart. Rather, it is the high level of institutionalized exchanges among networks of regulators and economic lawyers that might shape the impact of economic on political relations. The causal mechanism concerns the social embeddedness of markets in institutionalized relations, leading to socialization effects on actors that keep the relationship on a cooperative track. But are the institutions of the transatlantic relationships not in crisis too?

Institutions, Law, and Sovereignty

The authors in this volume profoundly disagree about whether the institutional framework of the transatlantic security community is in crisis or not. However, the different assessments have much to do with the issue areas concerned, on the one hand, and the types of institutions, on the other.

Let us start with the transatlantic economic relationship. Although McNamara argues that the transatlantic economic relationship has survived economic conflicts so far because of its embeddedness in highly institutionalized bilateral relationships of transgovernmental networks,[25] van Scherpenberg sees a serious and potentially dangerous lack of transatlantic institutions for dealing with bilateral trade disputes that are not subject to WTO rules. Both authors have a point in that they focus on different types of institutions. Van Scherpenberg is concerned with the lack of transatlantic *formal* institutions in the economic area that match the density of NATO and the security institutions. In contrast, McNamara's transgovernmental networks of like-minded regulators, bureaucrats, and lawyers constitute largely *informal* institutions.[26] In the end, the question remains: which type of institutional setting is more important to mitigate potential transatlantic economic conflicts?

As to NATO, most observers seem to agree that the North Atlantic alliance is experiencing a crisis that touches the core of the institution and has led to the "near death of the transatlantic alliance."[27] After 9/11, the NATO Council invoked article 5 of the North Atlantic Treaty for the first time in the history of the alliance—and nothing happened. It was not NATO that intervened in Afghanistan to uproot the Taliban and al-Qaeda network but the United States and a coalition of the willing, among them many European NATO partners.

25. On this point see also Anne-Marie Slaughter, *A New World Order* (Princeton: Princeton University Press, 2004).

26. Some of them, e.g., the Transatlantic Business Dialogue, are actually embedded in formal U.S.-EU institutions. On the TABD, see Maria Green Cowles, "The Transatlantic Business Dialogue: Transforming the New Transatlantic Dialogue," in *The New Transatlantic Dialogue: Intergovernmental, Transgovernmental, and Transnational Perspectives*, ed. Mark A. Pollack and Gregory C. Shaffer (Lanham, MD: Rowman and Littlefield, 2000). See also Mark A. Pollack and Gregory C. Shaffer, eds., *Transatlantic Governance in the Global Economy* (Lanham, MD: Rowman and Littlefield, 2001).

27. Pond, *Friendly Fire*.

When the Iraq crisis erupted, the NATO Council never did what it was supposed to do, namely, manage the transatlantic security partnership. It never discussed the conflict over Iraq, largely for fear that such an open dispute might lead to the collapse of the alliance. Instead, the dispute erupted in the UN Security Council. Moreover, if mutual consultation and joint decision making are constitutive norms governing the North Atlantic alliance,[28] these norms were severely violated during the past years—by both Americans and Europeans. Neither Jacques Chirac nor Gerhard Schröder bothered to consult NATO before they declared their opposition to U.S. intentions to invade Iraq.[29] Of course, the Bush administration also kept NATO out of its own decision-making process.[30] Last but not least, the U.S. administration's preference for coalitions of the willing is at odds with the decision-making rules of a multilateral alliance, which require consultation and serious efforts at joint decisions.

As Nau points out, however, Iraq may have shattered NATO at the political level, but the military cooperation functioned flawlessly during the Iraq War.[31] While political NATO almost collapsed over Iraq, military NATO took over its first "out-of-area" operation by assuming command of the International Security Assistance Force (ISAF) in Afghanistan in April 2003. NATO's role in the Balkans has also been largely successful. Finally, NATO enlargement has been a tremendous achievement and has been crucial in resocializing the eastern European military into the armed forces of democratic societies.[32]

Thus, the crisis seems to be confined to NATO's political structure in the sense that the North Atlantic Council has largely neglected its role as the prime manager of the transatlantic security relationship. At the same time, NATO as a military organization appears to be alive and kicking.

A security community does not only consist of formal institutions, however. What about the underlying understandings and collective normative commitments that are also constitutive for the transatlantic community? Conventional wisdom holds that there are deep and fundamental disagreements between Europeans and Americans concerning such foundational concepts as international law and sovereignty.[33] Interestingly, in this volume the two chapters that

---

28. For details, see Risse-Kappen, *Cooperation among Democracies*.

29. They did not bother to consult with the EU, either.

30. For details, see Pond, *Friendly Fire*; Gordon and Shapiro, *Allies at War*; Andrews, *Atlantic Alliance under Stress*; also Bob Woodward, *Plan of Attack* (New York: Simon and Schuster, 2004).

31. See also Helga Haftendorn, "Das Atlantische Bündnis in der Anpassungskrise," SWP Research Paper 2005/S 05 (Berlin: Stiftung Wissenschaft und Politik, 2005), 31.

32. See Alexandra Gheciu, "Security Institutions as Agents of Socialization? NATO and the 'New Europe,'" *International Organization* 59, no. 4 (2005): 973–1012.

33. See, e.g., Nolte, "Die USA und das Völkerrecht"; Michael Byers and Georg Nolte, eds., *United States Hegemony and the Foundations of International Law* (Cambridge: Cambridge University Press, 2003); Keohane, "Ironies of Sovereignty."

discuss these issues disagree with the conventional wisdom, albeit for different reasons. As to notions of sovereignty, Anderson argues that indeed the
United States and Europe differ profoundly in their conceptions of—
particularly—Westphalian sovereignty.[34] Continental Europeans especially
have adopted a notion of sovereignty that can be divided, shared, pooled, or
simply given up—and have done so in their practices in the process of European integration. Yet different conceptions of sovereignty cannot serve as a
crisis indicator because they have been with us for a while and certainly pre-
date the Bush administration. Disputes over multilateralism and unilateralism
have little to do with preparedness to relinquish sovereignty. Moreover, as Anderson points out, neither German nor French behavior during the Iraq crisis
showed much respect for multilateral institutions, including NATO and the
EU, and looked more like old-fashioned power politics rather than a postsovereign approach to foreign relations.

Finally, although the United States may remain the last Western power to
cling to traditional notions of Westphalian sovereignty, these differences between Europeans and Americans do not extend into the foundational rules
of international law, as Byers forcefully argues in this volume. Contrary to
what many Europeans, including international lawyers,[35] assume, even the
Bush administration does not see itself above international law but has
made sustained efforts to justify its actions in accordance with international
law. One may disagree with particular U.S. interpretations of international
law, but the Bush administration has not stepped out of the boundaries of
what constitutes legitimate readings of the law. And where it tried to over-
step, for example, with regard to an alleged right of "preventive self-
defense" or concerning torture and the Geneva conventions, the political
process or the courts have brought the U.S. government back into the mainstream, even though some serious disputes remain.

In sum, a mixed and complex picture emerges with regard to the institutional settings of the transatlantic community as indicators for a transatlantic
crisis. In the economic realm, a thin layer of formal bilateral institutions for
transatlantic governance coexists with "thick" transgovernmental networks of
experts, bureaucrats, and regulators. NATO continues to thrive as a military
institution, while it has largely failed to manage the transatlantic political relationship. And the United States and Europe disagree over notions of sovereignty and interpret international law differently, but they still share the same
fundamentally positive outlook toward international law in general. Thus, the
institutional framework of the transatlantic community is neither fully intact
nor in tatters.

34. On this notion see Stephen D. Krasner, *Sovereignty: Organized Hypocrisy* (Princeton:
Princeton University Press, 1999).
35. See, e.g., Nolte, "Die USA und das Völkerrecht"; Tomuschat, "Iraq."

Identities and Values

What about the sense of community, the collective identity, and the under-lying values of the transatlantic community? Are Americans increasingly from Mars, while Europeans seem to populate Venus?[36] Unfortunately, reaching firm conclusions about transatlantic identities constitutes a methodologically difficult endeavor, because there is little agreement in the literature about what can be used as valid indicators for a "sense of community."[37] Moreover, it is unclear how much collective identity is necessary for a transnational com-munity to work. Studies of the EU have shown, for example, that identifica-tion with Europe as a "secondary identity" (nation first, Europe second) is sufficient to ensure strong support for European integration.[38] We lack com-paratively sophisticated data on the transatlantic community to be able to reach firm conclusions.

On the one hand, Nau argues strongly that the transatlantic value commu-nity remains intact and has grown even stronger in the post–cold war era than it was before. Although the cold war community was primarily held to-gether by a common perception of the (Soviet) threat, the post–cold war community rests on collective values such as democracy, human rights, and market economy. In that sense, Nau suggests, the transatlantic relationship has only recently transformed itself from a security alliance into a security community.

On the other hand, Fuchs and Klingemann in their chapter and Hall in his point to potential cracks in the common value base. American and European citizens do belong to the same Western civilization when it comes to support-ing democracy, human rights, and the market economy in general. However, major differences between Europeans—particularly Germans and French—and Americans pertain to the way in which democracy is institutionalized. U.S. citizens support libertarian ideas such as a reduced state role in the economy, self-responsibility, and civic engagements. In contrast, a majority of Europeans prefer a strong welfare state that provides social equality and soli-darity. Yet Europeans are more heterogeneous themselves when it comes to fundamental values. Religiosity and national identification are cases in point. Regarding these two values, Poland is much closer to the United States than it is to its immediate neighbor Germany or to France. The popular notion that

---

36. See Kagan, *Paradise and Power*.

37. For a discussion, see Richard K. Herrmann, Thomas Risse, and Marilynn B. Brewer, eds., *Transnational Identities: Becoming European in the EU, Governance in Europe* (Lanham, MD: Rowman and Littlefield, 2004).

38. See, e.g., Jack Citrin and John Sides, "More Than Nationals: How Identity Choice Mat-ters in the New Europe," in Hermann, Risse, and Brewer, *Transnational Identities*, 161–85; Liesbet Hooghe and Gary Marks, "Calculation, Community, and Cues: Public Opinion on Eu-ropean Integration," *European Union Politics* 6, no. 4 (2005): 419–43.

Americans are religious whereas Europeans are secular should be taken with a grain of salt.

While Fuchs and Klingemann use macroquantitative survey data to analyze value orientations, Hall argues from a perspective grounded in historical sociology. In the *longue durée*, value differences between the United States and Europe have gained in significance, while similarities have been played down. As a result, mutual resentment seems to be growing but has not yet reached a breaking point. One should add that in Europe there is a long history of cultural anti-Americanism going back to the eighteenth century. Thus, anti-Americanism is not a new phenomenon but has historical roots dating back to when the United States was founded.[39] The history of anti-Americanism provides contemporary "anti-Bushism" with stereotypes that can be easily exploited by political elites. Although European criticism of U.S. foreign policy does not constitute anti-Americanism per se, it can be fueled by and therefore easily escalate into the latter. In the case of Germany, for example, the recent crisis over Iraq has triggered a wave of anti-Americanism on the political left *and* right, both of which have joined forces for the first time.

It is significant in this context that European views of U.S. leadership in world affairs in general and of President Bush in particular have reached all-time lows. Between 2002 and 2006, European support for U.S. leadership steadily declined from 64 percent to 37 percent. During the same period, European approval of President Bush declined from an already low 38 percent to 18 percent.[40] To put these numbers in historical perspective, I compare them to the approval ratings for U.S. policies and the U.S. president during another time of serious transatlantic tensions, namely, the early 1980s, the time of the "euromissile" crisis and of Ronald Reagan's presidency. At the time, Reagan and U.S. foreign policy were almost as unpopular in Germany as the current administration and its foreign policy were in 2006.[41] However, Reagan's image quickly recovered when the crisis was over and the first nuclear disarmament treaty with the Soviet Union had been signed.[42] Nothing in contemporary

39. For a comprehensive overview on the various anti-Americanisms, see Peter J. Katzenstein and Robert O. Keohane, eds., *Anti-Americanisms in World Politics* (Ithaca: Cornell University Press, 2006).

40. Data in the German Marshall Fund of the United States, "Transatlantic Trends: Key Findings 2006" (Washington, DC, 2006), 5, http//www.transatlantictrends.org. For a discussion, see also Reinhard Wolf, "America as the 'Other'? Europe's Security and Defense Identity in a Social Identity Perspective," in Peters, *Transatlantic Tug-of-War*, 143–80.

41. See data in Harald Müller and Thomas Risse-Kappen, "Origins of Estrangement: The Peace Movement and the Changed Image of America in West Germany," *International Security* 12, no. 1 (1987): 52–88.

42. Between May and December 1987, trust in Ronald Reagan increased from 44 percent to 60 percent among the West German public. See Forschungsgruppe Wahlen Mannheim, "Politbarometer 1987—Kumulierter Datensatz" (Cologne: Zentralarchiv für Sozialwissenschaftliche Forschung, University of Cologne, 1987), 100.

public opinion data suggests that the new honeymoon in German-U.S. relations alluded to at the beginning of this chapter has so far led to improvements in the U.S. image in Germany similar to the upturn it experienced during the 1980s.

This comparison has larger implications for the transatlantic community as a whole. The data and findings presented in this volume and pertaining to the sense of community do not allow us to conclude that there is an urgent and immediate crisis in the value basis of the transatlantic relationship. The data presented by Fuchs and Klingemann as well as the analysis by Hall point to long-term developments and underlying currents rather than short-term crisis events. We cannot interpret these findings as pointing to an immediate crisis of the transatlantic relationship. However, these arguments suggest that the collective identity of the transatlantic community rests on shakier grounds than Sunday speeches celebrating Western values pretend. As a result, the longer "anti-Bushism" continues, the more it can easily lead to increased anti-Americanism, further eroding what remains of a transatlantic collective identity. In other words, the value differences between Europe and the United States may become more salient and exploitable politically, the longer the current distrust of U.S. foreign policy continues among Europeans. Chancellor Schröder already demonstrated in the fall of 2002 how German leaders can exploit anti-American sentiments for electoral purposes.

Summary: A Lingering Crisis

The survey of the state of the transatlantic community yields mixed results (see table 12.2). When it comes to political interests and threat perceptions, the contributions in this volume overwhelmingly concur that the transatlantic relationship is in crisis. Regarding economic interdependence there is no crisis, but the economic ties are weaker than conventional wisdom assumes and, more important, are unlikely to save the political relationship when the latter is not in good shape. A mixed picture emerges with regard to the institutional framework of the transatlantic community. Although NATO as a *political* institution is in crisis, other parts of the institutional settings remain largely in-

Table 12.2. Transatlantic crisis scorecard

Elements	*State of the community*
Power and security interests	Crisis
Economic interdependence	Neither crisis nor "superglue"
Institutions and law	Mixed results
Identities and values	Enduring differences and increasing anti-Americanism in Europe

tact, including NATO's military integration and, interestingly enough, including the mutual commitment to international law. Last but not least, although there is no immediate breakdown in the sense of community, the collective identities and values beneath the transatlantic community are shakier than is often assumed.

In sum, the crisis scorecard does not sustain an alarmist picture according to which the transatlantic community is beyond repair. At the same time, however, none of the contributions to this volume allows the opposite conclusion either—that there is nothing to worry about. The emerging overall picture is one of a crisis beneath the surface; the predicament is lingering on, and any further trigger event may escalate into a full-blown and manifest crisis that could then shake up the Western order beyond repair.

Causes of the Transatlantic Crisis: A Synthesis

What are the underlying and proximate causes that led to the weakening of the transatlantic security community? In the following section, I go beyond a summary of our authors' conclusions about the evolution of the four elements that constitute the transatlantic security community (see also Ikenberry's introduction) and synthesize the findings of the volume into a more coherent causal story.

Note that the "dependent variable" to be explained here is the state of the Western order as a whole rather than particular events. The authors of this volume are not trying to explain, say, the transatlantic dispute over Iraq or some other policy disagreement of recent years. Rather, we are trying to explore what led to the crisis of the security community. We need to be careful methodologically, though. For example, take 9/11 and the ensuing differences in the intensity of threat perceptions (see chapter by Nau): one and the same event—the terrorist attacks on the World Trade Center and the Pentagon—cannot have caused differences in threat perceptions. Rather, some underlying and preexisting divergent interpretive frames could have caused the differences in threat perceptions that were then triggered by 9/11. As Katzenstein and others have argued, Europeans overwhelmingly view transnational terrorism as a threat to their internal security, which then triggers measures of crime prevention and criminal justice.[43] In contrast, Americans tend to view transnational terrorism as a threat to international security, which then leads to their support of military responses. George W. Bush's framing of the response to the 9/11 attacks—"war on terrorism"—may have triggered this perception.

As Hellmann argues in his chapter using Pierson's typology, most analysts of the transatlantic relationship employ causal arguments that highlight

43. See Katzenstein, "Same War—Different Views."

long-term structural changes with slowly developing consequences. Scholars mostly emphasize gradual transformations, not rapid and deep change. In Hellmann's terms, global warming would be the appropriate analogy (long-term cause, long-term consequence). This emphasis often leads to a failure to identify threshold points so that we can test the explanatory value of competing explanations. Realists' predictions of the end of NATO following the end of the cold war, but without specifying a timeframe, are as guilty of this methodological flaw as are constructivists who fail to indicate at which point and when increasing value gaps lead to the breakdown of a security community. As a result, the scholarly community so far has been much better at identifying the transatlantic crisis according to some indicators than at specifying its causes. Scholars have also been much better at clarifying underlying causes rather than proximate causes and/or trigger events.

It is nevertheless possible to use Hellmann's typology to synthesize the contributions in this volume and in the larger literature. Most underlying causes can be grouped under material or ideational "global warming" (long-term cause with long-term consequences), on the one hand, and under material or ideational "meteorite hit" (short-term cause with long-term consequences) on the other hand.

Material Global Warming: The End of the Cold War

Most analysts who take their theoretical points of departure from variants of realist thinking in international relations theory point to the end of the cold war as the most relevant underlying cause for the crisis of the Western community. Kupchan in particular argues that the current crisis constitutes a long-term consequence of the end of the cold war, which has led to diverging strategic interests between the United States and Europe, a gradual erosion of the sense of community, and a breakdown of the liberal internationalist consensus in the United States.[44] Van Scherpenberg appears to agree and argues that the end of the cold war has led to rising economic nationalism on both sides of the Atlantic, making the management of the economic relationship more difficult in the future. Others have suggested that the rise of U.S. unipolarity has increasingly affected the transatlantic relationship (see Ikenberry's chapter).[45] Nau also points to the end of the cold war as an underlying cause, but he draws the opposite conclusion, arguing that it has led to a strengthening rather than a weakening of the transatlantic sense of community.

---

44. Of course, this resembles to some extent the arguments by John Mearsheimer and Kenneth Waltz during the early 1990s. See Mearsheimer, "Back to the Future"; Waltz, "Emerging Structure of International Politics."

45. See also Ikenberry, *America Unrivaled*.

Strangely enough, however, the literature is unclear about the precise structural consequences of the end of the cold war for the transatlantic community. The original arguments by Mearsheimer and Waltz foresaw a multipolar order leading to short-term alliances rather than stable cooperative relationships, that is, multiple coalitions of the willing. Kupchan seems ultimately to share this view, because he predicts the rise of Europe and the EU as a "soft balancer" to U.S. power.[46] In contrast, Robert Kagan's argument about the end of the transatlantic community is based on the assumption of U.S. power and European weakness, that is, continuing unipolarity.[47]

These contradictions in the literature (which includes this volume) suggest that the end of the cold war as some kind of "global warming" can only serve as an underlying rather than a proximate cause of the current crisis of the Western order. As a result, most authors combine this account with other explanations.

Ideational Global Warming: Increasing Value Gaps?

Similar problems arise when we use "ideational global warming" as a potential cause of the transatlantic crisis. This perspective can be mostly identified with social constructivist reasoning, which emphasizes collective values and identities as a major component of security communities.[48] One way to work around the methodological problem of distinguishing between indicators and causes in this case is to distinguish between shared values on the one hand and collective identities on the other. The latter could be crisis indicators, whereas the former could be regarded as underlying causes in the following sense: increasing value gaps lead to a weakening of the sense of community as one of the underpinnings of a security community. Interestingly, we can easily falsify this hypothesis on the basis of the data and analyses presented in this volume.

As Fuchs and Klingemann point out in their contribution, the differences in attitudes between Americans and Europeans point to the persistence of value orientations that emerged in the eighteenth century, that is, long before the Western community came into being. Hall adds to this analysis that there has never been "pure love" across the Atlantic ocean but always various combinations of mutual admiration and resentment. The history of anti-Americanism in Europe alluded to earlier confirms that argument. As a result, there is not even "global warming" discernible in the data pointing to an increasing value gap. Rather, a combination of shared and diverging values has been with us for the duration of the transatlantic security community.

---

46. See also Charles Kupchan, *The End of the American Era: U.S. Foreign Policy and the Geopolitics of the Twenty-First Century* (New York: Knopf, 2003).

47. See Kagan, *Paradise and Power*.

48. See, e.g., Adler and Barnett, *Security Communities*.

Similar arguments apply to the frequent suggestion that Americans and Europeans are being driven apart because of differences in religious values.[49] Accordingly, Europeans are more secular, while Americans are becoming more religious. Differences in religious values cannot by themselves explain the transatlantic crisis, however. First, Europe is also becoming more religious as a result of the entrance of eastern European countries into the EU (see the data presented on Poland in the chapter by Fuchs and Klingemann).[50] Second, it is unclear whether Americans are becoming more religious, whether they are more polarized along secular versus religious values, or whether religion has become more politicized as a result of policies by the leaders of the Republican Party. In any event, differences in religious values alone cannot be used to explain current transatlantic conflicts.

In sum, the crisis of the transatlantic community must have different reasons. This conclusion does not mean that value gaps are irrelevant, but it suggests that value differences interact with other factors, leading potentially to a decreasing sense of community within the Western alliance. In the following sections, I suggest ways in which value differences and lingering anti-Americanisms can be brought back into a causal argument accounting for the crisis of the Western community.

Material Meteorite: 9/11 and Its Consequences

Both Kupchan and Nau—despite their differences—point to the significance of the events of 9/11 and of catastrophic transnational terrorism in accounting for the transatlantic crisis. In both readings, 9/11 has been a trigger event (or proximate cause) in the sense of Hellmann's "meteorite" with long-term consequences. Kupchan argues essentially that 9/11 served as a catalyst, pushing the lingering crisis of the Western community over the threshold toward a manifest crisis. His causal story can be summarized as follows: the end of the cold war gradually erodes the transatlantic community with regard to both interests and identities; 9/11 then pushes the transatlantic differences out in the open, leading to a full-fledged crisis in the relationship.

Nau's story is different. In his account, the effects of 9/11 are even more dramatic, given that the transatlantic security community was actually strengthened rather than weakened by the end of the cold war. The terrorist

49. See, e.g., Andrew Kohut, John C. Green, Scott Keeter, and Robert C. Toth, *The Diminishing Divide: Religion's Changing Role in American Politics* (Washington, DC: Brookings Institution Press, 2000); Braml, *Amerika, Gott und die Welt*.

50. See also Jürgen Gerhards and Michael Hölscher, *Kulturelle Unterschied in der Europäischen Union: Ein Vergleich zwischen Mitgliedsländern, Beitrittskandidaten und der Türkei* (Wiesbaden: VS Verlag für Sozialwissenschaften, 2005).

attacks against the United States on 9/11 then led to differences in threat perceptions that constitute the current crisis.[51] But as he argues in his chapter, this crisis only leads to an erosion of the transatlantic community if different domestic coalitions with diverging threat perceptions continue to govern on either side of the Atlantic. In other words, Nau's causal story requires a further ingredient, namely, a consideration of domestic politics.

Ideational Meteorite: The Significance of Domestic Politics

None of the authors in this volume talks a lot about the so-called neoconservatives in the Bush administration as "ideational meteorites" who may have triggered the transatlantic crisis. The "Wilsonians with boots" are often treated in the literature as primarily responsible for the post-9/11 U.S. foreign policy.[52] This group indeed dominated George W. Bush's foreign policy after the terrorist attacks and was also responsible for the invasion of Iraq.[53] Moreover, the neoconservative foreign policy outlook differs considerably from the views on international politics prevailing among the European political elites from the center left to the center right.[54] "Wilsonianism with boots" is a foreign policy outlook combining vigorous support for the promotion of human rights and democracy—a "liberal" perspective—with unilateralism and a preparedness to use military force to promote one's goals (militant internationalism). There is no stable domestic coalition to be found in Europe supporting such a foreign policy.[55] European liberals share the goal of democracy promotion but are adamantly opposed to unilateralism and more inclined to work through multilateral institutions. European conservatives, however, may be more supportive of using military force but do not think that democracy promotion should be among the primary goals of a nation's foreign policy. In that sense, they support a realpolitik outlook.

51. It is incorrect to use the "material meteorite" metaphor in this case. As I've argued, the same material event—9/11—led to different threat perceptions, which can therefore hardly be explained by material factors.

52. See Pierre Hassner, "The United States: The Empire of Force or the Force of Empire?" EU-ISS Chaillot Papers, no. 54 (Paris: Institute for Security Studies, European Union, 2002). See also Walter Russell Mead, *Special Providence: American Foreign Policy and How It Changed the World* (New York: Knopf, 2001).

53. For details, see Bob Woodward, *Bush at War* (New York: Simon and Schuster, 2002); Woodward, *Plan of Attack*.

54. See Thomas Risse, "Beyond Iraq: The Crisis of the Transatlantic Security Community," *Die Friedens-Warte* 78, no. 2–3 (2003): 173–93.

55. Tony Blair, President Bush's only real partner in Europe, actually underscores the point. The British Labour Party supported his foreign policy only reluctantly, as a result of which Blair had to spend enormous political capital to secure domestic support for the Iraq War.

Domestic politics looms large in the background of many contributions to this volume. Nau is most explicit about it, because his prediction about the transatlantic future depends largely on the degree to which European and U.S. domestic coalitions in charge of foreign policy hold shared threat perceptions. Kupchan argues that the erosion of liberal internationalism in the United States during the 1990s contributed substantially to the transatlantic conflict and that this effect was magnified when neoconservatives took over after 9/11.

Yet one should not confuse this explanation with an account that says, "It's all about George W." This assertion, at least, is only one of the potential conclusions. The "meteorite" metaphor implies that the rise of diverging domestic coalitions in charge of foreign policy on the two sides of the Atlantic serves as a catalyst (or proximate cause) in the causal story explaining the transatlantic crisis. The authors in this volume, as well as in the larger literature on the transatlantic relationship, disagree profoundly about what these developments mean for the future of the West. In the end, much depends on the weight one puts on the "global warming" factors looming in the background as compared to the significance of the triggering "meteorites" discussed here.

In sum, if we look at the causes for the crisis in the transatlantic order, we seem to find underlying ideational as well as material factors that continue to create trouble in the relationship. Among them are changes in the international system such as the end of the cold war. Yet these underlying causes are not much more than latent sources of transatlantic trouble. To manifest themselves in a crisis, they must be triggered by some event (such as 9/11) or by the deliberate actions of policymakers. Neither the end of the cold war nor value gaps nor anti-Americanism seems to be sufficient to *cause* transatlantic crises. Rather, material changes lead to changes in the configuration of interests and of domestic coalitions, which then trigger a transatlantic crisis. Value gaps as well as anti-Americanism in Europe can be tapped into by policymakers on either side of the Atlantic.

What do these different accounts tell us about the future of the Western order? Are we witnessing the gradual breakdown of the transatlantic community, its revival through a new "transatlantic bargain," or something in between?

Crisis Outcomes: Loosening, Adaptation, or Transformation?

As Ikenberry details in the introduction to this volume, the transatlantic crisis can have one of three outcomes. (1) It may lead to breakdown and the end of the West. (2) It may transform and fundamentally restructure the norms and institutions of the relationships within the Atlantic order. Or (3) it may lead to adaptation, that is, changes in some rules, while leaving most of the institutions intact.

Probably the most significant finding of this volume with regard to the future of the Western order concerns the fact that most authors reject thinking in binary terms: that the transatlantic community either collapses or survives without changes (see Hellmann's chapter on this point). Originally, both neorealist and social constructivist predictions oscillated between these two extremes.[56] The authors in this volume, irrespective of their theoretical orientations, mostly opt for scenarios somewhere in between. Two scenarios are considered most likely under current circumstances. The first is not contained in Ikenberry's three potential scenarios but represents a fourth possibility: the Western order can change toward a much looser transatlantic cooperative relationship than the tightly coupled security community of the cold war and the 1990s. The second scenario involves some adaptation, but also restructuring and transformation, in order to make the community fit for the challenges of the twenty-first century.

In their chapters Hellmann, Kupchan, Hall, and Nau (particularly the latter's, with his "conservative internationalist" scenario) all suggest that a complete breakdown of the transatlantic community is unlikely but that the West could develop a much looser relationship of temporary cooperation to solve common problems, of agreements to disagree in times of severe conflicts of interests, and of continuous coalitions of the willing. As Hall reminds us, a range of possibilities exists between pure love and divorce. In this case, we will probably witness a further deinstitutionalization of the relationship, maybe even the breakdown of NATO. Kupchan suggests in this context that the new Atlantic order could resemble the peaceful coexistence of the interwar period.

Such a loosely coupled transatlantic order would still leave the "democratic peace" intact.[57] As long as the United States and most European countries remain stable liberal democracies, they will not go to war against each other. The order will become far less cooperative, but the security dilemma will not return between the former allies. Europeans will not feel threatened by U.S. military power and thus will not be tempted to revert to traditional balancing behavior. For all the talk about "soft balancing,"[58] a return to the classic military balance-of-power system that prevailed between the United States and Europe during the nineteenth century remains unthinkable. The United

---

56. See, on the one hand, Mearsheimer, "Back to the Future"; on the other hand, Thomas Risse-Kappen, "Collective Identity in a Democratic Community," in *The Culture of National Security: Norms and Identity in World Politics*, ed. Peter Katzenstein (New York: Columbia University Press, 1996), 357–99.

57 See Bruce Russett, *Grasping the Democratic Peace* (Princeton: Princeton University Press, 1993); Russett and O'Neal, *Triangulating Peace*; Levy, "War and Peace."

58. See Frank Schimmelfennig, "Jenseits von Gleichgewichtspolitik und Anpassung: Chancen und Grenzen transatlantischen sozialen Einflusses," *WeltTrends* 11, no. 40 (2003): 76–81.

States and Europe will even cooperate on an ad hoc basis to protect mutual interests in the rest of the world. And, as Byers suggests, both the United States and Europe have a lot at stake in maintaining the international legal order, so an end to the transatlantic alliance would not necessarily imply the end of international law.

The second crisis outcome to which authors in this volume seem to subscribe concerns some degree of adaptation, coupled with transformation, that results in deeper changes in the norms and rules governing the relationship (see the chapters by Byers, Anderson, McNamara, and—depending on which threat perception prevails on either side of the Atlantic—Nau). There are several reasons why adaptation or transformation represents a likely outcome of the current crisis. First, the diagnosis of the current transatlantic crisis itself reveals that the security community is not beyond repair. Even the value gaps and the ruptures over core interests have not given rise to strong demands for a transatlantic divorce on either side of the Atlantic. Second, the value gaps, including European anti-Americanism and the differences in the interpretation of concepts such as sovereignty, are held in check by other factors that keep the community together.

Let me spell out in more detail what adaptation or transformation could mean. Adaptation requires adjusting the existing institutional framework of the community to the new post–cold war realities, including the new security environment. Adaptation of NATO, for example, must acknowledge two facts of life in the transatlantic order: first, that U.S. military power is unmitigated for the foreseeable future, and second, that the EU is rising as a foreign policy actor in its own right. Europeans must realize that the United States needs NATO much less for its security requirements than was the case in the past and that, therefore, there will be circumstances in which the United States acts alone rather than through NATO. The United States needs to realize that acting alone does not mean unilateralism. Both sides must then reaffirm the consultation rules of NATO, including the requirement that the North Atlantic Council discuss upcoming conflicts *before* national governments take a firm stance.

Furthermore, adaptation of NATO means that the institutional links with the EU and its foreign policy apparatus must be improved.[59] This requirement refers not only to the institutions of the European security and defense policy (ESDP) but to the EU's foreign policy role more generally. When it comes to conflict prevention, conflict resolution, and postconflict peace building, the EU has many more instruments at its disposal than NATO does. A comprehensive transatlantic security strategy requires closer coordination between NATO and the EU than is the case today.

---

59. For details, see Haftendorn, "Das Atlantische Bündnis in der Anpassungskrise."

Moving from adaptation to transformation, the latter implies a new "transatlantic bargain" that changes fundamental norms and institutions of the community.[60] Such a new bargain would have to start with the acknowledgment that the current transatlantic institutional framework is still a cold war leftover that has not yet taken into account the new security reality, particularly not the post-9/11 world. A new bargain would have to start with reforming the constitutive norms of the transatlantic order:

1. Multilateralism versus coalitions of the willing. The approach that prevailed during the Bush administration's first term, according to which the "mission defines the coalition," is inconsistent with a security community. It is unilateralism in disguise. The United States must reaffirm transatlantic multilateralism and the enduring partnership with Europe if the security community is to survive. At the same time, Europeans must accept that the United States sometimes will go it alone and that transatlantic consensus will not always be possible. Thus, an institutional mechanism is required for spelling out what it means "to agree to disagree."

2. International law and effective multilateralism. As Byers argues in his chapter, both Europe and the United States have a lot at stake in international law. However, this mutual commitment to international law and to effective multilateralism needs to be reaffirmed. Given the differences in the two security strategies that have been in put in place by the United States and the EU,[61] a new transatlantic bargain should entail some ground rules concerning "out-of-area" military interventions:
   - There should be a commitment by the transatlantic community to first seek approval by the UN Security Council for any "out-of-area" intervention. Transatlantic multilateralism must be embedded in a global multilateral order. This proposal, however, begs the question of how to enact the "responsibility to protect" if veto powers in the Security Council object (as was the case in the 1999 Kosovo War). Neither the United States nor Europe can forfeit humanitarian obligations just because semi-authoritarian Russia or authoritarian China objects to the proposed action. A rule of thumb might be that

---

60. See Andrew Moravcsik, "Striking a New Transatlantic Bargain," *Foreign Affairs* 82, no. 4 (July–August 2003): 74–89; Thomas Risse, "For a New Transatlantic—and European—Bargain," *Transatlantic Internationale Politik* 4, no. 3 (2003): 20–28.

61. See President of the United States, "The National Security Strategy of the United States of America" (Washington, DC: White House, 2002); European Council, "A Secure Europe in a Better World—European Security Strategy" (Brussels: European Institute for Security Studies, 2003).

it makes an enormous difference whether only one of the veto powers objects or whether a UN Security Council majority refuses to legitimize military action.

- Effective multilateralism also requires a joint understanding of what kind of military action is legitimized by article 51 of the UN Charter. The controversy centers around the notion of preventive action. Or, to put it more precisely: Where does preemption end and preventive war begin? And what do these notions mean in light of the new security threats, for example, transnational terrorism in combination with weapons of mass destruction? How far can one push the interpretation of article 51 without blurring the difference between self-defense and offensive warfare that would be disastrous for international law?

The transformation scenario would not stop with reformation of the norms governing the transatlantic relationship. Rather, transformation also requires changing the institutional framework of the order. In this context, some tough questions must be asked with regard to NATO:

1. Is NATO still institutionally adequate for managing the transatlantic alliance? Does it make sense to retain NATO's institutional framework when all future European NATO members are members of the EU (if Turkey joins, of course) and when the EU upgrades its foreign policy in the way foreseen by the 2007 Lisbon Treaty, including ESDP? What about a true "two-pillar" NATO, with both a North American and a European pillar? Of course, an EU caucus inside NATO implies a fundamental transformation of the North Atlantic alliance's political organization.

2. What about the future of NATO as a military organization? To what extent can it deal with new security threats such as failing and failed states, transnational terrorism, and the proliferation of weapons of mass destruction? The "new security agenda" requires a comprehensive strategy integrating political and military means. At present, NATO does not have the political instruments necessary for state building, postconflict peace building, democratization, and the like. The EU's foreign policy apparatus is much better equipped to deal with these political security tasks. Yet it still lacks the military power to back up its diplomatic strength. Transformation would require drastic improvements in the institutionalized relationship between NATO's military organization and the EU's political mechanisms.

Transformation would also require tackling the problems of the transatlantic economic order, as van Scherpenberg outlines in his chapter. Currently, there is no formal institutional framework outside the WTO to deal with transatlantic economic conflicts in a systematic fashion. A transformation scenario would probably require creation of a U.S.-EU institutional framework for resolving economic conflicts before they reach the level of adjudication by the WTO's dispute settlement system.

Which of the two scenarios—adaptation/transformation or a more loosely coupled transatlantic relationship—is the more likely? The issues with which the Western community must grapple so that it can adapt and transform itself to meet the challenges of the twenty-first century imply proactive engagement and strong leadership on both sides of the Atlantic. Indeed, as Hitchcock points out in his chapter, leadership has been crucial historically in helping the alliance out of a crisis. Papering over differences or allowing a crisis to linger is not sufficient. The conclusion is clear: in the absence of strong leadership and proactive policies for transforming the Western community, members of the security community are likely to give way to much less institutionalized, albeit still friendly, relationships with each other. A loosening of the Western order is the most likely outcome unless policymakers on both sides of the Atlantic actively adapt and transform the security community.

Concluding Remarks

The Western order is experiencing a severe crisis, but it is not beyond repair—a conclusion that can be drawn from most chapters in this volume. The West is in crisis mainly because policy conflicts pertain to core interests of either side, cover a whole range of issues, and are thus no longer confined to one policy field such as international security. Although the transatlantic economic ties remain strong, they cannot serve as a superglue that keeps the political relationship together. As for NATO as a core security institution of the Western order, its political framework is not functioning well, although the military organization has adjusted better to the new environment than many would have predicted. The West still shares a commitment to international law (while fighting over significant differences in interpretation), even though notions such as sovereignty are understood differently. Last but not least, the West still exists in terms of collectively shared common values, but this collective identity has enduring fissures that can be easily cracked open and can lead to confrontation through some triggering event.

Allowing the crisis to linger by papering over the differences will not suffice. Although the transatlantic "democratic peace" will remain intact, the transatlantic order will be much less institutionalized and cooperation will be much more ad hoc. In contrast, adapting and transforming the Western order for the twenty-first century requires proactive leadership on both sides of the Atlantic and includes working toward a new "transatlantic bargain."

We should not forget what is at stake in the larger scheme of things. U.S. foreign policy is currently experiencing one of the worst crises in its history. The United States is less and less capable of translating its still considerable military and economic power into influence and exercising its much-needed leadership in world affairs. As the years following the invasion of Iraq have amply demonstrated, the United States "can't go it alone."[62] Under these circumstances, loosened transatlantic ties and a deinstitutionalization of the Western order are disastrous for world order and global governance. Governing the global economy; tackling global security issues such as state failure, the proliferation of weapons of mass destruction, and transnational terrorism; dealing with the rise of China in global politics; preserving the global environment; and promoting democracy, human rights, and global justice—it is unthinkable that any of these challenges can be handled without close and sustained transatlantic cooperation. This conclusion makes it imperative that strong leadership be exercised on both sides of the Atlantic and that the Western security community renew and transform itself.

62. See, e.g., Joseph S. Nye Jr., *The Paradox of American Power: Why the World's Only Superpower Can't Go It Alone* (Oxford: Oxford University Press, 2002).

INDEX

Numbers in italics refer to figures and tables.